THE P̱ĀḌAENG CHRONICLE AND THE JENGTUNG STATE CHRONICLE TRANSLATED

THE P̱ĀḌÆNG CHRONICLE AND THE JENGTUNG STATE CHRONICLE TRANSLATED

Sao Sāimöng Mangrāi

Michigan Papers on South and Southeast Asia
Number 52

University of Michigan
CENTERS FOR SOUTH AND
SOUTHEAST ASIAN STUDIES

Library of Congress Catalog Card Number: 2002111502

ISBN 0-89148-087-0

Printed in the United States of America

Dunnigahassa lahuno yattha kāmanipātino
Cittassa damatho sādhu cittaṁ dantaṁ sukhāvahaṁ

Hard to control is the swift mind which wanders according to its whims;
It is good to tame the mind. A controlled mind brings happiness.

Dhammapada verse 35

Tumhehi kiccaṁ ātappaṁ akkhātāro Tathāgatā
Paṭipannā pamokkhanti jhāyino mārabandhanā

You yourself must strive; Tathāgatas only point [the way].
Those who enter the way and meditate are released from the bonds of Māra.

Dhammapada verse 276

Sabbapāpassa akaraṇaṁ kusalassa upasampadā
Sacittapariyodapanaṁ etaṁ buddhāna sāsanaṁ

Not doing any evil, cultivation of meritorious deeds,
Cleansing of one's own mind--this is the Teaching of all the Buddhas.

Dhammapada verse 183

In reverence
Is this Translation addressed
To the Theravāda Sāsanā of the Fully Enlightened One

CONTENTS

Jengtung State Chronicle

LIST OF FIGURES

INTRODUCTION

In this volume, the original edition of which appeared in 1981, Sao Sāimöng Mangrāi translates two Tai-language documents, which, despite their considerable value for Southeast Asian historiography, had been unavailable to scholars. The first document is the Chronicle of Vat Pāḍaeng, the Red Forest Monastery, which is one of the major monastic foundations in what is now the eastern sector of the Shan State of Myanmar (Burma). The second document is the official chronicle of the kingdom in which that monastery was located, namely the principality of Kengtung (Jengtung).

Each of these documents has its own virtues. The *Pāḍaeng Chronicle*, whose original manuscript is the property of the monastery, offers a partisan account of the fortunes of the New Ceylon Sect. Established at the Red Forest Monastery in Chiengmai in 1430, this sect spread throughout the Tai-speaking uplands of mainland Southeast Asia, becoming active in Kengtung some eighteen years later. Although the pre-fifteenth century sections of the chronicle are derivative and their chronology dubious, the account of the fifteenth and sixteenth centuries, which forms the great bulk of the narrative, speaks with a credible level of idiosyncratic detail and direct observation. Moreover, the dates from this section can be confirmed, in some cases corrected, by comparing them to contemporary stone inscriptions and to palm leaf documents from other Tai centers.

The *Pāḍaeng Chronicle's* overriding concern is to demonstrate the ritual purity of the New Ceylon sect and its superiority to the Garden Sect, which had its own monastery complex at Kengtung and was a constant rival for popular and more especially royal patronage. The superiority of New Ceylon monks, we are told, was demonstrated repeatedly by their firmer grasp of Pali grammar, which ensured the sanctity of monastic ordination procedures, as well as by their ability to exorcise evil spirits and to triumph over other sects in quasi-magical contests. Ultimately, in typical Southeast Asian Theravāda fashion, sanctity depended on the fidelity with which monastic rituals and traditions had been transmitted from Ceylon, which was regarded as the font of orthodoxy. Fifteenth-century Tais seem to have envisioned a hierarchy of sanctified centers, or more accurately, of centers with access to sanctified transmission, extending from Ceylon itself to coastal Ayudhya (capital of Siam) and Martaban, to Chiengmai and Chiengsaen in the interior, to Kengtung, and thence to the Sipsong Panna region and the Lu principality of Kenghung, which were yet farther removed from coastal scholarship. In short, the *Pāḍaeng Chronicle* allows us to reconstruct the routes, the organizations, and the psychological appeals by which Theravāda Buddhism spread into what in the early fifteenth century was still a substantially illiterate, animist universe. Beyond that, it offers rich detail on early Tai social structure and royal patronage, as well as incidental references to commercial and agricultural life and meteorological events.

As its title suggests, the second document, the *Jengtung State Chronicle*, is primarily a record of royal activities, both domestic and inter-state, compiled from annual court records. The reliable chronology extends from the thirteenth to twentieth centuries, with primary emphasis on the period c. 1400–1885. The *Gazeteer of Upper Burma and the Shan States* (Part II, Vol. 1, Rangoon, 1901, pp. 389-410) offered a summary and partial translation of the "Kengtung State annals," but that was a radically abbreviated, far less useful version of the present document. This chronicle provides information not only on what may be termed political structures – if we may so dignify what were in fact fluid personal relations – but also on the court's endemic factionalism and the interplay between family constellations and external alliances. We learn about indigenous concepts of legitimacy, which were at best partly Buddhist; about relations between Tai migrants and indigenous non-Tai inhabitants, about politicized ethnicity, hereditary social categories, and state revenues. Much information is available too on the constantly negotiated relation between Kengtung and outlying valleys, over whom Kengtung strove to maximize its practical and titular authority. At the same time, Kengtung's rulers sought to minimize their obligations to the Burmese empire, into whose orbit the state fell more or less permanently in the late sixteenth century. Thus this chronicle offers a classic image of interior Southeast Asia as an aggregation of solar polities with pulsating, overlapping gravitational fields, but without clearly defined notions either of borders or exclusive sovereignty. By checking these exceptionally detailed narratives and chronologies against Burmese and other Tai sources, we can construct a more faithful regional history.

It would be difficult to imagine someone more qualified to explicate and translate these documents than the late Sao Sāimöng Mangrāi, who was himself a prince in the Kengtung royal family. One might take a less trusting approach to traditional accounts of how Buddhism entered Southeast Asia than the author demonstrated in his introduction. But this small defect, if that is what it is, is overwhelmed by the rigor of Sao Sāimöng Mangrāi's scholarly enterprise, his intellectual honesty, his innate caution and modesty, and his heroic determination to remain faithful to the original text. We benefit too from his willingness to enlist other experts in arcane matters of astrology and textual interpretation, from his provision of copious supporting material (including introductory discussions of the Khün-Tai language and script, of chronology, ethnology, and Buddhism), and from his intimate familiarity with the culture, language, and geography of Kengtung. Western-trained scholars of Khün able to attempt such a translation are rare indeed. Of particular scholarly value are the photographic plates of palm leaves on which the *Pāḍaeng Chronicle* was inscribed, and the detailed footnotes that discuss uncertain references and textual discrepancies. In my opinion, both for its intrinsic value and the rigor of its scholarship, this is the most valuable historical publication the Center for Southeast Asian Studies has produced. Enthusiastic reviews of the original edition and requests for a book no longer in print suggest that my opinion is not unique, and it is indeed a pleasure to assist re-publication.

Victor Lieberman
Ann Arbor
May, 2001

INTRODUCTION

Over the past several decades much progress has been achieved in Tai studies around the world. The tremendous amount of research in various disciplines, the regular convening of the International Conference on Thai (Tai) Studies, the publication of the new journal *Tai Culture* in Germany, and the increasing number of translations of chronicles of the various Tai groups (Thai, Tai Yuan, Lao, Shan, Tai Le, Tai Lem, Tai Mao, Ahom, Tai Dam, etc.) into different languages including English, French, Chinese, Assamese, and Thai all attest to this growth.

Among translations, Sao Sāimöng Mangrāi's work on the *Pāḍaeng Chronicle* and the *Jengtung State Chronicle* stands out for the high quality of the original documents, painstaking and faithful translation, meticulous notes, insightful introductions, and priceless photographs. For over twenty years, since its first publication in 1981, Mangrāi's translation has been an invaluable source for scholars of Asia, especially Southeast Asia, and will remain so for many other years to come. It is unlikely to ever be superceded when one considers Mangrāi's intimate knowledge of Shan history, culture, and society as not only a Shan, but also a Shan prince, as well as a serious, intelligent, and diligent scholar with a rare grasp of languages — Shan or Khün, Tai Yuan, Thai, and Lao, Pali, Burmese, and English.

The two chronicles provide a wealth of information for reconstructing the history of the Tai in modern Myanmar (Burma), Thailand, China, and Laos with respect to political and social organization, Theravāda Buddhism, and inter-state and -ethnic relations from roughly the thirteenth to early twentieth centuries. Moreover, collating the chronicles with other Tai, Burmese, and Chinese records can shed additional light on many other subjects. As examples, accounts of the use of cowries as money and descriptions of the (gunpowder-propelled) rocket festival in the Jengtung (Kengtung) region provide information on certain monetary and cultural-cum-technological practices widespread in the Tai region. Likewise, the record of the eighteenth century succession dispute between two Shan princes in Jengtung offers an alternative view of the more detailed Chinese accounts to further illuminate the origins and nature of the Qing-Burmese war and the role Shans played in it.

More importantly, these two chronicles contain rich and rare ethnohistorical materials on northern mainland Southeast Asia, including Yunnan. The ethnic groups mentioned in the chronicles include the Mon-Khmer-speaking Yang (Riang), Sanjum, Lva, La, Mon, (Daiy) Doy, and Tai-speaking Lu, Laem, Shan (Yeu), Khün, Yon, Tai-no

(Daiy-no, or Chinese or Northern Shan), Lao, and Thai ("Ayodhiya people"). Others mentioned are the Sino-Tibetan speaking Burman and Chinese, and the Bong (unidentified by Mangrāi, but most likely the "Pong" people who still dwell in northern Burma).

There is another interesting and important group of people called "Kuy" in the *Pāḍaeng Chronicle* about whose ethnic identity Mangrāi is completely silent. The Kuy appear prominently in the chronicle between 1474–1508 and 1849. Among the total 222 paragraphs, 27 are about or mention the Kuy. They are referred to as monastery "subjects" (rather than "slaves," as Mangrāi has judiciously warned us) who were assigned numerous tasks related to the monastery and who had their own paddy fields and forest tracts. It is possible that this group is the same as the "Gui" people mentioned in some Tai Le accounts that may reflect the inter-ethnic relations when the Tai had just arrived in Sipsong Panna (Xishuangbanna) during possibly the seventh or eighth century. A similar term, "Kui" (one of many different spellings), refers to the Yellow Lahu, who have been living in northern Thailand, Laos, Vietnam, and especially the Kenghung (Jinghong)-Kengtung region to the present day (modern records about them first appeared in the early nineteenth century). Thus, it is not too farfetched to suggest that the "Gui" and "Kuy" should be identified with the Lahu-speaking Kui. It might be further concluded that prior to the arrival of the Tai, the Lahu people had been already residing in parts of northern mainland Southeast Asia, including the Kenghung-Kengtung region. If this tentative view proves to be true, it will clear the clouds shrouding the history of the Lahu people, who have long been thought to have arrived in modern Burma only during the eighteenth and nineteenth centuries.

Mangrāi in 1957 planned to write a history of the Shan (Tai) and G. H. Luce pointed out that it would be "the biggest and most important historical job still to be done in S. East Asia." This undertaking yet remains to be done, ideally through fruitful cooperation among scholars of different countries and different disciplines. If this work materializes some day, in the mansion of the history of the Tai people, Mangrāi's translation will certainly be one of the most important building blocks.

Sun Laichen
September 2001
Fullerton, California

FOREWORD

Occidental scholarship has had difficulty in reaching a just appreciation of the chronicles of Siam, the Shan States, and other lands where Tai languages predominate. In the first half of the nineteenth century it was hoped that these chronicles--whether dealing with kingdoms, principalities, cities, or Buddhist monasteries--would prove to be history, or something like it, which (if exaggerations and marvels were jettisoned) might yield an account of events that actually occurred at the stated dates.

A few chronicles, such as *Jinakālamālī* and the Luang Prasert Recension of the *Annals of Ayudhyā*, actually meet these standards, but they escaped the attention of Western scholars until the twentieth century. At the opposite end of the scale are compositions which might better be described as "pseudo-chronicles," being no more than collections of folktales with no historical basis at all. Most of the chronicles lie somewhere between the two extremes. Many of them are compilations in which the first section is borrowed from folklore, legend, or Buddhist commentarial literature; this is sometimes followed by a sort of protohistorical section which seems to contain confused recollections of real events; and finally comes the main section, which is often real history imperfectly transmitted. The men who preserved these chronicles by copying them from one manuscript to another were not infallible; they were liable to misread proper names and to insert passages in the wrong place or drop them out altogether; and they often had trouble with numerals, so that dates tended to become chaotic.

The various recensions of the *Annals of Ayudhyā* available in the nineteenth century, though the dates in them are corrupt, are now recognized as containing much valuable history. The discovery of the Luang Prasert Recension in 1907 cleared up the chronological problems. It is a highly condensed version of the *Annals*, compiled in 1680 A.D. at the command of King Nārāyaṇa. The dates in it are anywhere from six to twenty-one years later than those given in the other recensions. They are almost certainly right; many of them can be verified by reference to contemporary inscriptions or other trustworthy sources; and they provide a key to the proper dating of events that other recensions describe in much more detail.

In 1925 the late George Coedès published a French translation of the sections of *Jinakālamālī* dealing with Siam. This work, composed in Pali at Chiengmai in the sixteenth century, gives the dates in the Cuḷa Era, with the numerals translated into Pali and spelled out, and often the Pali translation of the name of the animal in the twelve-year cycle as well, so that the chances of corruption are greatly reduced. As in most chronicles, the narrative gains in accuracy as it approaches the author's own time and place; and the section dealing with Buddhism at Chiengmai from the late thirteenth to the sixteenth century is sober history, with an impeccable chronology.

Mūlasāsanā, a chronicle composed in the Tai-Yuan language at Chiengmai in the fifteenth century, tells how an order of forest-dwelling monks was introduced at Martaban from Ceylon in the fourteenth century, then spread to Sukhodaya, and later to Chiengmai. It throws much light on the different monastic orders at Chiengmai, including their disputes and vicissitudes. All the known manuscripts of *Mūlasāsanā* are flawed by obvious corruptions and a muddled chronology; but just as the Luang Prasert Recension makes it possible to correct the dates in other recensions of the *Annals of Ayudhyā*, *Jinakālamālī* can be used to correct many of those in *Mūlasāsanā*.

The publication of Sao Sāimöng's translation of the chronicle of the Red Forest Monastery at Kengtung is an important event. The translator complains, rightly, that the dates in the first few pages are hopeless, but they improve as the narrative advances; when it reaches events at Chiengmai and other cities in northern Siam in the fifteenth century, the errors are fewer in number and less in magnitude, and they can be set right, at least approximately, by working from *Jinakālamālī*'s chronological framework for the same events. When the narrative reaches Kengtung, several of the dates can be verified, or corrected, by reference to those given in a stone inscription, composed in 1451 A.D., which is preserved at the Red Forest Monastery itself.

Once the chronology is rectified, at least approximately, the chronicle gains in coherence and in historicity, and its many virtues become apparent. Most of the events from the fifteenth century and later must be real enough. Modern skepticism may smile at some of the anecdotes and the accounts of miracles; but they too are real, in the sense that they were believed at the time. The chronicle is valuable not only for the history it gives us, but also for the lively picture it conveys of the various sects of monks, their disputes over points of monastic discipline, ritual and the proper use of Pali, their relations with the royal family and officialdom of Kengtung, the management of monasteries, and the customs and beliefs of a premodern Shan society.

A. B. Griswold
Monkton, Maryland
December 1976

ACKNOWLEDGEMENTS

The *P̲āḍaeng Chronicle*

The Chronicle of Vat P̲āḍaeng is the property of that monastery, and it was very kindly loaned to me by the lord abbot, Brasāmī Sumana, when I suggested to him that it would be a good idea to translate it into English.

Brasāmī Khemacārī, lord abbot of Vat Jengyün, and Brabhikkhu Jutidhamma, lord abbot of Vat Khemin, have been most helpful in supplying me by post with information concerning the monasteries and Saṅgha of Kengtung relevant to the translation, and have helped in obtaining the photographs through the meritorious deed of the photographer, U Yee Subrohmmā. The Brasāmī of Jengyün is well versed in astrological calculations and has explained clearly points concerning the inauspicious days in paragraphs 130-36. Members of the Saṅgha of Kengtung, headed by Lord Ajnādham Bra Ñānavuḍḍhi, are gratified that the chronicle of one of their foremost monasteries will be published in an English translation by the Center for South and Southeast Asian Studies, The University of Michigan, Ann Arbor, and, through the two lord abbots, have requested me to convey their somanassa (pleasure) to the Center's director, to whom they also send their mettā (blessing) of long life, good appearance, happiness, and strength.

Mr. Alexander B. Griswold of the Breezewood Foundation, Professor Alton L. Becker of the Linguistics Department, The University of Michigan, and Professor Thomas R. Trautmann, director of the Center for South and Southeast Asian Studies, The University of Michigan, have patiently read through the translation in my untidy longhand and suggested appropriate amendments and emendations. Mr. Griswold's foreword and his letter to me of November 29, 1976, excerpts from which are reproduced in this volume, testify to the fact that he is an authority on the chronicles of Burma and Thailand.

Professor Madhav Deshpande of the Linguistics Department, The University of Michigan, has helped in the translation of many of the Pali words and sentences in the text, and especially in supplying citations for Pali rules from the grammatical treatise of Kaccāyana; he was often surprised to find the rules accurately quoted in the text in spite of the repeated copying that it must have undergone. Professor Hiram W. Woodward of the History of Art Department, The University of Michigan, has loaned me several chronicles of north Thailand, including those of Chiengmai and Yonaka. Mr. John K. Musgrave, Southeast Asian bibliographer, University Library, and Mr. John Grima of the Linguistics Department have given helpful advice on certain aspects of the transcription of Khün sounds.

Without the kind help rendered above the translation and notes would not be what they are. My deep appreciation and grateful thanks are due to those good people, especially when it is appreciated that they have to attend to their own work and business, spiritual or wordly, as the case may be.

I have done my utmost for the translation itself, and yet, like all things of this world, it is by no means perfect. This I admit in all humility. At least a beginning has been made, and the reproduction of the original side-by-side with the translation is a great help. It is for future scholars, rather than a mere translator like myself, to make further improvement. I regret the delay, and this is partly due to the long and difficult postal communication with Kengtung, the easternmost area of Burma.

Should this work ever reach Burma, it is my earnest hope that the Government of the Union of Burma would help the Saṅgha of Kengtung protect and preserve the Khün script and its use, thereby enriching the already rich and varied cultural heritage of the country.

The *Jengtung State Chronicle*

Here, as in my translation of the *Pāḍæng Chronicle*, I am indebted to Brabhikkhu Jutidhamma, lord abbot of Vat Khemin, and Brasāmī Khemacārī of Vat Jengyün for supplying me with meanings or confirmation of meanings of certain words and phrases of the Khün language, and also for elucidating certain manners and customs in Kengtung. In spite of the great distance separating Ann Arbor and Kengtung City, I have obtained what I wanted in most cases, except, as stated elsewhere, in regard to astrological terms. To Professor Hiram W. Woodward I tender my thanks for the loan of the chronicles of northern Thailand quoted in the notes and introduction. My grateful thanks also go to Mr. John Musgrave for the many sessions of fruitful consultation on various points in the chronicle. I also thank Professor Alton L. Becker for going through the manuscript and for suggesting improvements here and there. Finally, I appreciate very much the fact that the editorial board of the Michigan Papers on South and Southeast Asia, headed by Professor Thomas R. Trautmann, has decided to publish this translation of the *Jengtung State Chronicle* together with that of the *P̱ādaeng Chronicle*. This is most appropriate and the decision will be lauded, I am sure, by the people of Burma as a whole and by the Saṅgha and people in Kengtung in particular, and also by all students interested in the chronicles of Burma and Thailand.

ABBREVIATIONS

AN	Aṅguttara Nikāya
AP	Abhidhamma Piṭaka
BS	Buddha Sakkarāja
CS	Cuḷa Sakkarāja
CSC	*Chiengmai State Chronicle*
DN	Dīgha Nikāya
GPC	*Glass Palace Chronicle*
HM	*Hmannan Mahāyāzawindawgyi*
JKM	*Jinakālamālī(pakaraṇaṁ)*
JSC	*Jengtung State Chronicle*
JSS	*Journal of the Siam Society*
KV	*Kaccāyana-Vyākaraṇa*
KN	Khuddaka Nikāya
MLS	*(Tamnān) Mūlasāsanā*
MN	Majjhima Nikāya
MS	Mahā Sakkarāja
MV	*Mahāvaṁsa*
PC	*P̱āḍaeng Chronicle*
PED	*Pali-English Dictionary*
PB61	*Prajum Bongsāvadān,* [*Vol.*] *61*
PPN	*Dictionary of Pali Proper Names*
SE	Saka or Short Era
SP	Sutta Piṭaka
SN	Saṁyutta Nikāya
SV	*Sāsanāvaṁsa*
TMP	*Tamnān Mūlasāsanā Chapap Vat P̱āḍæng*
VM	*Visuddhimagga*
VP	Vinaya Piṭaka
YC	*Yonaka Chronicle*
U Kalā	*U Kalā Mahāyāzawingyi*

Bhamo
Namkham
Rājagaha
Tagaung
Hsenwi
Möngting
Küngma
Kunlong
Möngkā
Möngpaw
Möngban
Möngmit
Namtu
Lashio
Mogok
Hsipaw
Shwebo
Hanlin
Mandalay
Ava
Kyaukse
Pāngsāng
Möngläm
Möngmæn
Möngwang
Jengrung
Möngnông
Möngyāng
Möngma
Takawe
Dongdā
Möngbeng
Möngpu
Jengtung
Möngyawng
Möngbhyāk
Pagan
Meiktila
Lawksawk
Taunggyi
Loilem
Yawnghwe
Mt. Popa
Möngpan
Möngnai
Chiengsaen
Chiengrāy
Luangprabāng
Beikthano
Pyinmanā
Loikaw
Tharekhittarā
Toungoo
Chiengmai
Lambūn
Nān
Lampāng
Sandoway
Viengcan
Henzada
Pegu
Mt. Kelāsa
Sajjanālaiy
Sukhodaiy
Bassein
Rangoon
Thaton
Martaban
Moulmein
ANDAMAN
SEA
Lopburī
Ayudhyā
Tavoy
Bangkok
Rājburī
MILES
0
50
100
200
50
200
KMS.
N
Mrit
Tenassarim
GULF OF
SIAM

THE P̱ĀḌÆNG CHRONICLE

INTRODUCTION

The Shan States and Kengtung

Vat P̲ādaeng (Red Forest Monastery) is one of the great monasteries in the city of Kengtung in the Eastern Shan States of Burma. It is the chronicle of this monastery, the *P̲ādaeng Chronicle* (PC), that is being translated. This chronicle is not to be confused with the *Jengtung State Chronicle* (JSC), a translation of which comprises the second part of this volume. Before coming to the *P̲ādaeng Chronicle*, a brief description is necessary of the State of Kengtung and its set-up, the Khün̈s and their script, and of Theravāda Buddhism.

Administratively the Shan States of Burma were divided into Northern Shan States and Southern Shan states during the British administration. After the regaining of independence, the Shan States were called by the singular name, Shan State, to foster the idea of unity within the Union of Burma. During the British times there were the Shan States and Karenni States (now Kayah State). Now, since the new Constitution of Burma came into being in 1974, there are seven ethnic states, namely, Shan, Kayah, Kachin, Chin, Karen (Kawthoolei), Môn, and Arakan.

Almost all the Shan States, like other districts or provinces in Burma and Thailand, have two names--Shan (or local) and classical (or Pali). The classical name of Kengtung State is Khemaraṭṭha and its capital, Kengtung City, is Tuṅgapurī. The custom is also adopted for the names of some monasteries. Vat P̲ādaeng's Pali name is Sīhaḷarattārāma, and Vat Jengyün is known as Ṭiṭṭhārāmādhīpati.

The Khün̈s and Their Script

The traditional belief is that the original inhabitants of the valley of Kengtung were the Lva or Va. The *Jengtung State Chronicle* says as much and states that the Lva were driven out by King Mangrāy's orders and some of them were settled at Bāngham. Perhaps it was in deference to this tradition that at the consecration (abhiseka) ceremony of a new ruling prince of Kengtung the Lva of Bāngham had a role to play in that two of them would come and ceremonially open their food packets and eat the contents in the palace; but, before they could finish their meal, an official called Bhayā Lai would come and drive them away and then only would the prince be crowned. The Va of Va State have a tradition that their original home was in the Kengtung valley. It may also be noted that Mangrāy's forebears had the prefix Lāo or Lāv to their names.

When and how a Tai people called Khün came to settle in Kengtung valley still remain as vague as how the Tai peoples came to settle in territories stretching from the Brahmaputra to the Mekhong. The Khüns have held sway over what is now known as the State of Kengtung, except for territories added to it by the British in the east (the substates of Jengkhaeng and Möngyông), and in the west (the substates of Möngsāt, Möngpū, and Hsenyôt, which used to be a bone of contention between Kengtung, Möngnāy, and Chiengmai).

The Khün language is akin to Lü of Sipsôngbannā, Tai-Yuan of northern Thailand, and Lao. Like other Tai dialects it has five tones. For those who think that Khün has six tones, it would be more correct to say that there are six ways of spelling the five tones.

The Khün script with its two tonal marks is identical with that of Chiengmai (Tai-Yuan), Sipsôngbannā, and Mönglaem, and with some modification it is also understood in Laos. Prior to the sixteenth century, inscriptions in Kengtung had rectangular characters identical with those used in Chiengmai in the same period. Now the letters of this script in Chiengmai and Kengtung are round. This was probably due to Burmese-Môn influence from the time King Bayinnaung conquered Chiengmai, and all the Shan States in Burma submitted to him. While Burmese suzerainty over Chiengmai lasted a little over two hundred years, Kengtung has been with Burma ever since her submission in 1559.

At one time this Khün script seems to have been used in the Shan areas west of the Salween. Pali scriptures and their translation in this script, on palm leaves and Shan paper books dating back to the early eighteenth century, were found in Mönghnông, close to the Salween, and in Möngbeng, near Taunggyi. It is not known whether this indicates that Khün script was in general use or was used only in monasteries in those areas adhering to the Kengtung brand of Theravāda Buddhism. These books are now in the government museum in Taunggyi.

In areas where Khün script had been in general use until the early part of the twentieth century, namely, Kengtung, Mönglaem, Sipsôngbannā, Laos, and Chiengmai, there had been much intercourse between them from the legendary days of the chronicles and throughout their histories. For instance, the earliest legendary rulers of Kengtung, Kenghung, and Mönglaem were stated to be brothers, though the brother that was supposed to have ruled Kengtung has not been indicated in the dated parts of the *Jengtung State Chronicle*. Rulers of Laos, Kengtung, and Chiengmai used to send to each other such costly presents as articles of the royal regalia, elephants, and horses. They were also often at war with one another. In 1802 Chiengmai forces devastated much of Kenghung and Kengtung and deported thousands of their people whose descendants can still be found in and around Chiengmai and Lambūn. During the early 1850s northern Thai levies, headed by those from

Chiengmai and commanded by a member of the Thai royal family from Bangkok, laid seige to Kengtung City three times but failed to take it. In 1882 Kengtung forces overran Kenghung and Mönglaem and came away with the head of the Kenghung prince, Sao Saeng. In December 1932 the youngest son of the then retired chaoluang (great prince) of Chiengmai came to Kengtung to ask for the hand of a daughter of the ruling caufā (lord of the sky, "sôbwa" in Burmese) of Kengtung in British Burma. The marriage ceremony and the accompanying celebrations were on a scale never to be witnessed again in Kengtung or any Shan State of Burma.

Prior to the overlordship of Bayinnaung in the sixteenth century, a large part of what is now known as the Southern Shan States seems to have had a great deal to do with Chiengmai. Möngnāy, for example, figures quite prominently in the chronicles of Chiengmai from the time of King Mangrāy onward. A Shan dialect spoken in Samkā and Möngpāy, south of Inle Lake, still resembles that on the Thai side of the border, and its speakers are often the object of teasing by other Shans because of the different intonation. Alexander Griswold has suggested that Chiengmai probably was the paramount power in these regions. Certainly references are not lacking to the Ngios (Tai-Yuan word for Shans as distinct from Khüns) in the chronicles of Chiengmai of this period. There are also references to Chiengmai in the *Chronicle of Hsenwi* which I am translating.

Within the five above-mentioned states where Khün script was in general use, there seems to be little doubt that their culture and the Sāsanā came from Chiengmai, in the south, as recorded in the *P̱āḍaeng Chronicle*. In each of these states the ruler was called brayā or king; to his own people the ruler was rājadhirāja, king of kings. The mightiest of kings was also called brayā, like Brayā Asoka Dhammarājā.

Apart from the ruler or king being called brayā, the highest-ranking official of the brayā (ruler) was also given the title of brayā. In Kengtung the practice of giving this title was in vogue until 1935. How, then, is one to differentiate between brayā the king and brayā the high official? For one thing, the context should give a lead. In the second place, in Khün there is a slight difference in the spelling for the high official, which is bhayā--at least that is the current usage and the practice.

In Kengtung, besides the highest title of bhayā for the court officials, the following were titles for the more junior ones: ban, hmün, saen, bōk, and nāy. Up to the first three decades of this century when titles were conferred on officials of Kengtung, bōk and nāy were conferred on officials of the ruling prince's personal office; hmün was no longer in vogue except in substates or village circles; saen was conferred upon officials of both the executive and personal offices of the prince, as well as on others outside these circles. The bhayās of substates gave this title to their officials too. The prince's chief cook and two senior drivers in the early 1930s were saens. Ban was a title given to clerks in the executive office. In the *P̱āḍaeng Chronicle* we very often come across the titles of bōk and ban for personnel connected with the monasteries or religious affairs.

From the end of the eighteenth century the title caufā (lord of the sky) was beginning to be used for the ruling princes of Kengtung in the *Jengtung State Chronicle*. This title is cauphā in Shan, which has no phoneme /f/, and sôbwa in Burmese, and it is the proper Shan title for rulers of the Shan States in Burma from early times. The Burmese chronicles refer to Shan sôbwas frequently, especially from the sixteenth century onward. But, although references are found to the title of sôbwa or caufā in the *Jengtung State Chronicle*, it was mostly used by the Western Shans and the court at Ava. To his own people, the Khüns, the ruler of Kengtung had always been known by one of the four following titles:

a. somḍec bra̱pencau [majesty who is the excellent lord],

b. cauyôḍkhamôm [lord above the head],

c. caunöhō [lord above the head],

d. cauphaenḍin [lord of earth] from the Pali "paṭhavīssara."

The meanings of *a* and *b* are awkward and literal in English, the sense being that he is the highest lord.

As an indication of the extent that the Khün script had been in use and of the penetration of the Theravāda Sāsanā in Kengtung, it may be mentioned that the Tipiṭaka in translation can be found in Khün. One set has the whole Piṭaka, with their divisions and sections, in 170 volumes of palm leaves, each numbering over twenty to over fifty leaves. I have in my possession at my house in Taunggyi, Burma, a complete translation of the *Visuddhimagga* (VM). Khün versions of the Jātaka stories are also well known, especially the last ten Jātakas, namely, Temiya (or Mūga-Pakkha), Janaka, Sāma, Nimi, Candakumāra (or Khandahala), Bhuridatta, Nārada (Mahānāradakassapa), Vidhūrapaṇḍita, Mahosatha (Mahā-Ummagga), and Vessantara. The last Jātaka, Vessantara, is the best known of all.

These translations of the Tipiṭaka and the commentaries form a rich source of nearly forgotten Khün grammar and vocabulary and are a pillar of strength to the already strong Theravāda tradition in Kengtung.

The Khün script, then, had been in use in the court, offices, monasteries, and in the domains of the somḍec brapencau of Khemaraṭṭha from ancient times until 1962 when his administration and court were abolished and a new form of administration set up which is uniform throughout the whole of Burma.

When the somḍec's court was the center of all state activities in which fortunes were made and favors dispensed, the script was in a strong position. With the introduction of English and Burmese as official languages during the British times, along with the opening of motor roads (by Lord Paṭhavīssara himself in the twenties and thirties of this century), new ideas began to come in and the script's position has never been the same. Since independence in 1948, the horizon of the somḍec's subjects has expanded to the whole of the Union of Burma, and the script's position has become positively precarious. Burmese, the lingua franca that is understood throughout the whole union, is avidly sought after not only by non-Khün ethnic minority groups within the state but also by sons and daughters of leading Khün families. Even before 1962, when Khün was still the official language of the somḍec's administration, official circulars, orders, and communications left much to be desired in the way of spelling, syntax, and usage. Since 1962 the Saṅgha has been the only organized body to still use Khün script in its official communications, and it is encouraging the learning of Khün in monasteries--a brave and laudable effort. Much depends on the Khüns themselves--whether and how much they would think it worthwhile to keep up the use of their more perfect script (as compared to Shan) in a world of mass media and propagandized values. Should Khün script disappear, certain distinctive features of Khün culture would soon follow suit. But what must not be forgotten is that to know Khün thoroughly as a subject and for its own sake is scholarship, which is admired the world over. This the sons and daughters of Khün families must always remember.

Monasteries of Kengtung

One of the attractive features of the city of Kengtung is the existence of its numerous monasteries (vats) and their unique architecture, quite unlike anything found in the rest of Burma. Of the existing twenty-one monasteries within or very close to the city walls, the sites of many are several centuries old, even though few structures in them are older than one hundred years in age. There is no reason to disbelieve the account in the *Jengtung State Chronicle* that Vats Brahmai Hōkhōng, Brakaeu, Brakāng (par. 109 of the translation) and Cômsāng (par. 182) came into being around 1350 A.D. Almost all the monasteries mentioned in the *Pādaeng Chronicle* are still very much alive and their bhikkhus are busy teaching the Dhamma and giving spiritual guidance to their lay devotees who form the majority of the city's population. The sites of three or four monasteries of the chronicle which have long disappeared are still identifiable.

A few years back, the cetiya of Vat Brasingala Hōkāḍ, close to the city's eastern gate of P̲āḍaeng, was pulled down (!) so that a new one could be built in its place. (Devout Buddhists of Kengtung are very fond of doing this, but one wishes they would express their devotion by restoring old cetiyas or monastic structures rather than by replacing them.) Several hundred Buddha images of some soft metal alloy were unearthed in the process, each measuring about three and one-half by two inches, and all seem to have been produced from the same mold. Also found were some gilded bricks on which a date was inscribed. Unfortunately, the lord abbot of the monastery did not note the exact date, but he said he remembered that it was about six hundred years ago. The images and the bricks are now inside the new cetiya.

A monastery (or vat) in Kengtung has its own compound enclosed by brick walls within which are these structures: vihāra, rōng, uposatha hall, sālā, mondok (library), water well, and one or two other buildings used for classes or for cooking for public feeding on festive occasions such as a big dāna or the beginning of the vassā or its ending (Pavāraṇā).

The vihāra is the principal place for the morning and evening recitations of worship to the Three Gems by the bhikkhus and sāmaṇeras of the monastery and for ceremonial and dāna activities. Some of the vihāras are large, measuring perhaps over one hundred fifty by sixty feet, capable of holding comfortably several hundred people. There are two rows of lofty and impressive thirty- to forty-foot columns of timber or masonry supporting the girders and ceiling. These are also gilded with floral designs, harmonious with those on the four walls, reminding one of what the Chinese wrote in the eighth century about the ancient Pyū monasteries in Central Burma (cited below in the discussion of the mahātheras Soṇa and Uttara). At the back center of the vihāra, Buddha images are grouped on a raised dais five or six feet high and occupy the space between the first six columns. To the right and slightly forward is another, slightly lower, dais approximately four square feet in area. On it slender posts, decorated and gilded, support a series of square five- or seven-tiered roofs which taper to an ornate finial (called "thī" in Burmese). The Dhamma is preached on this dais. Beyond this dais there is a long low platform (maybe one and one-half feet high), about seven feet wide, stretching perhaps thirty or forty feet along, but at a little distance from, the vihāra wall; two rows of bhikkhus and sāmaṇeras sit here during dāna and other public ceremonies.

Adjacent to and slightly smaller than the vihāra, and joined to it by a large, covered verandah, is the rōng which is the dormitory for twenty to thirty bhikkhus and sāmaṇeras. The rōng may be on the left or right of the vihāra according to structural convenience. In modern times a monastery in Kengtung averages about two to five bhikkhus and ten to twenty sāmaṇeras; a larger monastery like Vat P̱āḍaeng may have more sāmaṇeras.

The uposatha hall may be located on either side of the vihāra, but is closer to the front of the monastery compound. Here, on full moon and new moon days, the Pāṭimokkha (227 rules or sīla governing the conduct of the bhikkhu) is recited. A bhikkhu in the congregation must speak up if he has transgressed any of the rules, in order to be absolved from wrongdoing and to be worthy of his robes.

Near the vihāra and rōng is the sālā which is opened on ceremonial occasions and is used as extra space to accommodate the Saṅgha or laity. In modern times the monastery's sālā is sometimes used as a classroom. "Sālā" is a Pali word meaning a large covered and enclosed hall, a resthouse, or a shed. To construct a sālā in or near a monastery, or along the highway for wearied travelers, is considered a meritorious work in the Theravāda Buddhist countries of Southeast Asia.

The cetiya and the mondok are usually situated behind the vihāra. The Boḍhi tree of Vat P̱āḍaeng is in this area. The water well and pit latrines are well to the back of the rōng; some monasteries have installed modern toilets either under the same roof as the rōng or in separate outhouses. Figure 1 is a rough sketch, drawn from memory, of the ground plan of Vat Hōkhōng in the 1920s; the main structures of the present-day monastery are still what they used to be except for new roofing.

A monastery has to do with lokuttara (supramundane) affairs. The uniqueness and beauty of the vats of Kengtung City are such that should the government of the Union of Burma see fit to allow even a guided tour of the city for foreign tourists, its lokiya (mundane) objective of earning foreign exchange would be more than achieved.

Saṅgāyanās and Tipiṭaka

Theravāda (Doctrine of the Theras) is the name of the oldest form of the Buddha's teachings in the Pali language, as contained in the Canon of Scripture mostly settled soon after the Parinibbāna (Nirvāna or Nibbāna) of the Master by the five hundred great theras at Rājagaha, capital of King Ajātasattu of Magadha. At this meeting, called Saṅgāyanā (council) in Theravāda countries, it is believed that all or almost all that the Buddha had taught and preached was recited and collected into the Tipiṭaka, the three divisions of the Piṭaka, namely, the Sutta Piṭaka (SP), Vinaya Piṭaka (VP), and Abhidhamma Piṭaka (AP). The Second Saṅgāyanā took place at Vesāli one hundred years after the first, and it was here that a rift developed between those who decided to adhere to the original teachings of the Lord, allowing no changes or modifications, and those who thought the words of the Lord could be modified.

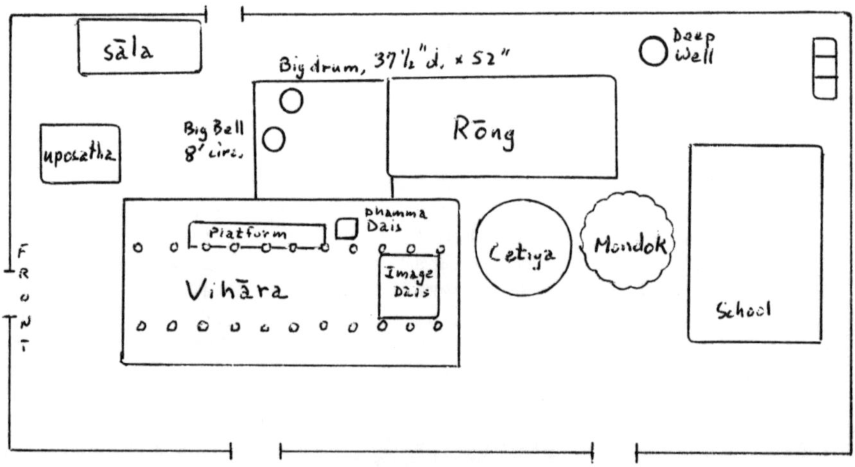

Fig. 1. Ground Plan of Vat Hōkhōng (not to scale).

The Third Saṅgāyanā took place during the reign of Emperor Asoka in the third century B.C. at his capital, Pāṭaliputta. Most probably the final form of the Tipiṭaka as we know it today was decided here. Some authorities doubt if the Abhidhamma was recited at the first two Saṅgāyanās because one chapter of it, "Kathāvatthu," is said to have been written by the president of the assembly, Moggalliputta Tissa Mahāthera, to refute dissenting doctrines. A definite break took place here between the orthodox and the nonorthodox, and it is said that the latter migrated to western India in the thousands to form a congregation of their own from which emerged the Mahāyāna Nikāya around the first century A.D.

Around 90 B.C. another Saṅgāyanā was convened by King Vaṭṭhagāmaṇī at Āloka Vihāra in Ceylon at which the entire Tipiṭaka, with its commentaries, was inscribed on palm leaves and submitted to checking and rechecking.

These four Saṅgāyanās are recognized by all Theravāda countries. The Burmese regard the one convened by King Mindon in

1868-1871 at Mandalay as the fifth, when the whole of the Tipiṭaka was inscribed on both faces of 729 marble slabs, each about a man's height, about three feet wide and four or five inches thick. The Sixth Saṅgāyanā of Burma was convened by the government under the premiership of U Nu; it was inaugurated in 1954 and completed in 1956, in commemoration of the twenty-five hundredth anniversary of the Parinibbāna of the Buddha.

How the First Saṅgāyanā at Rājagaha and the Second Saṅgāyanā at Vesāli were carried out can be read in chapters 11 and 12, respectively, of Culavagga, "Khandaka" division, of the Vinaya Piṭaka. They are also described in a condensed form in such chronicles as the *Mahāvaṁsa* (MV) and the *Jinakālamālī* (JKM), which also give some details of the Third and Fourth Saṅgāyanās. Details of the Sixth Saṅgāyanā, held in Rangoon, can be had from the Buddha Sāsanā Council of Burma, Kabā Aye Road, Rangoon.

These Saṅgāyanās have ensured that the Pali texts of the Tipiṭaka are as perfect as human effort can make them, and the Theravāda Buddhists have maintained that their form of Buddhism has not changed from the days when the Buddha himself was traveling and teaching in northeastern India more than twenty-five hundred years ago.

Mahātheras Soṇa and Uttara

There is a tradition firmly believed by the Theravādins that after the Third Saṅgāyanā in the third century B.C. the Sāsanā was taken by nine groups of mahātheras to various countries within and beyond India. The *Mahāvaṁsa* and most chronicles of Burma and Thailand that have anything to do with Buddhism mention this, probably all having the *Mahāvaṁsa* as their source. The mission to Ceylon was led by Mahinda Thera, Asoka's son; the mission to Suvaṇṇabhūmi, the "Land of Gold," which the Burmese and some chronicles of northern Thailand identify as Lower Burma, was undertaken by the Theras Soṇa and Uttara; and the Thera Mahārakkhita was sent to the country of the Yona ("Ionian," i.e., Greeks or perhaps Hellenized Iranians).

Western scholars take the mission to Ceylon more seriously than the one to Lower Burma because it is mentioned in the chronicles of Ceylon, and communication between North India and Ceylon in Asoka's time is confirmed by his inscriptions, while, the scholars maintain, the exact location of Suvaṇṇabhūmi cannot be determined. On the other hand, missions to the Hellenized states to the west tend to be accepted as fact, since Asoka himself says he sent embassies to states as distant as Egypt and Syria. The fact is, however, that Asoka's embassies are not known to be connected with the missionary work of the theras, and, in any case,

Greek and Latin sources say nothing of the Buddhist missions, or, for that matter (excepting the Greco-Aramaic inscription of Kandahar), of Asoka or his embassies.

Let us examine the possibility of the coming of Soṇa and Uttara to Lower Burma in the third century B.C. Throughout the period of European colonialism, Southeast Asia was regarded as very much of an appendage of India and China, and it was given the names of both India and China (Indo-China), or that of Further India or East India. Except for Siam, all the countries that comprise present-day Southeast Asia were colonies, and even Siam had to cede a large portion of her eastern territories to France besides conceding extraterritorial rights to all European and American powers as a price of her independence. Up to World War II it was customary for scholars to assume that there was little that Southeast Asia had contributed to the civilization of Asia and that there was little worthy of scholastic attention until the arrival of civilizing influences from India and China. Indigenous chronicles were regarded as fairy tales and were the butts of intellectual jokes--so much so that nationalists accused foreign rulers of teaching their compatriots to despise their own culture and civilization.

This was natural. More funds were available for archaeological explorations and excavations elsewhere. Then, as now, Southeast Asia was a fertile ground for commercial exploitation, not for excavation, by foreigners and natives alike, and scholars were the last people in the world capable of influencing government policies anywhere. Nationalists were too busy agitating to insist on excavations to prove their past. Indian scholars who were not politicians satisfied their nationalist aspirations by claiming, without proof, that Asoka's conquest of Kaḷiṅga and Kaniṣka's establishment of the Kuṣān empire in western India caused "waves" of Indian refugees, colonizers, and adventurers to emigrate and colonize practically all of Southeast Asia. Commerce was another theory put forward by scholars for the Indian migrational waves, without taking into consideration the return traffic by the seafaring Malays or Indonesians who are known to have blazed the sea trail to China and to have gone to, and actually colonized and settled in, Madagascar. Intermarriage was another reason given for the theory of Indian settlements, though there is no trace of either Indian blood or common dialects having been left behind.[1] In short, these one-way traffic theories were exactly what European powers, particularly the Portuguese, the French, and the Dutch, had been doing in their colonies from the sixteenth to the twentieth centuries. As for the export of scholars and brahmans from India, it is more likely that only those who could not make their way in their own homeland would emigrate. Even then it was admitted that when the "colonizers" arrived in Southeast Asia they met not savages but organized societies with a civilization of their own.[2] To admit Indian influences, yes; but to give Southeast Asian states from earliest days to the fourteenth or fifteenth centuries the name of Indian kingdoms,[3] no.

Since the end of the last World War, however, things have begun to look differently. Thanks largely to American scholars and archaeologists who went to Southeast Asia in the wake of their soldiers, archaeological finds in northeast and northwest Thailand have made scholars reassess past assumptions that every aspect of civilization in Southeast Asia had come from abroad. They now speculate seriously that Southeast Asia might have been the cradle of civilization for all Asia; they think that the first domestication of plants in the world occurred in Southeast Asia more than seventeen thousand years ago; bronze tools and Banchieng pots, some with beautiful fingerprint designs, found in northeast Thailand, may date to 4500 B.C.; there is a probability that bronze was exported from Southeast Asia to the Middle East, which is thought to have been the source of bronze for Europe.[4]

With these new and revolutionary ideas based on archaeological diggings it is possible to think that there were indeed organized societies and settled governments in Southeast Asia prior to the coming of Indian influences a little before and around the early centuries of the Christian Era, as revealed by excavations of the nineteenth and twentieth centuries. Perhaps the Theras Soṇa and Uttara were among the earliest of those influences.

To strengthen the foregoing, old Chinese writings state that there was a land route between China and India which passed through northern Burma in the second century B.C.[5] This means that the said land route was already in existence by the time mention was made of it in the Chinese writings, and no one can confirm or deny that it did not exist long before that.

As if to confirm that in those early days a part of Southeast Asia was indeed endowed with a civilization, the full significance of which has not yet been assessed, recent radiocarbon tests have pushed back the dates of the existence of old cities of Burma (namely, Tharekhittarā [Śrīkṣetra--old Prome], Beikthanomyo [Viṣṇu City] and Hanlin [near Shwebo in Upper Burma]) from pre-World War II estimates of 500-600 A.D. to the first century A.D. In a paper entitled "Later Evidence of Pyū Culture," U Aung Thaw, Director General of the Archaeological Department of Burma, draws the following conclusions:

1. The Pyū people had already established themselves in the region of Beikthanomyo, Hanlin, and Tharekhittarā by the first century A.D.

2. South Indian culture, which spread at the time, began to establish itself at Beikthanomyo. It would appear that a nikāya (sect) of Buddhism was established which did not worship images of the Buddha.

3. Tharekhittarā and Hanlin flourished at the same time as Beikthanomyo.

4. Beikthanomyo came to an end in the fourth century and Buddhism flourished in Tharekhittarā.

5. Tharekhittarā existed until the eighth century, and, from artifactual evidence, Tharekhittarā and Hanlin perished at the same time. It is certain that the Buddha Sāsanā at Hanlin did not prosper as radiantly as at Tharekhittarā.[6]

Here again, if Pyū cities in Burma were already in existence by the first century A.D., it is more than possible that they existed one or two hundred or more years before that, and they therefore vie with Funan (Cambodia) as being the earliest historical states in Southeast Asia. This will also do away with the sailor's legend which Ptolemy cites, and which was seriously believed to be fact by scholars before World War II (only because it was in writing), that the delta of the Erāvatī River was peopled by cannibals in the second century A.D.[7]

It will be interesting to see if competent experts will push back the dates of the funeral urns of Pyū kings, now that the capital of these kings, Tharekhittarā, is known to have been in existence as early as the first century. These funeral urns have Pyū writings on them. Inscriptions on the sides of three of these famous urns state that three kings of the Vikrama dynasty died in the years 50, 57, and 80 without mentioning any era. British scholars of old took the dates to belong to the present Burmese era, or Cuḷa Sakkarāja (CS), and added 638 to convert them into dates of the Christian Era; 50, 57, and 80 become 688, 695, and 718 A.D., respectively. Some Burmese scholars, however, interpret them as Saka Era (SE), or Mahā Sakkarāja (MS), and add 78 to make them 128, 135, and 158 A.D.[8] They maintain that, according to the Burmese chronicles, the Saka Era came into being in 78 A.D. during the Tharekhittarā period, while the present Burmese, or Cuḷa, era was inaugurated in 638 A.D. by a king of Pagan named Poppa Sô̂rahan.

The inauguration of the Saka Era at Tharekhittarā was attributed to the work of Sakka, king of devās, who had calculated it on a rock at a locality called Lokananda Kyauksaga when the Buddha Sakkarāja Era (BS) had reached 624; but, continues the chronicle account, astrological considerations decided that the new era (Saka) actually began in the year 622 of the Buddha Sakkarāja, and that therefore the year 624 would be reckoned as year 2 of the new era. What probably happened was that the court astrologers of Tharekhittarā at the time (some brahmans, most likely, who could not make ends meet in India) received the news of the commencement of the Saka Era in western India over a year later and recommended its adoption to their lord and master the king with astrological adjustments as stated. If this assumption is correct, one cannot help admiring the wit of the astrologers royal in converting "Saka" into "Sakka." It is important to resolve the 560 years' difference between the two views of the dates of the Pyū funeral urns in order to corroborate the antiquity of Tharekhittarā as determined by radiocarbon tests. Only experts can do this, but in view of the proven existence of Tharekhittarā in the first century A.D., is it not reasonable to assume that the dates on the funeral urns belong to the Saka Era (unless the script itself proves otherwise)?

What about Theravāda Buddhism during the Tharekhittarā period? The twenty numbered thick gold leaves of Tharekhittarā (unearthed before World War II) contain lines in Pali from the Tipiṭaka. Of the two stone inscriptions which used to stand at two of the Tharekhittarā city gates, one has lines from the Maṅgala Sutta and the Mora Sutta and the other lines from the Ratana Sutta. These suttas are among the well-known Paritta (protection) Suttas of the Theravādins, the recitation of which is believed to protect their hearers and surrounding areas from all dangers. It is plain that the lines on the stone inscriptions were meant to protect the city itself. U Aung Thaw, in the paper referred to above, says that the characters on the inscriptions belong to the fifth and sixth centuries. These are clear indications that Buddhism at Tharekhittarā from the fifth century onward was Theravāda, though the city itself had been in existence from the first century. Can one assume the possibility that the Theravāda Nikāya had been in existence some time before the gold leaves and the inscriptions? Scholars are quick to point out that here and there in Tharekhittarā evidence of the Mahāyāna sect and Brahmanism is also found. There is nothing extraordinary in this; even in modern times Hindu temples and Muslim mosques exist side by side with the predominant Buddhist pagodas and monasteries in Rangoon, Mandalay, and other big towns of Burma.

The probability of the existence of organized governments in Southeast Asia before the Christian Era, the land route between China and India through northern Burma in the second century B.C., and the existence of Pyū cities from the first to the eighth centuries (together with the artifacts mentioned and others of gold, silver, and semi-precious stones) certainly strengthen the possibility that Soṇa and Uttara came to Lower Burma in the third century B.C. Who can tell? The whole of Southeast Asia may have been flourishing at this period on a scale hitherto thought impossible; though solid evidence is lacking, circumstantial evidence would permit us to assume that possibility. Full reports are awaited of the excavations (cold season 1975-1976) by the Archaeology Department of Burma of one of the old sites near the town of old Thaton, traditionally thought to be the port of Suvaṇṇabhūmi, at the foot of Mount Kelāsa, on which a monastery is believed to have been built for the two theras. It has been said that a delegation of Rāmañña (Môn) Saṅgha, headed by the lord abbot of Kelāsa Monastery, was present at the consecration ceremonies of the great stupa built by Duṭṭhagāmaṇī, one of the great kings of Ceylon, in the second century B.C.[9]

Chinese writings of the mid-ninth century mention two land routes existing around the first four decades of that century between China and India which passed through north Burma, one of which went through a "Pyū capital."[10] Is this latter route one and the same as that of the second century B.C.? Scholars have not commented on this, but a layman would not hesitate to say yes. The following is the Chinese description of an unspecified Pyū city:

> Their king's name is Mahārāja. His chief minister is Mahāsena. When he goes on a short journey, the king is borne on a litter of gold cord; when he journeys far, he rides an elephant. His wives and concubines are very numerous: the constant number is a hundred. The compass of the city-wall is faced with glazed bricks; it is 160 li in circumference. The banks of the moat too are faced with brick. . . . Within the walls inhabitants number several myriad families. There are over a hundred monasteries with courts and rooms all decked with gold and silver coated with cinnabar and bright colours, smeared with kina and covered with embroidered rugs . . . the king's residence too is like this. . . . When they come to the age of seven, both boys and girls drop their hair and stop in a monastery, where they take refuge with the Saṅgha. On reaching the age of twenty, if they have not awakened to the principles of the Buddha, they let their hair grow again and become ordinary townfolk. . . . There are twelve gates with pagodas at the four corners. . . .[11]

This might have come straight out of any of the chronicles of Burma or Thailand, which are usually received with skepticism, but having come from Chinese sources scholars regard it as authentic.

There is no doubt from the description of the monasteries and the ordinations of sāmaṇeras and bhikkhus that they belong to the

Theravāda Nikāya, which is still true today, except for the ordination of girls. The king's journeys, his concubines, the twelve gates, the resemblance between the palace and the monastery all fit in with the chronicles and later historical records of kings and great cities of Burma. Remains of Pyū cities are dotted all over Central and North Burma. It is my belief that each walled town was a city-state independent of the rest except that one or two of the more powerful ones were likely to demand tribute from the weaker ones close by; and, furthermore, that it is a mistake to imagine a single Pyū city serving as the capital of all the Burmese Pyū city states, with particular reference to the old assumption that when Tharekhittarā was "destroyed" the "Pyū capital moved north" to Hanlin; in any case, this theory has been put to rest by U Aung Thaw's proven statement that Tharekhittarā and Hanlin perished about the same time only after the eighth century.[12]

The walls of Tharekhittarā are roughly circular in shape, measuring two and one-quarter miles east to west and two and three-quarter miles north to south. "And Sakra stood in the center of a piece of pleasant level ground and described a circle by means of a rope dragged round by the Nāga." So says the *Glass Palace Chronicle* (GPC), which goes on to give the dimensions of the city as one yojana in diameter and three yojana in circumference.[13] Could the Chinese be referring to Tharekhittarā in their writing when they say the Pyū city's circumference was 160 li? Some Burmese scholars think that this Pyū city is Rājagaha (Yāzagyo) in the Chindwin River valley midway between Môlaik in the north and Kalemyo in the south. The area is referred to as Kaletaungnyo in the *Glass Palace Chronicle*.[14]

That Tharekhittarā existed in the seventh century was certified in 648 and 675 respectively by Hsüan Tsang and I Tsing, the Chinese pilgrims to India.[15] Thus, the circumstantial evidence is strong for the continuous existence of Tharekhittarā for a period of nearly one thousand years.

From all this it is difficult to resist the temptation to assume that Theravāda Nikāya existed in Burma from the first to the ninth centuries A.D. If so, its origin could only have been traced to the coming of the Theras Soṇa and Uttara.

Authorities in Burma are excavating ancient sites near Thaton, as stated above, for it was at Thaton that Soṇa and Uttara are believed to have landed, and the *Chronicle of Thaton* maintains that since then there has been an unbroken line of theras down to historical times. Old Thaton was the capital and port of Rāmaññadesa (Môn country). Rāmaññadesa is identified as Suvaṇṇabhūmi in the Kalyānī Inscriptions put up by the Rāmañña king Dhammacetī (1472-1492).

The exact location of Suvaṇṇabhūmi is between the Sittang and the Bilin rivers, about twenty miles north-northeast of modern Thaton. This is where the excavations by the Archaeological Department of Burma are being carried out. Mount Kelāsa is to the west of the town of Bilin on the Bilin River and old Thaton is at the foot of these hills closer to the eastern estuary of the Sittang. One or two miles north of Bilin is a shrine traditionally believed to have been built over the ashes of Mahātheras Soṇa and Uttara, and the place is called Kusinārā, after the town of the same name in India where the Buddha attained Parinibbāna. Local people also believe that their area is called Suvaṇṇabhūmi because of gold dredging and panning from time immemorial in the sandy beaches of the Sittang and other streams and rivers. The gold of Decumpa, about ten or fifteen miles north of Pegu, has been very popular with past and present alchemists.

It is said that Professor G. H. Luce was able to locate Pyidôthākyun of the inscriptions and chronicles where Sôlu and Kyanzitthā fought Ngayamankan, because he was helped by local traditions and current conversation of the people of Kyundô. If so, traditional beliefs regarding Suvaṇṇabhūmi should not be lightly dismissed.

The Bhikkhu and His Upasampadā

To come back to the main topic, the Saṅgāyanās and the Pali Canon, then, are among the hallmarks of Theravāda Buddhism. Other important features of this orthodox Buddhism are its Order of the Saṅgha and its monastic system, which have been in unbroken existence since the lifetime of its founder, Lord Buddha, first in the country of his birth, India, and then in Ceylon and Southeast Asia.

A visitor to present-day Burma and Thailand is immediately struck by the pervading presence of the bhikkhus and their monasteries. Besides working for their own salvation, these bhikkhus are spiritual guides and Dhamma teachers to lay Buddhists everywhere. Since the recent political changes we do not know what has become of Buddhism in Laos and Cambodia, two formerly staunch Theravāda countries of Southeast Asia, or what may be the future of the Sāsanā there.

Sometimes these bhikkhus have been accused of leading an idle life. The accusation was certainly leveled against them during the British rule[16] in Burma by ignorant writers and by converts and preachers of other faiths, naturally jealous of the Saṅgha's predominant influence in the society, even under a foreign rule. The bhikkhus themselves regard such slander as part of the eight lokadhamma: lābha (wealth), alābha (poverty), yaso (fame), ayaso (obscurity), nindā (blame), pasaṁsā (praise), sukhaṁ (happiness), and dukkhaṁ (suffering). To the unbiased and to all Buddhists, however, their ascetic and celibate life alone evokes admiration and reverence.

Besides guiding lay devotees the bhikkhus must keep themselves free from any lapse in their adherence to the 227 Pāṭimokkha rules. This is done regularly on the full moon and new moon of every lunar month when the Saṅgha members congregate in the uposatha halls of their monasteries and listen to the recitation of the Pāṭimokkha. Bhikkhus of a monastery that has no uposatha hall or those whose number cannot form a quorum must go to the congregation of another monastery. Here, in the uposatha hall, a bhikkhu who has infringed any of the 227 rules must admit his fault by confession for which there are Pali formulae. Infringement of any of the four Pārājika rules (sexual intercourse in any form, taking a human life, stealing, boasting of possession of superhuman powers) results in the expulsion of the culprit from the Order. In actuality Pārājika confession is not necessary, for such lapses will be known publicly in no time and the guilty party forced to leave the Order; in any case, any bhikkhu who feels incapable of keeping to the rules has the liberty to leave the Order at any time. An infringement of any of the next 13 most serious rules, the Saṅghādisesa, can be purged by an assembly of the Saṅgha at a ceremony called Parivāsakamma (see note 86 of the translation). The remaining 210 rules are not serious enough to need any action other than confession.

It must be remembered that these rules are not commandments; and for laymen, except for taking human life and stealing, they constitute no more serious crime or sin than bad manners and lack of self-discipline and restraint. There is a story that once a bhikkhu in a village monastery was found to have infringed the celibacy clause of the Pārājika and when the villagers turned up in a body at the monastery to defrock him, he said, "What is all this fuss about an act which I have committed only once in my life; while you take it for granted every day!"

A layman may become a bhikkhu in two ways:

1. He receives pabbajjā (going forth) ordination to be a sāmaṇera (novice) at a young age from ten years up and stays in the monastery until he is twenty when he is qualified to undergo upasampadā (higher) ordination and become a bhikkhu.

2. If a layman is twenty and above and wishes to be a bhikkhu he receives both the pabbajjā and upasampadā ordinations on the same day. The important thing is that he must go through the pabbajjā ordination before the upasampadā ordination.

Up to the end of the last century, when the monastery was the sole fountain of learning, it was usual for a sāmaṇera to stay in the monastery for three or four vassā at least, during which he would learn the "three R's" and a certain amount of Dhamma. At the age of seventeen or eighteen the sāmaṇera might leave his yellow robes in order to help his parents or to get married. This was done for practical reasons, not because he could not withstand hunger during the evening, as often erroneously supposed. Many a boy would also choose to stay in the yellow robes until the age of twenty in order to become an ordained bhikkhu. Parents' opinions and the words of the lord abbot of the monastery played a big role in influencing the decision to stay in or to leave the monastery.

Under modern conditions, when the school has replaced the monastery as the place for education, sāmaṇeras in monasteries are not as numerous as formerly; however, in spite of the proliferation of modern schools, many boys still become sāmaṇeras in Burma and Thailand, as can be seen on the roads in towns and villages early in the morning when they are out on their alms rounds. The majority of Buddhist schoolboys, however, are ordained as sāmaṇeras in Burma during the summer vacation and they stay in the monastery as long as convenient to their families--anything from a few days to a few weeks--until the school opening is near.

That a bhikkhu has to follow the 227 Pāṭimokkha rules has already been mentioned. A sāmaṇera follows only the ten sīla as follows:

1. Abstaining from taking the life of sentient beings
2. Abstaining from taking what is not given
3. Abstaining from unchastity (sexual misconduct for the five sīla)
4. Abstaining from telling lies
5. Abstaining from taking intoxicants
6. Abstaining from eating after midday
7. Abstaining from dancing, singing, playing music, and witnessing shows and entertainments
8. Abstaining from wearing flowers and from using scents and beautifying cosmetics
9. Abstaining from using high and large beds
10. Abstaining from accepting gold and silver

In Thailand it is the custom for laymen (in fact they are encouraged) to be ordained bhikkhus for the whole three-month period of the vassā, and office workers are given three and one-half months leave for the purpose with full pay by their employers, especially the government. In Burma men above the age of twenty become bhikkhus for a period suitable and convenient to their families and circumstances. To be ordained for one vassā is also regarded as a special undertaking, although there is no sudden increase in the bhikkhu population as in Thailand during the vassā. I am not familiar enough with conditions in Ceylon to be able to say how and when laymen become bhikkhus, but I would think the practice is pretty much the same as in Burma.

In the monastery the bhikkhu follows two courses of conduct: Pariyatti (learning and study of the Dhamma) and Paṭipatti (practice of what has been learned, especially in the field of meditation). These two courses will enable him to attain Paṭivedha (realization of the Truth). In Theravāda countries there is no shortage of men who have dedicated their whole lives to the Sāsanā for their own salvation as well as that of their lay supporters. Just as the Buddha had taken upon himself the task of helping all creatures to cross the ocean of saṁsāra, all members of the Saṅgha are duty-bound to guide others on the path. It is wrong to say that the bhikkhu cares only for his own skin (see note 16). In helping others, he abides by the Four Brahmavihāra: mettā (loving kindness), karuṇā (compassion), muditā (sympathy), and upekkhā (equanimity).

In spite of all this, any time that a bhikkhu feels he cannot follow the ascetic life in the monastery, he is at liberty to beg the permission of the lord abbot to become a householder and to continue to support the Sāsanā from "without."

Seeing the bhikkhu on the road or in the monastery one must not forget the twenty-five hundred years of tradition behind him. Greatest importance is attached to the rites and procedures of the upasampadā ordination. Having attained the age of twenty the candidate must: be free from certain diseases considered incurable in ancient times; be free from debt and government service; have obtained his parents' consent; possess the aṭṭhaparikkhāra, or eight articles of necessity (a set of three robes, an alms bowl, cloth girdle, needle, razor, and water strainer); and have an upajjhāya (preceptor) to sponsor him at the ordination.

The ordination itself is conducted strictly in accordance with rules laid down in the Vinaya Piṭaka in a correctly consecrated uposatha hall by a quorum of properly qualified Saṅgha (minimum five, but usually between fifteen and twenty). A flaw in the consecration of the uposatha hall, in the qualifications of the candidate himself or of the ordaining Saṅgha, or in the words of recitation or ceremonial sequence during the ordination, would invalidate that ordination. That flaw may not have been noticed at the time but it would nevertheless invalidate successive ordinations that might come later. It goes without saying that monks of non-Theravāda Buddhist sects cannot take part in any Saṅghakamma (acts of the Saṅgha) of the Saṅgha of any Theravāda monastery.

This insistence on the most pure and most orthodox way of ordination forms the central point in all "purification" procedures of the Sāsanā by successive kings, ruling princes, and saṅgharājās (heads of the Saṅgha) in the chronicles and histories of Thailand and Burma. In the process of purification, bad bhikkhus are also expelled from the Order. It is this purification of the Sāsanā that has prompted the writings of the chronicles of Buddhism, such as the *Sāsanāvaṁsa* (SV) by Paññāsāmi Thera of Burma and *Jinakālamālī* by Ratanapaññā Thera of Thailand. The most famous record of such purification is the Kalyāṇī Inscription of Pegu, Burma, set up by the Môn king, Dhammacetī (1472-1492).

It is the purification of the Sāsanā in Kengtung which forms the subject matter of our text, the chronicle of the Sīhaḷarattārāma, otherwise known as Vat P̱āḍaeng, of the city of Keṅgtung, Eastern Shan States, Burma.

The Lay Devotees

The position of the Buddhist lay devotees in Theravāda countries is of the utmost importance, for without them there can be no Sāsanā. As the Saṅgha are not earning or working to support themselves, they must have patrons and supporters (dāyakā). The relationship between the bhikkhu and his dāyakās is one of mutual benefit. The dāyakā regards it as a privilege and a meritorious act to support the bhikkhu, and through him the Sāsanā, while the latter regards it as his duty to show the dāyakā the Dhamma ways and the way to Salvation. Moreover, having been supported by lay devotees, the bhikkhu feels duty-bound to make himself worthy of their respect and sacrifice. Such suttas as the Tevijja, Brahmajala, or Ambaṭṭha hint as much. For example:

> Whereas some samaṇas and brāhmaṇas, while living on food provided by the philanthropic and the generous, earn their living by wrong means of livelihood, by low arts, such as: prophesying long life, prosperity . . . divining by means of omens and signs . . . foretelling that our king will win the battle, the foreign kings will suffer defeat . . . there will be an eclipse of the moon, of the sun . . . foretelling an abundant rainfall, a deficient rainfall, a good harvest, a bad harvest . . . the bhikkhu refrains from such low arts.[17]

Generally speaking, the Theravāda lay devotees regard themselves as weak in pāramī (perfections), and, if they cannot forsake the life of a householder to practice the ascetic life of a bhikkhu, it is at least within their power to perform the three meritorious acts of dāna (liberality or giving), sīla (morality), and bhāvanā (meditation) whenever opportunities present themselves, in order to better their future rebirths in the saṁsāra.

Although the most noble dāna is given without ulterior motive or expectation for any return, except in the merit for a better kamma, it is believed that the more worthy the receiver of the dāna the greater the merit. This is the chief reason why the overwhelming majority of receivers of dāna are the representatives of the Three Gems, namely, the Saṅgha. The dāna to them can be anything from alms food during the morning alms rounds or their daily requirements (usually referred to as the catupaccaya, the four requisites: robes, food, shelter, and medicine) to pagodas and monasteries. The most common dāna to the Saṅgha takes the form of invitations to bhikkhus and sāmaṇeras for a meal before noon at one's house, or dāna of robes, accompanied by parcels or trays of such modern knick-knacks as sugar, a tin of condensed or powdered milk, a tin of tea leaves or coffee, matches, a bottle of cooking vegetable oil, a packet each of matches and candles, a bottle or two of indigenous or patent medicine for minor ailments, a cake of soap, a small hand towel, etc.

An earthen pot filled with drinking water at the gate of one's compound or in front of one's house for all to slake their thirst in the tropical midday sun; a few cents or a small cup of rice to the beggar at the door; contribution in cash or kind to the common or pool dāna of the village or the city ward; financially sponsoring the pabbajjā or upasampadā ordination of one's own children or those of others who are less fortunate and cannot afford the financial burden; construction of rest houses (sālā) on the highway or at well-known monasteries and pagodas--all are regarded as dāna that help to enhance one's meritorious kamma for the future. For the present, long life, good appearance, happiness, and strength (āyu, vaṇṇa, sukha, bala) will be the share of those who give dāna,[18] and to them the five blessings will also accrue, namely, the affection of many, noble association, good reputation, self-confidence, and heavenly rebirth.[19]

Although sīla is mentioned after dāna, the two go together, for good Buddhists must always observe five sīla as the minimum, and eight sīla whenever possible. The five sīla are:

1. Abstaining from taking the life of sentient beings
2. Abstaining from taking what is not given
3. Abstaining from sexual misconduct
4. Abstaining from telling lies
5. Abstaining from taking intoxicants

The eight sīla consist of the above five, but with absolute observation of celibacy in place of merely abstaining from sexual misconduct, plus the following three:

6. Abstaining from taking food after midday
7. Abstaining from dancing, singing, playing music, witnessing shows or entertainments, wearing flowers, and using scents and beauty cosmetics.
8. Abstaining from using high and large beds

The eight sīla are usually observed by both young and old in the monastery on uposatha days (first quarter, full moon, last quarter, new moon). These are also the days in the monastery when lay devotees of the Buddha Sāsanā, especially the senior ones, practice meditation (bhāvanā), as the home atmosphere is neither suitable for nor conducive to it. How the actual bhāvanā is carried out is described briefly in the next section, "The Theravāda Way."

This periodic meditation is different from what is happening in meditation centers all over Burma. (I understand that meditation centers are also spreading in Thailand.) At meditation centers, lay disciples, male and female, undertake to meditate for a period lasting from a week or ten days to six or eight weeks. The meditator observes the eight sīla and spends the whole period at the center, and is fed, besides a light breakfast at dawn, one main meal a day before midday with food from either the center's kitchen (where most workers are volunteers) on payment of a small fee, or from his or her home. Each person is given a cell, in the male or female hostel as the case may be. The routine during this period is rigorous: four hours in twenty-four are allowed for sleep; four for rest, eating, washing, and ablutions; sixteen for meditation. After the initial period of three or four days, no hardship is felt and the rhythm of life is one of peace and calm. At the end of the stay one has a feeling that one has not done enough, and that after attending to some urgent problems at home or business one may return to the center, perhaps in a few months time.

Besides dāna, sīla, and bhāvanā, Buddhists in Theravāda countries regard the Maṅgala Sutta[20] as their chief guide in the conduct of everyday life. It is said that when the British envoy, Sir Arthur Phayre, had an audience with King Mindon at Amarapura in 1855 (three years before he moved to Mandalay in 1858), he was told by the king that the Maṅgala Sutta could be an excellent textbook for a world citizen.[21] The sutta comes in twelve stanzas of Pali verse and contains the well-known thirty-eight maṅgala blessings) enumerated thus:

1. Dissociation with the foolish
2. Association with the wise
3. Reverence to those worthy of reverence
4. To live in suitable spot
5. Having done good deeds in past lives

6. Establishing oneself on the right path
7. Learning
8. Science
9. Well-trained in good discipline
10. Well-spoken
11. Support of one's mother and father
12. Cherishing one's wife and children
13. Following a peaceful livelihood
14. Giving dāna
15. Righteous conduct
16. Cherishing one's relatives
17. Deeds that bring no blame
18. Eschewing evil
19. Conquest of evil
20. Abstaining from intoxicants
21. Vigilance in righteous acts
22. Reverence to one's elders
23. Humility
24. Contentment
25. Gratitude
26. Hearing the Dhamma at proper times
27. Forbearance
28. Gentleness
29. Visiting holy persons
30. Discussions of the Dhamma at proper times
31. Austerity
32. Chastity
33. Perception of the Truths
34. Realization of Nibbāna
35. Not to be swayed by worldly conditions
36. To be free from sorrow
37. To be free from defilements
38. Tranquility

Another sutta which goes with the Maṅgala Sutta, and whose contents are regarded as equally worthy of striving after, is the Mettā Sutta.[22] Here it is taught that mettā (loving kindness) should be developed without bounds for all beings in the entire universe in the same way that a mother loves and protects her son, her only child, at the risk of her life. Such mettā should be generated and developed during the waking moments of one's life.

Perhaps not all Buddhists can live up to the high standards set by the two suttas, but they do try to follow the spirit of their teachings.

In Burma and Thailand there are women who are called "nuns" in English and whose lives are different from those of the ordinary householders. These nuns are not to be confused with the bhikkhunīs of the Buddha's time, nor are they so called in

Theravāda countries. In Thai and Burmese they are called the equivalent of "lady sīla-observers," and the colors of their dress range from white or off-white and pinkish white to very light brown, but never any suggestion of yellow. Besides the usual long skirt and long-sleeved jacket, each nun has a sheet of cloth over her dress. This sheet or robe leaves her right arm (in jacket sleeve) free in the manner of the bhikkhu and his yellow robes, but there are no regulations for its pattern or length.[23] It is long enough for one end to first go comfortably over the left shoulder with the other end going over the first and the overlap gathered and folded over the left shoulder, thereby leaving the right arm free and keeping the whole robe in place in a way that only pure cotton fabrics do, while the width may range from half-way down the knees to a little below the knees.

Some of these nuns live at home with relatives, but many live in "nunneries." The Sagaing Hills area (on the opposite bank of the Erāvatī from Mandalay) is specially famous for them in Burma.

These nuns are laywomen striving to live the holy life and they observe only the eight sīla. They do not constitute the Order of Bhikkhunīs (who observed their own 311 rules), which died out not long after the Paranibbāna of the Buddha. Inscriptions of Burma mention the existence of bhikkhunīs down to the fourteenth and fifteenth centuries, but it is not clear whether these were the bhikkhunīs of the Buddha's time or just the forerunners of the present-day lady sīla-observers.

The Theravāda Way

This is no place to expound the Theravāda doctrine, but for those unfamiliar with the subject, a brief description of its way to Salvation will not be out of place.

There is no creator God in Theravāda Buddhism, nor is there a faraway land where all beings who have done good deeds live in bliss forever. The Pali texts have never claimed that the Buddha was superhuman, and the term "Boḍhisatta" is applied only to him before he attained the Enlightenment and to nobody else. The Buddha's Enlightenment was attained through his diligent striving and his supreme intellect and wisdom. In Buddhist cosmology, a hundred thousand times ten million universes are not eternal and they arise and pass away in obedience to natural law. Although the existence of devās (supernatural beings) is not denied, no life is eternal for any being that inhabits the thirty-one realms of existence. All must be born as human in the human world in order to tread the path to Salvation.

A being is composed of five components (pañcakkhandhā): rūpa (physical body), vedanā (sensations), saññā (perception), saṅkhāra (tendency-formation or volition), and viññāṇa (consciousness). These five life-forming components are not an enduring entity, but undergo changes every moment in a dynamic process, subject to anicca (impermanence), dukkha (suffering), and anattā (nonself). When life comes to an end, this process is carried forward into a fresh existence. The volitional activities then bear their results, the good deeds producing happiness and the evil ones misery. These volitional activities are called kamma of which there are three: kāyakamma (deed), vacīkamma (word), and manokamma (thought); and the results are valled vipāka. In every life this dual process is carried on and fresh kamma and vipāka are in turn created, ad infinitum. In Buddhist terminology this endless process of life and rebirth is called saṁsāra.

The Buddha is represented as saying: "Without conceivable beginning is this saṁsāra. No beginning can be seen of beings hindered by ignorance [avijjā], fettered by craving [taṇhā], coursing through the round of births and deaths. The ancestors of a man are more numerous than the blades of grass and sticks and branches and leaves in India, more numerous than all the particles of dust that compose the earth."[24] Viewed in this light, especially when countless numbers of miserable existences are involved, the saṁsāra is frightening and is real suffering.

This suffering (dukkha) is the first of the well-known Four Ariya (Noble Truths) preached by the Buddha in the Dhammacakkappavattana Sutta[25] (Discourse on the setting in motion of the wheel of Dhamma) at the Deer Park of Isipatana, near Benares, two months after the Enlightenment on the full moon of July. This is usually known in English as "The First Sermon." These Four Ariya Truths are:

1. The Ariya Truth of dukkha (suffering or pain)
2. The Ariya Truth of dukkhasamudaya (origin of suffering)
3. The Ariya Truth of dukkhanirodha (extinction of suffering)
4. The Ariya Truth of dukkhanirodhagāminī-paṭipadā (practice whereby the extinction of dukkha is attained; this is also called Magga or The Way)

The first Truth teaches that all forms of existence are unsatisfactory and subject to dukkha. The second Truth teaches that the origin of dukkha is taṇhā (craving or desire) for sensual pleasures which perpetuates the saṁsāra. The third Truth teaches that the elimination of taṇhā is the extinction of dukkha and Nibbāna is realized. And how? As stated at the beginning of the Dhammacakkappavattana Sutta, this extinction of dukkha is not done by extreme measures of self-indulgence in sensual pleasure (kāmasukha) on the one hand, or self-torment (atta-kilamatha) on the other, but by the middle way (majjhima-paṭipadā), which is the fourth Truth, namely, the Eightfold Path (aṭṭhaṅgika-magga):

1. Sammā-diṭṭhi (Right Understanding): the correct view or understanding of the Four Truths.

2. Sammā-saṅkapa (Right Thought): thoughts should be free from greed and sensual lust (lobh and rāga), ill-will or anger (dosa), and delusion (moha).

3. Sammā-vācā (Right Speech): abstaining from telling lies (musavāda-vācā), calumnious words (pisuṇavācā), abusive and harsh words (pharusavācā), and flippant babble (samphappalāpa-vācā).

4. Sammā-kammanta (Right Action): abstaining from killing sentient beings, stealing, and sexual misconduct.

5. Sammā-ājīva (Right Livelihood): abstaining from a livelihood that brings harm to other beings, such as trading in arms, living beings, intoxicants or poison; slaughtering; fishing; soldiering; and avoiding deceit, treachery, soothsaying, usury, trickery, etc.

6. Sammā-vāyāma (Right Effort): developing and maintaining deeds and acts of a meritorious nature.

7. Sammā-sati (Right Mindfulness): this is the well-known bhāvanā (meditation) which makes the disciple mindful and aware of all movements of the body, of the feelings, of the mind and of mind-objects, during the waking moments, which is not unusual for those striving after perfection.

8. Sammā-samādhi (Right Concentration): concentration detached from sensual objects and demeritorious things, capable of inducing the four jhāna in the disciple, and eventual emancipation.

In the Dhammacakkappavattana Sutta, it is said that the first Truth of suffering (dukkha) is to be fully understood; the second Truth of the origin of suffering (dukkhasamudaya), which is craving (taṇhā), is to be abandoned; the third Truth, of the extinction of suffering (dukkhanirodha), is to be realized (dukkhanirodha equates with Nibbāna); the fourth Truth, of the path to the extinction of suffering (dukkhanirodhagāminīpaṭipadā) is to be cultivated.

The *Visuddhimagga* compares dukkha with a disease: the origin of dukkha, its cause; the extinction of dukkha, its cure; the path of dukkha, its medicine.[26]

The Eightfold Path is divided into three groups: Right Understanding and Right Thought come under paññā (wisdom); Right Speech, Right Action, and Right Livelihood under sīla (morality); Right Effort, Right Mindfulness, and Right Concentration under samādhi (concentration). No concentration is possible without the wisdom of what is involved, and both would come to naught unless they are based on high morality. When these have been understood, the Eightfold Path may be regarded in this light: all eight must be developed simultaneously, one cannot be neglected without harm to the others; then only will they pave the way to Nibbāna by controlling the mind and preventing the creation of that kamma energy which is the chief cause of rebecoming.

To control the mind one has to train and develop one's mental concentration through bhāvanā. This bhāvanā (meditation) is not mere desultory reflection, but a severe exercise in attention, discipline of the will and mind, and concentration of thought, and there are two types: samatha (tranquility) and vipassanā (insight). Samatha bhāvanā is believed to be capable of developing superhuman powers (abhiññā) in the disciple but does not lead to Salvation, and the true disciple uses it only as a step towards vipassanā-samādhi, the road to Salvation. It begins with concentrating total attention on the incoming and outgoing breath. One of the best-known meditation centers in Burma, Thāthana Yeikthā of the Mahāsī Sayādô in Rangoon, advocates the rising and falling of the abdomen when one breathes in and out as the center of attention. Both methods serve the same end. With intensive effort and mindfulness the mind is riveted to that one-pointedness (citt'ekaggatā) to the exclusion of all extraneous ideas and objects and this is samādhi. When this samādhi is sufficiently strong, the disciple will be able to carry on the bhāvanā continuously, day and night, without feeling any strain.[27]

Gradually the disciple becomes so detached that his own body and limbs cease to be "my body," "my leg," or "my arm," but are just objects of impersonal contemplation. The mind is so completely tamed and controlled that it becomes capable of perceiving the reality that lies beyond the ever changing mentality and corporeality or name and form (nāma-rūpa). "It then becomes a keen instrument, tempered to razor-edge sharpness, with which to cut through the bonds of ignorance [avijjā]." In other words:

> The mind, which up to that point had been constructing the moment-to-moment continuum of its illusory conceptions of selfhood, all at once breaks the sequence of that activity, is no longer tied to it, and at once enters into a fresh realm of knowledge. When this happens, the chain of cause and effect, which is linked by the emotional and intellectual reactions, is broken; there is

> no more kamma rooted in desire, and so no further projection into the future of saṁsāra. The incessant round of births and deaths comes to an end; in the Buddhist phrase, the fire of the passions is extinguished, and so Nibbāna is attained. One who has accomplished that is called an arahat.[28]

It is this desire for liberation that keeps Thai and Burmese bhikkhus by the tens of thousands within the confines of their monasteries voluntarily submitting themselves to the 227 rules of the Pāṭimokkha, and at the same time showing their lay devotees the way to the goal towards which they themselves are striving with diligence. Cannot this salvation be achieved by laymen? It is possible in theory, but in practice, as long as one is a householder, attachments are many, luxuries and responsibilities are great, and the mind can never attain that atmosphere of peace and equilibrium necessary for the prolonged and uninterrupted bhāvanā.

In the Mahāsatipaṭṭhāna Sutta,[29] the Buddha is quoted as saying: "This is the only way, O bhikkhus, for the purification of beings, for the overcoming of sorrow and lamentation, for the destruction of dukkha and grief, for reaching the right path, for the realization of Nibbāna, namely, the Four Foundations of Mindfulness."

It will thus be seen that in striving to attain the Salvation no man can help the next, only one's own effort can help one. It stands to reason that one must bear the consequence of one's action, bad or good, and no amount of praying by another man can absolve one's crime or sin, nor can any cursing by another take away the merit of the good deeds that one has done. The Dhammapada, verse 276, says: "You yourselves must make the effort, the Tathāgatas [Buddhas] are only teachers." Members of the Saṅgha will teach their lay devotees to follow the teachings of the Buddha, but the devotees themselves must act in accordance with the Dhamma. This is why the Theravāda Sāsanā is sometimes called the Buddhism of Salvation through self-effort. This is also why those casual students of religions, especially those in the first half of this century, often miss the point of this self-effort and arrogantly and ignorantly brand the Theravāda Nikāya as a selfish religion (see note 16).

The *P̄āḍaeng Chronicle*

The purification processes of the Sāsanā in Kengtung form the subject matter of the *P̄āḍaeng Chronicle*. The present copy in my possession belongs to Sīhaḷarattārāma (Vat P̱āḍaeng) itself and it was loaned to me by the kind abbot, Bra Sumana, the Lord Sāmī, who is very gratified that the chronicle is being translated into English. The Saṅgha of Kengtung is likewise pleased. For too long the ancient traditions and the Sāsanā of Kengtung have remained buried either underground or in the books of palm leaves and sā (Broussonetia) paper.

It is not known when the original of the present copy of the chronicle was written, but what is certain is that different portions of the chronicle were written at different times and that the whole has been copied and recopied many times, in the manner of all chronicles, by scribes who were not infallible. The short description of the life of the Buddha, of the three Saṅgāyanās, and how Buddhism reached Ceylon and Suvaṇṇabhūmi, is common to all chronicles of better-known pagodas and monasteries in Burma and Thailand, while the account of the coming of the old and new Sīhaḷa sects to Martaban, Ayudhyā, Sukhodaya and Chiengmai is an imperfect abridgement of the *Mūlasāsanā* of Chiengmai.

The text itself opens with several lines of Pali, which is customary for all chronicles, and the reader must not be put off when he comes across, here and there, Pali words at the beginning of a paragraph, such as "tato" (from then on, from this), and "atha" (then, at that time), which is also regular, especially when an important or dramatic moment is about to occur. A whole Pali sentence (see par. 80) indicates the acceptance by Ñāṇagambhīra Thera of the invitation to go to Kengtung. Three of the four documents appended to the chronicle have opening sentences in Pali (pars. 209, 213, 218).

For those not familiar with Kengtung usage it must be pointed out that the Garden and Forest sects have their synonyms as follows:

Garden: Sōndôk (garden of flowers); Pupphārām (monastery of flowers); Yang-gōng (name of a Garden Sect monastery).

Forest: P̱āḍaeng (name of monastery, red forest); Rattārām (Pali name of P̱āḍaeng, Red Monastery, sometimes misspelled as Nattārām); Mahāvan or Mahāvana (great forest, now only its site remains).

The name "Garden Sect" originated in Chiengmai when King Küṅā Sōndôkgham built Vat Sōndôkgham for Sumana Thera (par. 20). The word "sōn" means garden, hence the name of the sect. The name "Vat P̱āḍaeng" also originated in Chiengmai and spread to Kengtung, to its substates of Möngyông, Möngbeng, and Mönglaem, and, I am told, to Sipsôngbannā.

In spite of its shortcomings, the *Pādaeng Chronicle* is important and it lets us have a glimpse into the past history of Kengtung, its ruling princes, monasteries, Saṅgha, and people. It is idle to hazard any guess as to when different portions of the *Pādaeng Chronicle* were written without further study and evidence from Kengtung itself.

The *Pādaeng Chronicle*: Translation

In the translation I have tried to be as close to the original and to be as literal as possible, consistent with meaning and sense in English. The scribe or copyist of the present text was not overly careful in regard to tonal marks and sentence constructions which tend to be very concise for an ordinary reader unused to Khün script and language. For instance, paragraph 92 is incomplete (one or two sentences are needed at the end to clarify the meaning), and paragraph 145 seems to have something to do with a custom no longer understood now. The complaint of the present and last generations of readers of old Khün documents is that ancient writers were careless about tonal marks. Paragraphing was not the fashion and one knows the end of a vagga (chapter) only when one is told so.

The Khün text has been photographed and appears with its translation in this volume. With this in mind, and with due regard for clarity in English, I have tried to translate the *Pādaeng Chronicle* in such a way that should a person, especially one acquainted with Thai script and language, wish to read the original, he should be able to do so without much difficulty by following the translation; indeed, he could do so almost word for word and line by line for more than half of the text.

It is a common feature of Khün literary style to end a sentence with the words "han lae," as in the Tai-Yuan writings. The word "han" (third tone with its tonal mark) means "there." Most sentences in the *Pādaeng Chronicle* end with those two words or with "dībun hanlae" (over there). I think it is quite allowable to translate them into English as "there" or "over there."

Many Pali words which have become part of Khün and other Thai dialects and Burmese have been kept as they are in the translation with explanation or meaning in the notes; in any case, scholars of South and Southeast Asian studies or anyone familiar with Southeast Asia should have no difficulty in understanding these words without referring to the notes. Khün words for which I could find no equivalents in English have been treated in the same way. Certain Pali words, such as "thera," "bhikkhu," "Sāsanā," "kappa," "Dhamma," "Saṅgha," etc., would have found their way into the English language long ago had not scholars translating the Tipiṭaka insisted on translating every Pali word into English. Great and admirable as the English language is, it cannot translate every foreign word without losing something of the original meaning. It is wrong to call a thera "an Elder" (even with a capital *E*), for in Burmese or Thai that would mean an old man or some village or town elder, whereas there can be no quibbling about "thera." In the same way the Tipiṭaka should not be called the Three Baskets. "Dah," "punka," "thug," "karma," etc., are already in the *Concise Oxford Dictionary*, so why not "bhikkhu," "thera," and other Pali words of importance in Theravāda Buddhism.

Hitherto, Western as well as indigenous scholars and writers have rendered into English as "slaves" the literal meaning of the Burmese or Thai word for those people who had been dedicated to pagodas and monasteries. Prisoners of war were sometimes so dedicated, but not always, as will be apparent from the translation. They were not slaves as understood in the West, they were not harshly treated as many ordinary slaves used to be, and their duties were by no means unpleasant. In fact, to judge by the usual standard of earning merit in the Buddhist world, they must have regarded their jobs as meritorious, capable of bettering their kamma in future rebirths.

It is true that in Burmese and Thai the word for these people is the same as that used for ordinary slaves; but the sense is not the same and this is understood by Burmese and Thais, although it may not be so understood by people who know only English. In the same way, writers use the word "eat" in translating the privilege of enjoying the revenues of townships, provinces, or kingdoms in Burma and Thailand. Just like the word "slave," here again, the literal meaning is correct, but not the sense. Perhaps some writers with tongue in cheek use the word "eat" deliberately to create a crude picture of a lord eating chunks of earth of his fiefdom. On the other hand, the word for the first person singular pronoun in Burmese or Thai could also be translated as "slave," or "royal slave," which in fact has the sense of extreme courtesy, but this has not been done.

I therefore consider it more appropriate to use the English word "subjects" for people dedicated to Vat P̱āḍaeng. Pagoda or monastery subjects were no more slaves than the other subjects of kings, and in many ways they had more freedom than the latter in that they were not subjected to ordinary taxes or corvee work, nor were they summoned to fight in a war. Some people may think there is a stigma attached to pagoda subjects, but there seems to be no such thing in the *P̱āḍaeng Chronicle*. We are told, for example, that King Manuha of Thaton was dedicated to the Shwedagon Pagoda of Pagan;[30] it is difficult to imagine any stigma in this relationship when an eminent scholar like Professor G. H. Luce puts forward a theory (with which Burmese scholars disagree) that King Kyanzitthā (1084-1112) of Pagan gave his daughter in marriage to the grandson of Manuha. And apparently Manuha's son and grandson were still called princes.[31]

The *Pāḍaeng Chronicle*: Transcription

At the end of this introduction will be found a chart of Khün consonants and vowels (Fig. 2). A Khün or a Shan visiting Chiengmai or Bangkok finds on arrival that some dipthong sounds of Thai and Tai-Yuan dialects are the most difficult things for him to master, especially if he is an adult male whose "tongue has already hardened," as we say. A female visitor, as always, can adapt her tongue more readily and easily to the dipthong sounds of Thailand.

As I have said earlier, the Khün and Tai-Yuan scripts are identical, and so is their spelling; but pronunciation is not necessarily the same, especially for the Tai-Yuan dipthong words. For example, the word "Chiengmai" is written in Khün and Tai-Yuan exactly the same way--Jayaṅ Hmai--but Tai-Yuan pronunciation is "Jyaṅ Hmai," while Khün pronunciation is "Jeng Hmai"; the word "möang" (city, country, etc.) is pronounced "möang" in Chiengmai, but "möng" in Kengtung, as in other parts of the Shan States. It may be that since the sixteenth century, when King Bayinnaung of Burma received the submission of all the Shan States of Burma as well as Chiengmai, closer relations with the rest of the Shan States influenced Kengtung sufficiently to eradicate these two dipthong sounds (if they did exist) in Khün dialect. We do not know for certain. These two words are no longer pronounced with a dipthong sound in Khün.

In representing the sounds in the translation of the *Pāḍaeng Chronicle*, therefore, I do so by the present-day pronunciation, and not by transliteration, but by keeping the consonants as the original. Anyone wanting to check how the words are spelled can always do so by referring to the accompanying reproduction of the original.

Dates, Eras, and Year Names

All chronicles in Burma and Thailand use the Cuḷa Sakkarāja (CS), or Cuḷa Era, and the *Pāḍaeng Chronicle* is no exception. In addition, the *Pāḍaeng Chronicle* also uses the year names of the sixty-year cycle, and the year name always precedes the Cuḷa Sakkarāja. This is the custom in northern Thailand, Kengtung, Sipsôngbannā, and Möngalem, while Shan-speaking areas of the Shan

States of Burma and the Chinese Shans of southwestern Yunnan also have the same custom, although their pronunciation of some of the year names is slightly different but recognizable. This allows us to use the names to check the dates and vice versa.

At the end of this introduction a chart will be found (Fig. 3) in which the year names and the Cuḷa Sakkarāja dates are tabulated from the year Kaḍgai CS 1 to the year Kāgai CS 1345. This was compiled by me while in Burma, and I hope it will be found useful by readers of this and other works using the same system of year names and Cuḷa Sakkarāja, for it is not easy to follow arguments on this matter otherwise. The year which began on April 16, 1976, and ended on April 16, 1977, was Rāysī CS 1338, the year of the Nāga (Great Snake--Alligator in Shan). Mü̈ngsai CS 1339 began on April 17, 1977.

The cyclical names can also be applied to the Buddha Sakkarāja or Buddhist Era. When the last vassā came to an end on the full moon October 7, 1976, the Buddha Sakkarāja had attained 2520 in the year Rāysī. Working backwards with the sixty-year cyclical names in Figure 3, it will be found that BS 1 falls in Mü̈ngsai, which is the year of the first vassā after the Parinibbāna of the Buddha. The Thai BS 1 falls in Pü̈ksañā, a year later (Burmese/Ceylonese BS 2520 or Thai BS 2519). Strictly speaking, a new vassā is counted only after the Pavāraṇā on the full moon of October.

European scholars, basing their calculations on the coronation date of the emperor Asoka (218 years after the Parinibbāna) and on dealings his grandfather Chandagutta had with Seleucus Nicator, have placed the birth of the Buddha at 563 B.C. and the Parinibbāna at 483 B.C.

The traditionally accepted eras in Burmese chronicles are as follows: An "old era" of 8,645 years was abolished by King Añcana, grandfather of the Buddha, and an unnamed era set up by him. This new era ends after 148 years with the Parinibbāna of the Buddha, when Mahā Kassapa Thera and King Ajātasattu established the Buddha Sakkarāja. This Buddha Sakkarāja is used in the Burmese chronicles until BS 622 when King Thumondari (Sumundari) of Tharekhittarā, presumably on the advice of his brahman court astrologers, as stated earlier, established the Saka Era (SE) which is called the Short Era in Burmese and Mahā Sakkarāja (MS) in Khü̈n. When the Mahā Sakkarāja or Saka Era reached the year 560, King Poppa Sôrahan of Pagan did away with it and inaugurated the Cuḷa Sakkarāja, known in Burma as the New Kôza Sakkarāja.[32]

To obtain equivalent years in the Christian Era, the rules are:

1. For Buddha Sakkarāja dates, subtract 544 (e.g., BS 2520 - 544 = 1976 A.D.)

2. For Mahā Sakkarāja dates, add 78 (e.g., MS 560 + 78 = 638 A.D.)

3. For Cuḷa Sakkarāja dates, add 638 (e.g., CS 1338 + 638 = 1976 A.D.)

To obtain Cuḷa from Buddha Sakkarāja, subtract 1182 from the latter (e.g., BS 2520 - 1182 = CS 1338).

It should always be remembered that (1) Buddha Sakkarāja is reckoned in vassā if it is to be strictly correct, and a vassā occurs from the full moon in July to the full moon of October, a period of three lunar months; and (2) Cuḷa Sakkarāja is reckoned from mid-April to mid-April. It will therefore be seen that the conversions of either Buddha Sakkarāja or Cuḷa Sakkarāja dates into A.D. dates are only approximately correct.

The dates of events in the *Pāḍaeng Chronicle* are atrocious in their confusion, and from the beginning not a single Cuḷa Sakkarāja has the correct year name, and vice versa, until we reach paragraph 67, which is the beginning of the account dealing with Kengtung proper. The establishment of the Buddha Sakkarāja is vaguely mentioned in paragraph 5, while in paragraph 9 we are told that when the Buddha Sakkarāja had reached 560 the Order of the Bhikkhunī came to an end. In paragraph 10 Brayā Siriteja (Trīcakkhu, or Three Eyes) abolished the Buddha Sakkarāja and set up a new but unspecified era which, when it had reached 622, was abolished by Brayā Tambula who then established the Cuḷa Sakkarāja "until the present day." The names of the countries ruled by these kings are not mentioned.

Compared to the orderly Burmese eras described above, it can be seen where the confusion was introduced, and it is also clear that the Burmese chronicles were the sources of the new era creations in the *Pāḍaeng Chronicle*, the earlier part of which came from the *Mūlasāsanā* of Chiengmai. There seems to be little doubt that the Burmese chronicles were the source of the establishment of the Buddha, Mahā, and Cuḷa Sakkarāja eras in the *Pāḍaeng Chronicle* and in the four northern Thai chronicles I have come across.[33] The Buddha Sakkarāja date of the establishment of the Mahā Sakkarāja may vary in northern Thai chronicles, but all agree that it was King Trīcakkhu who did it; two make no mention of the name of his country, one says he was the king of Ceylon, and the fourth says he ruled over Pagan of Burma. The name Aniruddha (Anuruddha), the king of Pagan (1044-1077), is associated with the establishment of the Cuḷa Sakkarāja in the northern Thai chronicles mentioned above--two of them call him "Tambula

Anuruddha Dhammarājā of Angva" (Ava came into being in 1364 A.D. or CS 726), one says he was the king of Pagan, while the fourth associates him with Indra, the king of devās.

The *Pāḍaeng Chronicle* identifies one King Siriteja with Trīcakkhu. There is one King Thiririt (Sirirāja) of Tharekhittarā who unsuccessfully tried to establish a new era in BS 403, while the founder of Tharekhittarā, King Dwattabaung, is reputed to have possessed three eyes. The name "Tambula" could be a mix-up with the Burmese chronicles' "Thambula," a queen of King Kyanzitthā (1084-1111) of Pagan, and mother of Rajākumāra, author of the famed four-faced Myazedi inscription, or with "Tambadīpa" (Land of Copper) which is one of the names of old Pagan. In short, all point to either Tharekhittarā or Pagan as the source of the establishment of the Mahā and Cuḷa Sakkarāja eras.

This is not an unreasonable assumption. Tharekhittarā is now known to have existed historically from the first to mid-ninth centuries (see note 6), and Pagan had been in existence since its walls (the remnants of which can still be seen together with Tharaba Gate) were constructed in 849 A.D. The use in Lower and Central Burma of the Buddha, Mahā, and Cuḷa Sakkarāja eras could not fail to have an impact on her eastern neighbors. Many a thera is quoted in the *Mūlasāsanā* (MLS) as having gone to Pagan within historical times to study the Theravāda Sāsanā. Moreover, Chiengmai was the paramount power in northern Thailand from the thirteenth to the sixteenth centuries, and through its intercourse with Lower Burma it must have obtained various Môn and Burmese chronicles long before they were compiled into standard volumes as we find them today. The story of the lady who brought up an image of Lord Buddha from under the water, as described in paragraphs 165-69 of the translation, is also found in a Môn chronicle.[34] In the process of translation and copying, confusion would have naturally resulted between the Pali and non-Pali names, the year names, and the several varieties of sakkarāja, due to differences in languages and dialects and human frailties of the translators and copyists. In the same way chronicles of Chiengmai, China, Ayudhyā, Rāmaññadesa, etc., including Portugal, were also known in Burma. I am not competent to say if chronicles of famous pagodas in central and southern Thailand give accounts of the establishment of the Mahā and Cuḷa Sakkarāja eras.

I have spent many a day trying to unravel the sakkarāja dates and year names in the *Pāḍaeng Chronicle*, and to reconcile them to one another. It has led nowhere, even when read in conjunction with the *Mūlasāsanā* of Chiengmai, of which the *Pāḍaeng Chronicle* is obviously an abridged version before the account of Kengtung proper is reached. Fortunately, in my correspondence with Mr. Alexander B. Griswold, one of his letters has so disentangled the dates of this period, i.e., prior to the Kengtung account, that I cannot do better than to reproduce that letter, with his kind permission; this letter also gives further and relevant information on the subject. Mr. Griswold and his colleague, Dr. Prasert ṇa Nagara of Thailand, have done a great deal of work concerning the chronicles and inscriptions of Thailand, particularly those of Sukhodaya and Chiengmai, as attested by their numerous articles and inscription readings published in the *Journal of the Siam Society* (JSS). Currently the two scholars are preparing to publish in the same journal the reading and translation of the inscription of this selfsame Vat P̱āḍaeng, as mentioned in the letter below. Mr. Griswold, however, cautions that observations made by them on their present work "are tentative and subject to revision."

It only remains for me to clarify the name "Jayamantārāma," mentioned in Mr. Griswold's letter. As a monastery Vat P̱āḍaeng is known by the name Jayamantārāma, but as the chief monastery of the Sīhaḷa Nikāya (Ceylon Sect) it is known as Sīhaḷarattārāma. It is said that formerly the site of Vat P̱āḍaeng was a cemetery, and because recitations of appropriate suttas were made to rid the place of evil spirits and superstitions before the construction of the monastery, the name Jayamantārāma (Monastery of Victorious Sacred Recitations) was given to it.

As for the names Somacitta and Khemamaṅgala, it is possible that when Somacitta succeeded Ñāṇagambhīra as the rajāguru (par. 104) he was given the name of Khemamaṅgala (only his title is mentioned in the text). It should also be noted that Somacitta is mentioned on page 136 of the *Jinakālamālī* as the thera who took the Sāsanā to Kengtung: "In the year 810 of the Royal Saka Era [1448 A.D.] the Thera Somacitta established the Sīhaḷa Dispensation in the Khema Kingdom."

Extracts from Mr. A. B. Griswold's Letter
(November 29, 1976)

As you say, the early dates in the chronicle are atrocious. Successive copyists seem to have muddled them so completely that they would be very hard to correct, and I agree with you that the attempt would not be worth the trouble. For many of the later events, however, it should be possible to arrive at approximate dates by using other sources as a guide. Two of the most useful, I think, will be *Jinakālamālī* (JKM) and *Mūlasāsanā* (MLS).

Of all the chronicles of northern Siam, JKM has the best chronology. See Coedès, "Documents sur l'histoire politique et religieuse du Laos occidental," *Bulletin de l'Ecole Française d'Extrême-Orient* XXV/1, and Jayawickrama, *The Sheaf of Garlands of the Epochs of the Conqueror* (London, 1968); I prefer Coedès's translation, as he knew much more about Siam; and though Jayawickrama has profited from some improved readings of the Pāli text, he was misled on several identifications by the Bangkok Department of Fine Arts.

JKM's dates are usually given in CS, with the numerals translated into Pāli and spelt out, and often with the Pāli translation of the name of the animal in the twelve-year cycle, so that the chances of copyists going wrong were greatly reduced. The main section of JKM is in effect the chronicle of the "New Ceylon" sect and its chief stronghold, the Red Forest Monastery at Chieng Mai.

The main section of MLS on the other hand, is a history of the "Old Ceylon" sect, first at Băn (Martaban), then at the Mango Grove Monastery at Sukhodaya and the Red Forest Monastery at Sajjanālaya, then at Wat Pra Yün at Lampûn and the Flower Garden at Chieng Mai. The dates are corrupt, but I think Dr. Prasert and I have got them fairly well rectified in *Journal of the Siam Society* (JSS) 60/1:63-65.

I think it unnecessary for you to try to correct the dates in the first twelve paragraphs of your translation of PC [*Pādaeng Chronicle*]; it would be sufficient to make a general statement that most of them are impossible.

In paragraph 13, the date for Anumati's arrival at Băn should be CS 693 'rvaṅ met' (see JSS 60/1:55 and note 3). In paragraph 14 PC says Sumana and Anomadassī went to Ceylon before joining the community of Udumbara (Anumati), a statement which I think extremely improbable; neither MLS nor JKM mentions their going to Ceylon; and if they actually made such a trip, the author of MLS would certainly not omit it from the biographical details he gives regarding them. I think PC has confused them with two other monks. MLS's account is much more coherent; when they left Sukhodaya for the first time, they studied at Ayudhyā, not Ceylon, before joining Udumbara's order. The earliest possible date for them to have joined this order would be in CS 693, though of course it could have been a good deal later. Both PC and MLS say that they remained with Udumbara for five rainy seasons and then returned to Sukhodaya; the earliest possible date would be CS 698 (*not* CS 243!). They practiced the religion at Sukhodaya for the next five years, and then--after they had spent ten years altogether in the Ceylon order--Udumbara gave them the grade of Mahāthera and authorization to act as upajjhāya, and sent them back to Sukhodaya (the earliest possible date would be CS 703; for an estimate of the most probable date, see Griswold, *Wat Pra Yün Reconsidered* [Bangkok, 1975]:14-17). After becoming a Mahāthera in the Ceylon order, Sumana remained at Sukhodaya until his departure for the north in CS 731 (see JSS 62/1:108). He was at Lampûn, at Wat Pra Yün, from CS 731 to 733 (see *Wat Pra Yün Reconsidered*:23-38). Your chronicle paragraph 17 may be right in giving the name of Wat Pra Yün as 'Vat P̱ā Phai Hlvaṅ' ('monastery of the great bamboo grove'), which is what it may have been called before Kilanā erected the three new standing images in CS 731-732. This date, based on the inscription of Wat Pra Yün, is unquestionably right (see *Wat Pra Yün Reconsidered*:34-35); and it contrasts with the date CS 255 in paragraph 18 of your translation. In CS 733 Sumana moved to the Flower Garden Monastery at Chieng Mai (see *Wat Pra Yün Reconsidered*:38). He was Abbot of that monastery, and head of the (Old) Ceylon Sect at Chieng Mai (later known as the Flower Garden sect) until his death in CS 751 (JSS 60/1:53-54, note 2) in contrast to the date of CS 472 for his death given at paragraph 26 of PC; for the events of his career at Chieng Mai, recounted in paragraphs 20-21 of PC, compare *Wat Pra Yün Reconsidered*:38-44.

In the following account of the early history of the 'New Ceylon' sect, I take the dates from JKM except where otherwise noted. These dates, I think, provide a sound chronological framework for the events recounted in PC at paragraphs 35-65.

In CS 785, twenty-five Mahātheras from Chieng Mai, headed by the Mahātheras Dhammagambhīra and Medhaṅkara, and accompanied by eight Mahātheras from Kamboja [in this context, probably Ayudhyā], went to Ceylon, where the Theravāda doctrine was believed to be preserved in its purest form. Upon learning that their own ordinations were invalidated by irreparable flaws, they retired from the monkhood, and were then ordained in the Ceylon Saṅgha with the orthodox ritual prescribed in the Vinaya Piṭaka as interpreted in Ceylon. After returning to Siam, they spent some years at Ayudhyā, Sajjanālaya, Sukhodaya, and other places. In CS 792 the group headed by Dhammagambhīra and Medhaṅkara returned to Chieng Mai and established the 'New Ceylon' order at the Red Forest Monastery. After a time they ran into trouble, of which JKM gives only a veiled account; but MLS makes it clear what the trouble was: the New Ceylon monks were too stiff-necked and arrogant, openly denouncing the Flower Garden monks for their invalid ordinations, their relaxed discipline, their greed, and their careless performance of the rites. King Sām Fhāṅ Kèn, who favored the Flower Garden monks, feared a dangerous schism in the monkhood; so he expelled the New Ceylon monks from the capital, though allowing them to continue their activities in other parts of the kingdom.

According to JKM, they went to Lampâng, Lampûn, and other places in CS 794; and from CS 795 to 803 they stayed at Chieng Sèn and Chieng Râi. In CS 803 Sām Fhāṅ Kèn was deposed by his son Tilokarāja, who thereupon mounted the throne. JKM tells us that the New Ceylon monks--headed by Medhaṅkara, Ñāṇamaṅgala and Sīlvamsa--returned to Chieng Mai five months later, and received the active support of Tilokarāja. JKM does not mention Dhammagambhīra among them. Apparently he remained at Chieng Sèn or Chieng Râi. It is not clear whether he should be identified with the monk PC calls Ñāṇagambhīra; but I am inclined to think they were two different persons.

According to the inscription of Văt P̱ā Ḍèṅ, [Vat P̱āḏaeng], Khemamaṅgala, Abbot of the Jayamantārāma, was re-ordained in Dhammagambhīra's community in CS 796. Before joining this order, Khemamaṅgala was a Mahāthera in some other one, perhaps the Flower Garden sect. The re-ordination may have taken place at Chieng Sèn or Chieng Râi. In an unspecified year (which we think must have been CS 805, after Khemamaṅgala had spent ten rainy seasons in Dhammagambhīra's order), Dhammagambhīra gave Khemamaṅgala the authorization to perform the Acts of the Saṅgha, sent him back to Khemaraṭṭha, where he established a consecrated place (semā) for these acts. The inscription tells us that in the 'kā kai' year (presumably near the end of CS 805), Cau Brañā Srīsaddhammarājacuḷāmaṇi acceded to the throne (of Khemaraṭṭha) as a vassal of Chieṅg Mai. He then retired temporarily from the throne and was ordained as a monk in the community of Khemamaṅgala at Chieng Mai. After 'two years' (i.e., any period over one year and not more than two) he returned to Khemaraṭṭha and resumed the throne. The remainder of the inscription deals with the rebuilding of the 'cetiya in the form of a stūpa' (stūparūpacetiya) at the Jayamantārāma, in CS 812 and 813, and the deposit of some relics of the Buddha in it.

This inscription is the one I discussed with you when you were here last summer. Dr. Prasert and I worked from photographs, sent by the Burma Archaeological Survey to the Bangkok Department of Fine Arts before the Second World War. The photographs, which appear to have been made from rubbings rather than directly from the stone, are marked on the back: "Found behind the Hall and Thein at Wat Ba Lyang beyond the East Gate on the way to Lwai Mwe." I assume the inscription is the one which you saw at Văt P̱ā Ḍèṅ at Keng Tung, and which you begged the Abbot to look after "like a baby." Its contents consist chiefly of a history of the Jayamantārāma, which was evidently located at or near the city of Keng Tung, and which, after Khemamaṅgala returned to it as a Mahāthera in Dhammagambhīra's order, became a stronghold of the New Ceylon Sect.

For these reasons, and because the inscription was 'found' at Văt P̱ā Ḍèṅ, I took it for granted, before reading PC, that 'Jayamantārāma' is an alternative name for Văt P̱ā Ḍèṅ: the stone containing the inscription is so huge that it would not be likely to be carted around from one monastery to another. The failure of PC to mention the name 'Jayamantārāma' in discussing Vǎt P̱ā Ḍèṅ is no obstacle to the identification, as lots of monasteries have, or had, at one time or another, three or four different names with similar or different meanings.

In CS 810, according to JKM, the Thera Somacitta established the religion of Ceylon (i.e., the New Ceylon order) in Khemaraṭṭha (cf. par. 69 ff. of your translation). The succession of events in the inscription, however, shows that Khemamaṅgala established the semā at Keng Tung before the end of the 'kā kai' year (CS 805); and we may well ask why JKM ignores this event, or why it should have been necessary for Somacitta to establish the religion at Keng Tung in CS 810. The answer may be that, as Khemamaṅgala spent a good part of the years between CS 805 and 810 at Chieng Mai, the New Ceylon order did not become really active at Keng Tung before CS 810. I am inclined to identify Somacitta with Khemamaṅgala: 'Somacitta' may be part of a new title he received at Chieng Mai, although it would be natural for him to continue to use the name Khemamaṅgala in the inscription.

JKM's entry about Somacitta in CS 810 fits very well with PC's statement that the construction of the great uposatha hall of the Sīhaḷarattārāma was begun in that year (par. 84 of PC). I must admit, however, that if the Jayamantārāma is to be considered identical with the Sīhaḷarattārāma, it is puzzling that the inscription makes no mention of the building operations described in your chronicle (par. 82 ff. of PC). We might guess that the Sīhaḷarattārāma was built adjacent to Jayamantārāma, and that the latter retained its separate identity for several years, but was incorporated into the Sīhaḷarattārāma some time after the inscription was composed in CS 813. Otherwise it would be hard to account for the presence of the inscription at Vǎt P̱ā Ḍèṅ though it makes no mention of the Sīhaḷarattārāma.

Notes

1. Views on the subject by various scholars are beautifully summed up in Hall 1970:12-24.

2. Coedès 1968:15.

3. Coedès 1968, chapters 13 and 14.

4. Solheim 1971:330-39; Honan 1975; Gorman 1975.

5. Luce 1924:100-137; Luce and Pe Maung Tin 1939:264-82. These two articles have been republished in the *Burma Research Society Fiftieth Anniversary Publications 2* (1960) in which references to the land route across northern Burma between China and India appear on pages 207 and 385. The information is sketchy, it is true, but since it is now known that the Pyū city of Hanlin existed in North Burma by the first century A.D., it is reasonable to assume that the route must have been more used than hitherto thought.

6. Aung Thaw 1966.

7. See note 5. Reference to the cannibals is on page 232 of *Burma Research Society Fiftieth Anniversary Publications 2* (1960). As regards Ptolemy's *Geographia*, Hall quotes Paul Wheatley's recent research which shows that in its present form it was compiled by a tenth- or eleventh-century Byzantine scholar, and, although Ptolemy's principles were followed, the work contains only parts of the original book. See note 1.

8. Htin Aung 1967:18-19.

9. Htin Aung 1967:5-6.

10. Luce 1949:239-53; also in *Burma Research Society Fiftieth Anniversary Publications 2* (1960:307-22), in which two land routes between China and India are mentioned on page 316, and one of them passed through a Pyū capital.

11. *Burma Research Society Fiftieth Anniversary Publications 2* 1960:318-19.

12. Aung Thaw 1966.

13. Pe Maung Tin and Luce 1960:14. Dictionaries give the yojana anything from seven to thirteen and one-half miles. The diameter of Tharekhittarā is roughly two and one-half miles. By sheerest coincidence, I came across note 3 on page 114 of *Milinda's Questions* (1969) which quotes the *Cambridge History of India* (vol. I, p. 550) as saying that the "short yojana" is "about 2 1/2 miles."

14. GPC:2.

15. Luce 1924:138-205. Also in *Burma Research Society Fiftieth Anniversary Publications 2* (1960:239-306), in which reference to Hsüan Tsang and I Tsing appears on pages 260-61.

16. Sir George Scott has supplied us with much information on old Burma, even though from a superior height, but his opinion of

a Theravāda bhikkhu is quite incorrect as expressed on page 111, paragraph 2, of Shway Yoe's *The Burman: His Life and Notions* (1963).

17. Dīgha Nikāya (DN):3, Ambaṭṭha Sutta, "Mahāsīla" section.

18. Aṅguttara Nikāya (AN):IV, 57.

19. AN:IV, 34.

20. Khuddaka Nikāya (KN):I, 5.

21. Soni 1956:iii.

22. KN:I, 9.

23. Although there are no set rules for the nun's garments in Burma, the present-day practice is described by Daw Mi Mi Khaing in a book she is writing to be entitled *The World of Burmese Women*:

    The garb consists of an 'earth-stained' light brown sarong called a *khawut*, an apricot-coloured tight-sleeved jacket with cloth buttons in front called *letkyat*, a calf-length gown to be worn over this called the *kike*, a length of cloth over one shoulder and under another arm with ends brought together, called a *ko-yon*, and a folded cloth worn on the head or held over one arm called the *kaung-tin*. All garments are of cloth received white and dyed by the *thilashins* (sīla observers or nuns) themselves, except in the case of natural brown cotton. The total outfit needs ten and one-eighth yards of material. The cloisters requires an entering *thilashin* to have four such sets of habits, as well as a razor, umbrella, slippers, box, rosary, bedding and tray (for receiving alms). She should also have some pots and pans. . . . This initial equipment cost about one hundred kyats in 1964.

24. Saṁyutta Nikāya (SN):XV.

25. SN:LVI, 11.

26. VM:XVI, 87.

27. Such cases are not rare at vipassanā centers in Burma. A friend also told me that during his forty days at the Mahāsī Sayādô's Meditation Center, the last seven were carried on without either sleep or strain.

28. Chan Htoon 1958:8. U Chan Htoon is a retired justice of Burma's Supreme Court.

29. DN:22; Majjhima Nikāya (MN):10.

30. Harvey 1967:28.

31. Luce 1969:48-49.

32. Tet Htoot in Hall 1962:59.

33. *The Yonaka Chronicle* (YC) 1961:97-98, 116, 121-22; *Prajum Bongsāvadān 61* (PB61) BS 2479:99, 101; *Prajum Tamnān Bradhātu 1* BS 2485:34-35; *Prajum Tamnān Bradhātu* 2 BS 2510:74-75.

34. Halliday 1917:8-9.

Postscript

Several months after I had completed the translation of the *P̣āḍaeng Chronicle*, together with the introduction and notes, I came across a northern Thai chronicle named *Tamnān Mūlasāsanā Chapap Vat P̣āḍaeng* (TMP), kindly loaned to me by Professor William J. Gedney, Department of Linguistics, The University of Michigan. This chronicle has been transliterated from Tai-Yuan (Chiengmai) script into central Thai script by Sommai Premchit, and was published in January 1976 in mimeograph form by the Department of Sociology and Anthropology of Chiengmai University.

The TMP contains most of the events described in the *P̣āḍaeng Chronicle* prior to the arrival of Somacitta Thera at the court of Brayā Srīsudhamma Cuḷāmaṇī in Khemaraṭṭha Tuṅgapurī (city of Kengtung) in CS 805 (1443). The account of various events thus far in the TMP seems more orderly than in the *P̣āḍaeng Chronicle* and in all cases the year names correspond correctly with the Cuḷa Sakkarāja. But, as remarked by Professor Sommai, confusion and obscure meanings of words remain here and there.

According to the TMP, Ñāṇagambhīra did not set foot on the soil of Kengtung at all; he only sent Somacitta to do much of what the *P̣āḍaeng Chronicle* attributed to him. The TMP gives a brief account of the various places Ñāṇagambhīra stayed during the vassā in northern Thailand after his return from Ceylon and no mention is made of Kengtung; he died in Tausan CS 814 (1452) at the comparatively young age of forty-eight or forty-nine with only twenty-eight vassā in the yellow robe.

Some amusing details are given in the account of the dispute between the Garden and the Forest sects in Kengtung when the two sides had a public debate which the former lost through the untimely questioning by a lord abbot of the sect. While the *P̱āḍaeng Chronicle* mentions that the defeated lords were furious with their abbot and carried their books away in dejection and shame (*P̱āḍaeng Chronicle*, pars. 184-89), the TMP adds that the infuriated lords took the betel cuds from their mouths and threw them at the one who was the cause of their defeat (TMP, p. 29), an offense at least against the Sekhiya Rules of the Pāṭimokkha!

Where place names in Kengtung are concerned, those in the *P̱āḍaeng Chronicle* are readily identifiable in present-day Kengtung, while many in the TMP as they stand at present are not so. Like all chronicles, the TMP is not without some inconsistencies. For example, on page 22 we are given to understand that Ñāṇagambhīra stayed in Lampang for three vassā, but on page 24 it is stated that he spent only one vassā there. The account of the rules and procedures for ordination laid down by Mahā Varapañño in the TMP (pp. 28-29) is as unclear as is the account of those laid down by Mahā Varañāṇamaṅgala in the *P̱āḍaeng Chronicle* (pars. 145-46).

The detailed account of the construction of Vat P̱āḍaeng, of the uposatha hall therein, the dedication of the monastery subjects and their duties, the setup of the administration of the Sāsanā in Kengtung, the offices of the saṅkārī and lāmsaṅ, the inauspicious days to be avoided and the dire consequences for the disregard of those days (*P̱āḍaeng Chronicle*, pars. 130-36), the extent of the authority of the Saṅgha as revealed in the four documents at the end of the *P̱āḍaeng Chronicle*, etc., are to be found only in the *P̱āḍaeng Chronicle*.

Towards the end of the TMP (pp. 31-32), a list is given of six successive ruling princes of Kengtung who supported the P̱āḍaeng Sect, including the one who was assassinated because he went to "spread" the kaṭhina robes on a bad day. The list agrees with that in the *Jengtung State Chronicle*, but the dates of succession vary slightly in one or two cases. This list in the TMP is useful for checking the dates of accession of those rulers in Kengtung.

Having mentioned the rulers, i.e., the "external" side, a succession (paramparā) of lord abbots of Vat P̱āḍaeng is given for the "internal" side in paragraph 6 (TMP, p. 32) which states (my translation):

> In the direction of the Sāsanā, the Saṅgha parināyaka theras [the theras who were heads of the Saṅgha and who were] the somḍec [lord abbots] of Sīhaḷarattārāma since Somacitta and Khemamaṅgala,

> there were Brahmacuḷa, Indavij[j]ā, Ñāṇamaṅgala, until Hôsaensayu named Dhammamaṅgala, totaling twenty-eight lords. After that, from Mahā Puññavantā until after the Burmese [rule] there were twenty-nine. After the Burmese [rule and] beginning with the reign of Prince Sāmpī there were thus: Maṇīñāṇamaṅgala, Ariṭṭho, Suvaṇṇa[?-] Candaraṅsī, Kantikalamegha, Mahānāgo, Sirināma, Maṅgalarammati, Indo, Varamaṅgala, Jeyyevajira, Mahānāma, [and] Siridhamma.

From the preceding, Khemamaṅgala was the name of the thera who succeeded Somacitta, and was neither the title of the latter as the rājaguru, as I had thought (see "Dates, Eras, and Year Names"), nor one and the same person as Somacitta, as Mr. Griswold thought (see "Extracts"). Khemamaṅgala was the thera who erected the stone inscription which is still standing at Vat P̱āḍaeng, Kengtung (see "Extracts").

With reference to the Burmese rule, it may be mentioned that Kengtung (and all the Shan States of Burma) submitted to King Bayinnaung of Burma in the year Kaḍmeḍ CS 921 (1559) during the reign of Brayā Kaeuyôḍfānarindā. Between the latter and Prince Sāmpī, who succeeded in the year Tausaṅā CS 1064 (1702), there were eight rulers and 143 years.

The coupling of correct year names and the Cuḷa Sakkarāja in the TMP can only mean a more conscientious and careful writing or copying and/or a higher standard of literary proficiency in Chiengmai in those days when it was the center for Theravāda Buddhist civilization.

Professors Sommai Premchit of Chiengmai University and Donald K. Swearer of the Department of Religion, Swarthmore College, Pennsylvania, have translated the TMP into English and I understand that this is to be published in the *Journal of the Siam Society*. Dr. Swearer has very kindly sent me a copy of the translation. The publication of this translation will not affect my translation in any way, because the technique of one translation is different from that of the other, and also because the rich materials regarding life in Kengtung in those days as described in the *P̱āḍaeng Chronicle* are not available in the TMP. Besides, I hope the introduction and notes to my translation of the *P̱āḍaeng Chronicle* will give an insight into and an understanding of ancient and modern Kengtung, a Burmese Shan State.

From the TMP I have compiled the following relevant dates for comparison with those in the *P̱āḍaeng Chronicle*. (Note: Khün spelling, as in the *P̱āḍaeng Chronicle* translation, is adopted. Numbers in parentheses refer to pages in the TMP. Months quoted are those of Chiengmai which are one month ahead of those of Kengtung and two ahead of Bangkok.)

Rōngmeḍ 693: Matimā Mahāthera with four disciples left Martaban for Ceylon returning only after twelve years of study (p. 7).

Kaḍhmau 701: King Phāyū sent his son, Ceḍbantū, to rule Kengtung together with four theras who took the Sāsanā there (p. 6).

Rāyseḍ 708: Phāyū died; Ceḍbantū was to have succeeded but was murdered (p. 7).

Müngrau 719: Matimā was consecrated with the title Mahā Udumbara Svāmi (p. 7).

Rōnggai 733: Künā built Pupphārāma for Sumanaraṅsi who arrived from Sukhodaya with the Sīhaḷa Sect of the Theravāda Sāsanā (p. 9).

Kāpyī 736: Exruler of Kengtung, Samaṇa Cau Āy-ôn, arrived in Kengtung from Ayudhyā and Chiengmai with monks and images (p. 11).

Kāhmau 785: Ñāṇagambhīra went to Ceylon (p. 15).

Püksan 790: Ñāṇagambhīra left Ceylon (p. 17).

Kaḍrau 791: Ñāṇagambhīra arrived back in Ayudhyā (p. 17).

Rōnggai 793: King Sāmf̲angkæn died; Adittarājatilok succeeded (p. 19).

Koḍsan 802: Ñāṇagambhīra arrived in Chiengsaen for a stay of seven vassā (p. 20).

Kāgai 805: Ñāṇagambhīra dreamed about spirits haunting the palace in Kengtung, sent Somacitta and four bhikkhus to Kengtung. Somacitta returned to Chiengsaen after the vassā of 805 (pp. 20-21).

Kāpcai 806: Month Seven waxing 6th, Somacitta arrived back in Kengtung at the invitation of the ruler, Srīsudhamma Cuḷāmaṇī. Month Seven waxing 13th, Somacitta was invited to occupy Sīhaḷarattārāma Vat P̲āḍaeng (p. 24). In Month Jeṭṭhamāsa a severe storm broke but did not harm the monastery (p. 25).

Püksī 810: Month Seven waxing 8th, Thursday, was construction of the uposatha hall with sīmā stones planted on the full moon (p. 26). Month Eight waxing 80, lord of earth was ordained and left the Order on Month Nine waxing 4th (p. 26). Somacitta's dream (p. 25).

Tausan 814: Ñāṇagambhīra died at Muangvang near Lampang (pp. 23 and 24).

Rāysan 838: Month Four waxing 12th was the public debate between the Garden and Forest sects with victory to the latter (p. 29).

Münghmau 869: Another dispute occurred between the two sects. Inquiry was made and two names (Ñāṇagambhīra and Dhammakitti) were written on palm leaves to be tested by fire (p. 30).

Püksan 970: Rājaguru Varapañño laid down ordination rules (pp. 28-29).

A list of six ruling princes of Kengtung in succession who supported the P̱āḍaeng Sāsanā (pp. 31-32).

A list of lord abbots of Vat P̱āḍaeng from Somacitta to Burmese times (p. 32).

Figure 2

KHÜN SCRIPT TRANSCRIPTION

CONSONANTS

VOWELS

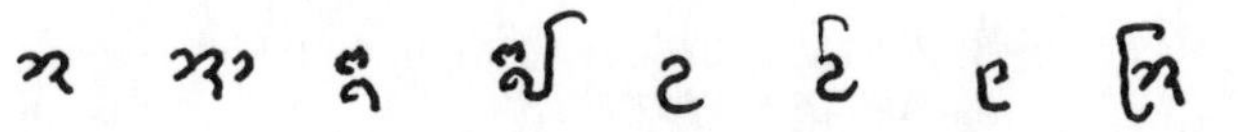

a ā i ī u ū e ō — basic form

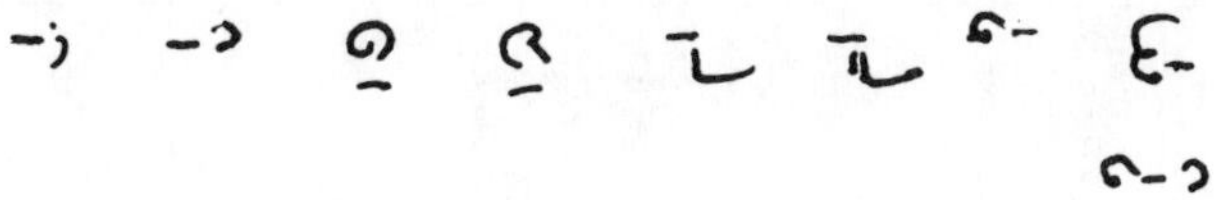

combination form

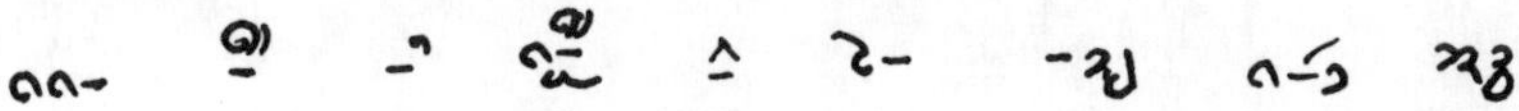

ae ü o ö ô ai āy au āu

iu eu æu uy ōy öy üy ôy

SAMPLES

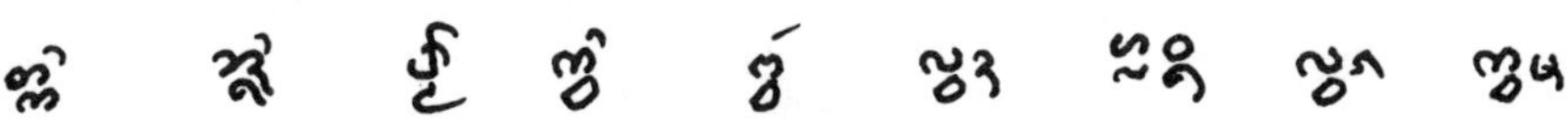

tok ong p̱om kō bōk lōḍ hlōng lōn kōm

kök köḍ köp mö möng hmön hlöm kô, pok

tôḍ tôn côm rek jeng geḍ ren phep dem

Figure 3

CHART OF THE SIXTY CYCLICAL YEAR NAMES AND CUḶA SAKKARĀJA

<table>
<tr>
<td>KĀPcai
26 506 926
86 566 986
146 626 1046
206 686 1106
266 746 1166
326 806 1226
386 866 1286
446</td>
<td>ḌAPp̱au
27 507 927
87 567 987
147 627 1047
207 687 1107
267 747 1167
327 807 1227
387 867 1287
447</td>
<td>RĀYyī
28 508 928
88 568 988
148 628 1048
208 688 1108
268 748 1168
328 808 1228
388 868 1288
448</td>
<td>MÜNGhmau
29 509 929
89 569 989
149 629 1049
209 689 1109
269 749 1169
329 809 1229
389 869 1289
449</td>
<td>PÜKsī
30 510 930
90 570 990
150 630 1050
210 690 1110
270 750 1170
330 810 1230
390 870 1290
450</td>
</tr>
<tr>
<td>KĀPseḍ
36 516 936
96 576 996
156 636 1056
216 696 1116
276 756 1176
336 816 1236
396 876 1296
456</td>
<td>ḌAPgai
37 517 937
97 577 997
157 637 1057
217 697 1117
277 757 1177
337 817 1237
397 877 1297
457</td>
<td>RĀYcai
38 518 938
98 578 998
158 638 1058
218 698 1118
278 758 1178
338 818 1238
398 878 1298
458</td>
<td>MÜNGp̱au
39 519 939
99 579 999
159 639 1059
219 699 1119
279 759 1179
339 819 1239
399 879 1299
459</td>
<td>PÜKyī
40 520 940
100 580 1000
160 640 1060
220 700 1120
280 760 1180
340 820 1240
400 880 1300
460</td>
</tr>
<tr>
<td>KĀPsan
46 526 946
106 586 1006
166 646 1066
226 706 1126
286 766 1186
346 826 1246
406 886 1306
466</td>
<td>ḌAPrau
47 527 947
107 587 1007
167 647 1067
227 707 1127
287 767 1187
347 827 1247
407 887 1307
467</td>
<td>RĀYseḍ
48 528 948
108 588 1008
168 648 1068
228 708 1128
288 768 1188
348 828 1248
408 888 1308
468</td>
<td>MÜNGgai
49 529 949
109 589 1009
169 649 1069
229 709 1129
289 769 1189
349 829 1249
409 889 1309
469</td>
<td>PÜKcai
50 530 950
110 590 1010
170 650 1070
230 710 1130
290 770 1190
350 830 1250
410 890 1310
470</td>
</tr>
<tr>
<td>KĀPsaṅā
56 536 956
116 596 1016
176 656 1076
236 716 1136
296 776 1196
356 836 1256
416 896 1316
476</td>
<td>ḌAPmeḍ
57 537 957
117 597 1017
177 657 1077
237 717 1137
297 777 1197
357 837 1257
417 897 1317
477</td>
<td>RĀYsan
58 538 958
118 598 1018
178 658 1078
238 718 1138
298 778 1198
358 838 1258
418 898 1318
478</td>
<td>MÜNGrau
59 539 959
119 599 1019
179 659 1079
239 719 1139
299 779 1199
359 839 1259
419 899 1319
479</td>
<td>PÜKseḍ
60 540 960
120 600 1020
180 660 1080
240 720 1140
300 780 1200
360 840 1260
420 900 1320
480</td>
</tr>
<tr>
<td>KĀPsī
6 486 966
66 546 1026
126 606 1086
186 666 1146
246 726 1206
306 786 1266
366 846 1326
426 906</td>
<td>ḌAPsai
7 487 967
67 547 1027
127 607 1087
187 667 1147
247 727 1207
307 787 1267
367 847 1327
427 907</td>
<td>RĀYsaṅā
8 488 968
68 548 1028
128 608 1088
188 668 1148
248 728 1208
308 788 1268
368 848 1328
428 908</td>
<td>MÜNGmeḍ
9 489 969
69 549 1029
129 609 1089
189 669 1149
249 729 1209
309 789 1269
369 849 1329
429 909</td>
<td>PÜKsan
10 490 970
70 550 1030
130 610 1090
190 670 1150
250 730 1210
310 790 1270
370 850 1330
430 910</td>
</tr>
<tr>
<td>KĀPyī
16 496 976
76 556 1036
136 616 1096
196 676 1156
256 736 1216
316 796 1276
376 856 1336
436 916</td>
<td>ḌAPhmau
17 497 977
77 557 1037
137 617 1097
197 677 1157
257 737 1217
317 797 1277
377 857 1337
437 917</td>
<td>RĀYsī
18 498 978
78 558 1038
138 618 1098
198 678 1158
258 738 1218
318 798 1278
378 858 1338
438 918</td>
<td>MÜNGsai
19 499 979
79 559 1039
139 619 1099
199 679 1159
259 739 1219
319 799 1279
379 859 1339
439 919</td>
<td>PÜKsaṅā
20 500 980
80 560 1040
140 620 1100
200 680 1160
260 740 1220
320 800 1280
380 860 1340
440 920</td>
</tr>
</table>

KAḌsai 31 511 931 91 571 991 151 631 1051 211 691 1111 271 751 1171 331 811 1231 391 871 1291 451	KOḌsaṅā 32 512 932 92 572 992 152 632 1052 212 692 1112 272 752 1172 332 812 1232 392 872 1292 452	RŌNGmeḍ 33 513 933 93 573 993 153 633 1053 213 693 1113 273 753 1173 333 813 1233 393 873 1293 453	TAUsan 34 514 934 94 574 994 154 634 1054 214 694 1114 274 754 1174 334 814 1234 394 874 1294 454	KĀrau 35 515 935 95 575 995 155 635 1055 215 695 1115 275 755 1175 335 815 1235 395 875 1295 455
KAḌhmau 41 521 941 101 581 1001 161 641 1061 221 701 1121 281 761 1181 341 821 1241 401 881 1301 461	KOḌsī 42 522 942 102 582 1002 162 642 1062 222 702 1122 282 762 1182 342 822 1242 402 882 1302 462	RŌNGsai 43 523 943 103 583 1003 163 643 1063 223 703 1123 283 763 1183 343 823 1243 403 883 1303 463	TAUsaṅā 44 524 944 104 584 1004 164 644 1064 224 704 1124 284 764 1184 344 824 1244 404 884 1304 464	KĀmeḍ 45 525 945 105 585 1005 165 645 1065 225 705 1125 285 765 1185 345 825 1245 405 885 1305 465
KAḌp̱au 51 531 951 111 591 1011 171 651 1071 231 711 1131 291 771 1191 351 831 1251 411 891 1311 471	KOḌyī 52 532 952 112 592 1012 172 652 1072 232 712 1132 292 772 1192 352 832 1252 412 892 1312 472	RŌNGhmau 53 533 953 113 593 1013 173 653 1073 233 713 1133 293 773 1193 353 833 1253 413 893 1313 473	TAUsī 54 534 954 114 594 1014 174 654 1074 234 714 1134 294 774 1194 354 834 1254 414 894 1314 474	KĀsai 55 535 955 115 595 1015 175 655 1075 235 715 1135 295 775 1195 355 835 1255 415 895 1315 475
KAḌgai 1 481 961 61 541 1021 121 601 1081 181 661 1141 241 721 1201 301 781 1261 361 841 1321 421 901	KOḌcai 2 482 962 62 542 1022 122 602 1082 182 662 1142 242 722 1202 302 782 1262 362 842 1322 422 902	RŌNGp̱au 3 483 963 63 543 1023 123 603 1083 183 663 1143 243 723 1203 303 783 1263 363 843 1323 423 903	TAUyī 4 484 964 64 544 1024 124 604 1084 184 664 1144 244 724 1204 304 784 1264 364 844 1324 424 904	KĀhmau 5 485 965 65 545 1025 125 605 1085 185 665 1145 245 725 1205 305 785 1265 365 845 1325 425 905
KAḌrau 11 491 971 71 551 1031 131 611 1091 191 671 1151 251 731 1211 311 791 1271 371 851 1331 431 911	KOḌseḍ 12 492 972 72 552 1032 132 612 1092 192 672 1152 252 732 1212 312 792 1272 372 852 1332 432 912	RŌNGgai 13 493 973 73 553 1033 133 613 1093 193 673 1153 253 733 1213 313 793 1273 373 853 1333 433 913	TAUcai 14 494 974 74 554 1034 134 614 1094 194 674 1154 254 734 1214 314 794 1274 374 854 1334 434 914	KĀp̱au 15 495 975 75 555 1035 135 615 1095 195 675 1155 255 735 1215 315 795 1275 375 855 1335 435 915
KAḌmeḍ 21 501 981 81 561 1041 141 621 1101 201 681 1161 261 741 1221 321 801 1281 381 861 1341 441 921	KOḌsan 22 502 982 82 562 1042 142 622 1102 202 682 1162 262 742 1222 322 802 1282 382 862 1342 442 922	RŌNGrau 23 503 983 83 563 1043 143 623 1103 203 683 1163 263 743 1223 323 803 1283 383 863 1343 443 923	TAUseḍ 24 504 984 84 564 1044 144 624 1104 204 684 1164 264 744 1224 324 804 1284 384 864 1344 444 924	KĀgai 25 505 985 85 565 1045 145 625 1105 205 685 1165 265 745 1225 325 805 1285 385 865 1345 445 925

Note on the Chart of the Sixty Cyclical Year Names and Cuḷa Sakkarāja

KĀPcai	ḌAPp̱au	RĀYyī	MÜNGhmau	PÜKsī
KĀPseḍ	ḌAPgai	RĀYcai	MÜNGp̱au	PÜKyī
KĀPsan	ḌAPrau	RĀYseḍ	MÜNGgai	PÜKcai
KĀPsaṅā	ḌAPmeḍ	RĀYsan	MÜNGrau	PÜKseḍ
KĀPsī	ḌAPsai	RĀYsaṅā	MÜNGmeḍ	PÜKsan
KĀPyī	ḌAPhmau	RĀYsī	MÜNGsai	PÜKsaṅā

KAḌsai	KOḌsaṅā	RŌNGmeḍ	TAUsan	KĀrau
KAḌhmau	KOḌsī	RŌNGsai	TAUsaṅā	KĀmeḍ
KAḌp̱au	KOḌyī	RŌNGhmau	TAUsī	KĀsai
KAḌgai	KOḌcai	RŌNGp̱au	TAUyī	KĀhmau
KAḌrau	KOḌseḍ	RŌNGgai	TAUcai	KĀp̱au
KAḌmeḍ	KOḌsan	RŌNGrau	TAUseḍ	KĀgai

The table above contains all the sixty cyclical year names of the chart, and the latter covers 1,345 years of Cuḷa Sakkarāja beginning with CS 1 in the year Kaḍgai and ending with CS 1345 in the year Kāgai. There are twenty-two Cuḷa Sakkarāja in each of the first thirty-five, and twenty-three Cuḷa Sakkarāja in the last twenty-five, of the sixty cyclical years, as indicated in the boxes. There is a difference of sixty years between one Cuḷa Sakkarāja year and the next in the same box.

Each year name has two syllables (Kāpsaṅā is often read as "Kāpsṅā"): the first, written in capital letters for easy identification, is called "mother of the year" and the second is called "child of the year." There are ten mothers and twelve children. In the chart the ten mothers are at the top of the ten columns of boxes and there are six boxes in the column under each mother. The names of the children are given in horizontal sequence in the sixty boxes. The ten mothers are:

1	2	3	4	5	6	7	8	9	10
KĀP	ḌAP	RĀY	MÜNG	PÜK	KAḌ	KOḌ	RŌNG	TAU	KĀ

The twelve children and the animals represented by them are:

1	2	3	4	5	6	7	8	9	10
cai	p̲au	yī	hmau	sī	sai	saṅā	meḍ	san	rau
rat	ox	tiger	hare	nāga	snake	horse	goat	monkey	cock

11	12
seḍ	gai
dog	pig

The numbering denotes only the required ordering of the names and has nothing to do with the ending numerals of the Cuḷa Sakkarāja.

The table shows how the mothers and children are combined (there can be no other combinations), with six of the children attaching themselves to each of the mothers. It will be noticed that mothers of odd numbers have only children of odd numbers, and mothers of even numbers have children of even numbers. Thus KĀP yields KĀPcai, KĀPseḍ, KĀPsan, KĀPsaṅā, KĀPsī, KĀPyī; ḌAP has ḌAPp̲au, ḌAPgai, ḌAPrau, ḌAPmeḍ, ḌAPsai, ḌAPhmau, and so on. Each mother then has six combinations making a total of sixty in the cycle, and there can never be a combination of odd and even numbers. On the other hand, when a child is considered as representing an animal, it will be seen that cai (rat) appears five times with different mothers as in KĀPcai, RĀYcai, PÜKcai, KOḌcai, TAUcai; p̲au (ox) has ḌAPp̲au, MÜNGp̲au, KAḌp̲au, RŌNGp̲au, KĀp̲au, and so on. Each child or animal thus has five combinations, making a total of sixty for twelve children in the cycle. This is important in horoscopic calculations.

To the question "What year?" a Westerner's answer is likely to be "1976" or "1338," if he prefers to refer to Cuḷa Sakkarāja. A Khün, however, will answer "Rāysī," and to him "1338" will be the "Sakkarāja" ("Cuḷa" understood) or "Sakkhāḍ," as it is often, but erroneously, pronounced. One day after the full moon of October 1976 is written as "The year Rāysī Sakkarāja 1338, Month Twelve waning 1st night." The day preceding nightfall in the foregoing statement goes with that night, because the waxing and waning refer only to moon phases and the moon can only be seen at night. Thus, a person can be born at midday on Month Twelve waning 1st night.

It is well known that the Chinese have the same sixty cyclical year system, and it is said that they have been using it since the twenty-seventh century B.C. There seems to be no doubt where the Southeast Asian cyclical systems came from. The ten "mothers" and twelve "children" of the Khün system are called "stems" and "branches" respectively in Chinese and they are combined in exactly the same way as in the table above except that the words are naturally different.

The ten Chinese stems, with Khün and Shan equivalents given below them, are:

1	2	3	4	5	6	7	8	9	10
CHIA	I	PING	TING	WU	CHI	KENG	HSIN	JEN	KUEI
KĀP	ḌAP	RĀY	MÜNG	PÜK	KAḌ	KOḌ	RŌNG	TAU	KĀ
KĀP	LAP	HĀI	MÜNG	PÜK	KAṪ	KHU̇T	HŌṄG	TAU	KĀ

Similarly, the Chinese branches, with Khün, Shan, and Thai equivalents added, are:

1	2	3	4	5	6	7	8
tzŭ	ch'ou	yin	mao	ch'ên	ssŭ	wu	wei
cai̤	p̱au	yī	hmau	sī	sai	saṅā	meḍ
caü	pau	yī	mau	sī	saü	sīṅā	mot
juat	chalū	khāl	thô	marōng	maseng	mamia	mamae

9	10	11	12
shen	yu	hsü	hai
san	rau	seḍ	gai
san	hau	met	kaü
vôk	rakā	cô	kun

The animals represented by the children or branches are the same for all except the following: for number 5, the Chinese have "dragon" and the Shans "alligator," for the Khün and Thai "nāga"; for number 8, the Chinese have "sheep" in place of "goat"; for number 2, the Shans have "buffalo," while the others have "ox."

The Ahom Shans of Assam, Namkham Shans of Burma, Chinese Shans of Southwestern Yunnan, and, I suspect, Shans in the Erāvatī and the Chindwin valleys of northern Burma, together with Shans of the Shan States of Burma west of the Salween, have the same sixty-year cycle system with identical names. Northern Thais (Tai-Yuans) and Laos also have the identical system. The Vietnamese, I am told, follow the same system in their own language. Central Thais and Cambodians use the twelve-year cycle, but the animals for the years are identical with those in the sixty-year cycle. Thais have a variation of the sixty-year system in that they use Sanskrit equivalents of one (eka) for KAḌ, two (do) for KOḌ, three (trī) for RŌNG, etc., prefixed to "śaka" (sakkarāja) up to ten (samriddhi - completing = ten) for PÜK, to denote the ending numeral of a Cuḷa Sakkarāja, thereby creating the ten mothers or stems in addition to their existing twelve animals. For example, while Thais of other regions have "The year Rāysī CS 1338," the Central Thais often, but not always, write "CS 1338 of the year Marōng Aṭṭhaśaka."

It will thus be seen that starting from eastern Assam practically the whole of mainland Southeast Asia follows the Chinese sixty-year cycle system and that the animal assigned to each of the sixty names is identical. Thus far the similarity is uniform throughout. But when it comes to assigning a year name to a particular Cuḷa Sakkarāja, there is a marked difference between the practice in the Shan areas west of the Salween as far as Ahom on the one hand, and in the whole trans-Salween Southeast Asia *and China* on the other. For the latter there is complete agreement that CS 1338 is in Rāysī of the nāga, Pingch'ên of the Chinese, in the sixty-year cycle, or Marōng (nāga) of the twelve-year cycle; but for the former, CS 1338 is in Koḍyī of the tiger in their sixty-year cycle. There is a difference of twenty-six years between Koḍyī and Rāysī if we count Koḍyī before Rāysī, or thirty-four years if Koḍyī comes after Rāysī. If we look at the twelve-year cycle, however, the difference is two or ten years, as the case may be. In short, the two regions agree on the animals and name combinations but differ in assigning them to a Cuḷa Sakkarāja.

I have raised this point because in working out the dates in *Ahom-Buranji* (chronicle of the Ahom kingdom), *Mürghmau Chronicle*, *Hsenwi State Chronicle*, and a Shan manual on horoscopes entitled *Cātisarañān*, I have discovered that the year names (called laknī) assigned to Cuḷa Sakkarāja are such that all four start CS 1 in Kārau, whereas the trans-Salween region's system of my chart starts CS 1 in Kaḍgai as stated. I have checked my chart with the Chinese and Chiengmai systems and the three correspond in every respect except the nomenclature. The cis-Salween Shan system is the "odd man out" and one is tempted to discard it out of hand, but the difference is worth looking into, even though one of my sources in Burma told me in a letter that many Shans in the Shan States of Burma doubted the soundness of their system regarding the cycle and Cuḷa Sakkarāja assigned therein. What is certain is that astrology or horoscopy of one system cannot be used by the other. Perhaps further investigation is needed with regard to the cis-Salween Shan system, and the result may rectify some of the discrepancies in the dates of the Shan chronicles quoted.

THE P̱ĀḌAENG CHRONICLE

TEXT AND TRANSLATION

Dedicated humbly to the
Theravāda Sāsanā

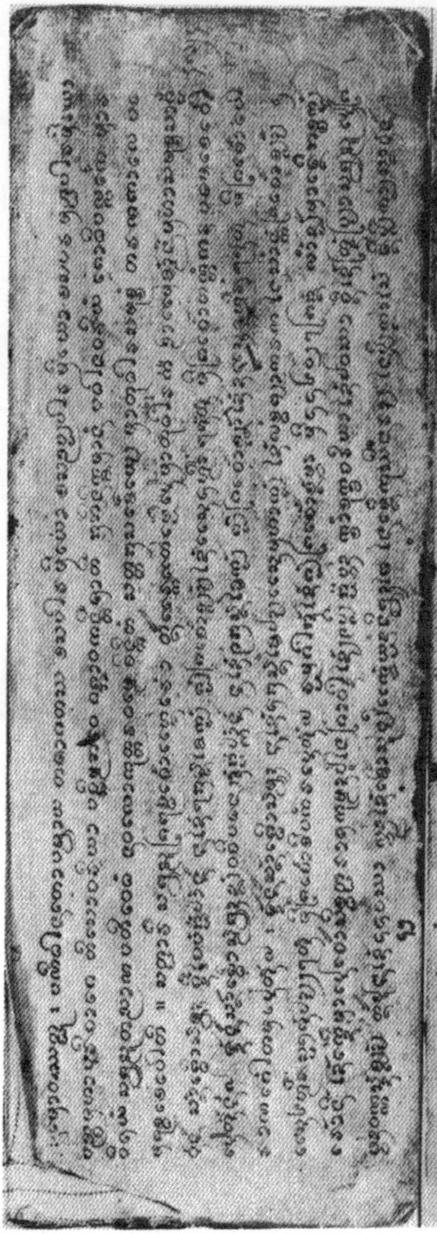

[1]

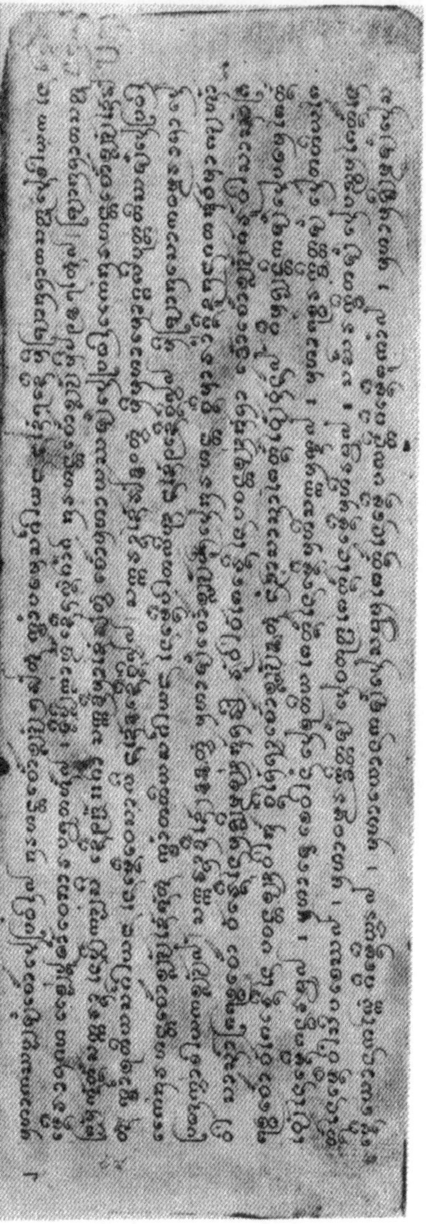

[2]

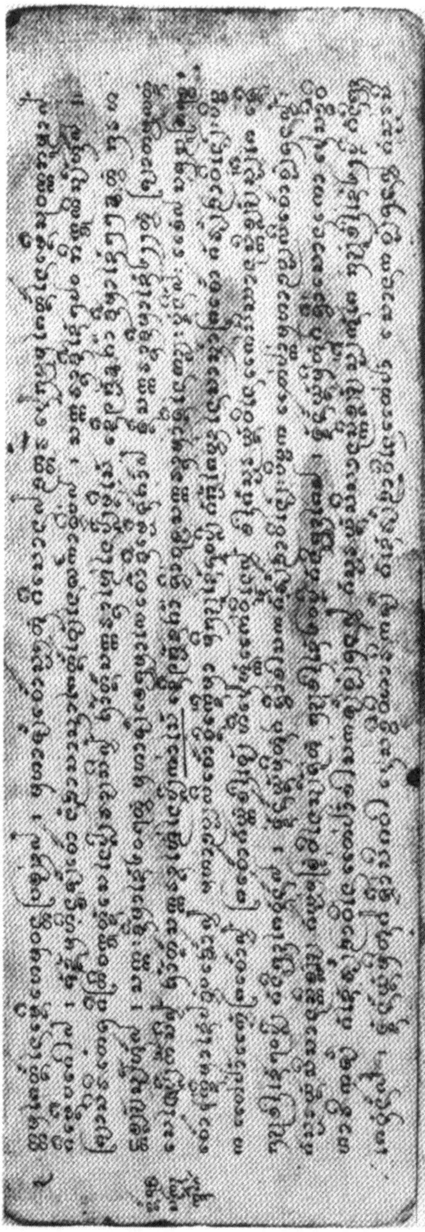

[3]

[4]

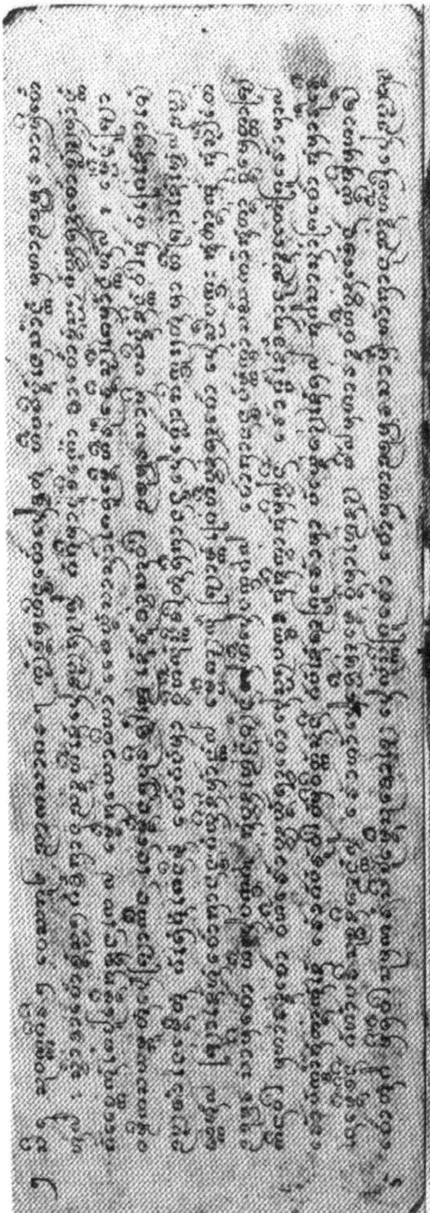

[5]

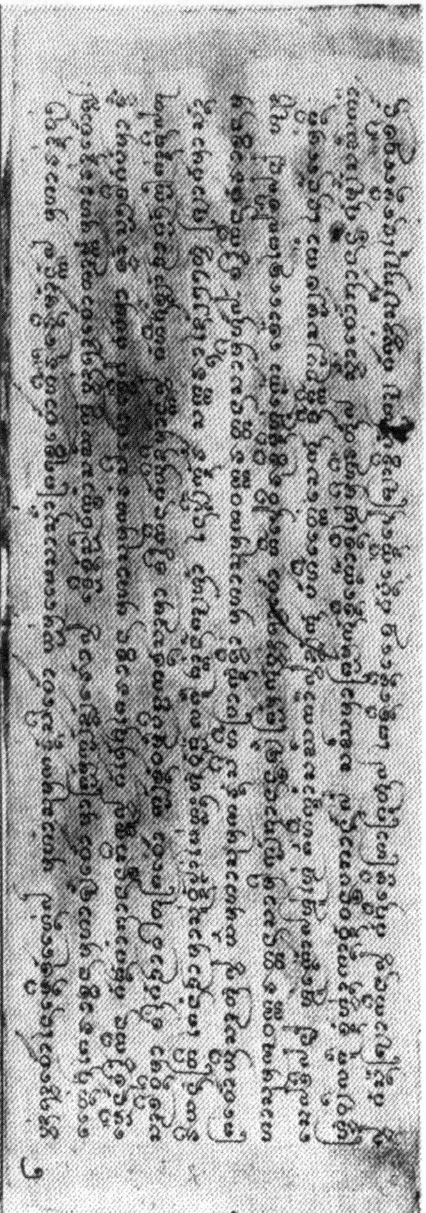

[6]

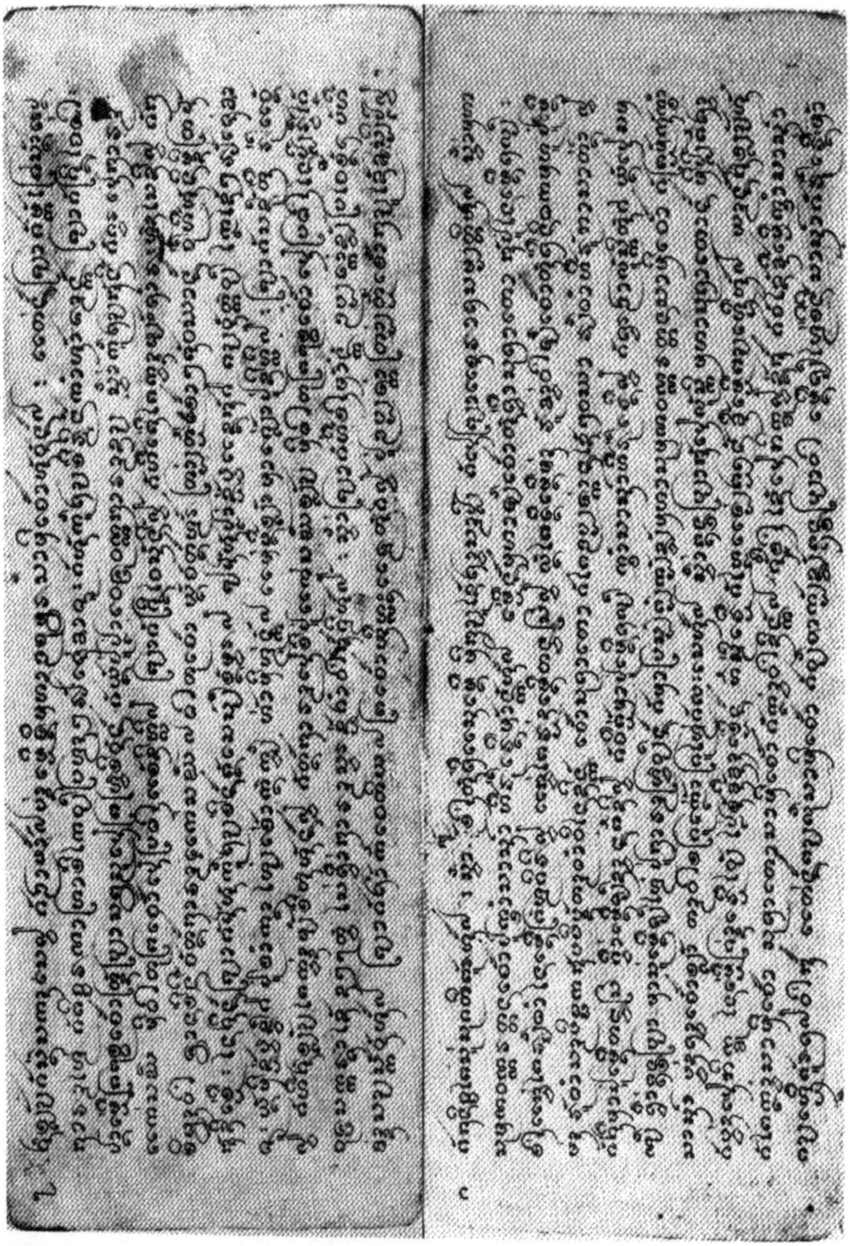

[7]

[8]

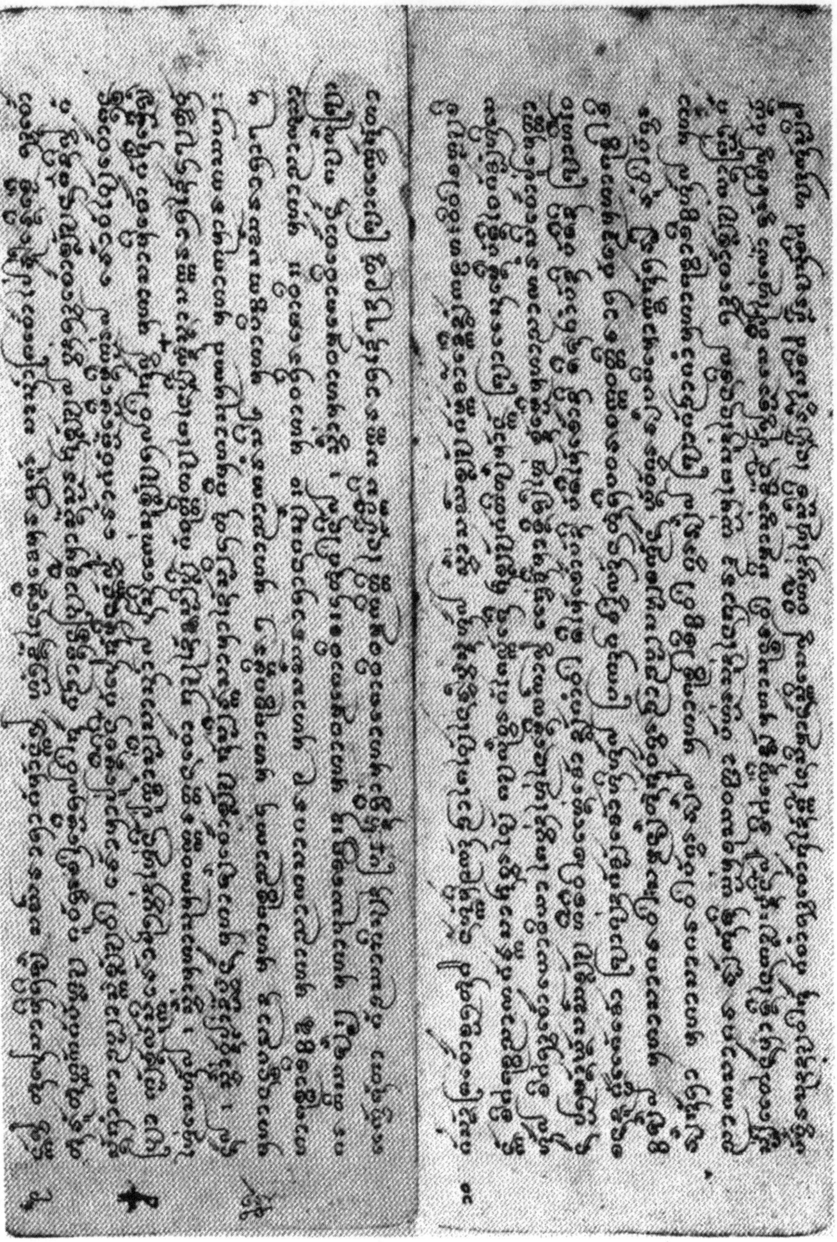

[9]

[10]

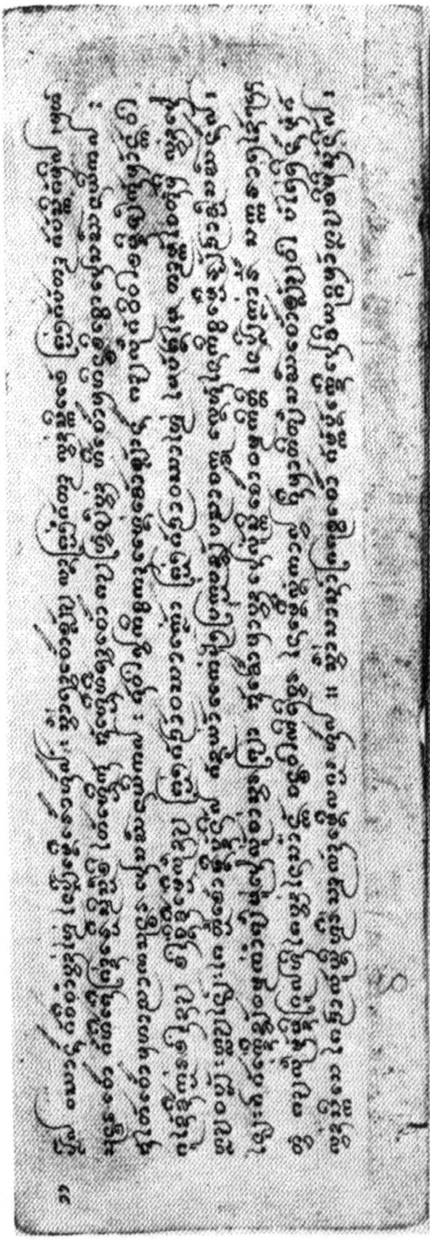

[11]

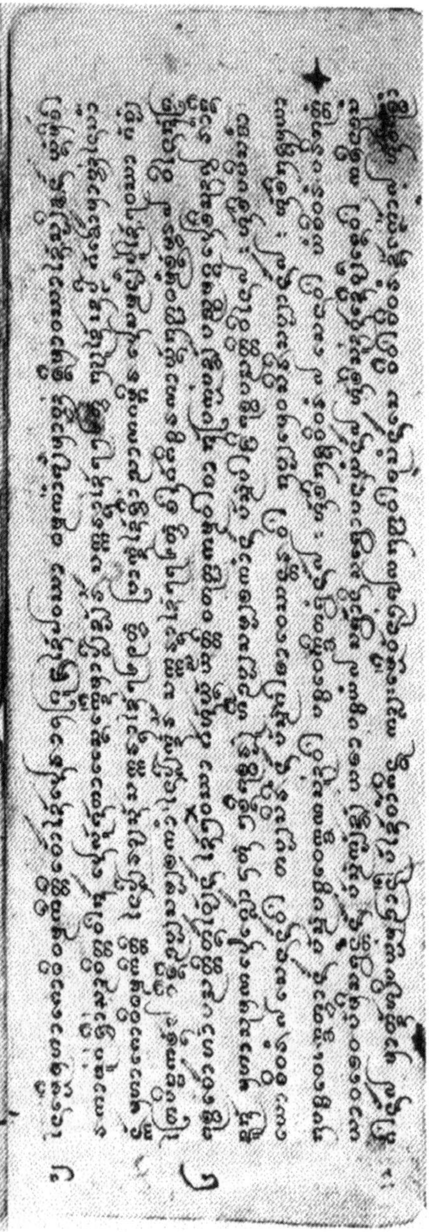

[12]

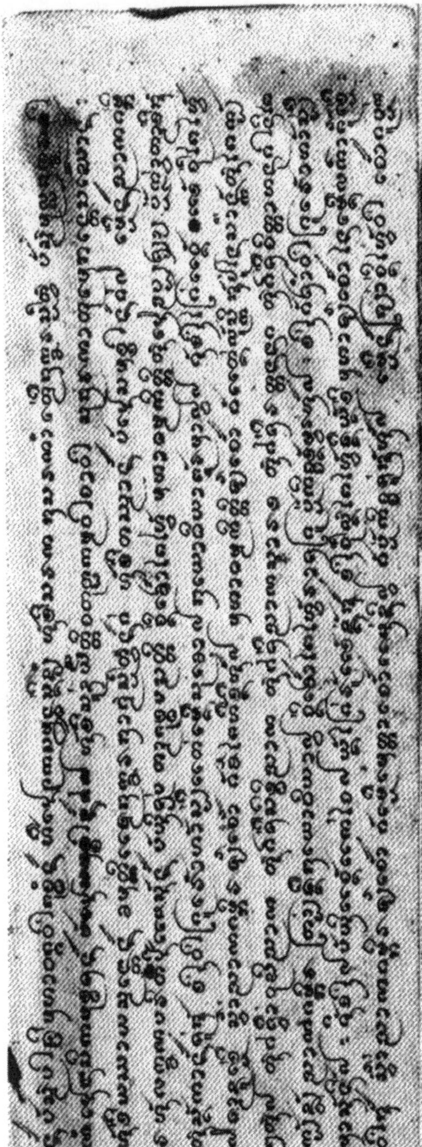

[13]

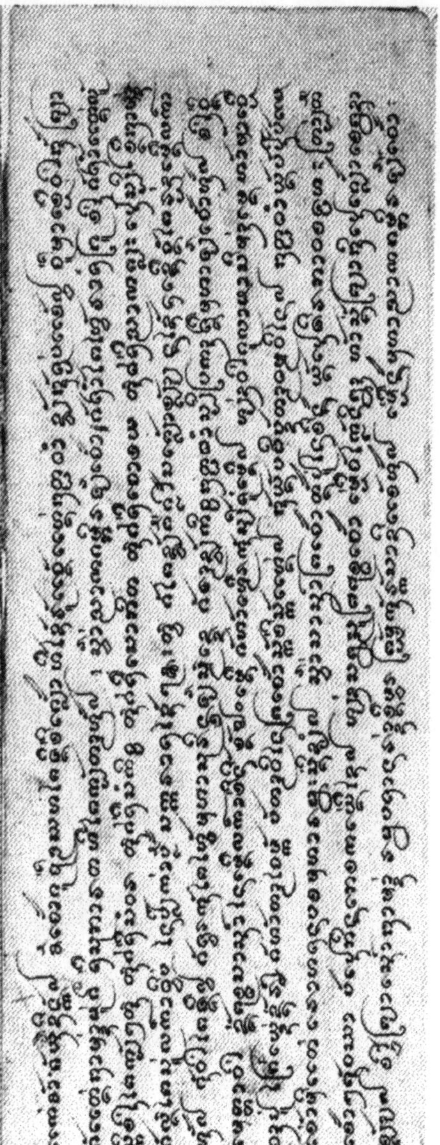

[14]

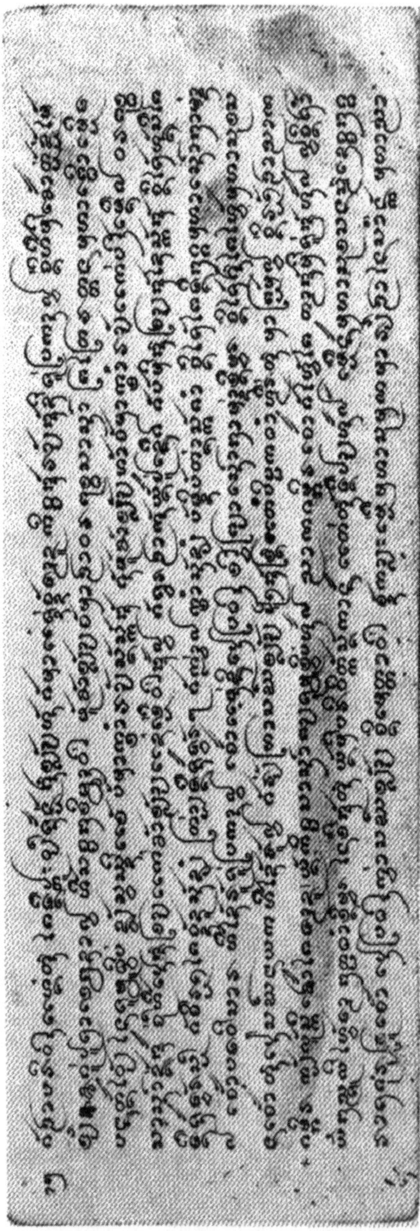

[15]

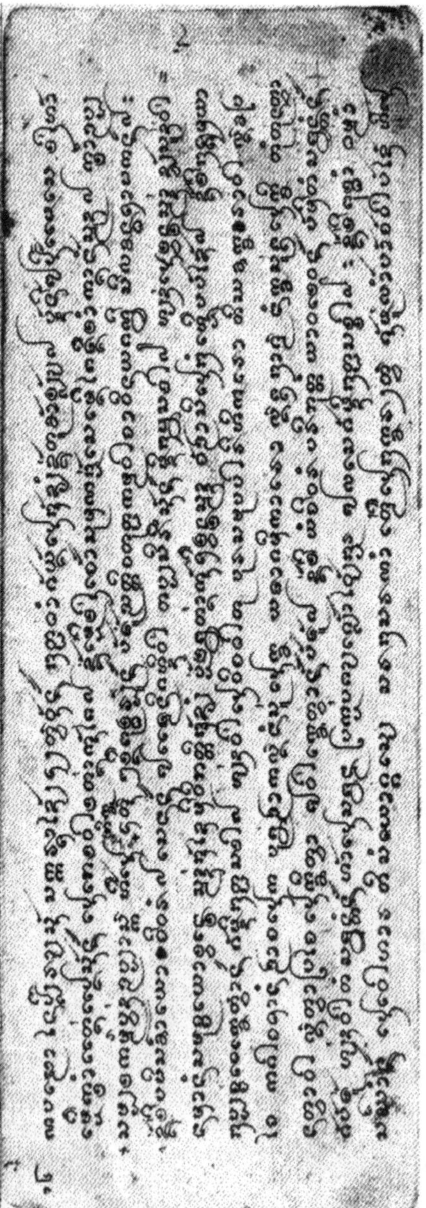

[16]

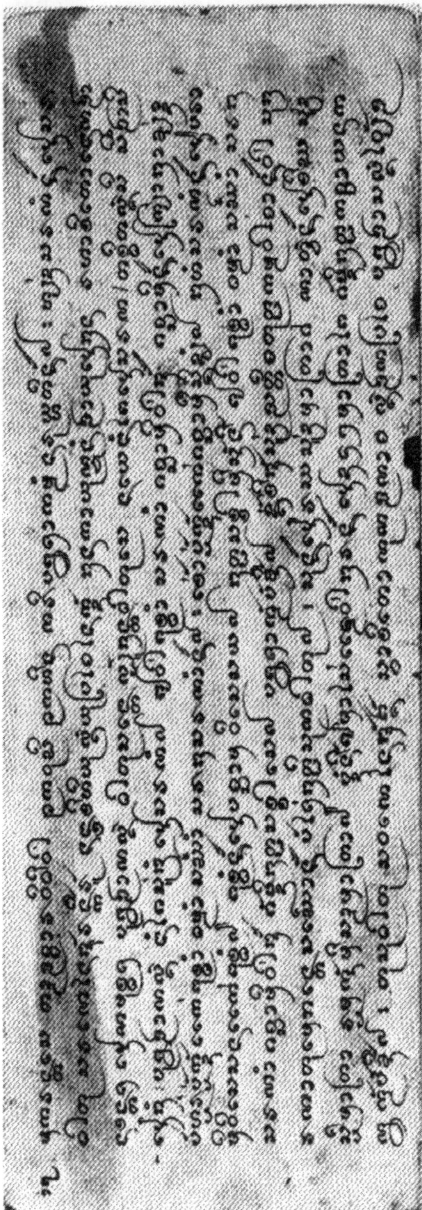

[17]

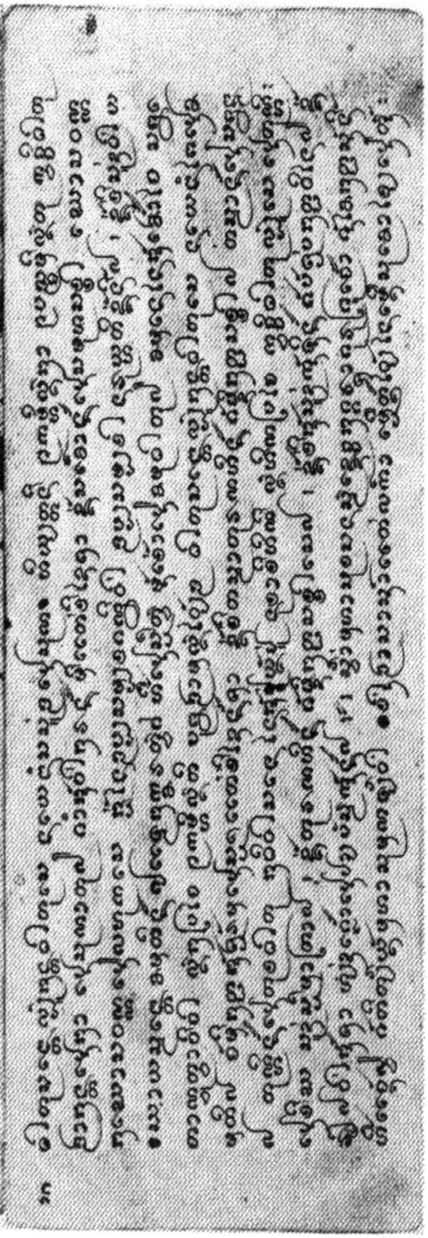

[18]

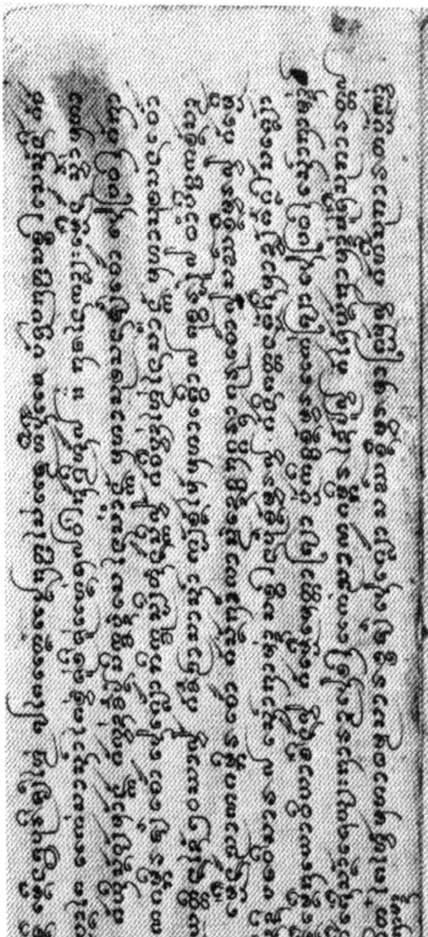

[19]

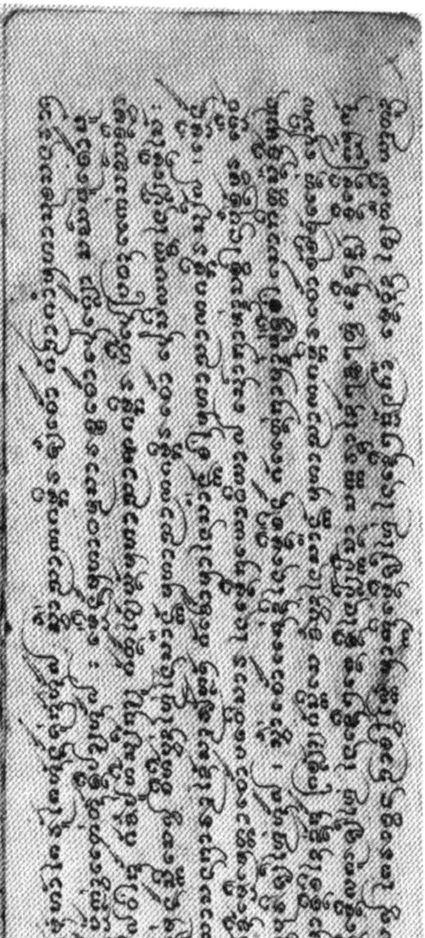

[20]

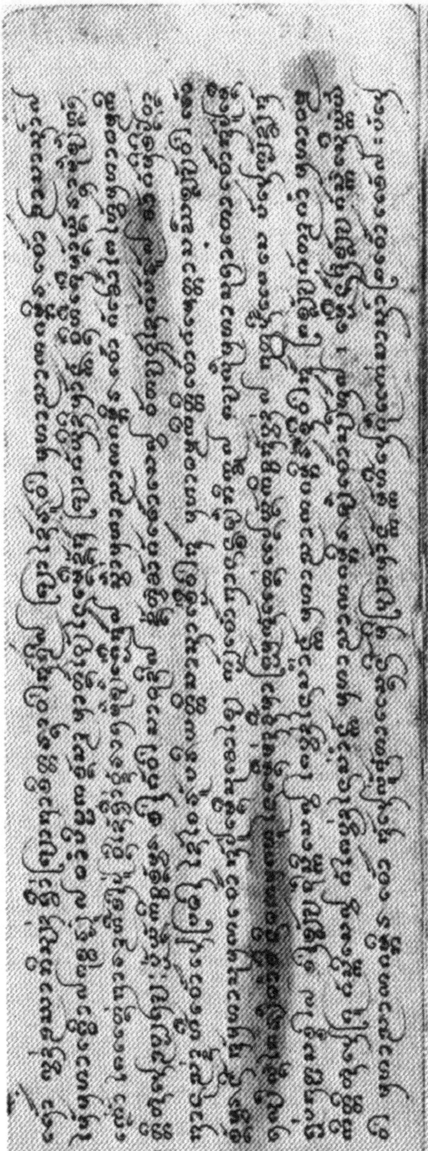

[21]

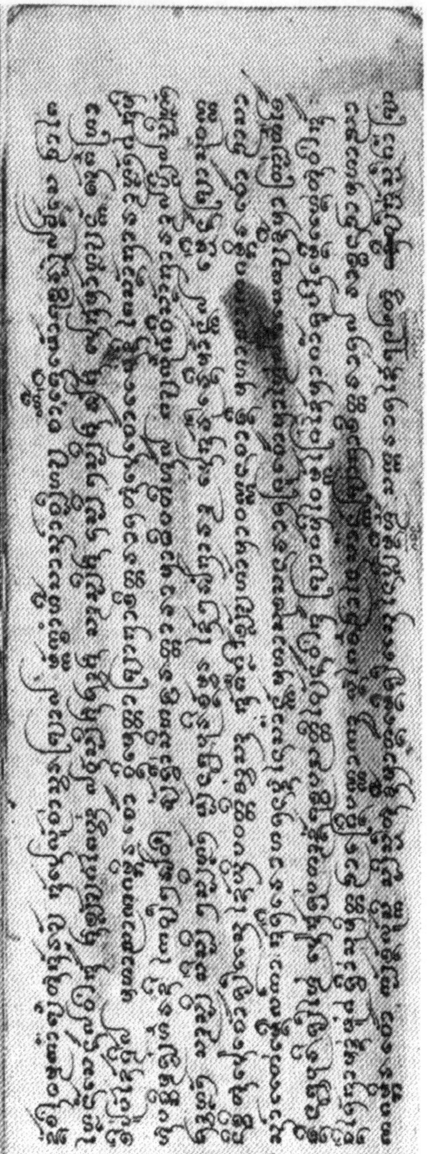

[22]

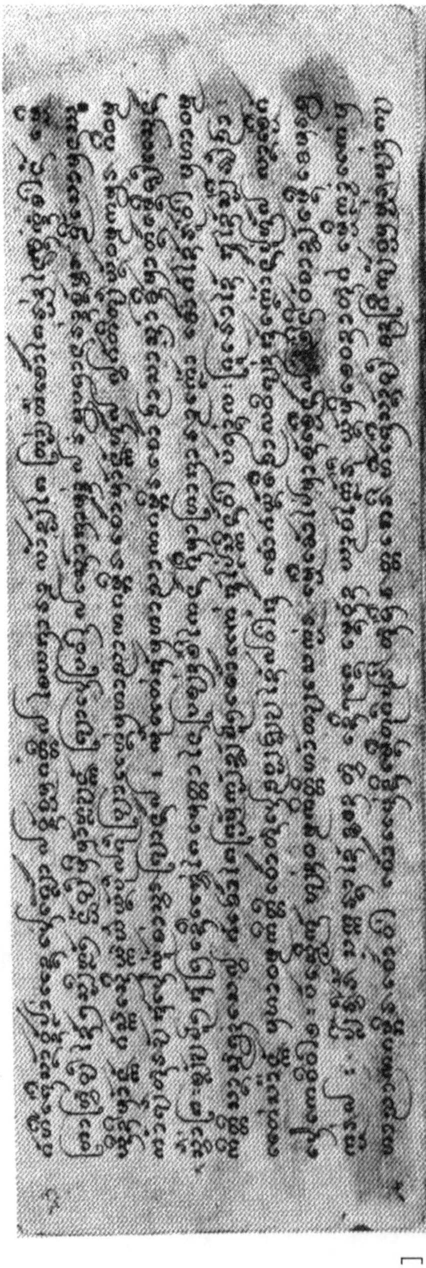

[23]

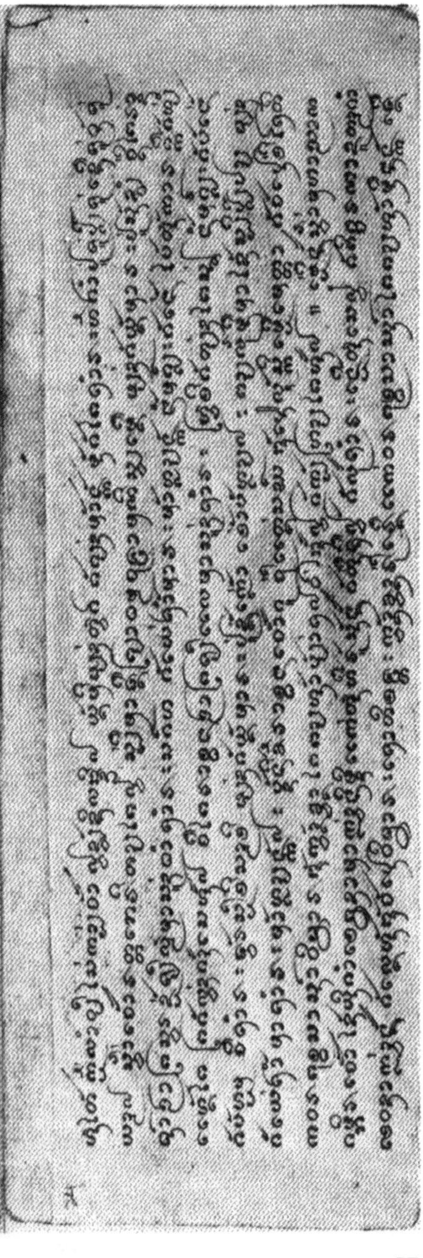

[24]

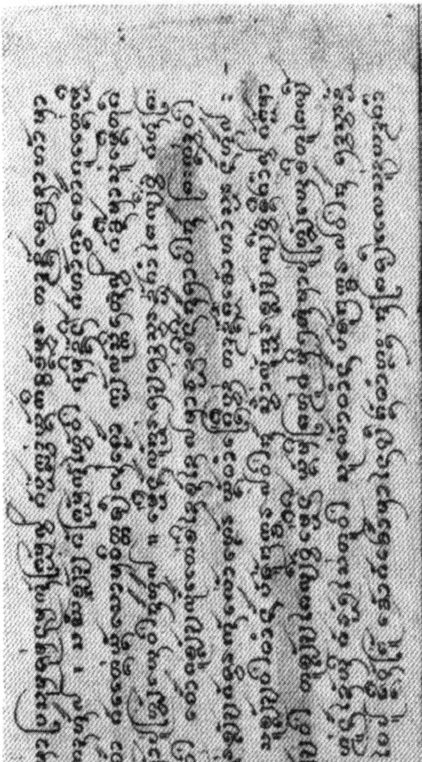

[25]

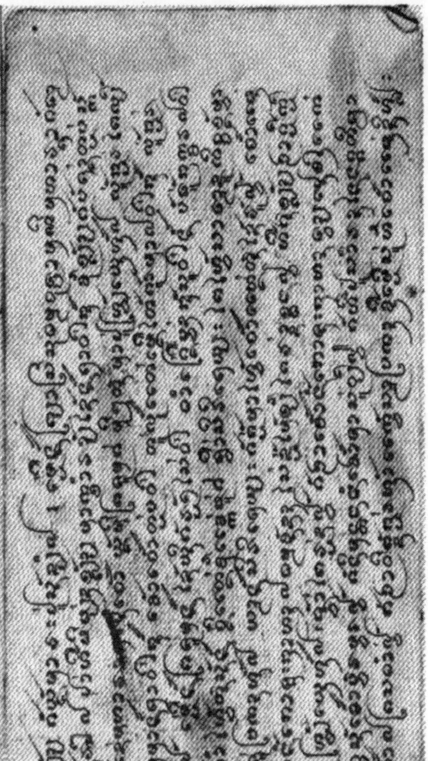

[26]

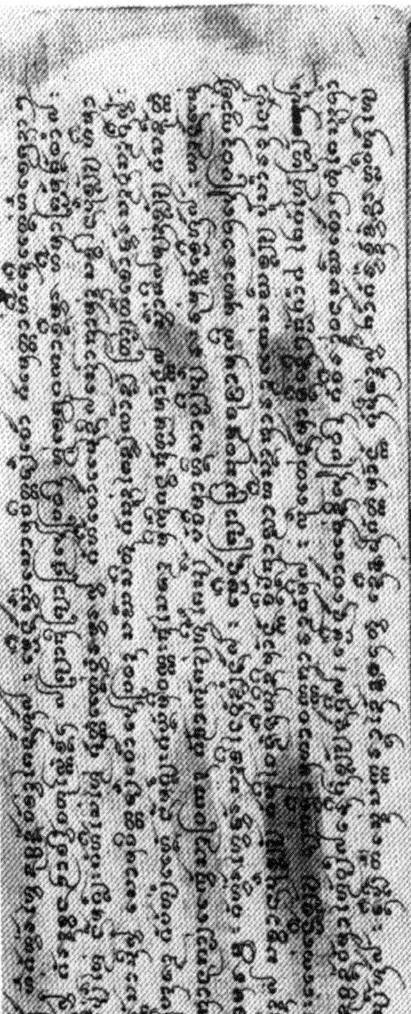

[27]

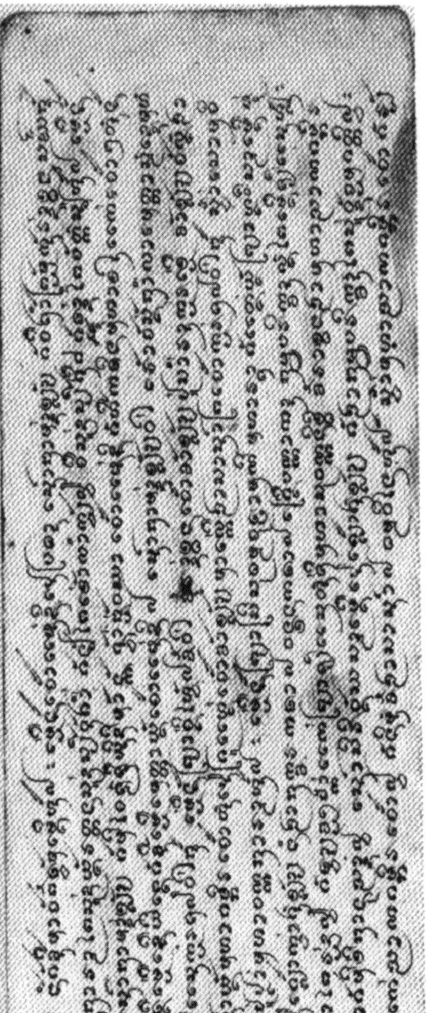

[28]

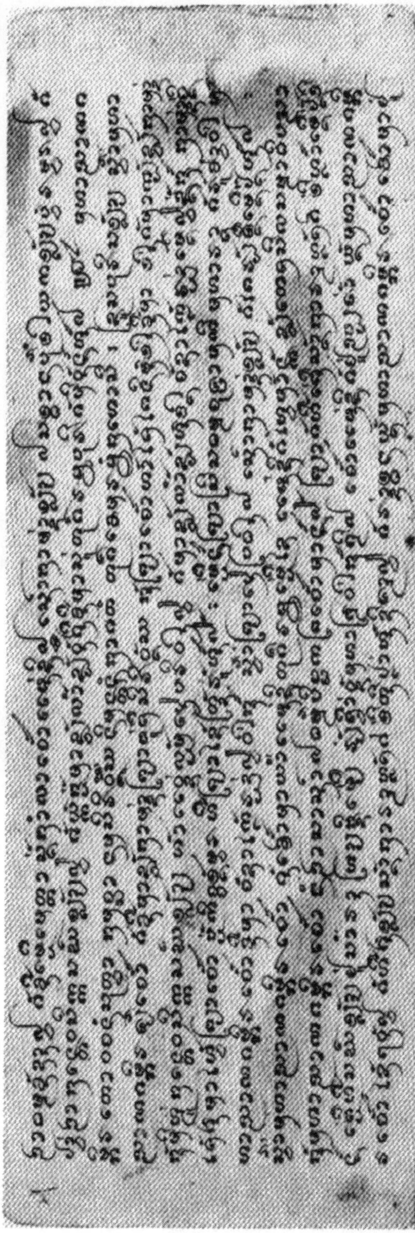

[29]

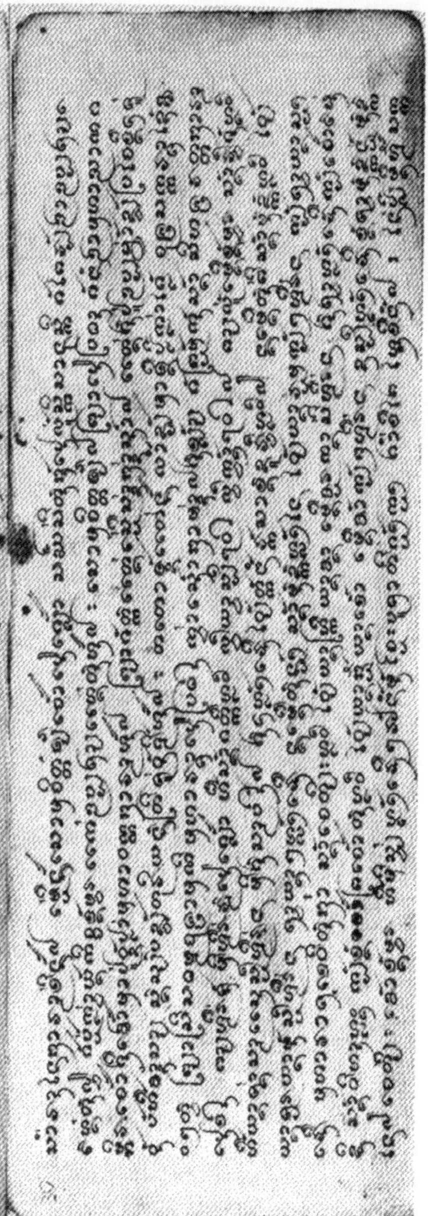

[30]

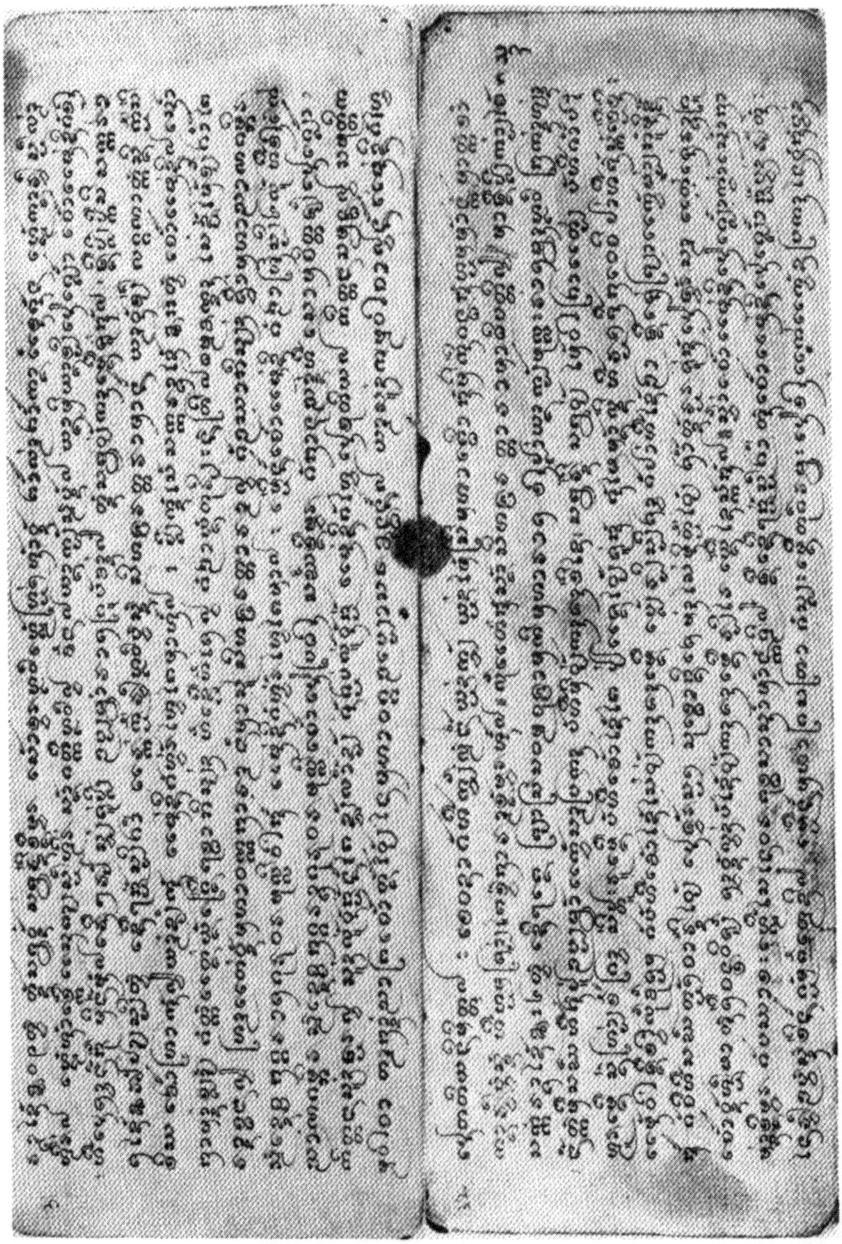

[31]

[32]

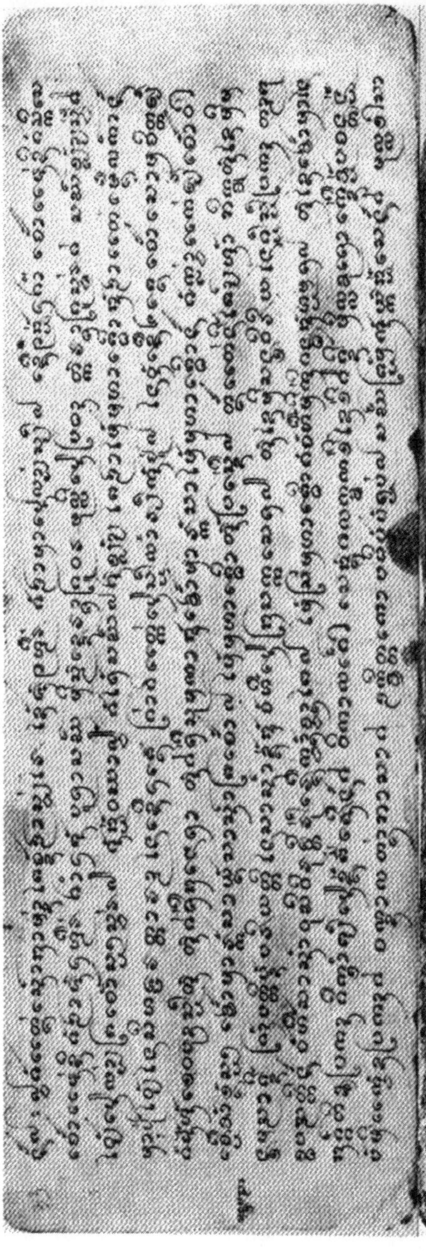

[33]

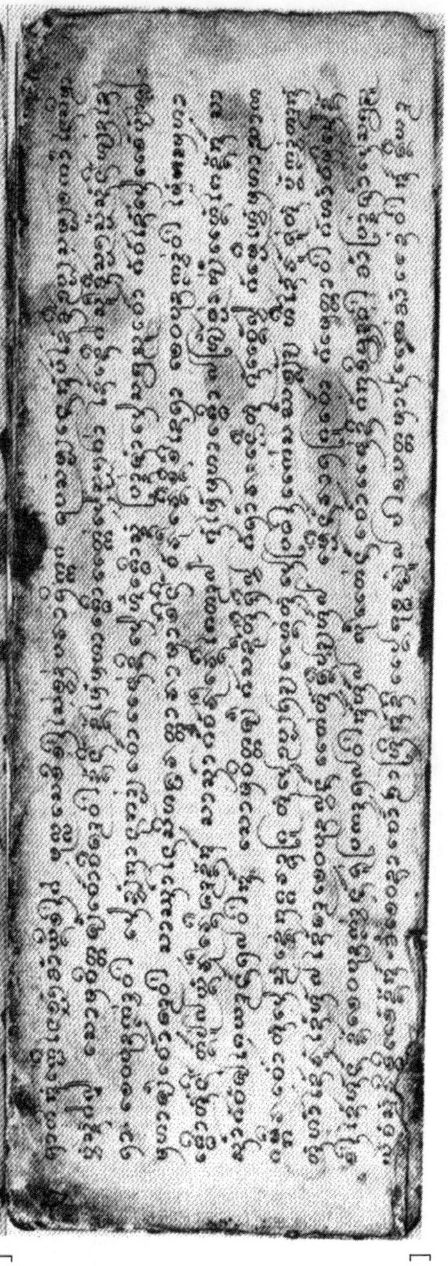

[34]

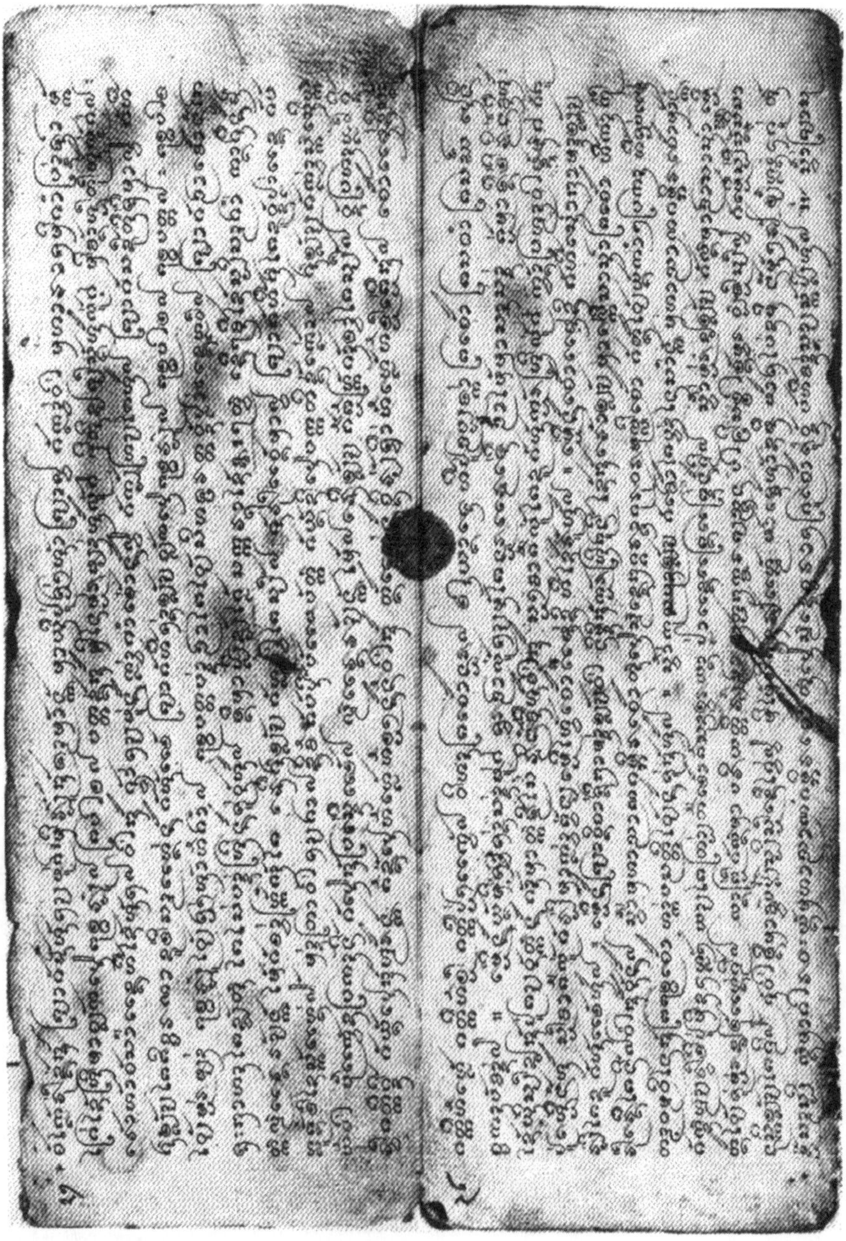

[35]

[36]

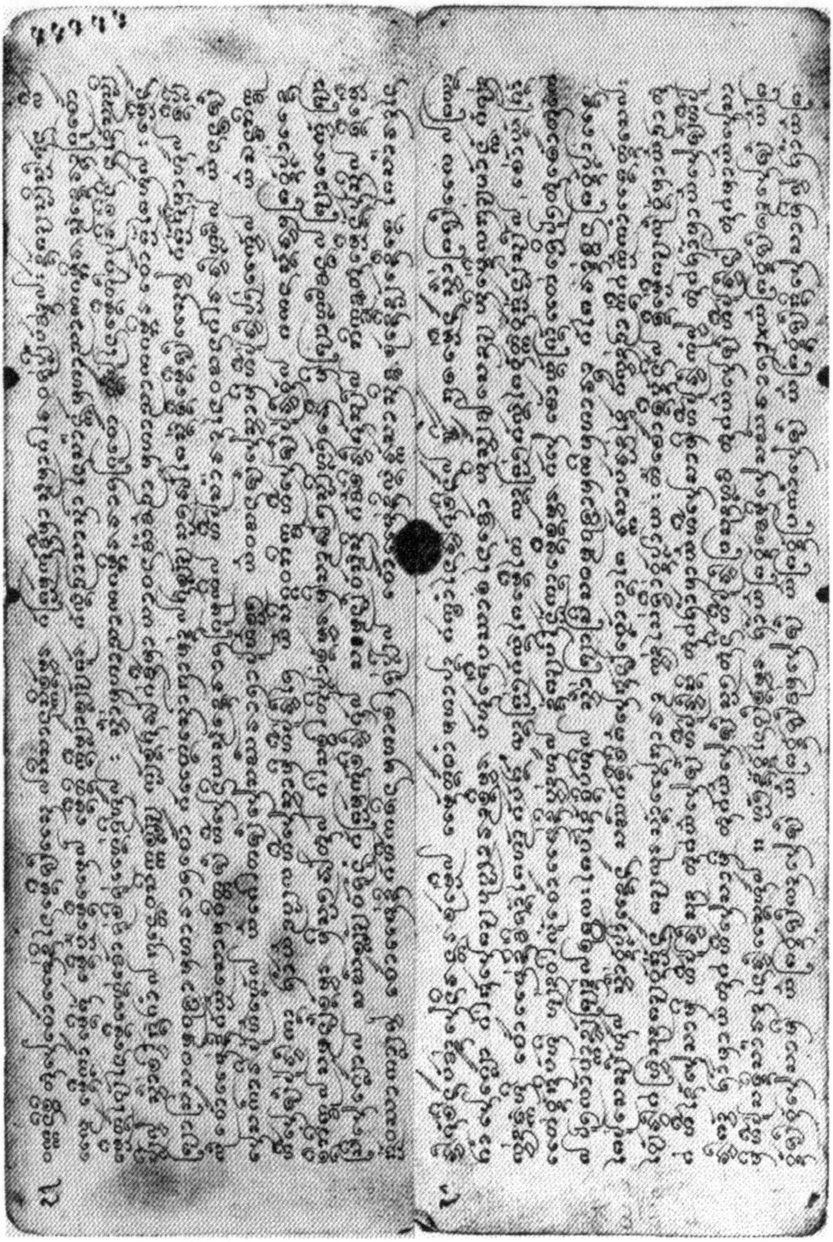

[37]

[38]

[39]

[40]

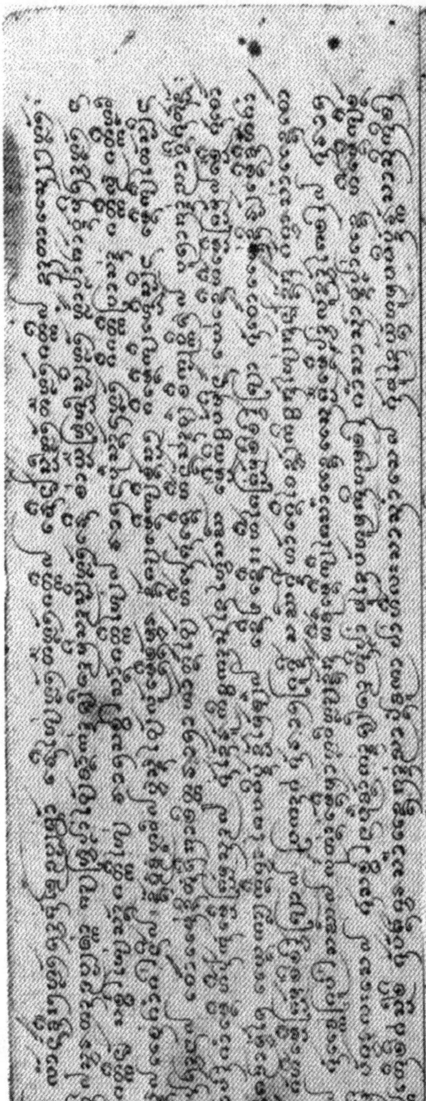

[41]

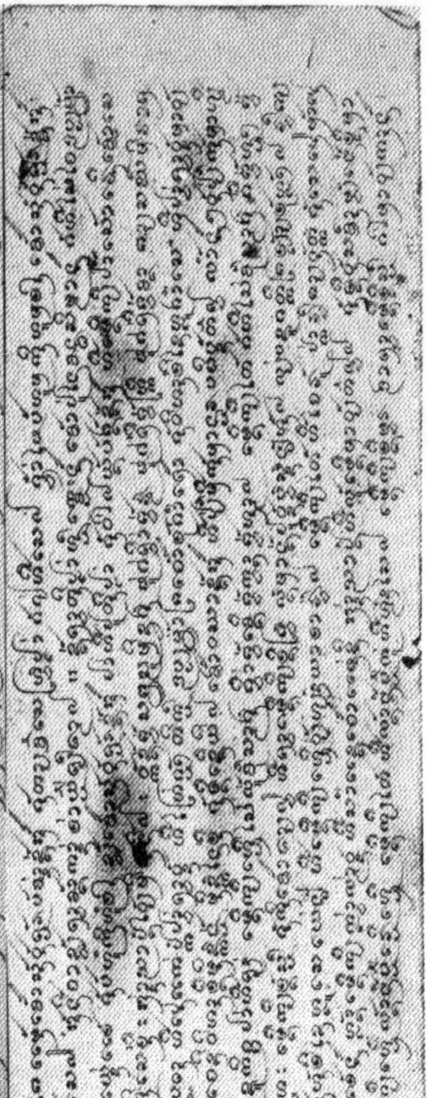

[42]

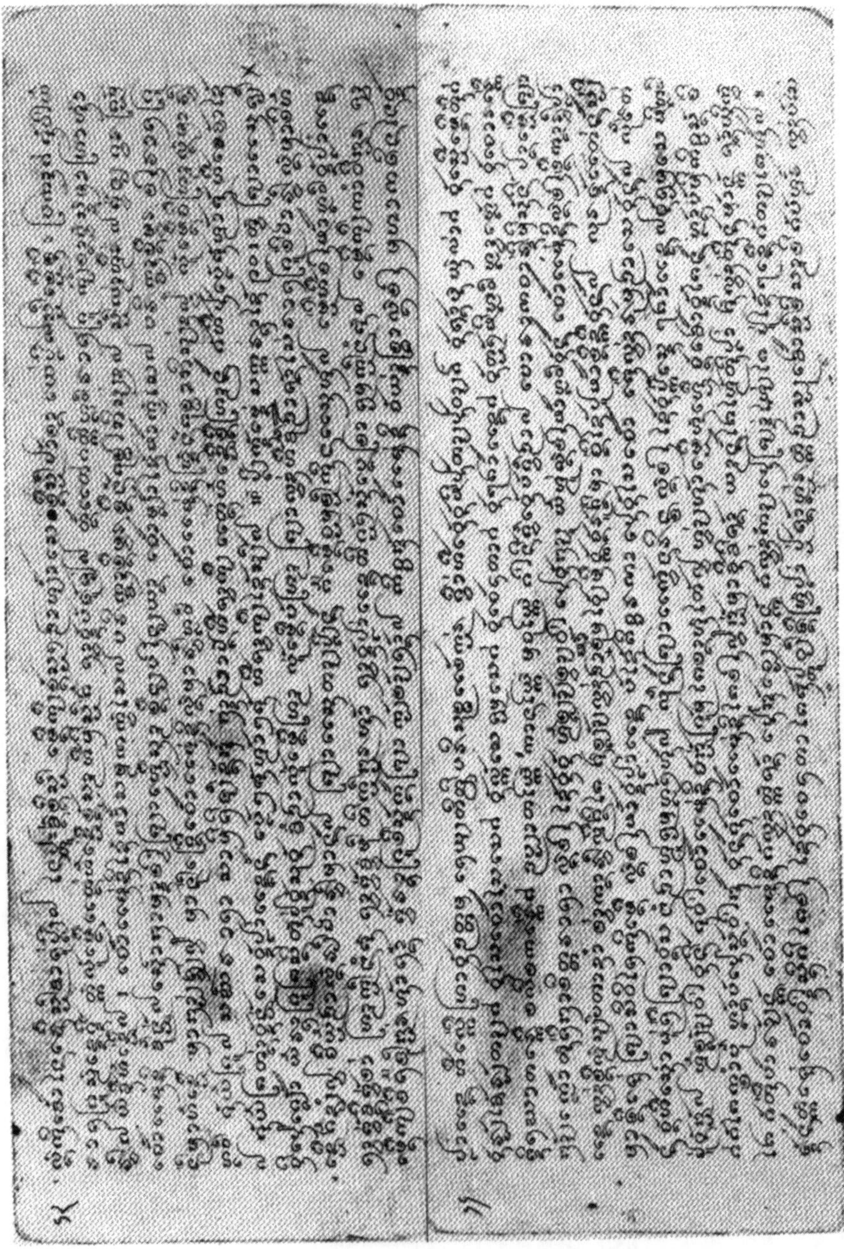

[43]

[44]

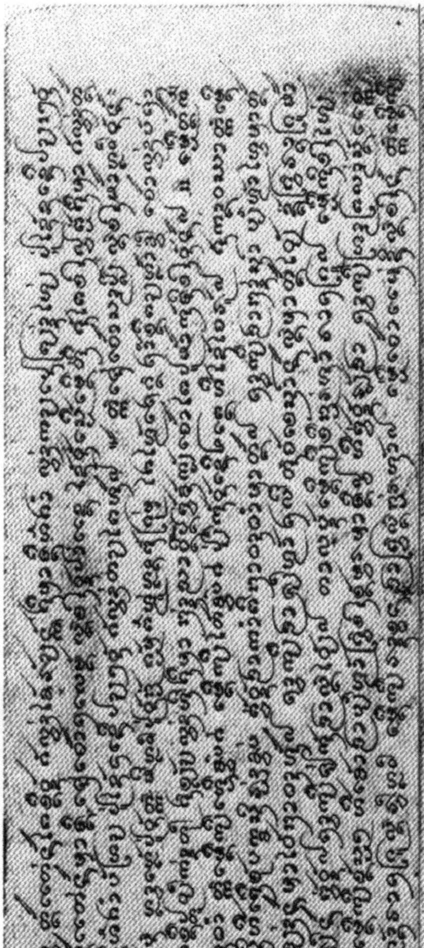

[45]

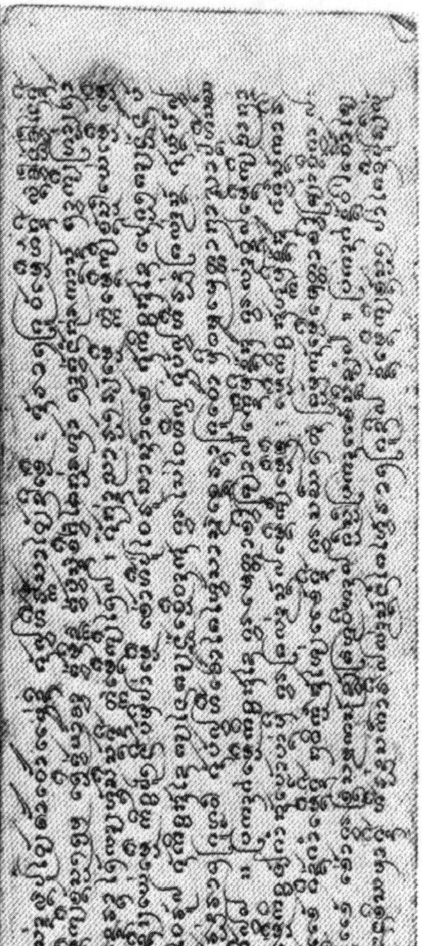

[46]

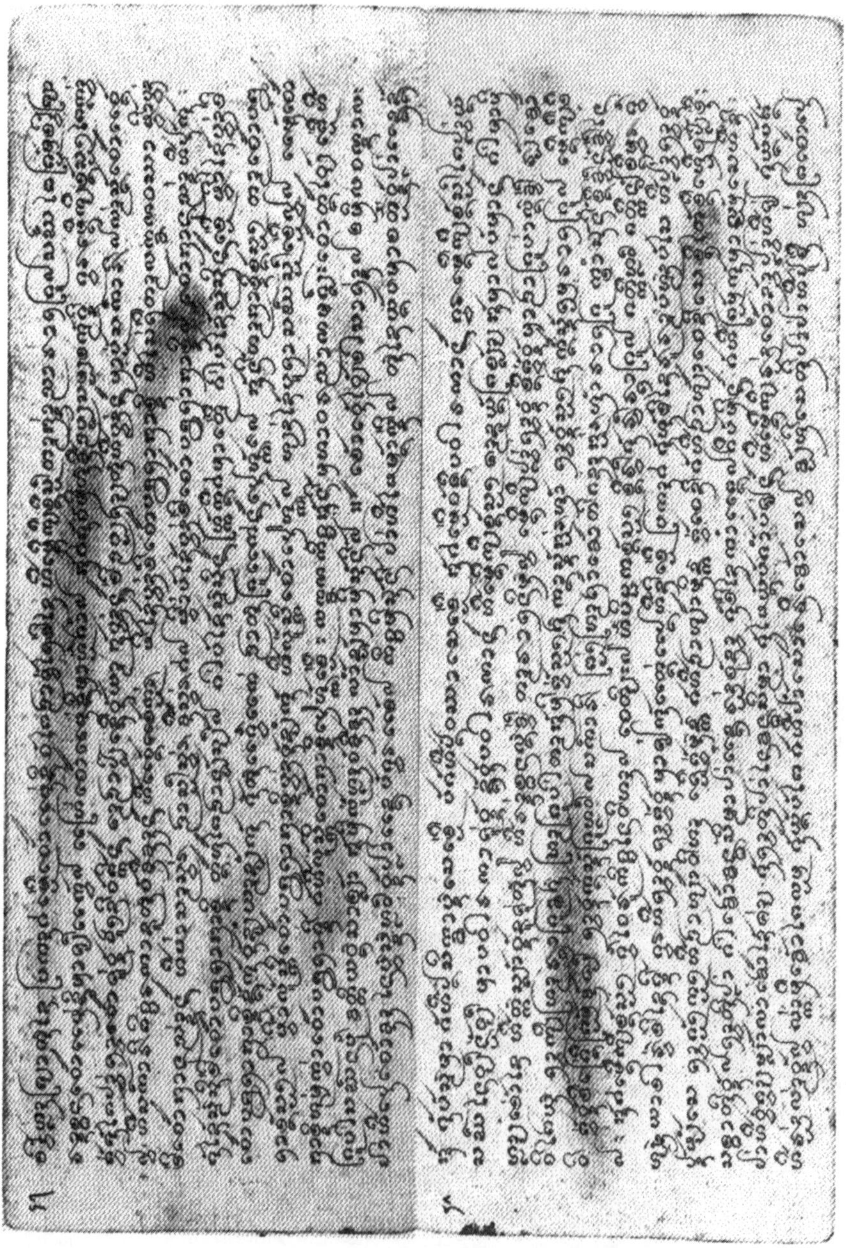

[47]

[48]

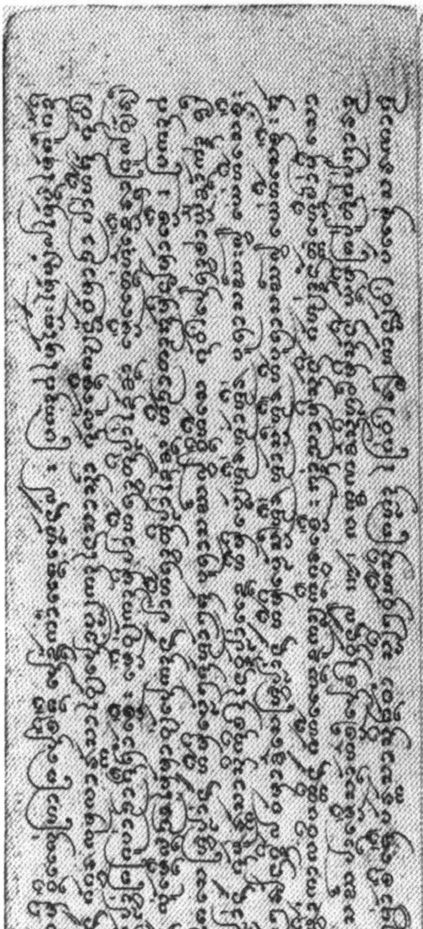

[49]

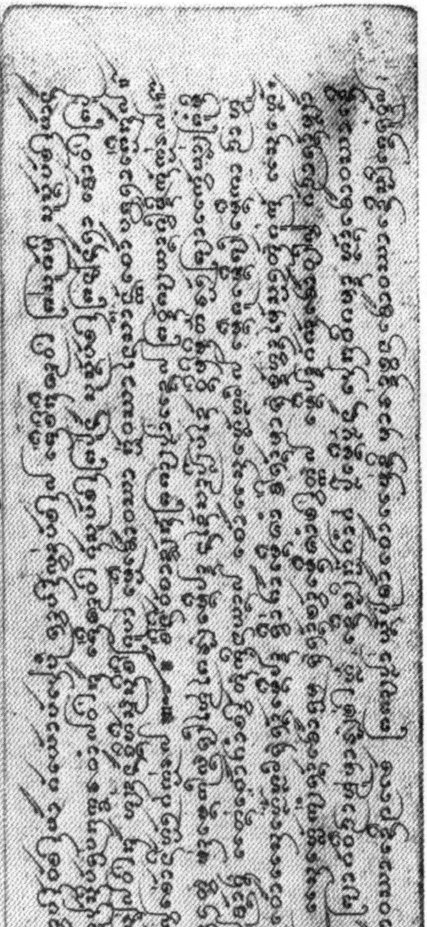

[50]

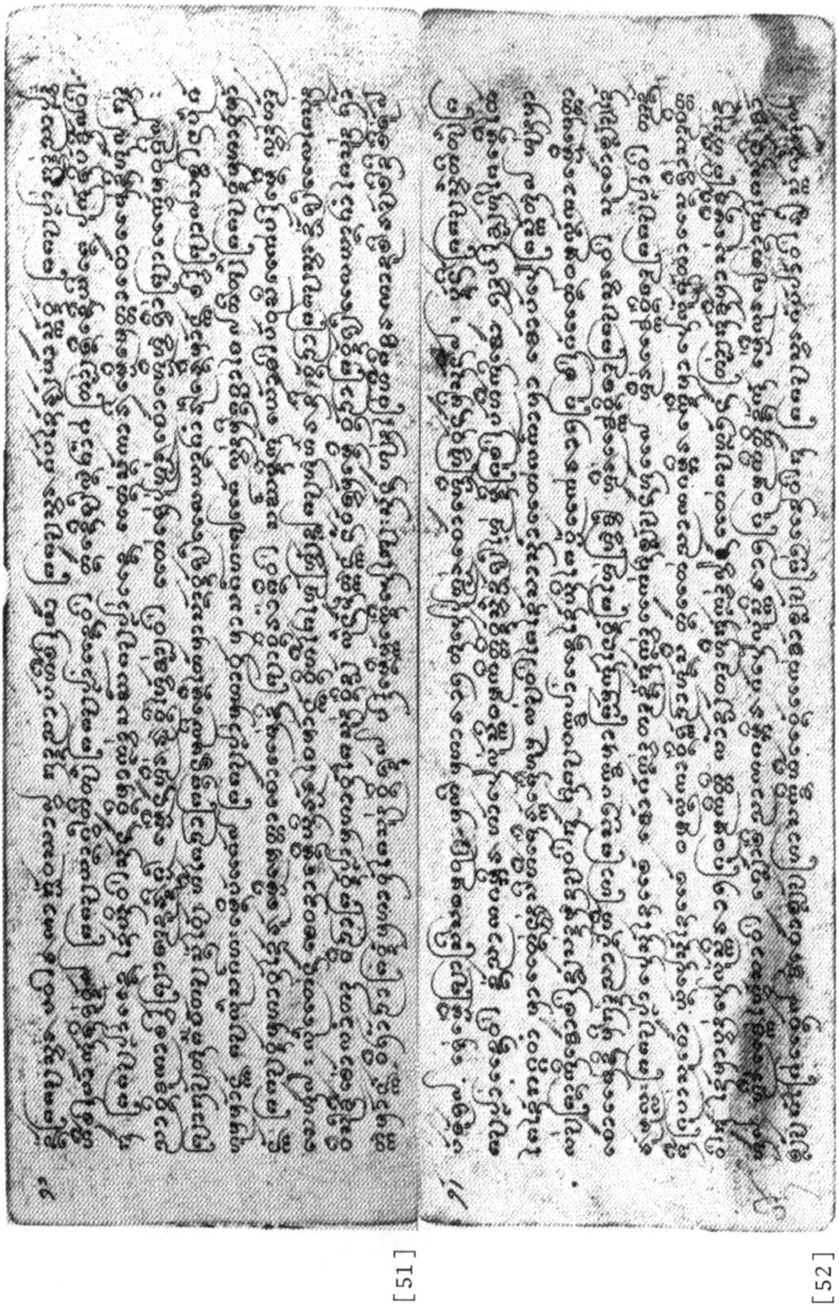

[51]

[52]

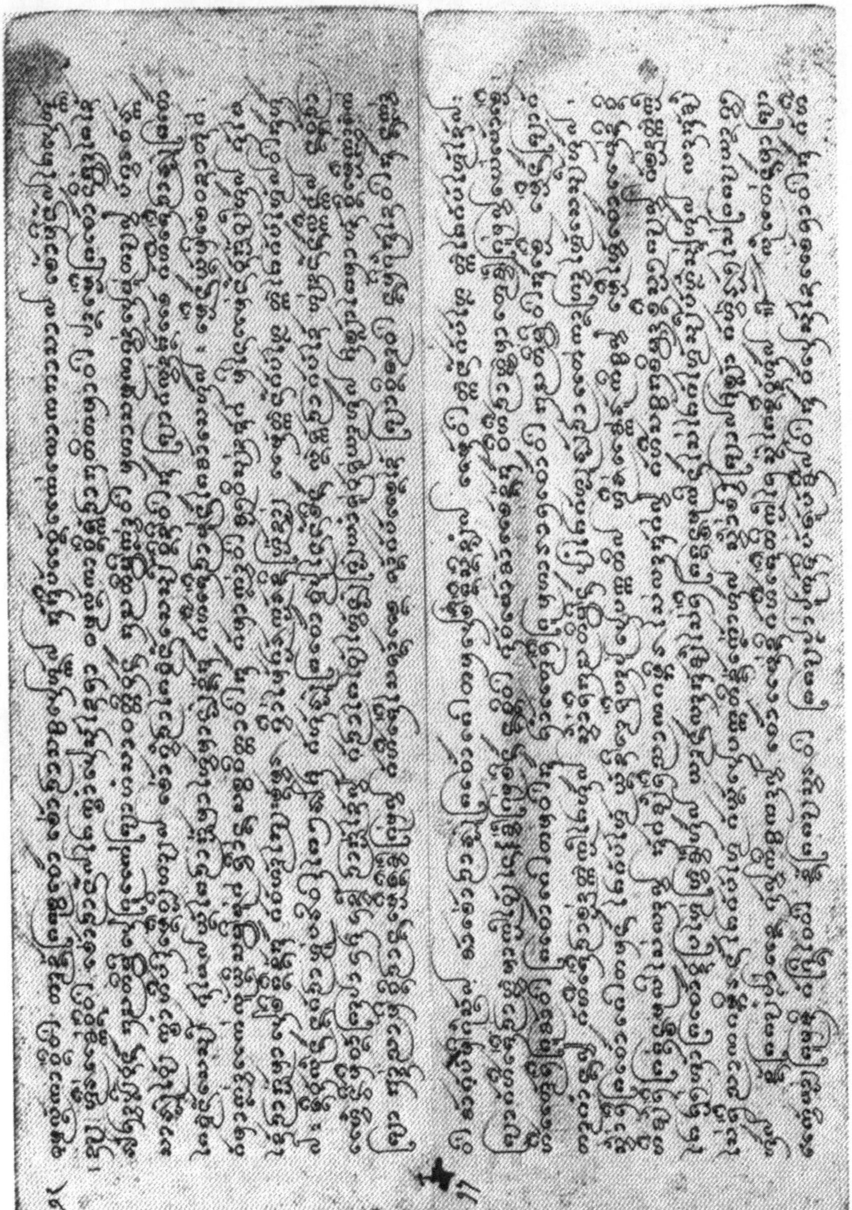

[53]

[54]

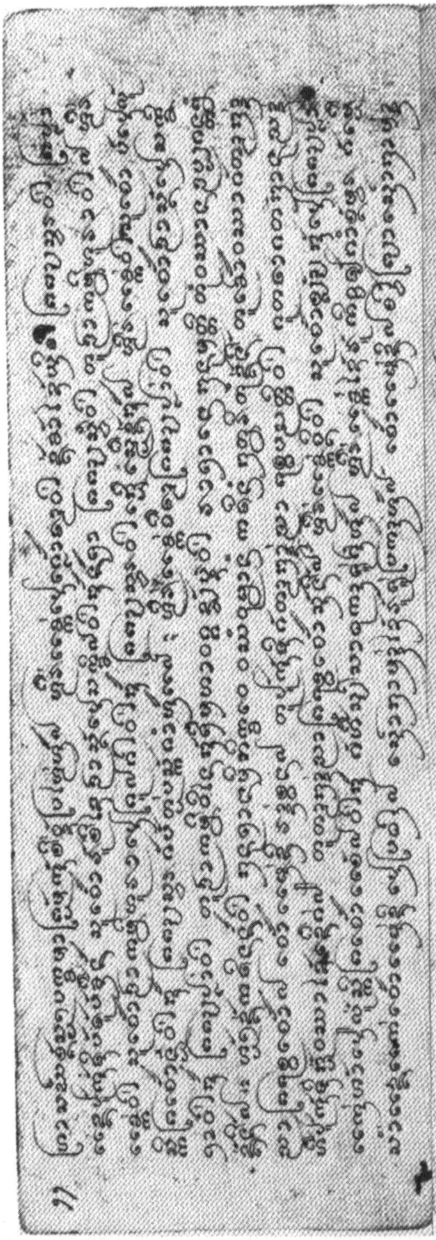

[55]

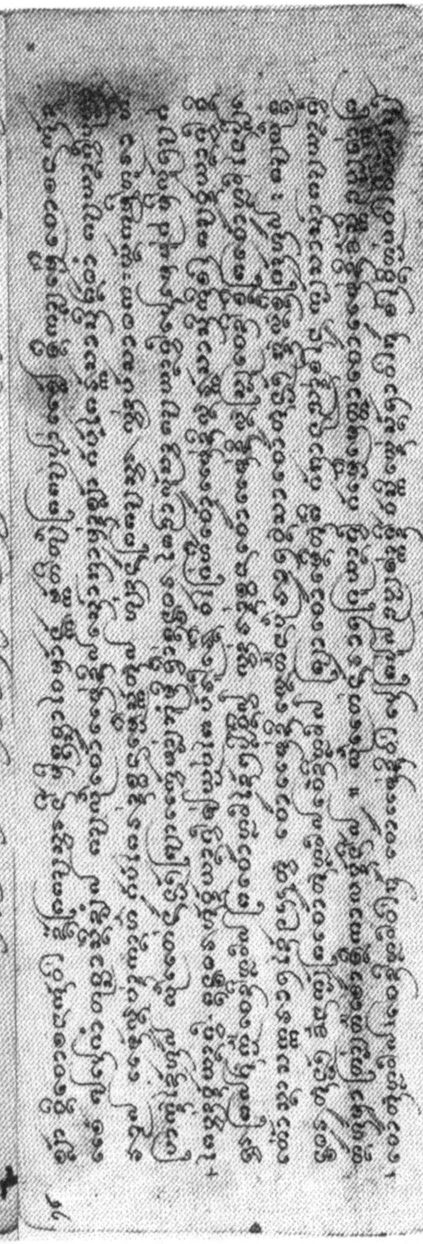

[56]

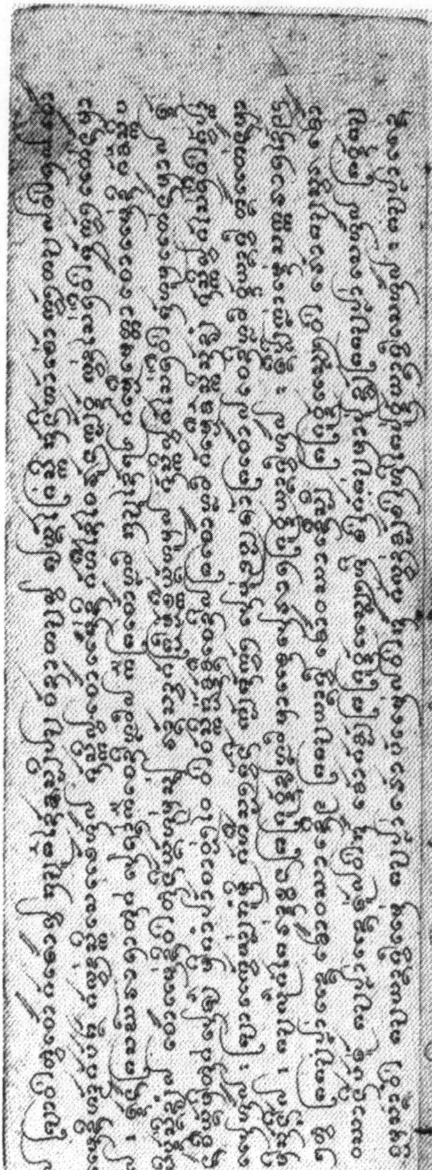

[57]

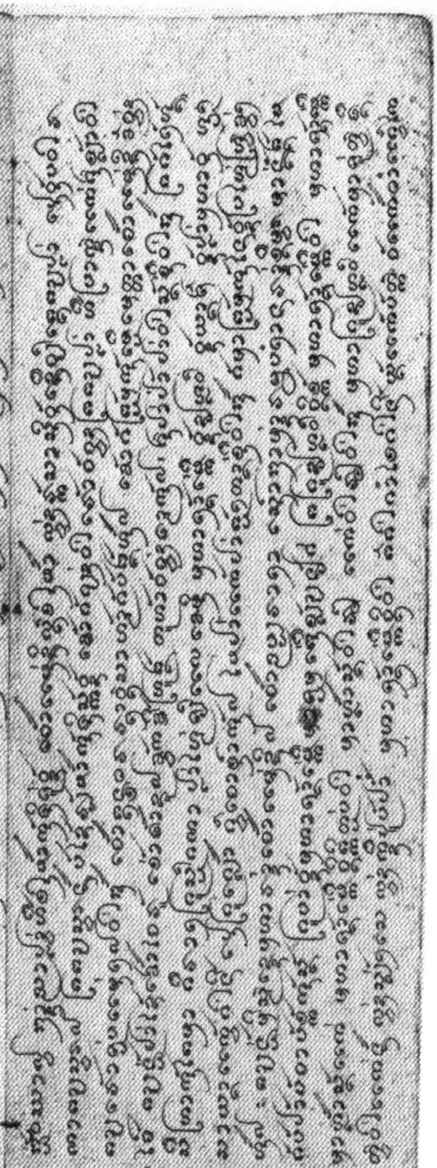

[58]

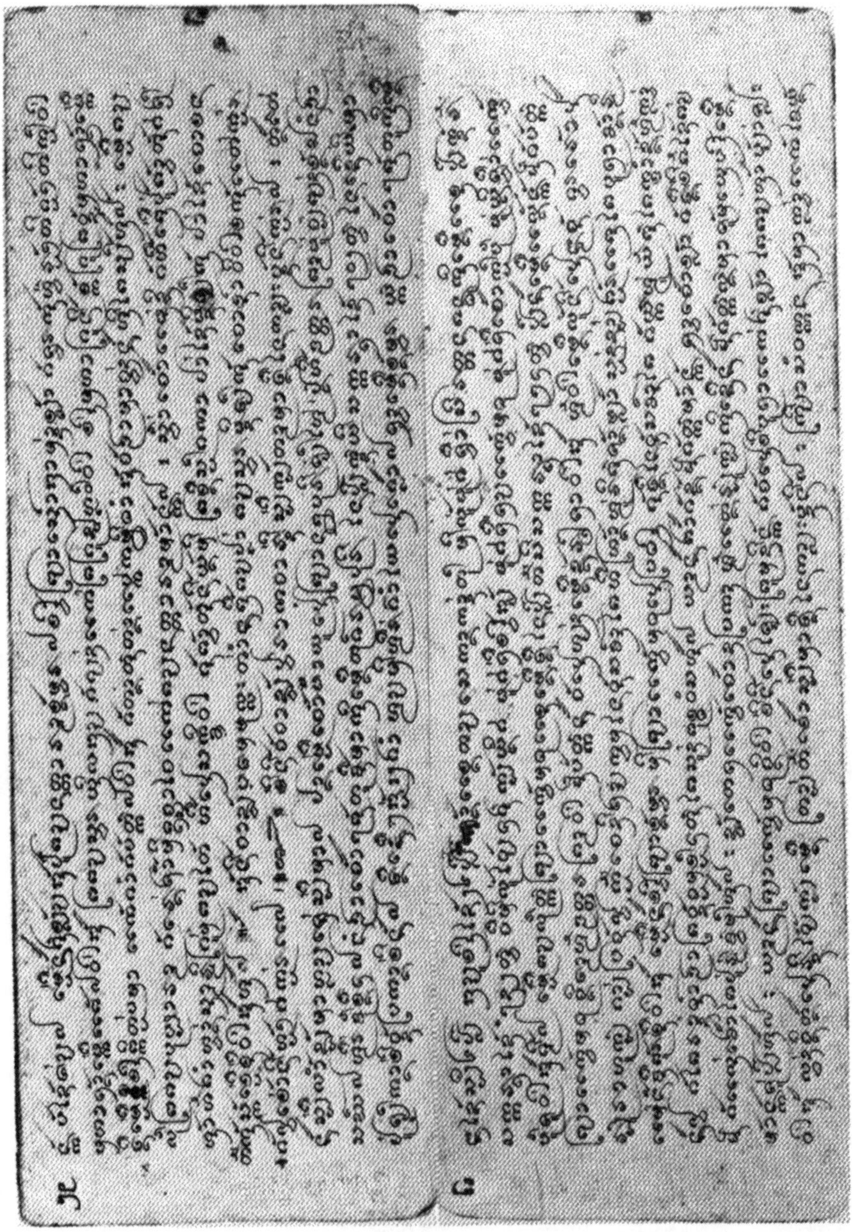

[59]

[60]

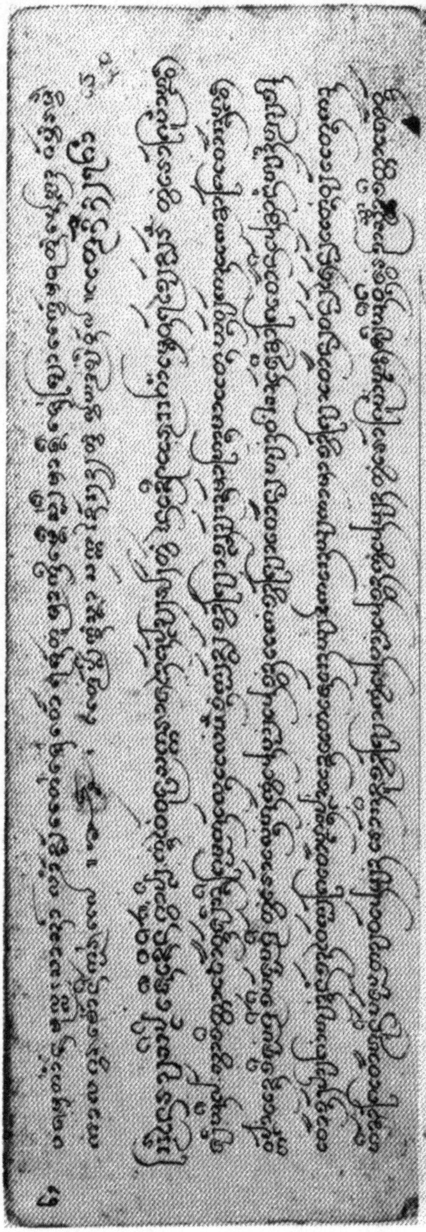

[61]

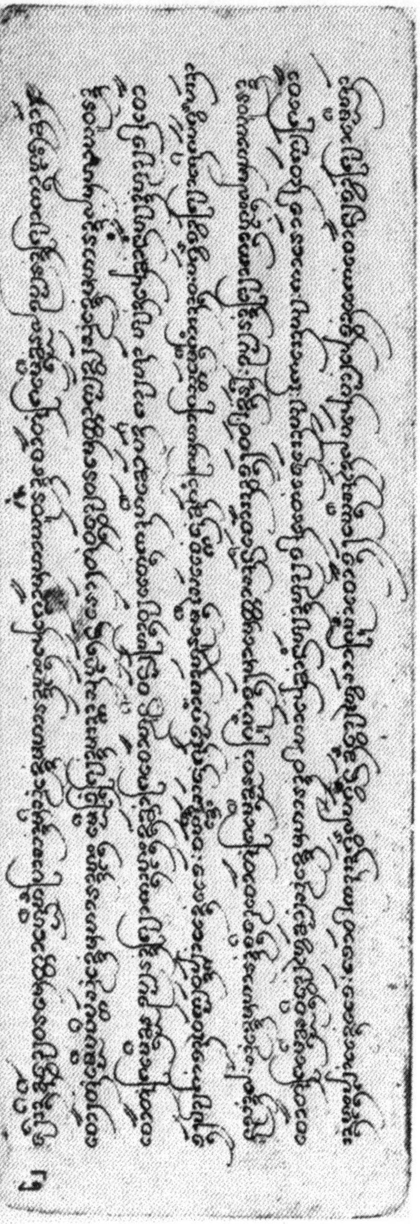

[62]

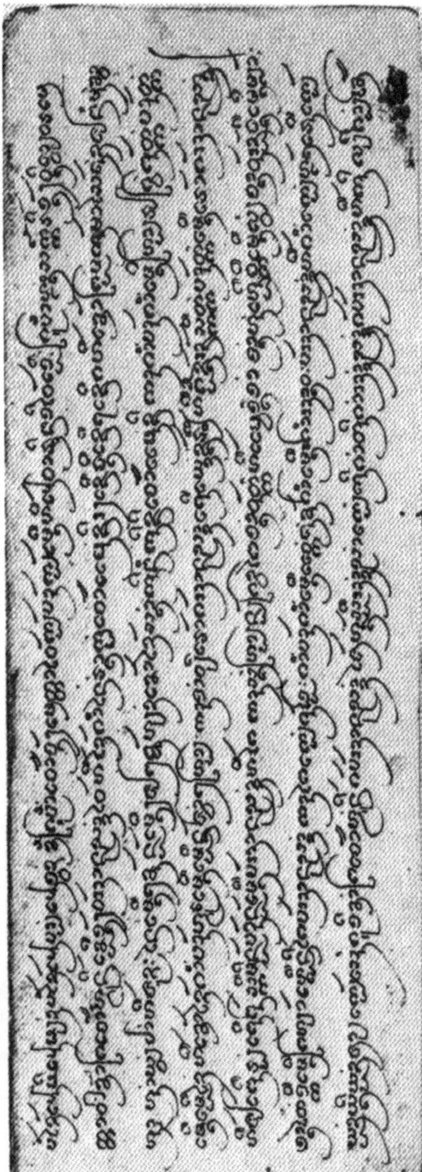

[63]

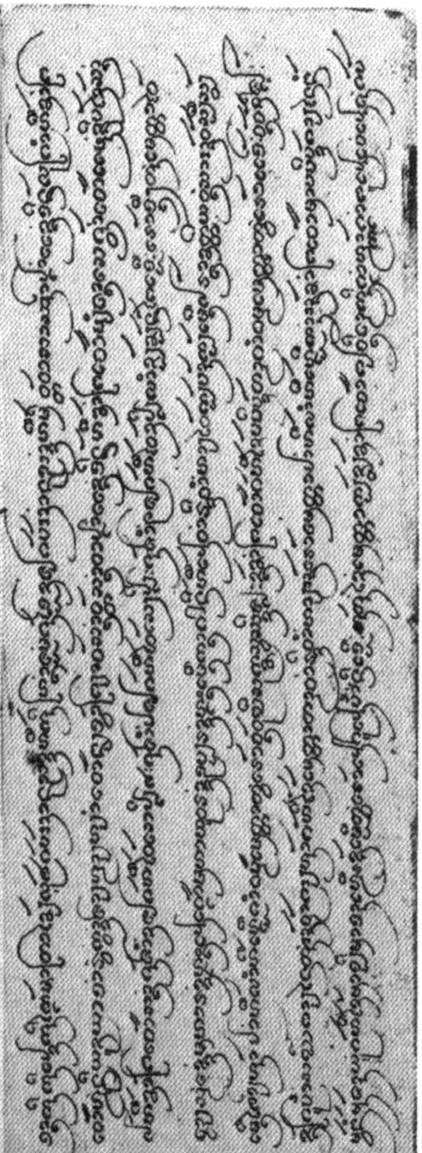

[64]

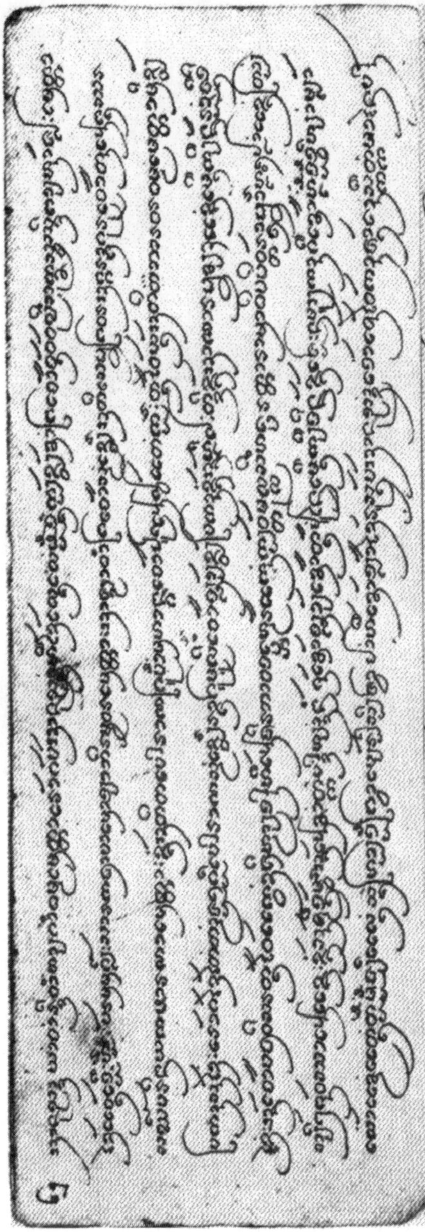

[65]

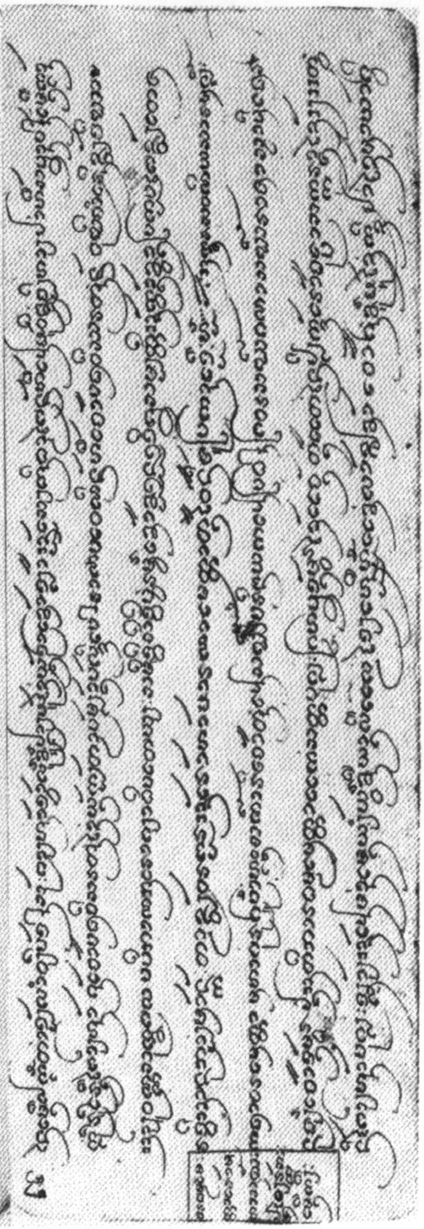

[66]

[67]

[68]

[69]

Contents of Translation

Pars. 107-115 Departure of Garden Sect Saṅgha; deserted monasteries filled by P̱āḍaeng; promotions of bhikkhus.

Pars. 116-129 Construction of Vat P̱āḍaeng; Möng Küy monastery subjects; their duties; different wards of the city and their duties towards P̱āḍaeng.

Pars. 130-136 Inauspicious days for rulers between 1474-1720.

Pars. 137-153 Duties of Möng Küy and city wards; some old traditions (pars. 145-46, 152).

Pars. 154-191 Sectarian disputes; a pious lady (pars. 165-69); validity of Pavāraṇā and spread of kaṭhina (pars. 172-73); the great debate (pars. 184-89) during Kaeuphāpbhummin's reign (1560-1597).

Pars. 192-195 Tradition of New Year ceremony from the reign of Kaeumadhu (1401-1416).

Pars. 196-197 End of a vagga (chapter); the year copy completed.

Pars. 198-208 Document I: how far monastery subjects could be used by the state.

Pars. 209-212 Document II: supplement to I.

Pars. 213-217 Document III: cutting of trees forbidden within the boundaries of Möng Küy.

Pars. 218-223 Document IV: boundaries of Möng Küy defined; names of headmen of Möng Küy.

The *Pādaeng Chronicle*

1. [1] Namotassatthu [Reverence to the Exalted One]. Paṇidhānato patṭhāya tathāgatassa dasapāramiyo dasaupapāramiyo dasaparamatthapāramiya pañca mahāpariccāge tisso cariyā pacchimabhave gabbhāvakantiṁ jātiṁ abhinikkamanaṁ padhānacariyaṁ bodhipallaṅke māravijayaṁ sabbaññutañāṇappaṭivedhaṁ nava lokuttaradhamme[1] [Beginning with his Resolve; considering in turn the Ten Pāramī (Perfections) of the Tathāgata (Buddha), the Ten Minor Pāramī and the Ten Major Pāramī; the Five Great Sacrifices; the Three Meritorious Acts; his Descent into the Womb in the last state of his existence; his Birth; the Great Retirement, the Great Exertion, his conquest of Māra on the throne of Enlightenment, his attainment of Omniscience, and the Nine Supramundane Conditions]. Cintitaṁ satta asaṅkheyye mātudhāra samuddaṁ taranakāle pathama buddha devoti[2] [From the time he took his mother across the ocean, the Bodhisatta (Buddha-to-be) made a Mental Resolve for seven incalculable world cycles to attain Enlightenment].

2. Sathā [the Master], that is to say, our Lord Sabbaññū [Omniscient] Buddha, from the time he was mātudhāraka [mother-carrier] when he took [his] mother across the great ocean, aspired to the Englightenment in his mind without speaking out for seven incalculable world cycles, [during which he] beheld one hundred forty-seven thousand Buddhas beginning with Taṇhaṅkara Pathamadevo Buddha. Next he aspired to the Enlightenment by word, for nine incalculable world cycles [during which he] beheld three hundred forty-seven thousand Buddhas beginning with Porāṇagotama. Next he aspired to the Enlightenment by word and body for four incalculable world cycles and one

---

So that the reader may follow the original text as closely as possible, these conventions have been used: (1) whenever the *Pādaeng Chronicle* contains Pali instead of Khün, the Pali is given in its entirety along with the translation; (2) the page numbers of the original manuscript are given in brackets in the translation, e.g., [6]; and (3) each paragraph of the translation is numbered sequentially in italics (e.g., *21*, *22*).

hundred thousand eons and received predictions in the residences of 462,027 Buddhas beginning with Dīpaṅkara Buddha. The total number of all Buddhas met was 446,027.[3]

3. During our present Bhada kappa [Bhadda world cycle][4] [he] was born as Prince Siddhattha, lived the household life for twenty-nine years, went forth,[5] practiced austerities for six years, attained Enlightenment, became Savior of all creatures for forty-four vassā[6] and entered the gem city of perfect Nibbāna at Möng[7] Kusinārāy in the year Kāsai.

4. Came that year Kāpsaṅā [2] Lord Mahākassapa Thera[8] heading five hundred arahantā lords performed the First Saṅgāyanā[9] lasting seven months, with Brayā[10] Ajātasattu as dāyaka [patron or donor], at the threshold of the vebhāra mountain cave in Möng Rājagaha.

5. Came the year Kāhmau, Month Four waning 1st night, arahantā lords numbering 69,872 and Brayā Ajātasattu together established [a new] Sakkarāja in the year Kāpsī, Month Nine waxing 11th night.

6. The Sakkarāja had progressed to one hundred, Lord Mahā Yasa Thera heading arahantā lords numbering [?] hundred performed the Second Saṅgāyanā in the city of Vesāli, completing it only after eight months duration.

7. The Sakkarāja had progressed to [? one] hundred and eighty, [and] Mahā Moggaliputta Tissa Thera heading arahantā lords numbering one thousand performed the Third Saṅgāyanā in the city of Pātaliputta, completing it after a duration of nine months, with Brayā Asokadhammarājā heading the dāyakas.

8. The Sakkarāja progressed to 288,[11] mahāthera lords who were arahantās deliberated the future [to see] if the Sāsanā[12] of Lord Buddha would prosper in Majjhimadesa [the Middle Country, or northeast India] or would prosper in Paccantadesa [the border regions], and the lords knew that the Sāsanā of Lord Buddha would prosper in Paccantadesa and directed eight lords to go and establish the Sāsanā then and there: that is, Majjhantika Thera was the first to establish [the Sāsanā], in Möng Bandharaṭṭha; Mahāthera Devāraṁ was the second to establish it, in Möng Mahisakkamaṇḍa; Mahābuddharakkhita Thera was the third to establish it, in Möng Vāsipadesa; Mahādhammarakkhita Thera was the fourth to establish it, in Möng Mahiraṭṭha; Sangharakkhita Thera was the fifth to establish it, in Möng Yonakalōk [i.e., Möng Yōn]; Mahāyonaka Thera was the sixth to establish it, in Möng Palanti [i.e., Möng Būkam]; Mahāmajjhima Thera was the [3] seventh to establish it, in Möng Hemavantapradesa; two mahāthera lords, namely, Soṇa and Uttara,

were the eighth to establish it, in Möng Suvaṇṇabhūmmā [i.e., Möng Pago]. As regards Lord Mahinda Thera, [he] took the Sāsanā and established it in Laṅkādhvīp.[13]

9. The Sakkarāja had progressed to 560, [and] bhikkhunīhood came to an end there.

10. Brayā Siriteja [i.e., Trīcakkhu] again terminated [the Sakkarāja] in the year Rāysī, again established a new Sakkarāja in the year Müngsai, Month Nine waxing 8th night. [When the Sakkarāja] had progressed to 558, arahantās came to an end there. The Sakkarāja had progressed to 607, Lord Mahāthera Debbamālai ascended to heaven. When the Sakkarāja had progressed to 622 Brayā Tambula terminated it in the year Tausī, and established a new Sakkarāja in the year Kāsai, Month Nine waxing 3rd night, called Cuḷa Sakkarāja until the present time, truly.

11. When Lord Sabbaññū Buddha had been born and attained the sixth year of age only was Lord Mahā Upāli born. At the age of forty [he] went to be ordained in the Sāsanā of the Lord and learned the Vinaya Piṭaka from the noble mouth of the Lord. The Lord raised him to be the authority on the Vinaya, and he taught the Vinaya to disciples continuously until his age reached seventy when he attained Nibbāna.

12. Next there was a Lord named Dāsaka who had learned the Vinaya Piṭaka to the end proficiently from the mouth of Lord Mahā Upāli and taught disciples, everyone of whom upheld the Vinaya. His age was sixty [when he] attained Nibbāna. Next there was a lord named Sonaka who was a coresident thera, [and] had learned the Vinaya to the end proficiently from the mouth of Dāsaka Thera and taught disciples continuously. His age was sixty-two years [when he] attained Nibbāna. Next there was a lord named Sigavā who was a coresident thera [and] had learned the Vinaya to the end proficiently from the mouth of Sonaka and taught [4] disciples continuously. His age was seventy-six [when he] attained Nibbāna. Next Lord Caṇḍavajira carried on. Next Lord Moggalliputta Tissa Thera carried on. Next Lord Mahinda Thera carried on. Next Lord Ariṭṭha Thera carried on. Next Lord Kulaputta Thera carried on. That is, Lord Tissa Thera, Lord Dattakāla Thera, Lord Cuḷasumana Thera, Lord Dīghasumana Thera carried on in succession from the residence of Mahā Ariṭṭha Thera in countless numbers until Lord Mahā Kassapa. [It was a] great and vast [affair] in Laṅkādhvīp over there.

13. The year Koḍyī, Cuḷasakkarāja 235, Lord Mahā Anumati brought the Sāsanā from the residence of Lord Mahā Kassapa and established it in Möng Bandharaṭṭha[14] for the first time when Brayā

Sutasoma was reigning in our Jumbūdhvīp.[15] The brayā, taking delight in the Sāsanā, raised by higher consecration Lord Anumati to the declared title of Udumbara Sāmī Thera there.

14. Next Mahā Sumana and Anomadassi, [and others totaling] five lords, went to Laṅkā for one vassā. On return one of them died at sea. The remaining four, taking an image of the Lord to join [the chapter of four bhikkhus] at an appropriate spacing, ordained one lay devotee [and their number] became five as previously. [They] disseminated the Sāsanā and ordained a great many lords for seven vassā. Later, having learned the news that Mahā Udumbara Sāmī was proficient in the Three Piṭaka and practiced [the Vinaya and Dhamma] extremely well, [the five bhikkhus] exhorted one another and went to study at the residence of Mahā Udumbara Sāmī for a period of five vassā and returned to Sukhodaiy in the Mü̇ngrau, Sakkarāja 243. Having disseminated the Sāsanā for five vassā and longing to see [their] guru [they] persuaded eight lords to go with them: namely, Ānanda 1, Buddhasāgara 2, Sujāta 3, Piyada- [5] ssī 4, Suvaṇṇagirī 5, Vessabhū 6, Ñānasāgara 7, with Lord Mahinda totaling 8, to practice at the residence of Lord Mahā Udumbara Sāmī there. As regards the two lords [Sumana and Anomadassi] they requested authorization to act as upajjhāya[16] and returned to their original place. The two lords ordained a great many lords and distributed them to live in Mȯng Ajjanālai [Sajjanālai] and Ayodhiyā spreading the Sāsanā to every country, making it shine with great radiance.

15. At that time Brayā Dhammikasayambhū, who was Brayā Kü̇nā in Mȯng Nabbapurī, Jenghmai, having heard the news that Udumbara Sāmī practiced extremely well and wishing to worship him in his country, sent men to invite him. The lord did not come but sent his disciple named Ānanda at the head of twelve bhikkhus for the brayā to reverence and serve there. The brayā saw Lord Ānanda and was exceedingly delighted.

16. Later the brayā wished to ordain the lords into two parties, different from each other: Let those ordained according to the tradition of Lord Udumbara Sāmī be one party; let those newly ordained outside the city be one party. Lord Ānanda did not like to perform a different act of the Saṅgha[17] and spoke to Brayā Kü̇nā saying: "Lord Mahārāja wishes us to ordain the lords into two parties different from what is already in existence [but as] we have not obtained permission from our guru we cannot do that which is different. We did not know there would be such ideas and had not asked our guru [about them]. It is not easy to do. Besides, the Sāsanā of the Lord which is prospering in this country is already pure and magnificent. We are but of Burmese-Môn origin, newly come. If the Mahārāja really wishes to ordain [bhikkhus], there is one lord mahāthera named Sumanaraṁsī residing in Möng Sukhodaiy who was a disciple of our guru, Lord Mahā Udumbara Sāmī, who had authorized him to be upajjhāya [6] to ordain the lords everywhere. Lord Mahā Sumanaraṁsī generally disseminates the Sāsanā of Lord Buddha exceedingly radiantly. The Mahārāja should commission men to go invite the Lord Mahāthera and then two of us would perform the act of the Saṅgha and ordain the lords in accordance with the wishes of the Mahārāja."

17. Then, Dāu Künā, having listened to the words of Ānanda Bhikkhu, sent men to invite Lord Mahā Sumanaraṁsī [who] did not come the first time; did not come the second time; came only the third time, bringing relics of the Lord with the Three Piṭaka. Dāu Künā was exceedingly glad and caused the populace to usher him in with gongs, drums, xylophones, harps, and musical instruments to Vat Ḻāphailōng [Great Bamboo Grove] east of Labūn, across the river.

18. In the year Kaḍrau, Sakkarāja 255, the brayā built three standing Lords, and then raised Mahā Sumanaraṁsī to the declared title of Mahā Sumana Vaṇṇaratana Sāmī there. Dāu Künā invited Mahā Sumana Vaṇṇaratana Sāmī together with Ānanda Thera to ordain the lords differently from the old group, only enlarging a little here and deducting a little there [so that] the old group and new group could perform acts of the Saṅgha together, not allowing a split. The act of upasampadā ordination[18] took place in the Ping River at the head of Labūn City,[19] in the middle of Vat Candapabhā. The Saṅgha, old and new, who came to assemble, numbered ten thousand.

19. At the completion of the act of Saṅgha, Lord Ānanda took leave of Brayā Künā and returned to his guru. At Möng Caem he fell ill without recovering and died there at Möng Caem.[20] [7] The populace performed the funeral ceremony and sent [his] robes and alms bowl to Lord Mahā Udumbara Sāmī there and then.

20. Now, the brayā, wishing to construct a new monastery, looked for a place about five hundred bow lengths from the city, personally saw a very beautiful sandy bank near the water and thought, "At the time when Lord Buddha attained Enlightenment, He stayed at the Veḷuvana Grove Monastery. This sandy bank should be a monastery for the Saṅgha headed by the Lord's relics." Having thought thus, the brayā had people sweep and clean [the sandy bank] nicely and made a solemn resolution, saying, "At this place shall I erect a monastery for the Saṅgha and the Lord's relics. If it will last throughout the five thousand vassā of the Sāsanā may I see a good dream." That night the brayā dreamed that the sandy bank was in ruins, but saw in the dream a grove of red lotuses five hundred bow lengths to the west of the city. There was one lotus at the center as big as a cartwheel, with flocks of birds and mother bees intermingling happily. The brayā woke up with a start. After dawn he had people go and sweep and tidy the place he saw [in the dream] and erected a monastery as living quarters for the Saṅgha having relics of Lord Buddha as chief in the year Rōnggai, Cuḷa Sakkarāja 357, and named it Sōndôkgham Monastery.[21]

21. The brayā gave dāna[22] lavishly supplying [the Saṅgha with] the four necessities[23] without break even for a day. The brayā, moreover, built a cetiya and another standing Lord, and served [the Sāsanā] until his age reached eighty years [when he] [8] died to go to the happy state over there. His son named Saenmöng, aged twenty-three years, succeeded to the throne. And Lord Mahā Sumana Vaṇṇaratana disseminated the Sāsanā, making it exceedingly radiant.

22. At that time a lord mahāthera named Sujāto, who lived in Möng Jaleng [Chaliang], went to study the Dhamma at Möng Brohmagirī [?]. He reached Möng Tanāusrī [Tenasserim of Burma], went down to Burma [where he] learned that a lord thera named Nidhakamahū living in Burma knew the Three Piṭaka and practiced according to the Vinaya. Lord Sujāto went to serve [the thera] for five vassā, studied various branches of the Dhamma and returned to Möng Tanāusrī [i.e., Möng Jengdāu] for an appropriate length of time and returned to live at Möng Jaleng.

23. Having made the Sāsanā radiant, [Sujāto] took one disciple, still a sāmaṇera, named Indaprayā [Intellect of Indra], and came to Jenghmai [where he] resided at Hroveng Monastery and met Lord Mahā Sumana Suvaṇṇaratana Sāmī and together promoted the Sāsanā and ordained the lords according to the creed of the old guru, abandoning the new guru there.

24. Indaprayā, the disciple of Mahā Sujāto, having just attained twenty years [of age], was ordained bhikkhu. When the sīmā boat had been constructed, [but] not yet used for ordination, it floated against the current northwards. When the populace saw [this, they] reported to the Lord Sāmī. Lord Sujāto Sāmī spoke thus: "Very good. When he has become a bhikkhu [he] will go and promote the Sāsanā in the north."

25. Later on the Lord Sāmī had a talk with Indaprayā, saying: "Here in Jenghmai the Sāsanā is already thriving greatly; [9] there are already a great many senior members of the Saṅgha, whereas in Möng Khemaraṭṭha[24] over there, learned lords are not numerous. I will take you [there]." So saying [he] took

Indaprayā up [to Khemaraṭṭha], instructed the populace [in the Dhamma], ordained many lords and, after an appropriate length of time, took leave of lay devotees, saying: "We have been in this country for a very long time; we will return ahead to our country; [we] will leave behind Lord Indaprayā and our newly-ordained disciples [to] promote the Sāsanā and give the sīla [precepts]." Having said so Lord Mahā Sāmī returned to Jenghmai.

26. Lord Mahā Sumana Vaṇṇaratana, having reached the age of eighty, died in the year Koḍsaṅā, Sakkarāja 472.

27. Regarding Vat Pādôkbō,[25] fourteen mahāthera lords continued to look after it: Mahā Sumana 1, Mahā Kumārakassapa 2, Mahā Nandapaññā 3, Mahā Buddhañāṇa 4, Mahā Buddhagambhīra 5, Mahā Ñāṇaraṁsī 6, Mahā Piṭakasaṅgharājā 7, Mahā Buddhādicca 8, Mahā Ñāṇasāgara 9, Mahā Saṅgharājā-nāgasena 10, Mahā Vajirabodhi 11, Mahā Ñāsasāgara-tissa Thera 12, Mahā Pussadebba 13, Mahā Dhammabodhi 14, this is all. As regards Lord Mahā Dhammabodhi, Brayā Kaeubantā[26] later consecrated him with the declared title of Mahā Bodhidhammakitti.

28. In the year Pük̈sī, Sakkarāja 739, Brayā Kaeubantā [10] constructed a brass [image of the] Lord, weighing nine million[27] [which was] taken and kept at the uposatha hall.[28]

29. Regarding the Saṅgha members, they were afflicted with disputes on many occasions. On one occasion, Buddhañāṇa kept bandits [who] later went to steal; the populace censured [him] greatly--Brayā Saenmöng was displeased and drove [him] away. On one occasion the lords of Yodhiyā who were ordained in Laṅkā came up to Jenghmai for a visit at the time Lord Mahā Ñāṇaraṁsī was in residence, intending to destroy the Saṅgha by urging them to adopt their doctrine with the words: "It is not good to carry staffs; it is good not to carry staffs; not good to carry silver and gold; not to carry, good." The brayā made people argue with them but could not beat them. The brayā was angry and drove them away.

30. One item. Dāu Lānnā[29] whose name was Pavara Cakkavattirāja asked Buddhādicca Thera and Mahā Sāgara if a sāmaṇera, suitable for upasampadā, should study Pāṭimokkha or should not study. Mahā Sāgara said, [he] should not study; Mahā Buddhādicca said [he] should study. The brayā took the words of Buddhādicca.

31. Mahā Ñāṇasāgara, receiving the kaṭhina[30] of dyed cloth, never recited [suttas] in the monastery, but generally went to recite them in the river. Some of the lords continued that [practice] up to the present day.

32. On one occasion, Mahā Sundara, saying "The sīmā[31] [stones] of this [Vat] Sōndōk have been planted, pulled up, and planted anew for the sixth time and yet it is not pure," made those lords who were ordained in that sīmā leave the Order and ordained them anew on two occasions, once in the year Rōngsai, another in the Rāysan, apart from each other by sixteen [11] years. [In] that vassā [he] caused [them] to be ordained anew in the year Mŭngrau. Some of the lords followed and actually left the Order; there were some who did not follow and did not leave.

33. Lord Mahā Sundara had the people construct sīmā boats at two places, south and north of each other. [He] caused the lords at the head of the city to be ordained at the north, making Lord Mahindādicco the Saṅgha president. Lord Mahā Ñāṇasundara was Saṅgha president of the south. When their business was over, [the lords] later quarreled bitterly, saying, "I ascended [the sīmā boat] before you; you ascended it only later." Some honored the old seniority; some honored the new seniority; no one obeyed anyone, [each acted] according [to] his heart's desire, creating many patterns, many methods until the present time, a painful spectacle to those endowed with wisdom-eyes who saw the happenings while helping to receive the offerings to the Saṅgha.

34. One incident took place when Dhammakamben [Dhammagambhīra], son of the brayā's chief gardener, came to be ordained as a disciple of Lord Dhammakitti in the year Kārau, Sakkarāja 744. Afterwards he quarreled with his guru, ran away to be ordained at the residence of Candavāṇījīcōn in Mŏng Laṅkā and returned to censure the Saṅgha who said that he was no ascetic, and he straight away left the Order and went to marry the daughter of Hmŭn Sāmlān at Mŏng Lagôn [modern Lampāng] there.

35. Thus was the Sāsanā of Lord Buddha greatly afflicted with unhappy events on many occasions.

36. [12] Dhammakamben came for ordination when Lord Mahā Bodhidhammakitti had been rajāguru for six vassā. At eighteen vassā, a boy named Sāmcitta was born to Ban Tāsæng in the year Ḍaprau, Sakkarāja 756. [When he] had attained the age of thirteen years [he] came for ordination at the residence of Mahā Bodhidhammakitti in the year Rāysan, Sakkarāja 769, and was named Ñāṇagambhīra. [After] having been sāmaṇera for seven vassā he finished the Three Tipiṭaka and reached upasampadā ordination in the year Kaḍrau, Sakkarāja 776.

37. Having examined for five vassā all the true Dhamma and Vinaya promulgated by Lord Buddha and seen to the end the five ways of Ñatticatutthakammavācā,[32] [Ñāṇagambhīra] considered that the act of upasampadā ordination performed by the four lords headed by Mahā Sumana with the image of the Lord as the fifth [member of the chapter] was not in accord with the Vinaya in Pali laid down by Lord Buddha. [He] saw that "Paṭisaṅkhāyo cīvaraṁ" and "senā" saying "tappsiriṁ" was not in accord with "gāthāvessantara" saying "appameva sirisappā"; saw that "ajjamayā apaccavekkhetvā" was not in accord with "Paccavekkhaṇa sutta," which had "paccavekkhitabbaṁ"; saw that "ajjacīvaraṁ" and "senā" reciting "yaṁ cīvaraṁ paribhuttaṁ yāvadeva" without "sabbantaṁ" was not in accord with "yathā paccayaṁ" and "sabbāni sabbopannāyaṁ"; saw that the recitation on Month One[33] full moon of only "kaṭhina dussaṁ," [while the cloth] was cut, stitched, dyed, and worn without dotting the "bindu," [and,] when the time came for wearing, the correct "dussaṁ" was left out and "cīvaraṁ" recited as before; saw that "Buddhāṁ" [13] was not in accord with Mahāvagga in Pali, which had "Buddhaṁ" with only single conjunction; saw that "saraṇaasaranaṁ" with two letters added, was not in accord with the original syllable "ṇaṁ," which was a voiced nasal-cerebral; saw the [incorrect] recitation of Ñatticatutthakammavācā of "su-araṇātu me bhante saṅgho"; saw the insertion of two [extra] letters in "yassāyasamanto khamati"; saw at "tassmā" that it was not correct. [Total number of irregularities, ten.]

38. Then, having seen that those perversities were not in accord with rules laid down by Lord Buddha, Ñāṇagambhīra approached reverentially Mahā Dhammakitti who was [his] upajjhāya and reported everything that he doubted. He [Dhammakitti] said: "Our guru descended from Möng Sukho and Ayodhiyā over there. If you wish to be really enlightened, go, [do] reverence and ask [there]." Lord Ñāṇagambhīra Thera begged to go then and there. Lord Mahā Dhammakitti Thera arranged five disciples in his residence, one lord named Vuḍḍhiñāṇa, one lord named Siddhiñāṇa, one lord named Ñāṇasārada, one lord named Ratananāga, one lord named Cittāhanu, this was all, to go with Ñāṇagambhīra until Ayodhiyā was reached. Then [having reached Ayodhiyā, they] approached, reverenced the rajāguru and told him all business there. He also said, "Our guru has handed down [the texts] thus. If you are not clear and wish to know truly, then, you should go and make reverence to the lord mahāthera in Möng Laṅkā over there." So it was said.

39. Then Lord Ñāṇagambhīra went to mettā[34] the lord of earth[35] and apprised him of every item of business. The brayā made reverence, saying, "My lord spoke [14] to me [and I am] greatly pleased. I beg my lord to persist and go to the place of origin and return only when [you] know the true Dhamma clearly and correctly." So saying, the brayā appointed one courtier named Subhārata to accompany [the thera]. Lord

Ñāṇagambhīra Thera again went and reverenced the rājaguru, who also arranged five of his disciples--one lord named Saṁvara, one lord named Saṅkicca, one lord named Sobhita, one lord named Codaya, one lord named Ñāṇabala, totaling twelve with the courtier, [and they] went down to Laṅkādhvīp in the year Kāpau, Sakkarāja 781, in merchant ships, reaching Möng Laṅkā only after a duration of four months.

40. After arrival [they] went together, paid reverence to Mahā Surinda Thera Somḍec[36] and asked the Lord Mahāthera about the ten divisions of the true Dhamma. He said, "The Buddhasāsanā in the sixty provinces of this Möng Laṅkā here is all the same everywhere, because foreigners, Muslims, Burmese, Môns are intermingling, everyone does whatever his heart desires, not following the Lord's Vinaya anywhere. The only place that still practices in accordance with the Vinaya and the true Dhamma without depravity is Rohajanapada Mahāraṭṭha,[37] where the Lord's Sāsanā is still strict and steady [and will be so] throughout five thousand vassā without split or schism in any way because Lord Sabbaññūbuddha, when nearing Nibbāna, had left word with Brayā In[da], lord of all debbaḍas, and kings and ministers and people together to preserve [the Sāsanā] diligently."

41. Then, Lord Mahā Ñāṇagambhīra Thera [15] took his entourage to the gate of the outer wall of the city. People saw them, and came to investigate [their] business, bad and good, in every way, had them worship the debbaḍas with popped rice, flowers, eight pairs of candles, with a solemn resolution, saying, "We have come to take the perfect Buddhasāsanā, the Three Gems, [and] the Mahābodhi[38] in order to establish them in the Jumbūdhvīp auspiciously. We have not come to do evil in any way. If we have come to harm the country and the perfect Buddhasāsanā, may calamities befall us." They rested for one month. No calamity occurred. Then they sent a letter to the second wall [and were] called for investigation in the same way, and, until the seventh wall was reached, they said and acted in the same manner [with] not a single wrong or different word. Only then did they send [messages] to the chief minister and lord of earth, informing them of everything.

42. Lord of earth at the head of ministers and courtiers then sent men to reverence and inform Lord Mahā Sudassana who was Saṅghanāyaka and to assemble ten thousand members of the Saṅgha who knew the Piṭaka. [They then] called Ñāṇagambhīra and disciples to ask about affairs of the Sāsanā in Jumbūdhvīp there. Lord Ñāṇagambhīra spoke[39] according to the existing conditions there. Then [he] raised his hands in reverence and asked questions from beginning to end about all the true Dhamma in which he had doubts.

43. Then, Mahā Sudossana Somḍec Aggarājaguru, the lord guru, head of all the Saṅgha, spoke, saying, "When Mahā Sumana studied in the residence of Mahā Ñā- [16] ṇapañño in the year Rāysan, Sakkarāja 242, the true Dhamma was one with ours. Now [it] has become perverted [because] he went and made those changes, creating a schismatic doctrine and differences. When Lord Sumana, having left the country [of Laṅkā], reached midocean and performed the act of upasampadā ordination to ordain the lay devotee with four bhikkhus [making a chapter of] five with an image of the Lord, [it] disagreed with Ñatticatuttha Kammavācā Vinayagaṇṭhī Sīlakkhandha Jāṭaka.[40]

44. "For 'Paṭisaṅkhāyo cīvaraṁ' and 'senā' to have a niggahita added, to read 'tappasiriṁ' like that, is against good grammar because it is dvandasamāsa[41] by the formula: 'Nāmānaṁ samuccayo dvando'; a samāsa [compound] has only one vibhatti [case ending], pointing to a different dabba [formation] called dvandasamāsa; 'si' cannot be turned into 'aṁ' above 'p'.

45. "'Ajjamayā appaccavekkhetvā' is also against good grammar because [it is] a 'vica' root; purasamupapārī hi karo-tissakhakkharā vā, with 'kha' as paccaya [affix]; kagācajānaṁ, turning 'ca' into 'ka'; pubba takes 'ka' to 'kkha'; yathāgamikāro, put down āgama 'i'; take 'kkh' to 'i' becomes 'kkhi'; tuṁtunatvā natvāvā, place tvā as paccaya becomes 'kkhitvā'; to say 'kkhetvā' is incorrect.

46. "'Yaṁ cīvaraṁ paribhuttaṁ yāvadeva' without 'taṁ sabbantaṁ' is also not correct, because 'taṁ sabbantaṁ' is 'sabba nām' attached to the beginning [should be] placed first; to leave it out is against good grammar.

47. "'Buddhāṁ, dhammāṁ, saṅghāṁ' are vohārati saṁyogaseyya; 'sara-a-ranāṁ' has two letters added; a person with a difficulty will not be able to say [it]; let it be [17] 'm' karanta according to Uccāravidhī which says 'ekavudhi ekahīna kari babbajjākammaṁ naruyhati', because 'saranaṁ' has 'sara' root, 'saraṇe' [equals] in the thinking of; nandādīhiyu, putting down 'yu' paccaya in kattar; anakāyuṇvunaṁ, turn 'yu' into 'ana'; rahāditonoṇa, turn dental 'n' into cerebral 'ṇ'; pubba puts down 'ṇ'; 'santo' root erases 'anta' root; 'naye' leads to 'saraṇa'; taddhita, put down 'si'; siṁ turns 'si' into 'aṁ'; pubba puts down 'ṇ'; taken to 'aṁ' becomes 'saraṇaṁ'. To say 'buddhāṁ saraṇāṁ gacchāmi' thus 'gacchāmi' is kiriyā akhyāta, never a kattar to 'buddhāṁ dhammāṁ saṅghāṁ sara-asaraṇāṁ', is kattar only to 'gacchāmi' alone. 'Ahaṁ saraṇaṁ' is parāmivisesana to 'buddhaṁ', 'buddhaṁ' is pacchāma visesaya, this is good grammar. To say 'buddhāṁ dhammāṁ saṅghāṁ sara-a-saranāṁ gacchāmi' is against good grammar; the pabbajjā ordination act is not valid.

48. "To recite Ñatticatuttha Kammavāca as 'su-a-raṇātu me bhante saṅgho' is not atthisuṇa root; 'su' is short being recited [as] one mātrā; 'ṇā' is long being recited [as] two mātrā, making a total of three mātrā; to add 'ara' [it] would become three, four, five mātrā, which is against the true Kaccāyana Grammar Treatise; the ordination act is not valid. 'Tusu' root 'savaṇe' [equals] in the listening [or hearing], svādito ṇuṇauṇāca, put down paccaya 'uṇa', pubba places 's' with 'u', [18]'santo' root erases 'anta' root, naye--takes 's' to 'u' becomes 'suṇa'; hiyyattanī-ekamhi 'ā', epañcamī 'tu', 'kvacci' root turns 'anta' into 'ā', becomes 'suṇātu'.

49. "Where is the word 'ara' from? That 'saṅkho' is samuhasaddā, ghosavaṇṇa aghosavaṇṇa, becomes 'lahuka'. It is quoted in the upasampadā ordination treatise 'upasampadā naruyhati' thus.

50. "The recitation of 'yassāyasamanto khamati' has one letter added [to it] making it two [letters], it is only 'khamu' root, 'khamane' [equals] 'in the understanding', sabbatoṇvutvāvīvā, take 'a' [as paccaya, ekamhi] puts down 'ti', pubba takes 'm' to 'u', 'santo' root erases 'anta' root; naye, take [it] to become 'khamati'. Where then is the rule for doubling the 'm'?

51. "That 'tasmāturaṇahi' is also against good grammar. 'Tasmā' is 'sabbanām'; 'tuṇhi' is 'tuda' root; 'adhivāsane' [equals] in residing, nudādīhiṇī, place hīna paccaya, erased by 'kvacci' root, becomes 'tuṇhi', which is a long vowel having two mātrā when reciting. Therefore, 'turaṇahi' is against good grammar.

52. "The recitation of kaṭhina is not according to the true Vinaya. Why is it so said? Because the beginning becomes the end, not compatible with each other."

53. Mahāsundassana Somḍec Agga Rājaguru the lord guru having thus explained lucidly, blamed Mahā Sumana Thera, saying, "He took the Sāsanā from Laṅkā and established [it] in Möng Sukhodaiy first, [19] spreading the Sāsanā to Möng Nabbaburī Jenghmai, added made-up words creating perversity not in accord with good grammar thus, and it would be immoral frivolity to the Sāsanā everywhere," so it was said there.

54. Atha, at that time, Lord Mahā Ñāṇagambhīra Thera, feeling greatly disgusted, begged permission to leave the yellow robes in the residence of Lord Mahā Sudassana Thera, at the head [of the Saṅgha], who gave permission then and there. Having left the Order, Lord Ñāṇagambhīra Thera and the ten bhikkhus he headed were ordained anew in the residence [of] Lord Mahā Sudassana on the day they left the Order. Having resided

after a duration of five vassā of study of the Dhamma, [Ñāṇagambhīra] asked for the Sāsanā together with Mahābodhi [saplings] and an image of the Lord and the Three Piṭaka. They [the Ceylon side] gave everything there.

55. Then Lord Ñāṇagambhīra took leave of Lord Somḍec Agga Rājaguru and all the Saṅgha, went to offer mettā to the lord of earth Pathavīsāra, ministers, courtiers, and lay devotees, and returned in merchants' ships without mishap until [they] reached Mӧ̈ng Ayodhiyā.

56. [At Ayodhiyā they] went to mettā the brayā and spoke about all business to the brayā at the head of ministers and courtiers [who were] exceedingly delighted. The brayā made people build a temporary monastery as dāna for Ñāṇagambhīra to reside in, sent the courtier named Subhārata and courtier Sobhita to pay reverence and invite Mahā Dhammasārada Thera at the head of the Saṅgha to assemble and asked Subhārata to describe [20] all the business, and everything that he had seen and heard. And Lord Ñāṇagambhīra Thera related from beginning to end the words spoken by Lord Mahā Sudassana Rajāguru there.

57. At that time Lord Mahā Dhammasārada, chief among the aged Saṅgha said, "Sādhu, very well," and begging to be allowed to live until death, created Mahā Ñāṇagambhīra the head of all the Saṅgha and made bhikkhus who were still young leave the Order and ordain anew in the residence of Lord Ñāṇagambhīra as the Sīla [? Sīhaḷa] Sect in the year Mӧ̈ngsai, Sakkarāja 786. Three hundred monasteries of the Sāsanā recognized the residence of Lord Mahā Ñāṇagambhīra completely.

58. Then Mahā Ñāṇagambhīra went to mettā Lord Pathavīsāra of Mӧ̈ng Ayodhiyā and ministers, courtiers, and lay devotees in order to return to Mӧ̈ng Nabbapurī, Jenghmai. The lord of earth in that country appointed the courtier named Sobhita to accompany [them] on Month One 1st waning night. Everywhere, wherever they stopped [on the way] many bhikkhus left the Order and begged to be ordained in the residence of Lord Mahā Ñāṇagambhīra as the Sīla Sect until Mӧ̈ng Labūn [and] Jenghmai were reached on Month Five full moon.

59. Came the year Pӧ̈ksañā, Sakkarāja 787, Month Four new moon, the whole kingdom, having performed the funeral ceremony of Brayā Kaeubantā, invited Dāu Lōk to reign over Jenghmai. In Month Five waxing 9th night, Tuesday, Daiy Tauyī[42] early [21] in the morning, [he] was consecrated and named Brayā Ādittarājā, so it was said. When the brayā learned that Lord Mahā Ñāṇagambhīra had brought the Sāsanā, the Mahābodhi tree, an image of the Lord, and the Three Piṭaka to repose in the city, the brayā was exceedingly delighted and made people dismantle

an old royal pavilion and re-erect it as a monastery for him to live in. It was named Vat Rājamunden [royal pavilion] for that reason.

60. Lord Mahā Ñāṇagambhīra went to reverence Mahā Dhammakitti who was his upajjhāya [and] gave a full report. He [Dhammakitti] said, "Sādhu. Very well. I am already old; I don't know when I will die. I allow you to be the head; be diligent in the study of the Sāsanā."

61. Lord Mahā Dhammakitti then spoke to all the Saṅgha, saying, "All of us ordained under ordination procedures brought by Lord Mahā Sumana of Sukhodaiy with Lord Ānanda Bhikkhu, and later by Lord Mahā Sujāto of Jaleng, who went to study the Dhamma under Nidhakamabahū in Burma and returned, have been ordained incorrectly, not in accord with the true Grammar. All of you will leave the Order and go for ordination at the residence of Mahā Ñāṇagambhīra." All the bhikkhus followed the words of Mahā Dhammakitti who was the guru, left the Order, and went to be ordained in the residence of Lord Mahā Ñāṇagambhīra Thera there.

62. Thereupon the people praised [him], saying, "This Lord Mahā Ñāṇagambhīra, son of Ban Tāsaeng, has great wisdom which is truly beneficial to the Sāsanā of the Lord. He is not [22] like Dān Dhammakāmben, the wicked one, who was the son of the chief gardener of the brayā, and who caused the Sāsanā to disintegrate and made people burn and bury the images of the Lord [or] cast [them] into the river." So saying people went to be ordained, each day ten men, twenty men, thirty men, forty men, fifty men, a hundred men, numerous in number, until living quarters could not be found. Lord Mahā Ñāṇagambhīra then requested Brayā Ādittarājā, who was lord of earth, to construct a monastery in the west-southwest, five hundred vā[43] from the city, called Sīhaḷarattārāmādhipati, there. Later on [the brayā] built each year ten monasteries, twenty monasteries, thirty, forty, fifty monasteries throughout all Nabbapurī totaling five hundred, all exceedingly prosperous.

Jengsaen

63. Now Brayā Suvaṇṇanidhi, Lord of Jengsaen, heard the news of merchants praising Lord Mahā Ñāṇagambhīra for having brought the Sāsanā anew from the residence of Lord Mahā Sudassana Rājaguru at Rohajanapada in Möng Laṅkā, which spread up to Nabbapurī Jenghmai [and] which is in accord with the Promulgation of Lord Buddha. Entertaining the desire to bring [the Sāsanā] to support [and] sustain his own country, the brayā dispatched one courtier named Sumitta with presents to the court of Brayā Ādittarājā asking permission to invite Lord Mahā Ñāṇagambhīra with twelve disciples. They arrived in Möng Jengsaen in the year Münghmau, Sakkarāja 796, Month One waxing 2nd night.

64. The brayā [23] had people construct Vat Pāḍaeng as the foremost [monastery] and Vat Cômgatti and Daiya Ārām, one after another, totaling fifty towards the head of the city, until Vongkot river landing was reached. Outside the city there were also a great many. The brayā, heading ministers and courtiers and the people of the country, was exceedingly happy and greatly praised the merits and virtues of Lord Mahā Ñāṇagambhīra, and blamed Dhammakambara, that is, Dhammakamben, the wicked one, who was the son of the chief gardener of the brayā.

65. Following the establishment of the Sāsanā by Lord Mahā Ñāṇagambhīra in Möng Jengsaen, when bhikkhus who had been away to distant lands returned to their old monasteries, they learned that Mahā Dhammakitti had died; they therefore went to confer with those older [bhikkhus] who had not yet left the Order, saying, "We cannot discard our guru and what we have learned from the residence of Lord Mahā Dhammakitti who was our upajjhāya." So saying they stuck to their old doctrine; sometimes [they] became factional and disunited because Dhammakitti had died before they returned.

Khemaraṭṭha Tungapurī

66. Here will be related the account of Möng Khemaraṭṭha.

67. The year Rōngrau, Sakkarāja 803,[44] Month Seven full moon, Tuesday, just before dawn, a devaḍā [devatā] spoke to Lord Mahā Ñāṇagambhīra, saying: "Lord of earth of Möng Tungapurī named Raṭṭabherī[45] [1416-1441] had people construct the city, digging the moat around Cômmônpheḍ[46] on [24] the south side, building the walls and battlements, finishing with bricks. There was one demon who was very angry and went to haunt the golden palace every year, every month, every day, every moment. Even after Lord Rattabherī had died and was succeeded by Brayā Dhamma Cuḷāmaṇī[47] [1441-1456], the demon continued to haunt in the same way. The brayā invited bhikkhus of Sōnḍôk Jenglom[48] to come and recite Dhamma for cleansing and protection, [the demon] came to haunt even much more, the holy water putrefied, leaves of the magic trees[49] withered, and the bhikkhus were defeated there. Bhikkhus of Jenglæ were then invited to come and perform the cleansing recitation. At first [the haunting] quieted down a bit--holy water did not putrefy, but there was no fragrance; the cleansing was done for the second and third time; the demon continued to haunt as of old, but not so much. Over ten years later, the demon continued to haunt on a big scale. Now [may I] invite my Lord to depute the Saṅgha who are your disciples to mettā [so that] it would be a pervasively great splendor to the perfect Sāsanā of Lord Buddha in the future, without a doubt." So saying [the devaḍā] vanished.

68. Lord Mahā Ñāṇagambhīra, having heard the words of the devaḍā as an omen to him and having been fully awake, arose to do personal cleansing, pondered over the words the devaḍā had spoken to him and saw what would be a pervasively great and steadfast splendor to the perfect Buddhasāsanā for a long time to come. Came [25] the time after breakfast [he] called all the Saṅgha to assemble together and spoke about all business in accordance with what the devaḍā had told him, letting the Saṅgha know everything. Together the Saṅgha reverenced [him] saying, "If this is so, my Lord should send a deputation."

69. Thereupon Lord Mahā Ñāṇagambhīra deputed Somacitta Thera as the head, and four disciples, who came up to Mӧṅg Tuṅgapurī there. After [their] arrival they went together to rest at Hrōy-yen.[50]

70. At that time young boys of Sōṇḍôkgham who went to graze cattle saw the five bhikkhus residing there. They approached to reverence them and asked, saying, "Where did my lords come from that you have arrived here?" The bhikkhus said, "We came from the southern kingdom over there."

71. The boys playfully practiced reciting ordination Dhamma according to what their fathers had taught them. When Lord Somacitta Thera heard [the recitation] he told them, "Your Dhamma recitation is not word-perfect."

72. Having grazed the cattle until dusk the boys returned home and told their fathers saying, "When we went to graze cattle today there was a group of bhikkhus residing at Hrōy-yen where we grazed the cattle and rehearsed the ordination Dhamma playfully. Hearing us, the group of bhikkhus shouted at us, saying, 'Your Dhamma recitation is not word-perfect.'" People of Sōṇḍôkgham became curious after hearing the words their sons had so spoken. Came the morrow and they [residents of Sōṇḍôkgham] entered the city to listen to the great Dhamma which the bhikkhus of Jenglae recited in the evening [26] to cleanse and protect the kingdom so. But the demons continued to haunt in the same way.

73. At that time Brayā Srīsudhamma Cuḷāmaṇī Mahārāja asked the ministers and courtiers, saying, "What should we do in order that the demons would not do any harm?" Not one of the lords was able to reply. At that moment the people of Sōnḍôkgham reverenced [the brayā] saying, "May it please Lord Mahārāja, there is a group of bhikkhus numbering five who have come and reside at Hrōy-yen there. Boys who went to graze cattle saw them and asked, saying, 'Where did my Lords come from?' They replied, saying, 'We came from the southern kingdom, over there'. When the boys who had learned ordination Dhamma recited it playfully, the group of bhikkhus shouted at them, saying, 'The ordination Dhamma which you recited is not word-perfect'. So they said, Sire."

74. Having heard the words of the people of Sōnḍôkgham spoken to him, the brayā deputed the officer in charge of guests named Sirijeyya to go and reverence Lord Somacitta Thera and ask about all the business. The thera explained everything clearly. Then Sirijeyya returned to reverence his lord to report to him. Lord of earth thereupon deputed Brayā Rôlōng as the head to take food, water, and a pedestal tray filled with flowers and candles to invite [the bhikkhus] and made people take gongs, drums, xylophones, harps, trumpets, conch shells, [and] musical instruments to Hrōy-yen there. On arrival they presented as dāna the food and water to Lord Somacitta Thera and others. Having completed the food consumption ceremony [the royal deputation] invited [the bhikkhus] to enter the capital where [they] were accommodated at Naggatiṭṭhā Monastery there. On the next day [the court] invited the Lord, the Dhamma, and, preceded by a palm leaf fan [tālapatta],[51] the Three Gems ascended the palace of lord of earth, there. [27] When [the Three Gems] ascended thus, the palace shook as if [it] would fall down.

75. At that time Lord Somacitta Thera gave mettā asking people to build five debbaḍā houses, beautifully decorated, and invite the four Dāucātulōk, Sakka, and Brahma[52] heading the concourse of devās to come together to hear the Dhamma. Magic trees were replaced with new ones; the holy water [bowl] was filled anew. When all arrangements were completed, lord of earth, ministers, courtiers, and lay devotees were invited to come together to hear the Dhamma and observe the sīla, while Lord Somacitta, heading the four Saṅgha, recited [Dhamma suttas] according to the program for the whole three days and three nights. The magic trees were fresh, beautiful, and did not wither; the holy water was beautifully clear with very sweet fragrance; all the ghosts and demons became terrified of the glory and splendor of the Three Gems and fled together, never to return to harm or haunt even once. It was then that the earth in Möng Tuṅgakhemaraṭṭha quaked three times in one

day. And Brayā Srīsudhamma Culāmaṇī Mahārāja, heading ministers, courtiers, and lay devotees, was exceedingly joyous at heart and gave orders for the construction of a monastery for the Saṅgha to reside in that forest there. All animals were given protection. [The monastery] was called by the name Mahāvana Ārām.

76. After that, came Month Five waxing 1st night. Hrōy-pūn[53] caught fire emitting smoke, [which] covered the whole city as if it would come and burn the capital and people's homes. Again, lord of earth heading [others] invited the five Saṅgha to recite cleansing suttas and the fire died down completely.

77. Came the year Tauseḍ, Sakkarāja 804, Month Eight, the rain fell very heavily. When the rain stopped, the sky split open[54] at Dônlōng Bridge[55] [with water volume] as big [28] as a great mat roll; the water rose, almost submerging the city.

78. At that time lord of earth, heading ministers and courtiers together, again invited the Saṅgha residing at Vat Mahāvana Ārām to recite the Ratana Sutta[56] the whole day until dusk; [the water volume] decreased to the size of a banana tree trunk. [The sutta was] recited all night, [the rain] stopped, not falling even a little. Thereupon, lord of earth and ministers and courtiers were exceedingly joyous at heart, and, at the end of the vassā, lord of earth gave a great dāna of kaṭhina [robes] to the five lords, everyone of whom accepted [them].

79. Arrived Month Five full moon, [the five lords] went to mettā lord of earth and ministers and courtiers saying, "May we mettā to take leave of Somḍec Mahārāja to return to Jengsaen?" The brayā reverenced and begged, saying, "I beg to invite my Lords to stay on. We would go down and fetch the Sāsanā and invite Lord Mahā Gambhīra, who is the guru of my Lords, to come and spread the Lord's Sāsanā." Somacitta Thera accepted the invitation to live at the forest of Mahāvana Ārām there. Brayā Srīsudhamma Culāmaṇī Mahārāja deputed Brayālōng Sāmmöng named Sirivaṁsa to head many persons to go to Möng Jengsaen carrying letters of friendship and salutation together with presents and the aṭṭhaparikkhāra.[57] On arrival the royal envoy presented gifts to the brayā of Jengsaen whose name was Mahā Suvaṇṇaniddhi and begged permission to invite Lord Mahā Ñāṇagambhīra [to Khemaraṭṭha]. The brayā granted permission and Minister Sirivaṁsa Sāmmöng, heading many persons, took the aṭṭhaparikkhāra to Vat Cômgatti and, after having presented them as dāna to Lord Ñāṇagambhīra, invited and begged for the Sāsanā and Dhamma Vinaya. Lord Mahā Ñāṇagambhīra accepted [29] the invitation and, after having taken leave of lord of earth and all the ministers, courtiers, and lay devotees, and having called his disciples, marched day and night to Tuṅga Raṭṭhapurī.

80. Mahā Ñāṇagambhīrato vacanaṁsutvā amaccā nāma Sirivaṁsa nimantanaṁ āgataṁ tuṅgakhemaratthaṁ ahosi [Having heard the words (? of confirmation) from Mahā Ñāṇagambhīra, an invitation had been sent to (? come to) the country of Tuṅgakhema by the minister named Sirivaṁsa]. O you Sappurisa [pious and worthy men], Lord Mahā Ñāṇagambhīra Thera came up with the royal minister named Sirivaṁsa, dispatched by the brayā to invite him. He came with the minister, surrounded by an entourage of disciples, by stages of the journey.[58] When [the party was] nearing the city, the minister dispatched men to reverence the brayā, informing him of all affairs. When Brayā Srīsadhamma Cuḷāmaṇī Mahārāja heard the news that Lord Mahā Ñāṇaghambīra would soon be arriving, he and ministers and courtiers went out to receive [the thera] at Mӧng P̱ong[59] there.

81. When Lord Mahā Ñāṇagambhīra put his feet down on the ground of Tuṅperaṭṭha, the earth quaked mightily because of the glory of his morality, meditation, and wisdom with which he brought the Sāsanā and the Lord's Piṭaka Dhamma. The brayā had people construct one monastery near Mӧng P̱ong, calling it Vat Mahābrohm, for the Saṅgha to rest to get rid of ṯheir fatigue. Lord of earth, having looked after Lord Mahā Ñāṇagambhīra for seven days, had people construct properly a monastery at Tīnp̱ā and invited Lord Mahā Ñāṇagambhīra to come and reside [30] in the monastery. Then Lord S̱omacitta Thera and the four Saṅgha who were the disciples [of Ñāṇagambhīra] went to receive their upajjhāya to whom a full report was given there. Then Somacitta Thera and the brayā heading others led Lord Mahā Ñāṇagambhīra to the forest monastery of Mahāvana Ārām there. The brayā also arranged to spread mats and seat cushions and had people serve the four requisites every day without break, accompanied by entertainment with musical instruments.[60]

82. Tato, from then until the year Kāgai, Cuḷa Sakkarāja 805, Brayā Srīsadhamma Cuḷāmaṇī Mahārāja headed the ministers, courtiers, and the populace, and they unitedly constructed Sīhaḷaratta Ārām to offer as dāna. Headed by Hmün Rom, Hmün Jan locality was assigned to construct a big brick building --length seventeen vā, breadth seven vā. All the retainers constructed the great homage hall. Yāngjāng, with three hundred twenty thousand paddy fields and a population of three villages, was to provide people numbering four houses to fetch water and see to the maintenance of the great hall. The elder sister queen constructed the great library[61] providing Yāngjôn, Yāngman, with twenty thousand paddy fields and five houses of Yāng[62] people. The younger sister queen constructed the inner library, providing Yāngrôm with fifty

thousand paddy fields and two houses of Yāng people. Mahārājadevī, the aunt, constructed the great cetiya, providing Yānghrük, Yangkhāng, Möngkhônkāng, forty thousand paddy fields, and twenty houses of people. Lord of earth constructed the great vihāra[63] and the great image of the Lord,[64] providing Yāng-ô, Yāngdau, Möngkhā, with fifty thousand paddy fields, thirty houses. People of the outer library, inner library, and of the cetiya, all of them, were to provide five hundred fief houses for the supply of worship oil and the beating of gongs and drums, lamps at night, water in the morning.

83. In the year Münghmau, Sakka- [31] rāja 809, all manner of services and usages were abolished. The single principal [wooden] pillar, north and in front of the monastery [was provided by] Fālām, Fākāng; the dais, Ban Nā; the pillar in the middle of the hall, the two Lāmhmüns; the pillar in front of the brick building, Sæn Bāy Sônghmün[65] [who], after the construction of the great brick building, begged for paddy fields and Yāngs with property--the Yāngs with Yāng Dip as the head. Lord of earth dedicated as dāna the people of Namun [Hot Spring] and each house was to supply five viss of oil as obligation every year and to constantly serve the rājaguru, [and] be exempted from all state labors, every item.

84. Came the year Püksī, Sakkarāja 810, Month Seven waxing 10th night, construction began on the great uposatha hall of Sīhaḷarattārāma at noon, laggana[66] fell on the Lion, and the laying of bricks from the four cardinal points towards each other was completed at the same time. The earth quaked to and fro.

85. The year Kaḍsai, Sakkarāja 811, lord of earth and ministers and courtiers prepared abhiseka paraphernalia and victory pavilions, invited [Ñāṇagambhīra] with musical instruments and a pedestal tray filled with flowers and gold candles, carried [him in a palanquin] from Mahāvana Ārām to Sīhaḷarattārām, and consecrated him with the name "Mahā Ñāṇagambhīra Somḍec Aggarājaguru Varamolī." The earth quaked to and and fro.

86. Then lord of earth donated sixteen [sīmā] stones to Lord Ñāṇagambhīra Somḍec Aggarājaguru Varamolī heading all the Saṅgha, [and the latter] allowed Somacitta Thera heading [others] to do the extolling recitation ceremony beginning with the recitation on the stone in the east, one after another. When [the recitation] came round to the eastern stone, the earth quaked to and fro for the second time.[67]

87. After the extolling recitation, the Sammuti Kammavācā [was recited] as laid down by the Lord in the uposatha section of the Mahāvagga division [of the Vinaya Piṭaka]. While the Kammavācā was being recited[68] the earth quaked [32] as the third omen. The devaḍās made the wind current bring the fragrant tender leaves of banana and of the Srīmahaboḍhi tree, which fell in the center of the uposatha hall impregnating the whole monastery with fragrance.

88. After the construction of Sīhaḷarattārāmādhīpati, came the year Kāpseḍ, Sakkarāja 816, Month Seven full moon, Brayā Srīsadhamma Cuḷāmaṇī Mahārāja donated Pāyāng [village] to the great Mūlarājaṭhān,[69] called the devās to witness, poured libation water on to the hands of the Saṅgha, and had the people minister to the Three Gems, exempting them from other labors and traditional services [towards the state], from any support to the state--not even one vā of bamboo or one sheet of thatch --from any journey-stage load corvee; they were not to journey beyond the four city gates, exempted in every way. Let any transgressor line the bottom of hell without ever coming out. Even during successive reigns they were not to be impressed into labor for the state; nor were they to be taxed for even ten, twenty cowries.

89. During the reign of Brayā Kaeuphāpbhummin[70] the Saṅgha were requested to inscribe [the exemptions] on a stone inscription for the second time. The Burmese Suddho Iṅjhe[71] in a royal order gave every exemption for the third time. From the time of the rajāguru, lord of Vat Hnôngphā named Candavijen, people of the monastery had never been impressed into state labor or taxed in any way. Meanwhile, lord of earth, at the head of all ministers and courtiers, had extremely radiant faith in the perfect Sāsanā of Lord Buddha.

90. Came Month Seven waxing 2nd night, the royal person of lord of earth at the head of one hundred were ordained; the uposatha hall was filled just comfortably. At that time the great monarch gave up Möng Tuṅgaraṭṭha as dāna to the Three Gems on that day of ordination [33] and then deputed ministers and courtiers to obtain a revenue of ninety thousand silver as [the monastery's] acquisition. Month Nine waxing 4th night, lord of earth left the Order and donated forty thousand silver and four thousand gold to the Saṅgha headed by Somḍec Rājaguru Varamolī: one portion fell to the rājaguru, one portion to the Saṅgha, two portions were set aside as Lord Buddha's share.

91. At the end of the vassā [the brayā] asked the Saṅgha and the populace to fetch the Mahāboḍhi tree brought from Möng Laṅkā and to plant it in the compound of Sīhaḷarattāram. On Month Four full moon, [the Mahāboḍhi's] one stem split into two standing side by side.

92. On Month Six full moon, Lord Somacitta Thera dreamed that two devapuḍs[72]--one named Anojā, one named Sumanā--who had come to tend the Mahābodhi, spoke to him, saying, "We two have come to safeguard the Lord's Sāsanā and the excellent Mahābodhi tree. Henceforth, any bhikkhu who is [too] slothful and lazy to practice and study the Dhamma in the Sāsanā will be forced to withdraw. Any lord who has desire and energy for the two courses as laid down by the Lord will cause the Sāsanā to flourish and spread radiantly and widely, and will cause the Srīmahābodhi tree to have fragrance. Any lord who comes under the eight items of evil practices, that is, to strive like a householder; vikārango, to have a deformity anywhere, one; candāla, different religion, one;[73] millakhujo, to be born in the outer rim of the paccanta region devoid of the Triple Gems, one; ukkhittako, to behave ill and be suspended by the Saṅgha, one; mūladāsā [34] jāti, to be born from the womb of a female slave, one; mūlasedi, to be guilty of a Pārājika[74] offense, one; dhupasampanno, not to have been ordained in an uposatha hall with proper boundaries, one."[75]

93. Lord Somacitta then asked, saying thus, "What is the reason for the Mahābodhi tree having split into two stems and grown to a height of two cubits within one month?" The devās spoke, saying, "Because of the glory and power of lord of earth who is a Bodhisatta and has resolved to be a Lord Sabbaññū. He would be one without a doubt."

94. Lord Mahāthera asked, saying, "On what will depend the flourishing of the Sāsanā in this Sīhaḷarattārāma?" The devapuḍs spoke, saying, "As long as this Mahābodhi tree stands flourishing and beautiful, the Sāsanā will flourish accordingly. If the Mahābodhi tree weakens and withers, the Sāsanā will then be decadent." So it was said.

95. Somacitta Thera, having been awake fully and having done personal cleansing, went at daylight to reverence Lord Mahā Ñāṇagambhīra, who was Somḍec Aggarājaguru and who was his upajjhāya, at the head of all the Saṅgha, and informed everyone of what he had learned, ṣeen, and inquired of the devapuḍs from start to finish. Then Lord Rājaguru spoke, saying, "It would be as you have seen and as the devās have told you in every detail."

96. After that, lord of earth made a solemn resolve, saying, "[If] my resolve to be a Sabbaññū would be fulfilled, may the devaḍās make an image of the Lord, a footprint, and an alms bowl out of some fine stone and give them to me." Came the time [35] just before dawn, the brayā dreamed that a very handsome man came and stood before him and said, "If Lord Mahārāja wishes to have some stone to sculpt an image of the

Lord, a footprint, and an alms bowl, there is one [stone] at Mônpheḍ, one at the foot of the Bengsang hills, one beside Lake Hnôngtung.[76] I will show them to you." Saying only those words the man vanished.

97. When the brayā woke up, [he] had people look at the places and they actually found [the three stones]. The brayā had craftsmen sculpt an image of the Lord, a footprint of the Lord, and an alms bowl of the Lord. The footprint of the Lord was kept at Mônpheḍ; the image of the Lord was kept in front of the golden palace; the alms bowl of the Lord was kept at Sīhaḷaratta Vat P̱āḍaenglōng. The brayā personally took food and water and placed [them] in the stone alms bowl every day.

98. Came the year Ḍapgai, Sakkarāja 817, Month Seven waxing 13th night, during that night there was a very severe rain and wind storm, [and] many trees and human houses fell down. At daylight, the brayā asked people to go and inspect Vat P̱āḍaeng. Nowhere was [it] damaged, even the roof-eaves and tiles did neither upturn nor fall, they were as good and normal as before. The populace spoke in praise saying, "The merit of the Three Gems is truly excellent. The wind was very violent; trees and houses broke and came down; both the vihāra and the hall buildings are still very firm as if they were iron pavilions and brass pavilions." From then [they] were called "iron pavilion," "brass pavilion" for that reason. Lord of earth constructed [36] the iron pavilion building, the brass pavilion building, the building with glass windows, and the vihāra for the Reclining Lord, and donated Yāngṅen to serve the Lord, the Dhamma, and the Saṅgha forever.

99. At that time there was a Jāngsāt[77] man who went with his son to spend the night in the forest looking for bamboos for weaving mats. On return when they were nearing the Namkhün[78] [they] heard the sound of a hill in the west falling near the Namkhün. The father and son went to have a look and saw a piece of rock about one vā in diameter floating in the water. The father and son rushed to tell the officials asking them to reverence lord of earth about it. When lord of earth had ministers and courtiers hasten to see [the floating rock] they actually saw [it] there. The brayā then spoke to the courtiers saying, "The omen of the floating rock is that we have purified the Sāsanā of the Lord and made it prosper brilliantly." So he said that day.

100. Lord Mahā Ñāṇagambhīra, who was the Lord Somḍec Aggarājaguru Varamolī, established the five kammas[79] in accordance with Dhamma Vinaya laid down by the Lord. A great number of men of good families went for ordination [in] the residence of Lord Mahā Ñāṇagambhīra. The living halls numbering thirty-four stretched to the end of the open fields of Pādaeng. Many hill people came down to take the Sāsanā back to every hill and mountain. Some of them came down to study and learn correctly and thoroughly the letters of the alphabet, Pali grammar, all, and returned home to teach pupils and disciples. And at the end of a complete year every monastery would come down with one hundred tooth-brushing sticks, three towels, three blankets, five viss of oil, and four pairs of large candles to pay homage to Lord Mahā Ñāṇagambhīra who was Lord Somḍec Rājaguru without a break in the line even for a year.

101. As for Brayā Su- [37] vaṇṇaniddhi, who was lord of earth in Möng Jengsaen and all [Ñāṇagambhīra's] disciples also came to pay homage every year without fail.

102. In Sipsôngbannā direction, Lü, Laem, Möngkā, Möngban, Möngpô, Möngmaen and Möngting, Küngmā,[80] over there, also came down to take the Sāsanā from the residence of Lord Mahā Ñāṇagambhīra Somḍec Rājaguru and established it in their lands everywhere.

103. As Mahā Ñāṇagambhīra, Lord Rājaguru had been living in Möng Tuṅgapurī here for thirty years, the royal person of the dāu [of Jengsaen] and disciples with one hundred men came to beg Lord Mahā Ñāṇagambhīra to return. Thereupon, Brayā Srīsadhamma Cuḷāmaṇī Mahārājacau deputed ministers and courtiers with two hundred men to send [him] as far as Jengsaen and then [they] returned there.

104. Came the following year lord of earth raised Somacitta Thera to be his own Somḍec Rājaguru Munī asking [him] to reside in the great hall [named] Vaḍḍhanagāra; raised Nanda Thera to be saṅkārī[81] to reside at the iron pavilion; raised Gota Thera to be saṅgharājā to reside at the brass pavilion; raised Vaḍḍhana Thera to be suāmī to reside in the hall with glass windows; raised Chanda Bhikkhu to be thera to reside at the middle hall; raised Uppala to be suāmī to reside at the hall of victory; raised Sivagga Bhikkhu to be thera to reside at the sandalwood hall.

105. The total census of the Saṅgha of Vat Pāḍaeng--all bhikkhus and sāmaṇeras--was two hundred. The number of all lay devotees of Ṫīnpā was three hundred and fifty houses having Brayālōng Khandha, Brayā Kaeu, and Brayā Srī as leaders.

106. [When] the Saṅgha assembled they did together at the homage hall. [When] the sāmaṇeras undertook to have the sīla [they] begged [for them] at the homage hall; eight bhikkhus would go, sit, and give the sīla.[82] When the time came for the end of the vassā, lord of earth offered Kaṭhina Mahādāna every year. Lord of earth observed the eight sīlas every new moon and full moon [when he would] go and spend the night in [38] the homage hall there without fail, always, all the time. Even the dāna of the Mahāpāng Dhamma[83] was also performed at the homage hall there.

107. Atha, at that time the bhikkhus of Jenglæ and those of Yānggham heading all belonging to the Pupphārām [Garden] Sect, not seeing the faith of the populace in them, felt jealous, envious, ashamed greatly, and angrily departed. Lord of earth, riding on an elephant, went to stop [them but they] would not listen--some went to the southern kingdom, some went west, east, to a man. Only Vat In[84] remained, without going away, because a son of lord of earth was ordained there. In the surrounding villages outside the capital, only those lords remained who were old, and suffering from illnesses and weakness--they could not go and therefore did not run away.

108. Brayā Srīsaddhamma Cuḷāmaṇī Mahārāja, then, invited the bhikkhus of Vat P̱āḍæng to go and reside in all [the empty monasteries] there. As for Vat P̱āḍæng itself, the Saṅgha became small, light, thin [in number] so that its upkeep was not thorough, and half was therefore walled off in which one hall remained on the far east side. Later a monastery was constructed [there] and named Vat P̱āya [modern Vat Cômhmai] until now. Only afterwards a lord was raised to be a sāmī to reside in the endmost hall; one lord was raised to be a thera to reside at the lion hall; one lord was again raised to be a sāmī to reside at the security hall; one lord was also raised to be a thera to reside at the coconut hall; yet one lord was raised to be a sāmī, one lord was raised to be a thera--these two lords were to reside at the great purity hall; one lord was raised to be a thera to reside at the little hall; one lord was raised to be a sāmī to reside royally in the gem hall there.

109. As regards all the monasteries in the capital, the bhikkhu of Vat Khemin was raised to be saṅgharājā; the bhikkhu of Vat Jengṅām was raised to be thera; the bhikkhu of Vat Jengcan was raised to be sāmī; the bhikkhu of Vat Jenglān was raised to be thera; the bhikkhu of Vat Jengkhum was raised to be thera; the bhikkhu of Prakam was raised to be thera; the bhikkhu of Vat Jeng-ing was raised to be sāmī; again the bhikkhu of [39] Vat Prasak was raised to be thera; yet the bhikkhu of Vat Prasö was raised to be thera; and again the bhikkhus of Vat P̱āmahāvan who were brothers were raised--the elder brother to be saṅgharājā, the younger brother to be sāmī, and they were to reside at Vat Mahāvaṇṇa [Mahāvana] Ārām there. All the Saṅgha went to congregate at Vat P̱āḍæng on the entry of the vassā, the coming-out of the vassā and uposatha days. As for Vat Prakaeu, Vat Prahmai, Vat Prakāng, in these three monasteries, lord of earth, angry, made no appointments.[85]

110. In the direction of Pupphārām there was a nobleman named Māḍsām, so it was said, [who] had people numbering twenty houses outside the city walls; they had no bhikkhus; so [the people] came in to share the monasteries in the capital every time [the need arose]. There was a low hill which was a burial ground where people disposed of their dead. People used to discard torn baskets, shredded hampers, and gins, looms, bamboo spinners at that place. It was therefore called Yānggōng Burial Hillock. Māḍsām and [his] people asked permission from lord of earth to construct a Vat on the Yānggōng hillock, and invited bhikkhus within the capital to go and preside over it. Not one would go, and the monastery was empty for one vassā. Afterwards there was a bhikkhu of the Garden Sect who was a son of an elder aunt of Māḍsām, suffering from the disease of the great wind [gastric ailment] and not able to live with others. [He] came up from Jenghmai alone and arrived at that place. Māḍsām and lay devotees invited that Bra Iraccaka to reside [at the monastery]. [He] instructed children according to the creed of the Garden Sect.

111. It is said that Vat In was originally called Vat Mônsut. It is said that there was a noble named Sāmavan who had a devout intention and had constructed a large image of the Lord with the half top of the image's head remaining unfinished. The next day [the image] was seen as finished, complete with moḷī, good and beautiful. The populace spoke out, saying, "Brayā In[da] must have come and helped in the construction." Not long after, however, the Vat In bhikkhu died; the noble named Sāmavan also died.

112. [40] There was a noble named Saen Lāmban [who] heading together with others went to invite bhikkhus in the capital [to reside at Vat In], [but] none would go. There was a bhikkhu residing at Vat Yānggōng named Bra Candaprayā, so it was said. Saen Lāmban, the granduncle, invited [him] to come and reside at that place, Vat In.

113. Later when [bhikkhus of] Vat Pupphārām side were not yet numerous, [they] at first used to go and beg the Forest Sect to assemble for Uposathakamma, Parivāsakamma, and Pavāraṇākamma,[86] following the doctrine of the Forest Sect. As time went on, bhikkhus of the Garden Sect became numerous, [they] agreed by common consent to regard Bra Iraccaka as their rājaguru there.

114. The Pupphārām Sect, their doctrine was not consistent. [Their] recitation of the sounds of the alphabet was not consistent; if they wanted to follow, they followed, if they did not want to follow, they discarded it. They followed the dictates of their hearts; they invented when they could, never following the sounds of the alphabet which Lord Buddha had laid down, saying "Akkharāpādayo ekacattāḷīsaṁ" [the letters of the alphabet also are forty-one].[87] That was why the Sāsanā of the monasteries of the Garden Sect was not consistent, tending to be frivolous, for that reason.

115. The narration of the chronicle of past events of the two sects, namely, Pupphārām and Nattārām [Rattārām], from the beginning, is here ended as a chapter.

Vat P̱āḍaeng

116. In here will be told the first origin of Vat P̱āḍaeng from start to finish, for the enlightenment in future times.

117. The year Mūnghmau Sakkarāja 819, Brayā Srīsadhamma Cuḷāmaṇī constructed the big brick building, three bōknāys constructed the bōsot; the three bōks of the interior[88] and a royal meritorious act constructed the vihāra; the big hall [was constructed by] four bōk [and] five nāys; the single pillar in the north, Ban Nā [and] Bōk Noi; the pillar at the center of Saṅgha dais, Ban Nā; the pillar in front of the rājaguru [dais], the two Lām Mūns; the pillar facing the Jensaen building and the big cetiya, Mahādevī and Ban Nā [of] Jengkhum; the building for bhikkhus of the monastery, people of Tīnp̱ā; the building in the direction of the road-mouth--Bô-kvāu and Tīn- [41] dong constructed.

118. Over and above that, the people of Bandōm served fifteen buildings--one big house per building, two small houses per building. Jencīn and Sōntān served twenty-five buildings in the direction of Tāsaen. Let Khāngkāḍ, Jengnām with thirty houses, Dāyô, Hōnông with ten houses, served [the buildings] at the head of the grove. There were bhikkhus for twenty buildings at the end of the grove. Small merit [capacity] constructed small buildings, greater merit constructed big buildings. Rājanāpun, constructed four buildings, namely, the prāsāḍ [pāsāda] building, the wind building, the great building, the uposatha building and the golden dais, this was all. As for the great meditation walk and the uposatha [building] let all the retainers [? construct, ? serve].

119. As for the two Möng Küys, namely, Möng Küy North with ten paddy fields, Möng Küy South with ten paddy fields, total, twenty paddy fields, lord of earth named Ādittarājā [1474-1508] appointed [their chief] to be Ban Jöng, [with the privilege] to sit on a felt mat, to wear a bamboo hat with silver summit,[89] to receive royal orders with a personal flower tree.[90] When there are words of state, [the Küy people] are to take turns to go for meetings at the state office; whatever they know, [they must] reverence the Saṅgha. When there is no business, [they are to] go once a month. If lord of earth is out on auspicious tours they must estimate a suitable time and seek an audience with flowers and candles. During Month Six and Month Eleven, they must go to assemble with the high officials.[91] When lord of earth accepts the state [or] ascends a new golden palace,[92] they must also go to assemble with the high officials.

120. One item. If the rājaguru or the Saṅgha are troubled in matters big and small, [Möng Küy] should inform lord of earth. If guests, senior Saṅgha, many of them, should come from other countries, officials of Möng Küy must inform Saen Bô-möng who would exhort the parishioners to go and give dāna. Should there be a royal thought, it should not be discarded.

121. Should the lay devotees of Khāngkāḍ, Jengñām, Tīnpā, whoever, be not fond of dāna or of support of the Sāsanā of Vat P̱ā-ḏaeng, let the two Möng Küys, remind them once or twice. If [they do] not listen, let royal orders be issued telling them not to discard the Sāsanā. Whoever is fond of observing the sīla and of giving dāna [42] throughout, not omitting even the daily food, when dead, should be buried at the head of the grove only when requested. Whoever is not fond of giving dāna and a daily spoonful of food, should not be allowed to be buried [there]. This concerns the people of Khāngkāḍ, Dāyô, Jengñām.

122. As the people of Tīnp̱ā [and] Hnôngkhe reside within the grove's boundary, they should be made to seriously serve and maintain [the monastery]. If [they are] not fond of giving dāna of a daily spoonful of food, forbid them from living in Tīnp̱ā. If the injunction is not obeyed let Möng Küy cut their house posts and drive [them] away. This is the royal order.

123. As regards sabbaññū officers,[93] there are three: one named Bōk Rom, one named Bōk Hrük, one named Bōk Khāng. On the Saṅgha side the rājaguru is to lead in urging the monastery people to sound gongs, to strike drums,[94] to attend to the Lord every morning and evening. If any part of the vihāra becomes dilapidated, call the monastery people to come and

work, including [repairs to] the buildings, cetiya, vihāra, outer library, inner library. When Month Two and vassā commencement arrive, take turns to come and sleep and work until [repairs are] completed. Moreover, every five days, take turns to visit and see to the work without fail. Mö̈ng Kü̈y North is to provide three officers, namely, Bōk Khö̈ng, Bōk Kvāng, Bōk Hnām. Mö̈ng Kü̈y South is to provide three officers, namely, Bōk Hnông, Bōk Vāng, Bōk Hra. The two Mö̈ng Kü̈ys, after [their] morning meal, are to make Mö̈ng Kü̈y people come with their belongings to sit at Vat Pōsoḍnôy,[95] make inspection rounds of every building for bhikkhus, and the halls in the east. Where minor damages are seen, Mö̈ng Kü̈y North is to do the repairs. Mö̈ng Kü̈y South is to pay attention to the halls in the west. For major, serious damages Mö̈ng Kü̈y has the duty of telling the monastery's secretary to inform lord of earth who will give orders to the retainers to come and work until the damages are repaired.

124. When the day of decay of the Sangkhān[96] comes round Mö̈ng Kü̈y North is to clean the well at Bōrö̈ North; Mö̈ng Kü̈y South is to clean the well at Bôkū[97] thoroughly. All [the two] Mö̈ng Kü̈ys are to take the people of the two Mö̈ngs who have come to work [43] to eat at the houses of the two[98] every year. Within the two pink gates the two Mö̈ng Kü̈ys are to get rid of the grass on both sides of the road, twice a year.

125. One item. At the consecration ceremony of the rājaguru somḍec, it is the duty of the retainers to build the three ceremonial pavilions which must have two necks;[99] the people of the monastery should not help. From the great hall the rājaguru will come round the uposatha hall towards the front of the [dormitory] hall and will be invited to ascend the temporary pavịlion. Lord of earth provides the ascetic silken robes, all the parikkhāra and the muddhābhiseka water.[100] The two lāmhmü̈n and officials, namely, outer officials, ministers and courtiers, high officials of the state office, village and field chiefs, and cavalry chiefs [should join lord of earth] in providing the silken robes and all parikkhāra to give as dāna to the rājaguru who will wear them to the ceremonial pavilion, for the ceremonial bath and cleansing, and put on the paraphernalia. Lord of earth comes to the great hall. When lord of earth has poured the muddhābhiseka water [on the rājaguru in a ceremonial bath] the retainers will carry [rājaguru in an open bamboo palanquin] to the great hall.

126. At consecration ceremonies for the gurus, saṅgharājās, sāmīs, and theras, royal orders command Kü̈y people to build ceremonial pavilions and to carry [the candidates] for a fee of one thousand cowries and one thousand areca nuts to be received by them. When consecrating other bhikkhus than those of Vat Pāḍaeng, five thousand cowries, five thousand areca nuts--Küy people are to receive all.

127. The year Kaḍmeḍ Sakkarāja 901, Brayā Saen of Jengcīn heading [others] consecrated Rājaguru Bra Sing who resided at Vat Suvan and requested the retainers to carry [the rājaguru]. The retainers would not carry; whereupon the brayā made officials place the rājaguru on an elephant from the wall of the hall to the single-neck ceremonial pavilion, after which [the rājaguru] was requested to come down at the wall level of the hall.[101]

128. Brayā Saen died that year. Bômöng Cômdông inherited the Saen paddy fields there.

129. At the dāna of the great robes[102] at Vat Pāḍaeng, the people of Bōk Khüng, Bōk Dā carry drums leading the forces; people of Bōk Khōmung beat drums out front; people of Vat Pāḍaeng beat the sanpengdrā gong[103] and follow the drums leading the forces. Möng Küy carries the palm leaf fan ahead; people of Möng Küy carry pennants and flags in front of the elephant; Bōk Rājaguru carries the white umbrella shading the brayā from the position of a hind-rider.[104]

130. On occasions when lord of earth proceeds to give dāna of mahākaṭhina in Vat [44] Pāḍaeng, the best day and the victorious moment of perfect purity must first be selected, that is, [these days] must be avoided: the day spirits give death and destruction, the day the yon is out hunting, the day the state's cloak is alarmed, the day death is received, the day of the prince's eviction, the day of secret burial and death, the day of the four squares, day 7 of the red sky, the day of the great ghost and iron javelin, the day of the robber's constellation, the day of the executioner's constellation, the day of the beggar's constellation, yoga of misfortune, yoga of the blind, and yoga of death.[105] These are all to be avoided, not to be accepted. Such is ancient tradition.

131. On the occasion when Brayā Āy Klau who was named Ādittarājā [1474-1508][106] proceeded to give dāna on a Monday, the astrologers predicted that it was the day of his age.[107] On that day of the dāna of the great robes, lord of earth proceeded with a force to the middle of the hall of Pāḍaeng, [where he] was afflicted with stabbing wind blackout[108] and fell down [unconscious] in the middle of the hall. People covered him with blankets for a very long time, then only did he become conscious and was able to spread the robes late that night.

132. Afterwards, Brayā Sivijaya [1509-1523] proceeded to give dāna of the robes at Vat P̱āḍaeng without considering it was the day of the prince's banishment; he was assassinated that day.[109] Only subsequently was a minister named Brayā Vangsa ordered to take charge of a force at the rear.

133. After that, Brayā Kaenarindā [1560-1597][110] gave dāna on Pük-seḍ day 7 of red sky, day of death after secret burial, the great ghost was in the east. The astrologers said, "Today if lord of earth leaves the palace and proceeds towards the south, then turns north and only then enters the monastery, there should be no trouble." It was also said that nothing should matter about going to perform meritorious deeds. That day, after having given dāna, lord of earth emerged to ride on an elephant. At that time Tīnpā was on fire [and] people stampeded. The elephant was afraid of the fire and became alarmed and greatly maddened. Lord of earth fell from the elephant and suffered greatly; this turned into a serious illness, [and he] lived for seven months and died there.

134. Next, Prince Vādsinggī [Oksing, 1678-1685][111] went to give dāna on a day of the four squares, [and he] had just passed the city gate and arrived at Hrōpā, [when] the elephant [tusk] rings fell off; they were put on two or three times but were not firm, and therefore they were not put on. [45] Lord of earth became ill with fever from then, and the fever worsened on arrival at the monastery, becoming very severe on his return to the golden palace. He lived on for three months and fifteen days and died.

135. Since then, Prince Jalemang [1685-1702][112] went to give dāna at Vat P̱āḍaeng on the day the kingdom's cloak was alarmed. After the dāna and on return to the golden palace [the brayā] immediately had aches and pains, never recovered, and lived for four months and five days and died.

136. Prince Sāmplī [1702-1720][113] went to give dāna of the great robes on the day that was a Sunday, Daiy Kaḍhmau named Jāng-bon, the iron rod was in the east, the great ghost was in the west. The procession had just passed the palace gate when fire broke out at Jhegong and Lākhōng[114] and the lord could not proceed, and had Brayā Saen carry [? him] to the city gate of Kāḍtung.[115] The populace ran back. A royal order was issued for Bōk Khan to go with the lord to spread kaṭhina robes on that day.

Duties of Monastery Subjects

137. The custom was established [that] straw seats, pillows, [and] ādhāndham[116] are the responsibility of Möng Küy North for one complete year; Möng Küy South, one complete year. Be mindful to change on the full moon day of Month Six. During the vassā, Möng Küy is to perform the ceremony of the invocation of the Dhamma and request for the sīla on behalf of others, on every uposatha day for a complete year. Bōk Vat is to set up the kambī ādhāndham. Küy people are to bring the cushion-seats[117] and trays of offerings, Bōk [? Vat] is to bring the palm leaf fan and to set up the Dhamma to be preached on the ādhān there. Küy people will bring and set up the spittoon and straw seat of the lord who is going to preach. The paraphernalia of the rājaguru, post-covering cloth, cushion-seats, spittoons, are to be brought by Bōk Vat and Küy people. Möng Küy will carry the tālapat[118] before the rājaguru.

138. During the big dānas attended by lord of earth, the two Möng Küys are to bring trays of offerings and all the articles for the dāna, which on arrival are to be taken over by Bōk Vat. The Küy people will carry [on a palanquin] the lāmsaṅ[119] and distribute [the dāna article] in accordance with usage. On occasions when preparations are made for the rājaguru to come to the great hall Möng Küy is to proffer the invitation and to precede with the paraphernalia. When lord of earth comes for the dāna, the two Möng Küys [46] are to remind Bōk Ban to bring mats and spread them awaiting lord of earth's arrival; and when done with to store them properly.

139. When the rājaguru visits the palace, goes to Outer Khōng or Inner Khōng, or anywhere, the two Möng Küys are to follow him; people of Bōk Phākhāu, Bōk Mindok, Bōk Pōsot go in front carrying the paraphernalia; people of Bōk Nam-un shade [him] with the white umbrella; the Küy people bring up the rear with food baskets. When somḍec rāja[guru] wishes whatever letters to be sent, Möng Küy will carry them. When royal summons call, go only when they concern the two Möng Küys. When there are errands of state, during Month Six or Month Twelve,[120] go; do not go when there are no errands--only be attentive to the Sāsanā in all seriousness.

140. Affairs of the mundane world the people of the two Möng Küys should not concern themselves with. Whatever affairs, internal or external, when mixed, should be attended to, to the finish; if not finished, they must reach the lāmsaṅ; if not yet finished, they must reach the saṅkārī;[121] if not finished, they must reach the great rājaguru; if not finished, they must go and reverence lord somḍec rājaguru who will issue orders to all the Saṅgha to assemble and deliberate them to the finish.

141. One item. Should affairs arise which should go to the high officials, the lāmvat [monastery messenger] and Mö̤ng Küy should take the order of the Saṅgha and go. When business and words arise, light in nature, the lāmsaṅ and Mö̤ng Küy should go. When affairs are serious the saṅkārī should go to mettā. When affairs are really serious, that is, words of state or really big affairs, four Saṅgha together should go to mettā the high officials, then only [will it be] appropriate. The person who is lord somḍec rājaguru himself should observe only the ascetic tranquility with Brahmavihāra[122] and the Two Courses [of study and practice of the Dhamma].[123]

142. Another item. When the free lords[124] come from outlying monasteries or from different directions, they must go to the saṅkārī and the lāmsaṅ who are to take them to reverence the rājaguru in an appropriate manner.

143. The two Mö̤ng Küys are not to go up and stay on a level with the offspring of [47] any high official.

144. One item. When lord of earth is on an auspicious journey, both Mö̤ng Küys are to follow the orders of the rājaguru and Saṅgha, and go and confer with high officials to invite [in a ceremony] lord of earth to return to Jengkaeu,[125] and to be in the procession leading lord of earth to the golden palace.

145. One item. Should there be lords for upasampadā ordination, the two Mö̤ng Küys should inform Bōk Ban to inform the lords of every monastery suitable for ordination, ask for the year, month, day, and moment of ordination from the upajjhāyas who gave the ordination, and come and report to the lords saṅkārī and lāmsaṅ so that the saṅkārī will examine properly the lords for ordination. If ordained by Lord Pabbajjā Ādiḍ, enter names according to vassā seniority. If ordained by Lord Ānuññāḍ split [the offering packets] into three portions, take two portions, return one portion. If ordained by neither Lord Pabbajjā Ādiḍ nor Lord Ānuññāḍ, give equally. If the sīla were received from Lord Pabbajjā Ādiḍ from there, count [or take] all. As long as the sīla are not received, bring one-half [of the packets] to add to those for not receiving the sīla. If ordained by Lord Pabbajjā Ādiḍ together on the same day, at the same time, give weight to the one whose guru is the senior one. This is in accordance with [agreement between] the two, Ādiḍ and Lord Pabbajjā. If the disciples of Lord Pabbajjā Ādiḍ are ordained on the same day let his disciples be the weighty [senior] ones because homage has been paid twice to the Saṅgha. Even if Lord Ādiḍ is younger than Lord Pabbajjā, let the lord's disciple's be the weighty one.[126]

146. Lord Mahā Varañāṇamaṅgala established this pattern of ceremony in order that the senior Saṅgha, the field of merit,[127] and members of the royal family who have sons and grandsons for ordination [will know that] the procedure is this. But excepted are those born of slaves and low-caste Damiḷa[128]--they are not to be ordained in the great uposatha hall of Vat P̱āḍaeng, it is not done. Such is the procedure; let no one destroy it. If a lord has wronged Vat P̱āḍaeng [48] and has not begged for exoneration, make him leave the Order or make him give up his vassā.

147. One item. At the approach of the Pavāraṇā[129] the two Möng Küys should inform the Saṅgha inside the capital, outside the capital, every monastery, to come to the Pavāraṇā. Regarding the Pavāraṇā day itself let the two Möng Küys ask the bhikkhus who will come and who will not come, how many will come, and after examining every lord by lot, invite them to come down to the Khōng according to royal invitation. Möng Küy will inform the monastery people and Bōk Wat to take the grūbā[130] to the Khōng and receive charcoal-toasted glutinous rice cakes. Eight Küy men will carry the rājaguru, carry the grūbā with available men; two men carry white umbrellas in front; two monastery men shade the rājaguru with white umbrellas; Möng Küy carries the palm leaf fans, monastery people carry the paraphernalia together with pedestal trays and spittoons; monastery people shade the great guru and the saṅkārī with white umbrellas; some carry food baskets and beat the flat gong ahead of the rājaguru. These are to be done both at Outer Khōng and Inner Khōng.

148. One item. The two Möng Küys should be familiar with the work inside the vihāra and the cetiya and the two Piṭaka pavilions, together with the homage hall, the rājaguru's hall, big buildings, small buildings, all. Where repairs to leakages and painting are necessary, [they] should have people of the monastery, of Bōk Vat come and help to make good properly. Another item. Where dilapidation and uncleanliness are seen, they must make known to the monastery people to clean and tidy up; gong and drum people are to get rid of the vihāra grass; people of Bōk Mondok, the library grass; Bōk Cetiya, the cetiya grass, both south and north, every year. The lay devotees of Tīnvat and people of Tīnp̱ā, all within the group of the sīmā of P̱āḍaeng, every parish̄, should make enclosures where walls and moats do not exist, so that cattle and horses cannot enter with ease. People within the group of the sīmā, whoever does not support or help, let Möng Küy tell the parish people to urge [the defaulter] to help. If still disobedient, report to the lāmvat to drag their hands to make enclosures. If they still do not go, cut down their house posts, and then drive them away from Tīnpā, forbidding them to stay, because the Lord is [49] their benefactor--only when there are troubles would [they] run to the Lord seeking refuge as an iron wall.

149. One item. Various kinds of bamboos[131] born within the sīmā group should be looked after for the support of the Sāsanā. Should outside retainers come to take the bamboos, forbid them to cut. If disobedient, tell the lāmsaṅ to urge Bra Grūbā to take all back. When there is work, let not Tīnpā people begrudge [the bamboos]. When constructing ceremonial pavilions for the rājaguru and elephant platforms, horse platforms, for lord of earth, let not Tīnpā people begrudge the bamboos to be taken by the retainers who have come for the construction, let them take as little or as much as needed.

150. One item. When Tīnpā people die and are to be buried at Hrōpā, [they] must honor the Saṅgha with five thousand cowries, five thousand areca nuts, then only permit the burial. If it is the people of Dāyô, Khāngkāḍ, Jengṅām who die and are to be buried at Hrōpā, if they observe the sīla, eat and give dāna[132] in Vat Pāḍaeng, [they] must honor the Saṅgha with ten thousand cowries, ten thousand areca nuts, then only permit [the burial]. Outside of that, if lords of twenty paddy fields or lords of five hundred paddy fields are to be buried at Hrōpā, [they] must honor the Saṅgha with twenty thousand cowries, twenty thousand areca nuts, then only allow the burial. This is for times of prosperity; if times are hard, make estimates to suit the occasions.

151. Royal orders are thus and libation water had been poured on to the palms of Somacitta Thera at the head of the Saṅgha when the brass pavilion was constructed and offered as dāna that day.

The Great Sīla

152. The way of soliciting the great sīla[133] is as follows. There was a grandfather bhikkhu residing in the monastery at Tīndong who made his grandson go forth to serve him at a place where people did not come to observe the sīla or hear the Dhamma. Every fifteen days he gave the sīla to the grandson. He recited whatever pleased him, not at all in accord with the formula of the Three Refuges [50] and the ten precepts. The villagers wanted to offer the robes as dāna but suspected that it would not be meritorious. People elsewhere asked [the villagers], saying, "You have your own bhikkhu, why don't you offer robes as dāna?" They said, "Our grandfather bhikkhu gives the sīla not in accordance with the letter of the Dhamma." People asked, saying, "If you don't offer dāna to the grandfather bhikkhu, why don't you offer it to the sāmaṇera?" They said, "The grandfather bhikkhu's giving of the sīla to the sāmaṇera is not in the least accurate." For that reason, the sīla must be obtained from the grūbā at the commencement of the vassā and the ending of the vassā at the residence of Lord Pubbajjā.

153. The narrative of the origin of Vat P̲āḍaeng is here concluded as a chapter.

Disputes Between Garden and Forest Sects

154. Here will be told the dispute between the bhikkhus of Vat P̲āḍaeng and the bhikkhus of Vat Yānggōng.

155. The year Müngplau, Sakkarāja 934,[134] the Burmese Mingaung[135] [?] went down to Jenghmai to attack Möng Pāḍ[136] lasting three years but did not conquer it. Only then [Mingaung] sent royal orders summoning Brayā Kaeu Phāpbhummin [1560-1597] for assistance. Brayā Kaeu pitched camp by the bank of the Salween, ordered Lord G̲hamdāu, lord of the Yāng paddy fields, and Lord Saenhleklōng and Möng Bū, Möng Beng, Möng Kā and forces to attack Möng Pāḍ lasting seven days. Lord Saenhleklōng had an elephant fight with [the lord of] Möng Pāḍ named Fāmöngṅam, who came on an elephant to fight at a place between a pair of two trees. Saenhlek toppled Möngṅam's elephant which fell down leaning against one tree. Saenhlek urged his elephant to attack further; Möngṅam fell down [from his elephant]. Möng Pāḍ was defeated, fled into the city and presented Brayā Kaeu with elephants and horses. The brayā brought his forces to fight [at] Dāhlô [Ferry] on Month Ten waxing 1st night.

156. That Müngplau year was an adhikamāsa year[137] when the vassā should commence in Month Ten. Bhikkhus of the Garden Sect actually commenced the vassā in Month Nine. Bhikkhus of the Forest Sect waited for lord of earth to invite every monastery to commence the vassā on Month Ten full moon. [51] After the Garden Sect had had the Pavāraṇā ending the vassā, royal orders forbade the dāna of [kaṭhina] robes to bhikkhus of the Garden Sect--not a single monastery received the robes. Royal orders [on the other hand] urged the dāna of [kaṭhina] robes to bhikkhus at every monastery belonging to the Forest Sect.

157. Bhikkhus of Yānggōng criticized bhikkhus of P̱āḍaeng saying, "From Month One waning 1st night to Month Two full moon the spread of kaṭhina robes is not valid." Bhikkhus of P̱āḍaeng, having heard that, reported to the Saṅgha of P̱āḍaeng [who then] deputed the saṅkārī to mettā lord of earth. A royal order directed high officials to inquire into traditions and customs.

158. Then Hmün Rom made obeisance, saying, "There was one of Your Highness' ancestors whose name was Brayā Kaeumadhu, [1403-1416] to whom his royal father, Brayā Āy, before dying, left word that Bra Indamolī be fetched from the southern kingdom to construct Vats Jenglæ and Yāngg̱ham. [The two monasteries] flourished shiningly, and were patronized by high officials and pious devotees. Later, they could not cope with the cleansing ceremony for the capital;[138] whereas bhikkhus of Mahāvan Forest Sect performed the cleansing ceremony successfully. Therefore the Garden Sect became jealous and severely criticized bhikkhus of Vat Mahāvan. Bhikkhus of Vat Mahāvan came to know about it and reported to lord of earth. The brayā considered that a dispute between the Saṅgha might not be auspicious for the country, and stopped it.

159. "After that the guardian devaḍā of the state was worried and caused the valleys and hills in the southwest to be on fire. When bhikkhus of the Garden Sect of Jenglæ were taken to recite the suttas, the flames rose to the height of the palm tree. Bhikkhus of Vat P̱ā Mahāvan were taken to recite the suttas; then only the fire died down. After that the rain fell abundantly [as if] the whole country would be flooded; and when bhikkhus of Vats Jenglæ [and] Yāng̱ham were taken to recite the suttas, the rain fell even more. Bhikkhus of Vat Mahāvan were again taken to recite the suttas, then only the rain stopped. The state is liable to encounter such dangers; for that reason [I beg you to] ponder over the bad and the good, the right and [52] the wrong. Such was the situation during the reign of Brayā Srīsudhamma Cuḷāmaṇī Mahārāja who was Your Highness' ancestor."

160. Now the Garden Sect bhikkhus criticized the P̱āḍæng Sect by saying, "Ñāṇagambhīra originally was a disciple of Dhammakitti of Vat Sōndôk, Jenghmai, quarreled with his guru who starved him, and the lay devotees drove him away to the southern kingdom. He managed to obtain a Gavampati image[139] [and] made an ointment to act as a popularity potion[140] [and] lied that he had obtained the Sāsanā from Laṅkā. None of them was a bhikkhu because they told lies, and ate people's rice by chanting mantras." So they said. People belonging to the P̱āḍæng Sect heard [the criticism] and reported to the rājaguru who deputed Dhammalaṅkā to mettā lord of earth. [The latter] issued royal orders to get bhikkhus of the two sects to assemble at Vat Brahmai Hrôkhōng.

161. Hmün Khaek then asked bhikkhus of the Garden Sect, saying, "What do you know about the origin of the Forest Sect?" They stated what they had told the populace.

162. Hmün Khaek thereupon asked bhikkhus of the Forest Sect, saying, "According to the history of your grūbā, what is the truth?" Dhammalaṅkā pulled out documents [concerning events] from the time Ñāṇagambhīra was born as a son of Ban Tāsaeng with the name of Sāmcitta and was ordained as a disciple of Rājaguru Dhammakitti, stage by stage, as related before, until the end when he came up to the Khün state here.

163. Hmün Khaek made reverence, saying, "Originally Ñāṇagambhīra was the disciple of Rājaguru Dhammakitti; [up to this point the stories of the two sects are] similar to each other. How later differences came about thus we would like to know. Could my lords find evidence to make it a little clear to us." So it was said.

164. Bhikkhus of the Garden Sect did not utter one word.

165. [53] Dhammalaṅkā then said, "Just as Lord Buddha gave weight only to Truth, other matters are not comprehensible to the worldly language. Only water and fire are of importance." Hmün Khaek asked, "What happens when only water and fire are taken into account?" Whereupon Dhammalaṅkā referred to the past, saying, "One hundred and twenty years after Lord Buddha had attained Nibbāna, an aññatiṭṭhī [heretic] was guru to Brayā Haṁsāvati at that time. The aññatiṭṭhī said, 'Mahā Samaṇa Gotama is a dead person; [one] should not preserve his image; it would bring catastrophes to the country; [one] should sink it in the water; then only all would be well.' The brayā solemnly obeyed and had people sink all images of Lord Buddha in the water. Whoever brought up [an image] for reverence, [the brayā] would have that person executed.

166. "At that time there was a devaḍā who came and told a daughter of a treasurer, named Nāng Saddhacittā, saying thus, 'There is an object of miraculous powers in the river east of the city. Whoever could bring it out and worship it as an object of refuge would be protected from all dangers, namely sticks, staves, rocks, spears, and swords, and will not perish by water or fire.'

167. "The next day she went with five hundred members of her entourage and saw the image of the Lord submerged in the water but was unable to retrieve it because the water was too deep.

She therefore took off her rings and hired four fishermen with four rings. [The image] was taken out [of the water] and taken by her to reverence every day, every moment. The populace, going and coming, saw it and went to report to the brayā. Royal orders had her taken to the palace ground and had an elephant urged to gore her; the elephant was unable to gore her. The brayā thereupon asked her, saying, 'What meritorious excellence have you?' She said, [54] 'I have no excellence; I only take an image of Lord Gotama as my one refuge, and will not perish by water or fire.'

168. "The brayā made people bring and pile up firewood in the palace ground there, and she said, 'If [you] will really burn me, do so only when the palace ground is filled with firewood. Write the name of my guru as "Lord Gotama Buddha," and then write the name of Lord Mahārāja's guru as "Aññatiṭṭhī," thus.'

169. "Thereupon the brayā followed her words and make people drop the two names into the fire mass. The name 'Aññatiṭṭhī' was received by the fire flames midair and was completely consumed, whilst the name 'Lord Gotama Buddha' was not burned, but remained whole, beautiful, and fresh as normal."

170. Having been acquainted with the situation, Hmün Khaek went to reverence the brayā who caused to be inscribed on a palm leaf the name "Bra Indamolī" and the name "Ñāṇagambhīra" on another palm leaf, and, the two sides having been made to declare solemn resolves, [the two palm leaves] were dropped into the fire mass in front of the Lord's image of Vat Prahmai Hrōkhōng there. At that moment the palm leaf with the name "Bra Indamolī" inscribed, when dropped into the fire, was burned without anything remaining. The palm leaf with the name "Ñāṇagambhīra" inscribed the fire did not burn, remaining normal as of old. Thereupon high officials and the populace hooted and shouted at the bhikkhus of Yānggōng Sect. As for the bhikkhus of P̱āḍaeng Sect, at the conclusion of the affair, lord of earth had people beat victory drums and send them to their monasteries.

171. Afterwards Brayā Kaeu Phāpbhummin [1560-1597] thought thus, "The Garden Sect bhikkhus said that the Forest Sect bhikkhus spread the kaṭhina robes incorrectly and invalidly. What is the real situation?" Having thought thus, [the brayā] had [55] the Saṅgha of the two sects assemble at Vat Prahmai there.

172. Heading other officials, Hmün Khaek asked, saying, "I have heard the Garden Sect bhikkhus state that P̱āḍaeng bhikkhus spread kaṭhina robes incorrectly, invalidly. Where did you learn this from, what do you have as evidence?" Bhikkhus of the Garden Sect said, "We speak from the profound text on astrology." Hmün Khaek said, "Do you regard the profound text on astrology as your guru?" Bhikkhus of the Garden Sect said, yes, always. Hmün Khaek said, "Then you are not disciples of the Lord, right?" Bhikkhus of the Garden Sect replied not one word there.

173. Hmün Khaek then asked bhikkhus of the Forest Sect, "What do you take as evidence?" Bhikkhus of the Forest Sect said, "We follow the profound text of the Vinaya called Mahāvagga by the sentence: 'Rājāno anumatituṁ vassāna upagantabbaṁ' [One should observe the vassā with the king's permission]. The section concerning the kaṭhina says, 'Anujānāmi bhikkhave vassaṁ vuṭṭhānaṁ kaṭhinaṁ attharituṁ' [I allow, O bhikkhus, the spread of kaṭhina robes for those who have lived the vassā]. We commence the vassā according to the orders of Lord Buddha and according to the invitation of lord of earth. We spread the kaṭhina according to the orders laid down by Lord Buddha which says, 'The Tathāgata sanctions the spread of the kaṭhina one month after the Pavāraṇā.' We obeyed the orders of Lord Buddha thus." Hmün Khaek then said, "All of you who are bhikkhus of the Forest Sect are the true disciples of the Lord." So it was said, and everyone gave the acclamation, "Sādhu."[141]

174. Having learned all the facts, Hmün Khaek went and reported everything to lord of earth at the head of ministers and courtiers. Lord of earth and high officials, ministers, and courtiers [56] said among themselves, "These bhikkhus of the Garden Sect entertain too much jealousy, always blaming bhikkhus of the Forest Sect; but when it comes to a real debate, they are only empty words."

175. Afterwards lord of earth, ministers and courtiers did not go to observe the sīla or to hear the Dhamma at Yānggōng Pupphārām; even during the alms bowl food-offering ceremony in the middle of the palace, did not invite a single bhikkhu [of Yānggōng]. For that reason, bhikkhus of the Garden Sect did not succeed in making the study of astrology outstanding.

176. After that a younger brother of Brayā Kaeu Phābhummin named Indadhara went and took a Yānggōng daughter as wife [and they] had a son who went to be ordained at Vat Yānggōng.

177. Indadhara saw the low state of Vat Yānggōng, without brilliance, and, wishing lord of earth to patronize Vat Yānggōng Sect, led bhikkhus and people in the construction of a big cetiya and a great image of the Lord, completing them only after five years. Then [he] invited lord of earth to consecrate the cetiya and the great image of the Lord in the year Tausaṅā, Sakkarāja 944. For the sake of the meritorious act of the younger brother, prince of the royal family, lord of earth forbearingly went with reluctance. Later Indadhara, the younger brother, asked for paddy fields to be dedicated to the great image of the Lord and the great cetiya. The brayā, lord of the land, the elder brother, gave permission for the dāna of paddy fields to the Sāsanā of the Yānggōng Sect until the present day.

178. After that, the rājaguru of Yānggōng went to mettā lord of earth asking permission to leave bhikkhuhood in order to serve the great image of the Lord and the great cetiya. Lord of earth said, "As a bhikkhu you could serve just as well, why do you wish to leave?" He answered, saying, "The fruit of bad kamma has not yet come to an end." [57] The brayā said, "You yourself are already old, your age is over eighty, nearing death, and yet you want to leave. You must be saying this in a delirium of death." [He] would not hear of any hindrance by lord of earth, and actually left the Order. After the rājaguru had left the Order, lord of earth urged him to be mindful of the monastery's paddy land and gave him the title of Ban Kuang from then.

179. Next, one Bra Saṅgharājā, architect of the construction of the great cetiya and the great image of the Lord, aged seventy-six, went to mettā lord of earth asking permission to leave bhikkhuhood to serve in the same way. Lord of earth said, "This lord is still a trifle youthful, an age still popular with divorced women and unmarried virgins." After leaving bhikkhuhood he was given the title of Ban Hum.

180. Next there was yet a lord who was a thera with a fluent tongue who, saying he would leave in order to polish and attend to the cetiya and the great image of the Lord, went and asked permission to leave bhikkhuhood in the same manner. After leaving [he] was given the title of Bōk P̲ākp̲aen.

181. Brayā Kaeu Phāpbhummin made these two bōks and Ban Kuang[142] serve the Lord and the great cetiya of Vat Yānggōng from that time. Later [lord of earth] invited Bragrū of Vat Dôyhlōng to be rājaguru at Vat Yānggōng as replacement.

182. Came the year Kāmeḍ Sakkarāja 945, bhikkhus of P̲āḍaeng Sect commenced the vassā in Month Nine; bhikkhus of Yānggōng Sect commenced the vassā in Month Ten. Bragrū of Vat Salaeng said thus, "We of the Garden Sect commenced the vassā incorrectly. The P̲āḍaeng Sect is correct." They drove Bragrū of Vat Salaeng away; he came and lived with bhikkhus of the Forest Sect. A bhikkhu of Vat Cômsāng said, "Yānggōng Sect is correct; we of the Forest Sect are not correct." [They] drove him away to Vat Yānggōng.

183. The Pādaeng Sect [58] having ended the vassā, royal orders went out for the dāna of kaṭhina robes to every monastery. Lord of earth went to offer dāna of the robes and straight away observed the sīla on full moon of Month One of the Forest Sect, which was the Pavāraṇā day of the Garden Sect.

184. Bhikkhus of the Garden Sect did not receive kaṭhina robes, not a single monastery. They were furious and said, "We will debate with the Forest Sect bhikkhus to make it plain to the populace that our sect is righteous and true." Prince Indadhara Rājavongsā restrained [them but they] would not listen. They went in a body to mettā lord of earth and asked for the debate time and again. "The External Side is not to interfere. Just look on and listen with ear-wax picked. We will debate and argue by ourselves. Lay people are not to speak, are not to say anything." So they said.

185. The bhikkhus sent letters to each other to and fro, namely, the rājagurus of the two parties, Pāhmai, Jenglae, Khemin, Mahā Jāngphök, Vat Dôyhlōng, Vat Yāngjhô, Vat Pā Mahāvan, Nôngsā, Yāngkaeu. "These are the chief gurus who should debate with each other; no one is to answer or to argue for anyone." So saying, [the Saṅgha] came and assembled in Vat Brahmai Hrōkhōng.

186. The External Side consisted of the somḍec mahārāja, lord of earth and lord uparāja, ministers, courtiers, and all citizens, sitting attentively with no one speaking, saying, or pointing out anything.

187. The grūbā of Vat Mahājāngphök came a little behind others. The grūbā of Dôyhlōng greeted Mahājāngphök, "Mahājāngphök, mā hlā sang kae?" ["mā," come; "hlā," late; "sang," why; "kae," so]. Mahājāngphök returned with the answer, "Mā hlā sang vā rü?" ["vā rü," how do you say it?]. Mahāguru of Dôyhlōng answered every word until the word "kae" when he was confused and kept silent. Mahājāngphök then said, "Such a mere Shan word you cannot answer; to answer points of the Dhamma would even be far [59] away--it cannot be easy."

188. Then all the populace on the side of Nattārām [Rattārām, or Forest] Sect and all high officials, ministers and courtiers shouted, beat the drums, beat the gongs and said, "Mahājāngphök has won!"

189. Bhikkhus of the Garden Sect felt ashamed and were furious at the bragrū of Dôyhlōng, and said, "This reverend mahāguru greeted the grūbā of Vat Mahājāngphök but when he countered with questions could not answer them." So saying, each lord carried away his volumes of the Dhamma with which he had hoped to debate, and all ran away. Afterwards bhikkhus of the Pupphārām Sect were even more jealous of the Nattārām [Rattārām] Sect.

190. Lord of earth, on his part, had people plant a coconut tree in front of the golden palace between [the latter and] the state office near the south wall of the palace, letting it be the testimony that, "As long as this coconut tree exists, bhikkhus of the two Sects shall not quarrel, shall not confront each other ever." So it was said.

191. This, the narrative of the first original chronicle of how the Forest Sect and the Garden Sect quarreled, argued, and disputed with each other in the old days, is here concluded as a chapter.

The New Year Festival's Frog

192. Here will be told about an ancient tradition handed down from then continuously through many reigns until the present time without a break.

193. At the time Prince Phāyū was the brayā of Nabbapurī Jenghmai, Uttara Brāhman, well-versed in the three vedas, by royal orders, headed the Saṅgha and four noblemen in bringing up Prince Cedbantū [1350-1367] to rule Möng Tuṅga Raṭṭhapurī in the year Koḍyī Sakkarāja 702.[143] In Month Two [the prince] came and stayed at Jengkāng at Vat Prakāng there. Came Month Five waxing 12th night, it was recorded that Hmün Ghamyai led all the people to elevate Prince Cedbantū to the throne. [60] His reign lasted sixteen years. His age was twenty-six years [when he] was gored to death by an elephant in the middle of Kāḍ-tung. [He] had a son named Srī Ratanabandhu who succeeded in the year Kaḍrau Sakkarāja 732. [Ratanabandhu] had four children including one girl--one named Dāu Āy, one named Jāy Kaeumadhu, one named Prince Kôngpun, a girl named Kaeubunjū.

194. Later, after Brayā Kaeumadhu had succeeded, came the year Tausī, Sakkarāja 754, and there was great drought in the land that year; the rain did not fall. Brayā Kaeumadhu then asked the astrologer Uttara Brāhman saying thus, "What is wrong with the state that the rain does not fall?" The astrologer said thus, "This state belongs to the Monday nām; we should fashion an image of Rāhū the frog holding the moon in its mouth and build a sand cetiya covering it on the day the Saṅgkhān departs[144] and a force of soldiers, elephants, horses, and sword-and-shield dancers to pay homage [to it] on the bank of the Khün river."

195. At that time, when the departure day of the Saṅgkhān arrived, all high officials, with Brayā Kaeumadhu leading, proceeded with forces to do as directed by the astrologer, and then invited four bhikkhus of Vat Cômdông to recite Buddhavaṁsa Sutta[145] there. At that moment the sky roared and so much rain fell that the lords had to run away from the rain to the shelter of Khō-mung [covered or roofed bridge]. Because of the power of the Three Gems, the astrologer fashioned an image of the frog devouring the moon, rain poured down so much cooling the land every year. At that moment, Brayā Kaeumadhu proclaimed, "This place is the excellent Earth of Victory, which would be a place of worship for all people in time to come without a doubt." So saying he established the tradition for the land which has lasted until this present time.

196. Krīyā saṅvaṇṇanā--the narrative unfolding [61] the first chronicle of the origin of the Sāsanā, from the reign of Prince Ceḍbantū who came to rule, in succession, until the reign of Brayā Kaeumadhu, the grandson, is here completed in appropriate time.

197. Written in the year Koḍsaṅā Sakka[-rāja] attained 1232, completed at midday. Written in Month Three waning 7th night.[146]

Document I

198. In the year when the zodiac is inclining towards this month, that is, year Koḍcai Cuḷa Sakkarāja 1202, Month Nine waxing 11th night, Saturday, Daiy Daplau, our person [I] the great grūbā of Jengyün and the old svādittā of Vat Jeng-ing, having seen the legitimate way and the illegitimate way in which high officials assign conscripted labor to the subjects of the great Lord of Vat P̱āḍaeng, are apprehensive that it would be a sin, a crime for the high officials and royalty, because these Sanjüm[147] subjects of the Lord have been the occasion of libation water to commemorate the dāna which lords of the two sides[148] have offered to the great Lord of Vat P̱āḍaeng since the former reigns of royal ancestors. It is not legitimate for high officials and royalty to assign conscripted labor indiscriminately to this group of subjects of the Lord --[offenders] will become demons at death.

199. Having compassion on high officials, lest they would commit a sin, a crime and become demons at death, our person [I] the great grūbā of Jengyün therefore exhorted the old svādittā of Vat [62] Jeng-ing to go [with me] and offer the excellent mettā at the palace where there were the great somḍec mahārāja at the head of mahāyuvarāja, the excellent lord Prince

Möngkhôn, and uparāja, the great Brayā Kāng, the two [latter] having gone for an audience with the great somḍec mahārāja who was suffering from the illness, carbuncle on the back.

200. We two lords begged to offer excellent mettā to the somḍec mahārāja and mahāyuvarāja the excellent lord Prince Möngkhôn and uparāja the great Brayā Kāng [as follows]: "It is not good for the future to assign conscripted labor indiscriminately to this group of subjects of the Lord because they have been the occasion for libation water commemorating the dāna which lords of the two sides have offered to Vat P̱āḍaeng. It is not appropriate to make them contribute to the beg-pardon silver[149] for support of the state and for the distribution of silver and gold pedestal trays to the great monarch of the golden realm of Ava; it is not appropriate for high officials to enjoy [the dues]; it is not allowed."

201. The somḍec mahārāja thereupon asked the excellent lord Prince Möngkhôn, saying, "The two grūbās having come to mettā thus, what have the two royal uncles to say?"

202. Uparāja the great Brayā Kāng and mahāyuvarāja the excellent lord Prince Möngkhôn begged to offer reverence to the somḍec mahārāja, saying, "They are truly subjects of libation water to commemorate the dāna by our royal ancestors to the great Lord of P̱āḍaeng. But as regards what is appropriate and what is not, we beg to reverence the two lord grūbās [to advise us] how it would not be a sin, a crime to royalty and high officials in the future, [63] [so that they] would not become ghosts and demons, would not commit a sin, a crime. We beg the two lord grūbās to mettā so that it would become a tradition, a duty, for the state."

203. The great grūbās--the two saṅkārīs--offered excellent mettā, saying, "We two will allow this group of subjects of the Lord to support the royal treasury of lord of earth for twelve months: during Month Seven, Month Eight, let them come and pay three viss of silver, of fineness 'nammon khāuhnām hnāyōy',[150] without shortage, fifty within the state, two viss fifty without the state,[151] because they obtain livelihood out of the water and ground of lord of earth. Whenever there is carrying to be done in support of the state, let them carry twenty-five pole-loads. Work within the capital we also allow--whatever others do, so let them do. Should war fall within the state, we also allow them along with others to fight, to cut. Should there be wars outside the state, we do not allow them to go.

204. "The journey stages for carrying pole-loads: in the west, to reach Dongdā; in the north, as far as Möngḥlōy; in the east, to reach Möngmlā; in the south, as far as Möngbrayāk. To go beyond this is not allowed.

205. "The collection of beg-pardon silver to support the state and for the distribution of silver and gold pedestal trays at the golden city of Ava, is not allowed. Collection of dues on houses, of dues on male and female youths, of lists of married couples, from this group of subjects of the Lord, is not allowed also. To use royal orders to collect fees for the feet and the royal orders, is also not allowed. To feed [officials, etc., from the capital] with meals, [64] eatables, duck, chicken, even one egg, is not allowed. The conscription of beg-pardon dues of three viss is also not allowed to exist.

206. "Should the monastery of the Sāsanā at P̲āḍaeng fall into disrepair, let this group of subjects of the Lord do the repairs, stop the leaks, sweep the sand, pull the grass. When royalty and high officials are going to construct buildings at P̲āḍaeng, let subjects of the Lord tidy and clear the sites. If constructions are not undertaken by lord of earth, but subjects of the Lord are made to do them, if three viss are spent, exempt [them from paying the tribute of the three viss of silver] for one year; if six viss spent, exempt for two years; if nine viss spent, exempt for three years, and so on according to that scale.

207. "We two lords have offered mettā thus to the great somḍec mahārāja, heading the mahāyuvarāja and the great uparāja Möngkāng so that it would be an immemorial and recorded custom for the state. Let no members of the royal family who should succeed to the state in the future transgress our words of the Dhamma-mettā, then only would they prosper and be blessed with happiness. Subjects of the Lord, too, must definitely act according to the words of our Dhamma-mettā, then only all would be well. The grūbās and the Saṅgha of the Internal Side who will come into being in the future must also mettā according to the immemorial and recorded custom which we have just spoken--let there be no work in excess of what subjects of the lords have to do for the Internal Side. Let the dāna of oil, charcoal, and brooms be offered in the same manner as whilst our person is the grūbā.

208. "For any lord to tell subjects of the Lord and ask to chew betel which costs cowries and silver, is also not [65] allowed. To wreck the words of our Dhamma-mettā is also not allowed. Let [the Saṅgha] look after subjects of the Lord, then only would they prosper and be blessed with happiness." Mettā for information.

Document II

209. Paramamaṅgala sārakathā pāmodyābhiramma varamettā [Greetings to the one who is exceedingly auspicious, the one who speaks only the essential, and the one whose mettā is excellent]. The Ājñādham Bracau[152] Somḍec Atiseṭṭha Bra Vara Aggarājaguru, the lord who is the perfect head of the Saṅgha sends pervading mettā [as follows]: Whatever former obligations established by grūbās and senior bhikkhus of the past in their excellent Dhamma-mettā, we have followed faithfully those usages of the ancient somḍec rājagurumolī lords.

210. As for the authoritative state boundaries of Möng Küy, wherever they may reach, lord of earth has established and demarcated them as firm, solid, and permanent commemoration of the dāna to Vat Mūla Siṅhaḷarattārāmādhipati, the great royal monastery of P̲āḍaeng, for the duration of the five thousand vassā.

211. All Sanjüms who are subjects of alms bowls and libation water, while they reside in that place, Möng Küy, let them know nothing about the twelve kinds of labor, namely, rice dues, measures of horse fodder and reeds, construction of temporary structures and huts, carrying of pole-loads by journey stages, collection of monetary dues--it is not allowed, with the exception of affairs of elephants and wars which have arrived in [66] the state, and the construction of military fortresses and city walls, from which they are not exempted.

212. In future, should any succeeding official and noble take them out to pay dues and do labors, let that person be ruined and destroyed, let the state not be prosperous. Whichever lord of earth follows, does not destroy or abandon, the ancient customs, may that lord of earth grow and prosper with long life, beautiful complexion, happiness, strength, intelligence, freedom from illnesses, kingly supremacy, and be totally accomplished in overflowing wealth, vast celestial fortune, accompanied by power, magical might and glory in every way, in accordance with the excellent blessings we have set up in this pervading mettā.

Document III

213. Akkhara savaniya sāramaṅgalakathā varamettā [Greetings to the one whose words are memorable, whose speech is to the point and auspicious and whose mettā is excellent]. The great mahāguru grūbā, lord saṅkārī, who is Saṅgha parināyaka, head of the excellent assemblage of the Saṅgha, saṅgharājā, svāmī, senior and junior theras, hereby proclaims a specially solemn Dhamma-mettā for the information of all sentient beings and lay persons.

214. From the year Kaḍrau Cuḷa Sakkarāja 1211, onwards, all persons who are Burmans, Mȏns, Shans, Yōns, Khüns, Yāngs, Lüs, Laems, Northern Shans, Chinese, Las, Dȏys, serfs of lords, men, and noblemen, whosoever, are forbidden to disturb, [67] chop, or cut timber and firewood in this forest of Möng Küy, because lord of earth had demarcated and offered it as dāna to the lord of Vat Mahārājaṭhān Ṗāḍaeng from the time of former successive khattiya royalty [ruling princes] for the duration of the five thousand vassā of the Sāsanā.

215. For that reason any person whom we the Saṅgha have forbidden with this mettā of injunction, who would not listen but would come and disturb and cut timber and firewood in this forest of Möng Küy, when dead would become demons and ghosts, and after remaining in that state [for a period] would later go to hell for the duration of one hundred thousand aeons.

216. Furthermore, for the present world, should we the Saṅgha come to know that this person or that person has come and taken timber and firewood in this forest of Möng Küy, it would be a great crime.[153] Mettā for information.

217. All Sanjüms, the forest keepers themselves, are not to disturb or to cut [timber and firewood] for sale. Even to cut trees for rai cultivation,[154] they [the Sanjüms] should look for suitable places for cultivation, for cutting; otherwise it would also be a great crime.

Document IV

218. Imasmiṁ rājasīmā vibhāgaraṭṭhadinnā buddhañ ca dhammañ ca saṅghañ ca parikkhepenakkhette samantācakkaparimaṇḍalaṁḷapitaṁ yāvapañcavassasahassāni upatthambhako jotika buddhasāsanaṁ siṁhaḷarattārāmādhipati [Here in this (region) the royal boundary is given in the division of the kingdom, in the neighboring land, to the Three Gems. This district is offered for the five thousand years by the supporter of the Sāsanā of Lord Buddha (and the monastery of) Siṁhaḷarattārāmādhipati].

219. Now, the year Kaḍrau Cuḷa Sakkarāja 1211, Month Seven full moon, Sunday, Daiy Taucai, [68] nakkhatta rökfā [contellation] is Anurādhā 17,[155] antarabāhira [inside and outside] the two parties, Internal and External: the Internal consisted of mahāguru the great grūbā, lord saṅkārī, who is the perfect head of the Sangha, residing at Titthārāmādhipati Vat Jengyün, at the head of the excellent Sangha Party, sangharājā, svāmīs, senior and junior theras, all the lords; the External consisted of the Somḍec Seṭṭha Paramapôbitra,[156] the excellent lord of earth, who is known by the special title of Khemāraṭṭhamahāsīha Pavarasudhammarājā Bhummindanarindādhipati,[157] [the two parties] have come together to assemble in unity and harmony in order to make a firm agreement to be kept with the great monastery of Möngküy, to endure, firm and solid, throughout the five thousand vassā.

220. According to the boundaries demarcated and offered as dāna to the Great Lord of Vat Mūla Rājaṭhān of Pāḍaeng by ancient Khattiya royalty of old, for the benefits of the Sāsanā of all Rattārām Sect, the Sanjüms are to preserve Möngküy [territory that receives] all the water that drips into it as follows: from the main road to Kiusāi, thence to Hrohnôngpük, to the Precipice of Mailôhô, to the fence of Dang-gvāi, going down to Hronā of Bāncöng, ascending to Hrōyhlōng, to the Rock of Jāngnôn, and then ascending to Dôy Bengsum, up to Kiu Hlāgān, to Cukbengvaen, rising to Kui Pājhānglōng, ascending to the Precipice of Pāpaek, following the ridge and up until the small Boḍhi tree of Mônlān, to Hronông Bengseau, along the ridge ascending to Yāngkeng in the middle of the hill, up to Hrinkông Kāngkiu, ascending to Hmākhrin Rūpmlā, ascending to the summit of Jôphāhrak, descending to Kiulōng at Bōktātaek, along the ridge descending to Hrinkông Hālūk, down to Hrinkông Pāngcaeng, down to Vat Sanat; down to the road to Ghrākāṣ, again descending [69] along the road to Kiu Sālā Brabāḍ, downwards to Hrinkông Hrōhrōy, to Khutkhumthāng, to Hrōhrōy Udenhnông, along the road to Hrinkôngsut, to Hmākhrintūp, to Hrin Āpāk to Cumpōk Dhātu, to the road to Tham-aen, downwards to Hrōy Vangkheu, descending to Hrohnông Bāndum, crossing over to Tonmōng Jāngtāi, emerging at the main road at Kiusāi.

221. [These are] Dhamma-mettā of the Mahāsangha and royal orders of lord of earth given to Möngküy. Whoever comes and disturbs the jungle, the forest of Möngküy commits a great crime. For all to know; with loving kindness and compassion.

222. [Added to the text in a different hand] Here will be recorded headmen of the Sanjüms: Möngküy has Bô Hong, Pāngfāk headman is Nāy Num, Hôpong headman is Nāy Ghamhöng, Hmākhrinlāp headman is Kaejhaeng, The Sanjüms outside Möng[küy] have Hmün Jai. Kaesaeng is the head of all headmen.

Notes

1. Paṇidhānato, etc. This Pali passage comes from the introduction to the Ratana Sutta which consists of twelve beautiful stanzas of Pali verse in praise of the Three Gems, and this was how it came to be recited.

   Vesāli (modern village of Basrah in Muzzufferpur District of Uttar Pradesh, India), capital of the Licchavis, was afflicted by evil spirits, diseases, and famine resulting in death and despair, and the Licchavi princes decided to invite the Buddha to come and purge the city of the three pestilences. This was the fifth year after the Enlightenment. The Buddha came from Rājagaha and was met on the northern bank of the Ganges by the Licchavi princes. The moment the Buddha set foot on the ground a severe storm came up and there was a heavy fall of rain which washed all the corpses into the river and the city was thus cleansed. In the evening the Buddha stood at the gate of Vesāli and taught the Ratana Sutta to Ānanda Thera. Ānanda received the sutta from the lips of the Master together with the alms bowl containing holy water and went to the city gate with the Licchavi princes. Standing there he meditated on all the merits of the Buddha as stated in the Pali passage in the text. Having done so Ānanda Thera entered the city and during the three watches of the night went about within its three walls reciting the Ratana Sutta and sprinkling holy water from the Buddha's alms bowl.

   The considerations referred to in the Pali passage, the Five Great Sacrifices (pañca mahāpariccāge), are possessions, children, wife, parts of the body, and life. The Three Meritorious Acts (tisso cariyā) are in behalf of the world, in behalf of his kinsmen, and for the sake of the Enlightenment. The Nine Supramundane Conditions (nava lokuttaradhamme) are the Four Paths (sotāpatti-magga, sakadāgāmi-magga, anāgāmi-magga, arahatta-magga), the Four Fruits (sotāpatti-phala, sakadāgāmi-phala, anāgāmi-phala, arahatta-phala), and Nibbāna.

   The full story of this episode is in the Commentary on the Dhammapada, verse 290 (Burlingame 1969:168-76).

2. Cintitaṁ, etc. The full story of how the Buddha carried his mother across the ocean and made his first Mental Resolve to Englightenment, is given in JKM:3.

3. 446,027. The actual total number of Buddhas in this paragraph is 956,027.

4. Bhadda kappa. There are two kinds of kappas: Suñña kappa in which no Buddha is born, and Asuñña kappa in which Buddhas are born. Asuñña kappa is of five kinds: (1) Sāra kappa in which one Buddha is born; (2) Maṇḍa kappa in which two Buddhas are born; (3) Vara kappa in which three Buddhas are born; (4) Sāramaṇḍa kappa in which four Buddhas are born; (5) Bhadda kappa in which five Buddhas are born. The present is Bhadda kappa, and four Buddhas have already been born, viz., Kakusandha, Koṇāgamana, Kassapa, and Gotama. The fifth Buddha, Metteyya, will be born at some future date, and at the end of his Sāsanā the world will be destroyed by fire.

5. Went forth. To go forth means to leave home and worldly life and take up the life of a bhikkhu. The Khün word in the text is "ôk pōd," as in Thai "ôk puat," from Pali "pabbajita" or "pabbajjā." A sāmaṇera, or novice, receives pabbajjā, or first stage, ordination, which is essential before he can be given, at the completion of the age of twenty, the upasampadā, or higher, ordination of bhikkhuhood.

6. Vassā. This is from the Pali word "vassa" meaning "rain" or "rainy season," but, like a few other Pali words that have become part of Khün vocabulary, the vowel of the last syllable has been lengthened to read vassā. The monsoon regions include northeastern India, where the Buddha was born and Buddhism was established. There the rainy season lasts four months, from June/July to October. In the Buddha's time this was the period when traveling was not easy, with clouds and rain above and mud, slush, and floods below. Sometimes bhikkhus fell ill or while traveling trampled on people's crops and teeming small creatures during the rains. When complaints reached the Buddha, he laid down the rule that all bhikkhus must stay in one place during a three-month rainy period or vassā. This could begin from the full moon of June/July (until the full moon of September/October) or it could begin with the following full moon. In modern times, however, it is the unanimous practice in all Theravāda countries to commence the vassā on the full moon in July and to end it on the full moon in October. The ending of the vassā is called Pavāraṇā. During the vassā no bhikkhu may leave his monastery except by permission on grounds of compassion, or monastic and Sāsanā affairs. The seniority of a bhikkhu is counted by the number of vassā he has been through. The Sāsanā is also reckoned in

vassā, which is sometimes wrongly identified with years. The vassā is fully explained in the Vinaya Piṭaka (chapter 3 of Mahāvagga).

7. Möng. This is how the word is pronounced in Khün at present and within living memory. It can be transliterated as "Meüng," rendering it somewhat like the Thai "Muang" in pronunciation. The word, in all dialects of the Tai language group, means kingdom, continent, country, town, city, capital, or province.

8. Thera. This word, in Khün, is pronounced "then," but alphabetically transcribed it would be "thayar," which would be an unusual way of rendering the word "thera." The meaning and significance of "thera" are so well known in all Theravāda Buddhist countries and India that it is not necessary to translate it as "elder" as many scholars do. "Elder" retranslated into Burmese or Thai languages would mean "aged person," "old man," etc. Whenever the word "then" occurs in the text, it is rendered as "thera."

   A thera is a senior bhikkhu those standing is at least ten vassā old. Sometimes it is a title conferred upon a bhikkhu by the local populace or authorities. The next higher title is mahāthera. Sometimes the word "mahā" is added by courtesy. An arahantā (arahat) of old was always called "thera."

9. Saṅgāyanā. "Saṅgāyanā" has also been appropriated into the vernacular vocabularies of Burma and Thailand. See the introduction for a brief description of various Saṅgāyanās.

10. Brayā. Transcribed as written in the text. Its modern pronunciation is "phya" or "phaya." In the dialects of the Tai language group east of the Salween, from Mönglaem down through Jenghung, Kengtung, Laos, and all of present-day Thailand, the word "brayā" in ancient literature means king or monarch.

11. 288. The year of the dispatch of Buddhist "missionaries" after the Third Saṅgāyanā is placed at 235-236 after the Parinibbāna. See note 13 in the introduction.

12. Sāsanā. Again, in incorporating the Pali word "Sāsana" into its vocabulary, the Khün dialect, along with Thai and Burmese, has the final vowel lengthened. This word has been variously translated as "Message," "Teaching," "the Doctrine of the Buddha," or "Dispensations." In Southeast Asian traditions, "Sāsanā" means the five thousand vassā after the Buddha's Parinibbāna during which the teaching of Gotama Buddha will endure. Why five thousand? An ancient Indian era has reached such a huge number that it must be divided by five thousand to make it easy to remember, and the Buddha Sāsanā of five thousand

years follows this custom (YC:109-111). The Sāsanā is reckoned in vassā. At the end of the vassā on the full moon of October 1976, the 2520th vassā of the Sāsanā for Burma and Ceylon was completed; it was the 2519th for the Thais.

13. Laṅkādhvīp (Laṅkādīpa, Ceylon). By tradition the dispatch of the missions to disseminate the Sāsanā was done at the instance of the president of the Third Saṅgāyanā, Moggalliputta Tissa Thera, soon after the big event itself. There were nine missions including that of Mahinda to Ceylon, which took place in BS 236 (JKM:64). The date of the Third Saṅgāyanā is variously placed at BS 234 (JKM:62), BS 235 (MV:lix), and BS 236 (*Hmannan Mahāyāzawindawgyi* [HM], p. 158). So the missions must have been dispatched within, or soon after, one year of the Saṅgāyanā. It is interesting to note that northern Thailand (Mö̇ng Yōn) is identified with the Yonakalōk, and Pagan (Būkam) with Palanti. The MV gives the account of the missions on page 82.

14. Bandharaṭṭha. Martaban, opposite Moulmein, at the mouth of the Salween, Burma.

15. Jumbūdhvīp. From the Pali "Jambudīpa" (country or continent of the rose apples [*Eugenia jambolana*]), India. This is a rare instance in which Southeast Asia is given the name usually reserved for or identified with India.

16. Upajjhāya. Usually translated into English as "preceptor." I am keeping the term "upajjhāya," as it is well known throughout Theravāda countries. A bhikkhu or sāmaṇera must have an upajjhāya for his ordination.

17. Act of the Saṅgha. Saṅghakamma is an act or ceremony performed by a quorum of the Saṅgha in the uposatha hall. In such an act, a ñatti, or motion, is put to the Saṅgha assembly which is asked three times to accept or reject it. There are many kinds of such acts for appropriate occasions, e.g., upasampadākamma, whereby a bhikkhu is ordained; uposathakamma, which approves the recitation of the Pāṭimokkha; parivāsakamma, which puts bhikkhus on probation; tajjaniyakamma (censure); pavāraṇākamma (vassā-ending ceremony); pabbājaniyakamma (banishment); and so on. The *Pali-English Dictionary* (PED) mentions eleven kammas on page 190, column 2.

18. Upasampadā ordination. Ordination of a bhikkhu. This is different from the pabbajjā, or first stage, ordination of the sāmaṇera (novice). Before a man can become a bhikkhu he must first receive the pabbajjā ordination before the upasampadā ordination is given. A sāmaṇera, when he has reached the age

of twenty can take the upasampadā ordination straight away. See also note 5.

19. The head of Labūn City. In the Khü̈n, Shan, and Chiengmai dialects, head of a city is the "beginning" of a city, i.e., the main thoroughfare within its walls. If the thoroughfare is in the southern part of the walls, that direction would be the "head" of the city, as in the case of Kengtung where the ruler's palace also faces south.

    Hōveng is the head of the "veng" (city), as opposed to Hāngveng or Lāveng ("hāng" and "lā" mean tail end).

20. Mö̈ng Caem. Probably modern Bān Maecaem, on the river Maecaen south of Chiengmai.

21. Sōndôkg̲ham. "Sōn" (garden), "dôk" (flowers), "g̲ham" (gold), or garden of golden flowers; "g̲ham" also has the meaning of beautiful, wonderful, excellent, etc. It is from here that the Khü̈n word "bāy sōn" originated, and I have translated this "bāy sōn" as the "Garden Sect" of the Saṅgha of Kengtung. There is still a Vat Sōndôk in Chiengmai.

22. Dāna. Meritorious offering(s) to the Three Gems or others with the object of obtaining meritorious kamma in the coming rebirths.

23. The four necessities. From "catupaccaya," the four necessities for a bhikkhu, namely, the (three) robes, alms food, a dwelling place, and medicines.

24. Khemaraṭṭha. The classical name of Kengtung is Khemaraṭṭha Tuṅgapurī: "khema" (serene, calm, tranquil), "raṭṭha" (country, state, kingdom), "tuṅga" (high, prominent), "purī" (city, capital, fortress).

25. P̲ādôkbō. Grove of the Lotus. Vat Sōndôkg̲ham is meant (see par. 20). Variations of the same name are a common phenomenon in the text, as the reader will realize as he reads on, which is confusing for one not familiar with its style and language.

26. Kaeubantā. This king, Kaeubantā, of Chiengmai seems to be the same person as Sāmf̲angkaen who succeeded Saenmuangmā and ruled from 1411 to 1442 (YC).

27. Nine million. This weight of nine lān, or million, is calculated this way:

    1 ban equals .75 viss
    1 hmü̈n equals 7.5 viss
    1 saen equals 75 viss

1 lān equals 750 viss
9 lān equal 6,750 viss

As one viss equals 3.6 pounds, then nine lān are 24,300 pounds or 12.15 tons.

28. Uposatha hall. Called "rōng pōsoḍ" in Khün, a hall for upasampadā ordination, Pāṭimokkha, and other ceremonies. Sometimes it is translated into English as "chapter house." Anything connected with the mundane world, such a house, should not be within a monastery compound, hence the impropriety of the translation of "chapter house." See also "sīmā," note 31.

29. Lānnā. "Lānnā" means one million rice fields, and it is the designation of the old kingdom of Chiengmai. In Khün and Chiengmai (Tai-Yuan) scripts the word carries the meaning of one million rice fields. A change in the tone for "lān" in the Central Thai dialect gives the meaning of a vast stretch of rice fields to the word, and this is the meaning now taken by Central Thais. "Dāu Lānnā" means the king of Lānnā. Laos has been known to Kengtung as "Lānjāng," (the land of) one million elephants.

30. Kaṭhina. Kaṭhina robes are offered to bhikkhus during the month following the end of the vassā (Pavāraṇā). Since the Pavāraṇā is on the full moon of October, kaṭhina ceremonies take place around the full moon of November. When such a ceremony is held, the season for the acceptance of robes by a bhikkhu is from the full moon of October to the full moon of March, the remaining seven months being the wrong season. If no kaṭhina ceremony is held the "robes season" lasts only one month, from the full moon of October to the following full moon in November.

Among the 227 rules for a bhikkhu, a whole section of 30 rules, called Nissaggiya-Pācittiya, is devoted to the robes and related matters. Details about kaṭhina robes can be had in full in chapter 7 (on kaṭhina) of the Mahāvagga in the Khandaka division of the Vinaya Piṭaka.

The "spread of kaṭhina robes" is often used to describe the dāna of the robes. The word "spread" comes from Pali "atthāra" in chapter 7 of the Mahāvagga, mentioned above. It is used, not literally, but in a technical sense, in that the cloth is spread out in the process of being stitched.

In the Mahākaṭhina the yarn is spun, the cloth woven and stitched into robes and dyed all in one day. In Burma this is still practiced at the kaṭhina dāna of the Great Shwedagon Pagoda every year; in Burmese this is called "Matho-thingan."

31. Sīmā. The word literally means "boundary" or "limit." In the Theravāda Buddhist context it is the boundary formed by the eight or sixteen (see par. 86) stones around the uposatha hall (see note 28). Often the word "sīmā" is taken to mean the uposatha hall itself. There are rules and ceremonies as to how the sīmā stones are to be planted. There is a superstition that while rites are being performed by the Saṅgha in the hall, no shadow of a female must fall on any sīmā stone, or else the rites are invalid.

32. Ñatticatutthakammavācā. "Ñatti" is the announcement of a motion put before an assembly of the Saṅgha; "kamma" is the proceedings or ceremony performed by a lawfully constituted chapter of bhikkhus, often translated as "formal act"; and "vācā" is text or word. If the ñatti is put once it is ñattidutiyakamma; if the ñatti is put three times it is ñatticatutthakamma. If the assembly remains silent at the end of the ñatti, first or third intonation as the case may be, the motion is carried. "Kammavācā" is the text of the Saṅgha kamma or formal act.

33. Month One. Called "Dӧnceng" in Khün. It is Month Twelve in Bangkok and in the Shan States west of the Salween; but in Chiengmai it is Month Two. It is during this month that kaṭhina robes are offered to the monasteries, especially on the full moon, which occurs sometimes in November.

34. Mettā. The usual meaning of "mettā," loving kindness, is well known to people familiar with Buddhism; but in the parlance of the Saṅgha in Kengtung the word is often used as a verb, as in this case. It would be awkward to translate it as "spoke with loving kindness to the lord of earth." Where the original text warrants it, I will use the word "mettā" as a verb, meaning say, speak, or tell.

35. Lord of earth. This has been the literal translation of the word "cauphaenḍin" for many centuries past. According to page 25 of the TMP, the term originated when there was an earthquake on the occasion of the completion of the construction of Vat P̱āḍaeng when libation water was poured by Brayā Srīsudhamma Cuḷāmaṇī, the ruler. It is more likely the term was derived from the Pali "paṭhavīssara" (spelled "pathavīsara" in the text). Lü, Laem, Chiengmai, and Central Thai dialects use the same term to refer to kings and rulers.

36. Somḍec. This is a very exalted title used in Kengtung for the ruling prince and the highest and most senior bhikkhu. In Thailand it is part of the king's title, and sometimes it is conferred by him upon senior princes or highest ranking officials or bhikkhus. Its origin is believed to have been

Cambodian, meaning majesty, great one, supreme, excellent, eminent, etc.

37. Rohajanapada Mahāraṭṭha. Rohaṇa is the south and southeastern part of Ceylon, with its capital at Mahāgāma. The name in the text is somewhat confused.

38. Mahābodhi. The Mahābodhi or Bodhi tree (*Ficus religiosa*) is the tree under which the Buddha sat in meditation and attained the Enlightenment.

39. Spoke. The Khün word used here is "hvai," which means literally "to reverence" (act of putting two hands together, etc.) or "make obeisance." "Hvai" and "hvaisā" have the same meaning. When used by a layman in addressing a bhikkhu, or by a commoner in addressing a prince, the word also means "tell," "speak," or "report." There are many such instances in the text. In such a context the word can mean "respectfully beg to state."

40. For "Ñatticatutthakammavācā," see note 32.

"Vinayagaṇṭhī" (or "vinayagandhi") is a "tīkā" (explanation) of difficult passages in the Vinaya commentaries by Mahāvajirabuddhi Thera of Ceylon. It is also called "vajirabuddhitīkā" (*Dictionary of Pali Proper Names* [PPN]).

"Sīlakkhandha Jāṭaka" (? Jātitka): pertaining to the sīla section.

41. I am grateful to Professor Madhav Deshpande of the Department of Linguistics, The University of Michigan, for his patience and help in clarifying the Pali words and grammatical rules in paragraphs 44 to 51. It surprises him to see how the rules were accurately quoted purportedly 550 years ago by the Theravāda Order of the Saṅgha in defense of orthodoxy of their Nikāya. Professor Deshpande remarks that, although the passage as it stands has its own obscurities, the main lines of argument are quite clear.

The Pali words in the dispute between the Garden and Forest sects concern recitation formulae in the pabbajjā and upasampadā ordinations, such as: (1) taking refuge in the Three Gems ("Buddhaṁ saranaṁ gacchami," etc.); (2) recitation of the four necessities of a bhikkhu, namely, the robes, food, shelter, and medicine, each of which begins with the words, "Paṭisaṅkhā yoniso...,"; and (3) recitation of the kammavācā during the upasampadā ordination in the uposatha hall which always begins with the words, "Suṇātu me bhante saṅgho...." In (1), the Garden Sect would add "ara" to the syllable before the cerebral *ṇ* and recite "Buddhāṁ sara-ara-ṇaṁ gacchāmi"; in (2) there are, according to the text, grammatical errors in their recitation; and in (3) they would say "Su-ara-ṇatu me bhante saṅgho." This was still the practice in Kengtung in the 1930s. To refute these inaccuracies, the Forest Sect quoted the rules in the Kaccāyana Grammar Treatise, putting the words in the mouth of Ceylon Theravāda authorities as stated in the text.

The grammar treatise in question is the *Kaccāyana-Vyākaraṇa* (KV), which by tradition is ascribed to Mahā Kaccāyana Thera, an arahat during the lifetime of the Buddha. Kaccāyana was the son of the chief brahman of King Caṇḍapajjota of Avanti (capital of Ujjeni). After he had succeeded his father, the king sent him to invite the Buddha to visit Ujjeni. The Buddha ordained him and, having attained arahatship, he returned to Ujjeni as the Master's representative in order to establish the Sāsanā there. He was reputed to be a brilliant grammarian and to have founded the famous school for grammarians at Avanti. Most probably the KV was a compilation which traced its origin to this school of grammarians (PPN).

The recitation on the four necessities of a bhikkhu or sāmaṇera shows the ascetic nature of the Theravāda monastic life:

> Reflecting carefully I wear the robes for the purpose only of warding off the cold, the heat, the contact with gadflies and mosquitoes, of wind and sun, and snakes, and for covering the body for decency.
>
> Reflecting carefully I eat the alms food, not for sport or sensual enjoyment, not for adornment or beautification, but solely to sustain the body in life, to keep it unharmed, to aid in the practice of the holy life; thus I may dispel the old pain and shall incur no new; and everywhere shall I be without discomfort and free from blame.
>
> Reflecting carefully I make use of a shelter for the purpose only to ward off cold, heat, the contact of gadflies and mosquitoes, or wind and sun, and snakes; only to avoid the dangers of the climate and to obtain privacy for mental development.
>
> Reflecting carefully I make use of medicines only to remove sickness and painful feelings that have arisen and only to preserve my health.

What follows is Professor Deshpande's elucidation of the Pali words and KV rules in paragraphs 44-51.

Par. 44: dvandva-samāsa (dvandva compound), a compound xy where the meanings of x and y are both prominent and are simply added together, e.g., "John and Tom."

Nāmānaṁ samuccayo dvandvo. This is rule 331 of the KV, defining the dvandva compound.

"Vibhatti" is case ending. As a rule, a compound word takes only one case ending, and the member words do not take case endings separately.

Par. 45: Purasamupaparīhi karotissa khakhara vā tappaccayesu ca, KV:596.

Kaga cajanam, KV:625.

Yathāgamamikāro, KV:607.

Tuṁtūnatabbesu vā, KV:622.

Par. 46: Sabbanāma (pronoun).

Par. 47: Makārānta (ending in *m*).

"Uccāravidhī" seems to be a reference to a Pali text on pronunciation. This text is not listed by Otto Franke in his *Pāli Grammatik und Lexicographie* (1902).

Pali "saraṇam," in this context, actually corresponds to Sanskrit "śaraṇam," and is not historically connected with Sanskrit "smaraṇam," or Pali "saraṇam" (to remember).

Nandādīhi yu (KV:549): "After the verbs nand, etc., the affix yu (equals ana) is added in the sense of action or object." This rule does not proscribe the affix "yu" in the sense of "kattar" (agent) as claimed by the text.

Anakā yuṇvūnam (KV:624): "The affixes yu and ṇvu are replaced by ana and aka."

Rahādito no ṇa (KV:551): "After verbs ending in *r* or *h*, the sound *n* of ana is changed to *ṇ*."

Naye paraṁ yutte (KV:11): "A consonant without a vowel, if connected with the following syllable becomes a part of the following syllable" ("sar" plus "ana" equals "saraṇa").

"Si" is the accusative affix.

Siṁ (KV:219): "The affix si after neuter nouns ending in *a* is always changed to aṁ."

Pubbamadhoṭhitamassaraṁ sarena riyojaye, KV:10.

Visesana (attribute, adjective); the meaning of "parāmi" is unclear (? preceding).

Visesaya, substantive (qualified).

Pacchāma, unclear meaning (? following).

Par. 48: One could conceivably think of the root "suṇa" in the verb "suṇātu," but the expression "atthisuṇa" is unclear.

Svādito ṇuṇāuṇā ca, KV:450.

Hiyattanī (past tense), ekamhi (singular).

Kvacādimajjhuttarānaṁ dīgharassā paccayesu ca, KV:405.

Par. 49: Ghosa-vaṇṇa (voiced consonants), aghosa-vaṇṇa (unvoiced consonants).

Par. 50: Kaccāyana lists the verb root "kham" as "khamU," with the letter *U* as a metalinguistic marker.

Sabbato ṇvutvāvī vā, KV:529.

The verb root "tud" is given as "tudA" with *A* as a metalinguistic marker.

Par. 51: "Adhivāsane" is a strange meaning for "tud" which normally means "to strike." "Adhivāsanā" means "assent," "forbearance," "endurance."

"Nudādīhi ṇi" is not found in Kaccāyana's grammar. What it means most probably is as follows: "Add the affix 'ṇī' after verbs 'nud', etc."

42. Daiy Tauyī. This is the cyclical name of the day. The names are identical with the year names, beginning with Kāpcai, Ḍapp̱au, etc. By naming the days thus, any day can be pinned down with certainty by one who knows the system.

43. Vā. A "vā" equals the length of the outstretched arms of a man; nowadays reckoned as six feet in Burma or two meters in Thailand.

44. Rōngrau, Sakkarāja 803. For the first time in the text the sakkarāja date and year name coincide. By comparing the year names and the sakkarāja date in the text and those in the "Chart of the Sixty Cyclical Year Names and Cuḷa Sakkarāja" (Fig. 3), the reader will know which are correct or nearest to the correct ones.

45. Rattabherī. This is Brayā Kông Ratanabheri who ruled Kengtung from 1416 to 1441 A.D. He was succeeded by his son, Prince Sām (1441-1456) who assumed the title of Srīsudhamma Cuḷāmaṇī at the coronation, and who is much involved in the "purification" of the Sāsanā as brought in by Ñāṇagambhīra of the "Forest Sect."

46. Cômmônpheḍ. This is one of the hillocks within the walls of Kengtung City: "côm" (summit), "môn" (hillock), and "pheḍ"

(demon or ghost). The origin of the word "pheḍ" is the Pali "peta."

47. The name of this ruler appears in our text in three different forms: Dhamma Cuḷāmaṇī (par. 67), Srīsudhamma Cuḷāmaṇī (pars. 73, 75, 79, 159), Srīsadhamma Cuḷāmaṇī (pars. 80, 82, 88, 103, 108, 117), the last of which is problematical. Since the *Jengtung State Chronicle* calls this king Srīsudhammacuḷāmaṇīrāja (par. 119), we may suppose that "Srīsadhamma" is in error, the scribe having forgotten to add the vowel stroke which changes inherent *-a* to *-u*. However, the Vat P̱āḍæng inscription, as published in JSS, has Śrī Saddhammarājacuḷāmaṇi (i.e., "sat" + "dhamma," rather than "su" + "dhamma"), which may be the original form of this king's name.

48. Sōndôk Jenglom. This monastery was one of the monasteries in Kengtung City. Note the prefix "Sōndôk" which denotes the tradition of Sōndôkg̱ham of Chiengmai (see note 21). "Sōndôk" means garden of flowers; hence, the "Garden Sect" in Kengtung.

49. Magic tree. Called "kārabük" tree in Khün (Burmese: "padethā" tree). It is an imitation tree made of bamboo with a square bamboo base for firm standing on the floor, and is about eight or nine feet high. About three feet from the floor a cylindrical frame (with a slight bulge in the middle) is fitted onto the main bamboo stem or "trunk" of the "tree." This frame is sparsely crisscrossed diagonally with bamboo laths, and its size is about three to four feet long by two and a half feet in diameter. On the lattices of the cylindrical frame are hung articles for dāna offering. In modern practice, the following would be tied on to the frame of the "tree": the eight articles of necessity (aṭṭhaparikkhāra, see note 57), a folding reed mat (six feet by two and a half feet), a rug or small carpet, a blanket, a pillow, a mattress (six feet by two and a half feet) stuffed with cotton one inch thick, a pestle and mortar (of wood), cooking utensils, a kerosene lamp, an alarm clock (possibly a Big Ben in the 1920s and 1930s), a water goblet, a glutinous rice steamer, a glass water jug, a mug, a teapot, teacup and saucer, one or two food plates (enameled or china), candles, cheroots, matchboxes, sugar, jaggery, tea leaves, etc. --in short, the modern idea of satisfying the four requisites (catupaccaya) of the bhikkhu, viz. robes, food, dwelling place, and medicine.

In Buddhist cosmology such "magic trees" existed on the North Island, the inhabitants of which would pluck from them whatever was wanted to keep life and soul together.

Sometimes "kārabük" in Khün is also written "kālabük." In Thai it is called "kalpabrük" (from the Sanskrit "kalpabṛkṣ"), corrupted into "kālabrü̈k," from which the Khün "kālabük" is derived. In Burmese it is "padethā-bin."

50. Hrōy-yen. A small vale outside the city of Kengtung, about half a mile from the city gate in the south, which during the British rule (and perhaps before) was the place where death sentences of condemned prisoners by hanging were carried out. Its present name is Hômḍa, often erroneously pronounced "Hômla."

51. Palm leaf fan. For the Saṅgha, the palm leaf fan is about eighteen to twenty inches across, and round in shape, with a handle, the end of which is looped like a conch shell. The handle is held by a bhikkhu so that the base of the loop rests on the floor and the round fan shields the holder from the head down. Recitations, etc., are done behind the fan on ceremonial occasions. These "fans" are never used for cooling during the hot weather.

52. Debbaḍā . . . Brahma. "Debbaḍā" is derived from "devatā." "Dāucātulōk" are the four Guardian devās or gods of the human world. "Sakka" is Inda, or Indra, king of all devās. "Brahma" means "the devās of the Brahma world."

53. Hrōy-pūn. Another small vale to the southwest of Kengtung City, at the foot of the hillock on whose summit stands a part of the city wall.

54. Sky split open. It seems this is a tornado!

55. Dônlōng Bridge. This bridge is over the Namkhün River to the north-northwest of Kengtung City. The Namkhün rises among the mountain ranges in the west, emerges into Kengtung valley in the west, flows north, and, after being joined by the Namlāp stream (which flows past the city walls in the east), leaves the valley in the north to join the Namhlōy River, a tributary of the great Mekhong.

56. Ratana Sutta. This is one of the Paritta (protection) Suttas. The Ratana Sutta was first recited at Vesāli, at the behest of Lord Buddha, by Ānanda Thera. See note 1.

57. Aṭṭhaparikkhāra. The eight necessities for a bhikkhu, viz., the three robes, the alms bowl, a razor, a needle, the girdle, and a water strainer.

58. The journey. The journey from Chiengsaen, on the Mekhong, to Kengtung City would take seven nights by easy stages.

59. Mö̈ng Pong. This is a well-known hot spring village about four miles south of the city of Kengtung, on the main route to Thailand.

60. Musical instruments. For some of the items, see paragraphs 17 and 74.

61. Great library. A monastery's library in Kengtung is known as "mondok," sometimes written as "ƀindok" or "vendok." This is where all palm leaf books are kept.

62. Yāng people. Two meanings can be attached to the term "Yāng people." (1) Many village names within the Kengtung valley are preceded by the word "Yāng" (which means an open field or space), like those in the text. In this case "jāuyāng" would be people from these villages. (2) Certain tribal peoples of Môn-Khmer stock are also called Yāngs and still populate the central parts of the Shan States. These are what the census authorities write as "Riangs." Since the Riangs (or Yāngs, as Shans call them) are supposed to be the original inhabitants of the Shan States, it is more than possible that the Yāngs in the text were such people and that many derived their names from them originally in the Kengtung valley. The Yāngs in paragraph 83 are definitely Riangs.

63. Vihāra. This is the chief structure in a monastery in Kengtung. It is the chief place of worship, and images of the Buddha are kept here on a raised dais, five or six feet high.

The rōng, or hall where bhikkhus and sāmaṇeras live, is usually a structure next to the vihāra.

64. Great image of the Lord. In the vihāra of a monastery in Kengtung, there are several seated images of the Buddha on the dais among which the principal one is called the great image--"ƀracau tonhlōng" or "ƀracau hlōng"--which is taller than the rest, often as tall as ten or twelve feet, and in one or two cases fifteen feet or more.

65. Saen Bāy Sônghmün. I am not too sure if this is an official's title. It can also mean the officials, "saen," on the side of the two hmüns, i.e., the two preceding lāmhmüns. Bhayā Lāmhmün was one of the highest-ranking titles for officials in the Kengtung establishment.

66. Laggana or lagana. An auspicious moment or time fixed as lucky by astrologers for the beginning or performing of any work, project, or function.

67. The second time. This should be the third time, the first two earthquakes having taken place in paragraphs 84 and 85.

68. Recited. These recitations in paragraphs 86 and 87 are part of the ceremony to validate and sanctify the uposatha hall and the sīmā stones.

69. Mūlarājaṭhān. "Mūlarājaṭhānhlōng" or "Rājaṭhānhlōng" was an additional designation to a monastery patronized by the ruling prince of Kengtung. Vat P̲āḍaeng was the former Rājaṭhānhlōng; within the last hundred years or so it was Vat Hōkhōng which took the title. Both the monasteries still retain the title.

70. Kaeuphāpbhummin. This ruler of Kengtung could be either Brayā Ratana Bhumminda Narindā (1560-1597) or Brayā Kaeuphāpnarindā (1621-1638). The first was the twenty-third ruler, the second the twenty-fifth. The scribe of the text has mixed the two, as he has done with other names of places and monasteries. From the text it seems that Ratana Bhumminda Narindā is meant, as he was the first to confirm the exemptions, while "the Burmese Suddho Iṅjhe" was the second to do so. It could not have been Kaeuphāpnarindā, as he was contemporary with King Thālun (Suddho) of Ava (1629-1648). See note 71.

71. Suddho Iṅjhe. A Burmese king by the name of Fā Suddho is mentioned in the *Jengtung State Chronicle* during the reign of Brayā Kaeuphāpnarindā (1621-1638); this was Thālun Min of Burmese history who was also known as Thado (Sado Suddho) Dhammarājā (1629-1648). Iṅjhe ("eiṅshe" = front palace) is a title for a Burmese crown prince. Perhaps the royal order was given while Thālun was crown prince.

72. Devapuḍ. From "devaputta" (son of a devā), but generally he is regarded as a male devā.

73. Different religion. This is a mild translation of the word "caṇḍāla," which means a man of a certain low tribe or an outcaste.

74. Pārājika offense. Among the 227 rules for a bhikkhu, the four most serious offenses are called Pārājika; the transgression of any Pārājika forces a bhikkhu to leave the Order. These four Pārājika rules forbid bhikkhus from: committing sexual intercourse in any form; killing and causing to be killed a human being; stealing anything worth five māsaka (anything that has any commercial value); boasting about any extraordinary attainment (such as supernatural powers or enlightenment).

75. Any lord . . . proper boundaries, one. This whole sentence is incomplete--something is definitely missing to round off the ending.

76. Mônpheḍ, Bengsang, Hnôngtung. Mônpheḍ (see note 46) and Bengsang are localities inside Kengtung City. Hnôngtung is a small lake, perhaps one hundred fifty by five hundred yards, within the walls of Kengtung to the west of the palace. The legend is that the lake is all that is left of the immense

sheet of water that once covered the whole Kengtung valley, roughly five by twelve miles, and was drained by a hermit called Tuṅga Rasī, hence the names Tuṅgapurī (the classical name for Kengtung) and Hnôngtung.

77. Jāngsāt. A village two or three miles west of Kengtung city gate, formerly inhabited by mat weavers as the name indicates: "jāng" (craftsmen), "sāt" (mats).

78. Namkhün. See note 55.

79. The five kammas. "Kamma" here refers to the Saṅghakamma (note 17). The *Pali-English Dictionary* mentions (p. 190, col. 2) that "the number of officially recognized Kamma is eleven." The five referred to in the text, as understood by the present-day Saṅgha of Kengtung, seem to be those that deal with normal activities of the Saṅgha, and they are:

1. Upasampadākamma (ordination of a bhikkhu);
2. Uposathakamma (Pāṭimokkha recital on new moon and full moon days);
3. Pavāraṇākamma (ending of the vassā);
4. Parivāsakamma (undergoing a probationary period for violating one or more of the Saṅghādisesa rules of the Pāṭimokkha);
5. Kaṭhinakamma (accepting the kaṭhina robes).

80. Lü. A small branch of the Tai race, the Lüs inhabit the region covering Sipsôngbannā of Jengrung (Kengrung; Cheli in Chinese), eastern border substates of Kengtung, and Möngsing opposite the latter across the Mekhong in Laos. The Laem (Lem) are another branch of the Tais. Mönglaem State is due north of Kengtung and directly east of Burma's Va States. This group of Tais seems to have escaped the attention of American ethnic mapmakers. Khüns of Kengtung, Lüs of Jengrung, and Laems of Mönglaem are very close to one another in their histories. In the old days both Mönglaem and Jengrung paid tribute to the kings of Burma, as well as to the Chinese governor of Yunnan.

The remaining six, namely, Möngkā, Möngban, Möngpô, Möngmaen, Möngting, and Küngmā, are small states inhabited by what the Shans call Tai-nö (Daiy-nö or northern Thais), generally known in English as Chinese-Shans. Due to disturbances in their areas in the eighteenth and nineteenth centuries, many thousands of these people migrated to Kengtung, and they have settled just outside the Kengtung city walls in the east and southeast and in many villages a mile or two east of the city. They still speak their Tai-nö dialect. They are hardworking and prosperous and support many monasteries of the Forest Sect of their own. In the old days many of them entered the service of the ruling prince as his bodyguards and policemen. I am trying to trace how and when exactly they came over to Kengtung.

81. Saṅkārī. This word is the shortened form of "Saṅgha kārī." ("Kārī" is derived from "kāra," meaning "service" or "deed.") The saṅkārī was a very senior member of the Saṅgha in Kengtung whose duty was to administer the Saṅgha Order or the Sāsanā generally and to see to the discipline. His assistant was the lāmsaṅ (see note 119). Some of the work and duties of both the saṅkārī and lāmsaṅ are mentioned in the text. Neither of the two titles is in use in Kengtung at present.

82. Give the sīla. Just as bhikkhus have to go through the Pāṭimokkha rites every new moon and full moon in order to ensure that all 227 rules are being observed by them fully and conscientiously, sāmaṇeras have to have the sīla "given" to them by a competent bhikkhu on the same days of new moon and full moon. The assumption is that between the periods of sīla-giving the sāmaṇeras may have transgressed unconsciously one or many of the ten sīla through deeds, words, or thoughts, just as a bhikkhu may have done with reference to the 227 rules. A bhikkhu or sāmaṇera who, by deeds, words, or thoughts, has slackened any or parts of the rules governing his daily activities is like a weakened battery which must be recharged periodically to have absolute efficiency. Otherwise, the bhikkhu or sāmaṇera will not be worthy of the respect or esteem paid to him by laymen.

83. Mahāpāng Dhamma. Mahāpāng Dhamma, or "Dhamma of the Great Epoch," is known in Chiengmai and Bangkok as Mahājāt or Mahāchāt. It is the most popular form of the more expensive dāna at which the versified translation (with a great deal of imaginative embellishment) of the Vessantara Jātaka (Jātaka no. 547) is recited for a whole day, from predawn to about seven or eight in the evening. A day before and a day after, other Jātakas or Suttas are read out or recited and "sermons" preached before the libation water is poured by the chief dāyakā to commemorate the dāna and mark its completion. This three-day ceremony is still very much in fashion in Kengtung and it is done in monasteries. The chief dāyakā, relatives, friends, and elder "parishioners" of the monastery concerned practically eat and sleep within the precincts of the monastery's vihāra for the duration; it is also great fun for the children.

84. Vat In. Its full name is Indapupphārām (Monastery of Indra's Flowers), and it still flourishes in Kengtung, close to one of the northeastern gates of the city. As the name "pupphārām" indicates, it belonged to the Garden Sect.

85. Except for Vat Prasak and Vat Pāmahāvan (the eighth and tenth mentioned in the paragraph) all the other monasteries are still functioning in Kengtung City. The site of Vat Prasak was where the Roman Catholic mission now stands, just inside the western city gate; that of Vat Pāmahāvan was about half a mile further west at the foot of Cômsrī Hill.

86. Uposathakamma is the act or ceremony of reciting the Pāṭimokkha before an assembly of ordained bhikkhus (Saṅgha) in the uposatha hall of a monastery on uposatha days of the full moon and new moon. See also the "Introduction."

Parivāsakamma is the act of undergoing a probationary period for a bhikkhu who has transgressed any of the thirteen rules in the Saṅghādisesa section of the Pāṭimokkha. Temporary huts of bamboo and thatch or hay, each with an area of about ten or twelve square feet, are constructed for as many as there are probationers in the compound of a monastery chosen for the purpose. Each bhikkhu stays in a hut for the duration of about ten days, and the ceremony usually takes place after the harvest in December or January. The probationers assemble in the vihāra of the monastery about three times a day for confession, recitation, and other solemn rites between dawn and nightfall, otherwise their time is spent in the huts in silent meditation or caṅkama (meditational walk).

While the Parivāsakamma is strictly a Saṅgha affair, the help and cooperation given by lay devotees create quite an ado for the locality. Local inhabitants flock to the place to offer food to the alms bowl at dawn, the main meal before midday, and other dāna items. Outside the monastery a mini-bazaar comes to life to be patronized by laymen (and their children) connected with the Parivāsakamma, and an air of festivity hangs over the location throughout, as does the morning and evening Shan winter mist. This is a typical Parivāsakamma ceremony in Kengtung in modern times.

Pavāraṇākamma is the ceremony on the full moon day of October for the ending of the vassā for the bhikkhus in all Theravāda countries. It is also an official act or Saṅghakamma, like the foregoing two, to be performed in the uposatha hall. On the Pavāraṇā day, lay devotees of the parish come to the monastery early in the morning, and while the Saṅgha conduct the Parivāsakamma in the uposatha hall, they prepare special dāna and food for the Saṅgha at 11:00 A.M., followed by a meal for the laity. At about 1:00 P.M., when both the Saṅgha and laity are ready, the bhikkhus and sāmaṇeras of the monastery enter the vihāra and take their places on the Saṅgha-dais. Soon there take place the ceremonies of paying homage to the Three Gems, of calling upon all the devās to witness the dāna and share the merit, of giving the five and eight sīla to the lay congregation by the head of the monastery, of presenting the dāna offerings to the Three Gems, and, finally, of pouring the libation water. The day practically ends here at about 3:00 P.M. for most of the lay devotees who return home to attend to the household chores. For the more devout and senior laymen, however, the main business has just begun, for they stay behind in the monastery to observe the eight sīla, to discuss Dhamma topics and to meditate far into the night. These people return home the next morning.

The Pavāraṇā day just described takes place in the present-day Kengtung State, especially in the capital itself.

See also note 6 on the vassā, note 17 on the Saṅghakamma, and note 28 on the uposatha hall.

The complete 227 rules of the Pāṭimokkha comprise division I of the three divisions of the Vinaya Piṭaka, namely, Suttavibhanga, while the recitation ceremony of the Pāṭimokkha (uposathakamma) is given in detail in the Vinaya Piṭaka, division II (Khandaka), section 1 (Mahāvagga). Subsection 2, Pavāraṇākamma, can be read in detail in the Vinaya Piṭaka, II.1.4.

87. Forty-one letters. KV, rule 2.

88. Bōks of the interior. In the old days the ruling prince of Kengtung had his own privy council and officials here were given the rank titles of bōk, nāy, saen, and brayā. These officials belonged to the "inside" or "interior."

89. Silver summit. Round bamboo woven hats are still worn in parts of the Shan States. They are worn over the turban as protection against the rain or sun. In the old days the summit of the hat would have a convex silver cap about three inches in diameter with a pointed top fitted to it. This denoted the rank of the wearer according to the text. Princes or higher officials would have the summits of beaten gold, embossed with floral designs.

90. Flower tree. This "flower tree" consists of thin bamboo sticks about twelve inches long stuck into a cut-away piece of fruit, such as papaya, which forms the base. At the tip of each stick is a very thin, square sheet of silver kept in place by two small pieces of papaya. The size, thickness, and number of the silver square sheets depend on the occasions and purposes for which the "flower tree" or "ton-dôk" is needed. The size can be one square inch or four square inches. The smaller squares usually go with dāna offerings in monasteries. In the past, the bigger ones denoted official ranks, and the few top officials and princes had them made of gold. I believe the tributes from Shan ruling princes to the court at Ava included the golden squares.

91. High officials. This word in Khün or Tai-Yuan, "dāubrayā," seems to have been used in Burmese too. High officials during the reigns of Tabinshwehti and Bayinnaung are also referred to as "dobañā" in the *Hmannan Mahāyāzawindawgyi* and *U Kalā Mahāyāzawingyi* (U Kalā) chronicles of the period.

92. New golden palace. When a prince succeeds to the throne, and before coronation, he is supposed to "accept" the state from the people in an appropriate ceremony. When a new palace has been built and is about to be occupied, there will be a ceremony of occupation and the prince is then said to "ascend" the new palace. A commoner will also "ascend" his new house.

93. Sabbaññū officers. It seems that these officers were specially appointed to look after the image(s) of the Lord. The word for "officers" in the text is "bōk," an official title.

94. Drums. In every monastery in Kengtung City there is a large two-faced drum measuring four feet long, with each face about two and a half or three feet in diameter, hanging either at the far end (from the images) of the vihāra, or outside the covered space between the rōng (hall or dormitory) and the vihāra. On a convenient high shelf nearby are kept two large gongs, one measuring about two feet in diameter and the other slightly smaller, and a pair of large brass cymbals about eighteen inches across. Most of the monasteries outside the city also have these musical instruments. On uposatha days or special occasions when lay devotees come to the monastery to offer dāna, these instruments will be played at the commencement and at the end of the rites and ceremonies for the day. Not infrequently the gongs and the cymbals are played by women while the drum is almost always struck by a man. They are played in the following rhythm:

	1	2	3	4	1	2	3	4	.....
Drum			x	x			x	x	.....
Gongs		x		x		x		x	.....
Cymbals		x		x		x		x	.....

This rhythm is played for about one and a half to two minutes and then stops while the drum trails off without any rhythm for eight or nine strokes. When the instruments are played the second time, late in the afternoon, the households within the parish know that the ceremonies are over and that members of their families will soon be home.

The music is played in homage to the Three Gems, dāna, sīla, and other metitorious deeds in the monastery. The text seems to indicate that in the old days the instruments were played every morning and evening.

95. Pōsoḍnôy. This seems to mean "the small uposatha hall."

96. Day of decay of the Sangkhān. The Khün "Sangkhān" is the Burmese "Thingyān" ("Saṅkrān") or the Thai "Songkrān," and the story is as follows. A Brahma and the Sakka had a wager over a mathematical calculation with the forfeiture of the loser's head as the penalty. The Sakka proved right and the Brahma's head was cut off; but the head could not be put down or else a universe-consuming fire would break out, so it was placed on a pedestal tray and seven of the Sakka's goddesses were made to take turns carrying it. Once a year the head is transferred from one goddess to the next, and the process takes three days: the day the handing over begins is called the "coming" or "the fall of the Sangkhān" (this is usually on April 13); the next day, the day of decay, is when the transferring process takes place; the proper New Year Day takes place the next day when the Brahma head has reached the new goddess. The middle day, the day of decay, is considered unlucky for any venture except for merrymaking, while the third day, the New Year Day, is the lucky day and the old year's bad luck and ill omens are washed away with the hair-washing ceremony that people perform at home on this day.

Scientifically, Sangkhān is the time when the sun passes into the zodiacal sign Aries. Thus, the lunar year is made to coincide with the solar one at this time. Before the Julian calendar was corrected by Pope Gregory XIII in 1582, the Sangkhān Fall day of Cuḷa Sakkarāja took place between March 27 and March 30. Since 1582, from CS 944 to CS 1250, it has taken place between April 9 and April 13. Within living memory the Sangkhān Fall day has been April 12 or 13. (See Billard 1963).

97. Bôkū. Also called Bôkūd (place of ferns). This well is in a grove called Dongbôkūd within the city walls to the southwest. Its water is very soft and suitable for drinking. Up to the 1930s the drinking water for the palace was fetched from this well, and this well only.

I am not aware of the significance of the well at Bôrö in modern times. The reference could be to the shallow pond of Bôrö which is still in existence just below the hillock on which stands the eastern city wall. Vat Bôrö can be seen from the road leading to the airfield across the largish pond covering perhaps two or three acres. Buffaloes are often seen wallowing in the pond which is covered with tiny, green, scummy water plants.

98. The houses of the two. The meaning of "the houses of the two" is not clear, as their names have not been mentioned. Perhaps they have been left out through oversight.

99. Two necks. There must be two "necks" so that the roof will have three tiers.

100. Muddhābhiseka water. This literally means "consecration of the head," but in practice it is the ceremonial bath of purification for a ruler, or, as in this case, for a senior member of the Saṅgha when he is raised to be the head of the Saṅgha Order.

101. Wall level of the hall. As the refusal of the retainers to carry the palanquin was not anticipated, a temporary (i.e., bamboo) platform had not been provided for mounting and dismounting the elephant. The wall of the hall was therefore used for the purpose.

102. Great robes. Kaṭhina robes are sometimes called "the great robes," because the word "mahā" is prefixed to "kaṭhina," as in par. 129, and also because the dāna of kaṭhina robes is regarded as a specially meritorious deed. Technically mahā-kaṭhina are those special kaṭhina robes for which the cotton yarn is spun and the fabric is woven, cut, and stitched into robes, dyed, and made ready for offering in one day.

103. Sanpengdrā. The instrument or instruments cannot be identified. I am tempted to think of the Burmese "saingwaing," but this is a drum-circle which would require a professional musician to play, while the text seems to indicate that the instrument(s) could be handled by anyone, like a gong beaten in rhythm.

104. Hind-rider. A hind-rider sits (with knees folded) astride the elephant behind the howdah. There is a broad strap which goes round his waist and is hooked onto the lower portion of the howdah to keep him from sliding down the elephant's sloping back.

105. Death and destruction . . . yoga of death.

1. The day spirits give death and destruction is obviously a bad day.
2. The day the yon is out hunting: "Yon" is from the Pali "yanta" meaning a machine, but is understood in Khün vocabulary to be a supernatural machine carrying a blade capable of killing people. A sudden death with little or no illness is attributed to the yon's handiwork.
3. The day the state's cloak is alarmed: the cloak refers to the guardian spirits of the kingdom or state who will not be able to do any protection when alarmed.

4. The day the weapon of death is received: A wealthy man used to throw down from the upper story of his house a long knife to his gardener below. The gardener used to receive the knife adroitly and safely, but, one day, he missed it and the knife plunged into his neck causing instant death.

5. The day of the prince's eviction: The prince in this case is Prince Suppabuddha, father of Devadatta and Yasoddharā (mother of Rahula, i.e., Siddhattha's wife before he attained the Enlightenment). The astrology has it that Suppabuddha was driven from his palace by a mob and was swallowed up by the earth as he reached the ground. The actual death of Suppabuddha by the earth is told differently in story 12 of book 9 of the Dhammapada Commentary illustrating the Dhammapada verse no. 128 (Burlingame 1969: 291-93).

6. The day of secret burial and death: A certain wife was unfaithful and kept a lover whom the husband killed one day. Not wishing to publicize her infidelity, the wife cut the dead lover into two halves and secretly buried one half during the night. The next night she took the second half for another burial, unconscious that the husband was following her. At the bank of a river the husband pushed the wife and her burden into the water.

7. The day of the four squares: The twelve animal year names, cai, p̱au, yī, hmau, etc., are placed in the four squares, four at a time, and calculations are made from which inauspicious days would emerge.

8. The day 7 of the red sky: The sixty cyclical year names (kāpcai, ḍapp̱au, rāyyī, etc.; see "Chart of the Sixty Cyclical Year Names and Cuḷa Sakkarāja," Fig. 3) are also applied to the day, which is then designated as "daiy" (e.g., Daiy Ḍapp̱au, etc.). Now the twelve lunar months of the year have their bad days as follows: months One, Five, and Nine have bad days which begin with "koḍ" and "kā"; months Two, Six, and Ten, "kāp" and "ḍap"; months Three, Seven, and Eleven, "kaḍ" and "pük"; months Four, Eight, and Twelve, "tau" and "rāy." Only the "heads" of the names are given, e.g., there are six names headed by "kāp," viz., kāpcai, kāpseḍ, kāpsan, kāpsaṅā, kāpsī, and kāpyī. Any daiy day with the above cyclical names would be bad in months Two, Six, and Ten, and doubly bad if the day happens to be the day seven, i.e., Saturday.

9. The day of the great ghost and iron javelin: Two enemies after their death became the great ghost and the iron javelin. On certain days they are in certain points of the compass: Sunday and Friday, west; Monday and Saturday, east; Tuesday and Wednesday, north; Thursday, south. One

should not travel towards those cardinal points on the days named.

10. The day of the robber's constellation: The robber's constellations are nakkhatta constellations 3 (Kattikā), 12 (Uttara-phaggunī) and 21 (Uttar-āsāḷha). Obviously these are bad nakkhattas. See note 155 for the nakkhatta constellation names.

11. The executioner's constellations are: nakkhatta constellations 7 (Punabbasu), 16 (Visākhā) and 25 (Pubba-bhaddapadā).

12. The beggar's constellations are: nakkhatta constellations 1 (Assayuja), 10 (Maghā), and 19 (Mūlaṁ).

13. It is plain from the names of the next three yoga that they are bad.

106. Ādittarājā. This is Ādittarājā I, who ruled from 1474 to 1507, and his name is Āylau, not Āy Klau as stated in the text. Ādittarājā II ruled from 1638 to 1660.

107. His age. "Āyu" is the word used in the text. Strictly speaking this Pali word means "life" or "longevity," but it has also come to mean "age" by usage, as when one says, "My āyu is so many years." In the text it could mean either his birthday or the day his age comes to an end.

108. Stabbing wind blackout. Throughout India and Southeast Asia the ancient idea persists that the human body is made up of the four elements of solidity, fluidity, wind, and heat. Many internal illnesses of human beings are believed to be caused by the malfunction of the wind element. "Stabbing wind" would be the Western concept of gastric pain.

The equivalent of "blackout" in Khün or Shan is literally "black eye" or "tāḍam." When one's eyes see black they cannot see anything else.

109. Brayā Sivijaya. This ruler's full title was Sivijeyyarājā and he ruled Kengtung from 1511 to 1523. Due to his misbehavior people rose against him. He went to Vat P̱āḍaeng and took refuge there as a bhikkhu. Officials and people captured him inside the monastery and executed him publicly at Kāḍtung inside the city gate about five or six hundred yards from Vat P̱āḍaeng's walls (*Jengtung State Chronicle*).

110. Brayā Kaeunarindā. This ruler's full title was Kaeuyôḍf̱ā Narindā and he ruled from 1523 to 1560. He submitted to King Bayinnaung of Burma (capital in Pegu) in 1559 and in return received the five royal regalia, the Tipiṭaka and other presents (*Jengtung State Chronicle* and Burmese chronicles).

111. Vādsinggī. This was Prince Oksing (Surindarājā) who ruled from 1678 to 1685, and is said to have been a powerful ruler.

112. Prince Jalemang. This was a title obviously given to a Kengtung prince while he was at the Ava court; the king at Ava must have made him a ruler at Sale in Central Burma before he succeeded in Kengtung. He was Prince Kaeubunmā (also known as Prince Mönglek) who ruled Kengtung from 1605 to 1702 with the title of Udeyya Traisaṅvacara (? Udaya Traisaṅvacchara).

113. Prince Sāmplī ruled from 1702 to 1720. He was the son of "Jalemang" and is said to have been powerful and to have rebelled against Ava three times in 1708.

114. Khōng. A "khōng" is an open ground. The best known khōng in Kengtung City is in front of the south wall of the palace. This space was also known in the old days as Khōng Gvāyjon (buffalo fight ground). Since the palace faces south, this Khōng Gvāyjon is in front of the palace. From within the palace, this khōng is also called Khōngnôk (outer khōng). Its southern limit is marked by Jhegong. From the nineteenth century up to the mid-1930s, Jhegong was also known as Adīju, from the Burmese "atīzu" (quarters for musicians), as the court musicians lived there. To the east of Khōng Gvāyjon is Hōkhōng (head of the khōng) which rises forty or fifty feet above the general level to the road that goes past the west wall of Vat Hōkhōng. Lākhōng (tail end of the khōng) is to the west towards the present city ward of Nôngkhe.

Within the palace's southern wall and adjacent to Khōng Gvāyjon is a khōng known as Khōngtai (lower khōng) of the palace. On a different level, ten to fifteen feet higher, and immediately in front of the palace building is Khōngnö (upper khōng). The upper and lower khōngs are joined by stone steps about twenty feet wide flanked by five-foot-high parapets; otherwise, the two meet at the bottom of a brick walling, ten to twelve feet high, topped with a low two-foot-high parapet which forms the limit of the upper khōng. The khōng within the palace is known as Khōngnai (inner khōng).

In the old days, public ceremonies and festivals (known as "pwe" in Burma), religious or worldly, were held in these khōngs. From the 1950s, half of Khōng Gvājon in the west (towards Lākhōng) was expanded and turned into a soccer field while the eastern half (towards Hōkhōng) became a shedded bazaar called Kāḍkhōng.

There is no doubt that the khōngs referred to in the text are those described, because the palace or the royal invitation is always mentioned along with them.

115. Kāḍtung. This gate was named after the old bazaar of Kāḍtung ("kāḍ" meaning bazaar, and "tung" from Tungapurī). It is now called P̱āḍaeng Gate (see Fig. 4). The old bazaar was just within the city wall. From here the bazaar was moved in the late 1920s by Prince Kônkaeu Intraeng to the present bazaar called Kāḍhmai (new bazaar). The modern hospital compound is just outside this gate, bounded on the west by the city wall and on the east by the western wall of Vat P̱āḍaeng.

116. Straw seats . . . ādhāndham. A straw seat is made of paddy straw. Several strands of straw are gathered together to the size of about one and a half inches in diameter, and held tightly in place by other (single or double) strands of straw, so that a straw "rope" of some length is obtained thereby. This "rope" is then coiled into a circular shape. From the beginning at the center the first coil is held fast to the second, the latter to the third, and so on, by more strands of straw, until the circular shape has reached a diameter of about eighteen or twenty inches with a thickness of about two inches. This large straw disk is then covered with yellow cloth, usually on both sides, and is now ready for seating a bhikkhu. This is called "j̱halī" in Khün. A sāmaṇera is not allowed to sit on one.

Pillows are square, half-moon, or triangular in shape, somewhat tightly stuffed with cotton or silk cotton (*Bombax malabaricum*). Their sizes: square, approximately eight inches wide by twelve or fourteen inches long; triangular (equilateral), twelve to fourteen inches from the apex to base and about fourteen to fifteen inches along the sides. The first two are used as sleeping pillows at night and as armrests during the day. The triangular one is used only during the day as an armrest or for leaning against while one is reclining.

An ādhāndham is a portable rack with a folding support, often carved and gilded, with pegs for holding palm leaf books. It is sometimes called "ādhān" for short (see Fig. 10). Its full name as stated in the text is "kambī-ādhāndham" from Pali "gambhīra" (deep or profound), "ādhāra" (support or stand), and "dhamma" which in this context means the written or inscribed Dhamma on the book or books of palm leaves.

117. Cushion-seat. Called "ādsanā" from the Pali "āsana." It is round in shape and folds in two halves. It is stuffed with cotton or silk cotton (*Bombax malabaricum*) in sewn segments. Size: about twenty inches in diameter and two inches thick.

118. Tālapat. This is the proper name for the palm leaf "fan" (see note 51) used when a bhikkhu is giving the sīla or reciting a sutta. In a congregation of bhikkhus before lay

devotees, the former sit in a row and only the most senior may have the tālapat. On special occasions senior bhikkhus, who are seated in the front row, may each have a tālapat while while reciting suttas.

In the text the tālapat is being carried by a Möng Küy man walking before the most senior thera from his place of residence to the vihāra or wherever he is invited outside the monastery. Once the thera has reached his destination the tālapat is placed beside him to be picked up and used by him as and when necessary.

119. Lāmsaṅ. The lāmsaṅ used to be the general secretary of the Saṅgha in Kengtung. In Khün, "lām" means a messenger or general factotum of an organization. A government office, or a village, has a lām to carry messages to outside persons. Lāmsaṅ, therefore, is the lām of the Saṅgha. A monastery has or used to have a "lāmvat." In the Saṅgha organization in Kengtung, lāmsaṅ was the chief assistant to the saṅkārī (see note 81).

120. Months Six and Twelve. These two months are of special importance because one, Month Six, concerns the New Year festivals and ceremonies, while the other, Month Twelve, has to do with Pavāraṇā (end of the vassā) and the accompanying festivities. These months correspond with months Five and Eleven in central Thailand and the Western Shan States and to months Seven and One in northern Thailand.

121. See note 81.

122. Brahmavihāra. The four Brahmavihāra items are mettā (loving kindness), karuṇā (compassion), muditā (sympathetic joy), and upekkhā (equanimity).

123. The study and practice of the Dhamma. This is from the well-known Pali phrase of Pariyatti and Paṭipatti.

124. Free lords. The word used in the text is "caudaiy" (free lords), and it is a word used for referring to members of the Saṅgha in the same way as "jāucau" was used earlier in the text. The usage was common throughout Kengtung and northern Thailand in the old days.

125. Jengkaeu. This is the Khün name of the present city of Kengtung. The *Jengtung State Chronicle* states that originally it was a Lva fortified town, and that the present city walls were built during the reign of Brayā Āy-ôn (? 1377-1398).

126. If ordained . . . weighty one. It is not easy to make out the sense or meaning of this paragraph from "If ordained at Lord Pabbajjā Ādiḍ . . ." to the end. I sent a xerox copy of the original page to the Saṅgha at Kengtung, and they replied that the scribe or copyist did not make himself clear or had left out words or sentences here and there, or the customs in those days of the text must have been different from those now prevailing with regard to certain procedures and rites before the actual upasampadā ordination. Further research is necessary for the full understanding of the passage.

127. Field of merit. The idea being that the institution of the Saṅgha is the place where one performs meritorious acts, thereby gaining the good kamma for future rebirths.

128. Damiḷa. One of the legendary names of Kengtung, before acquiring the classical "Tuṅgapurī," was "Dammilāp" (from "Damiḷa"). It is quite definite, I think, that the original inhabitants of Kengtung were not Tamils of South India. On the other hand, chroniclers of Kengtung through their reading of such books as the *Mahāvaṁsa* must have known that the Tamils (Damiḷas) were the arch enemies of ancient Ceylon. The original inhabitants of Kengtung were Lvas or Vas, as is traditionally believed, and their dark skin was perhaps associated with that of the Damiḷas. But, then, Theravāda Buddhism never discriminates against anyone who wishes to enter bhikkhuhood, as long as he is a free man and free from certain incapacities laid down in the Vinaya rules.

129. Pavāraṇā. The ceremony of the termination of the vassā. See also note 86.

130. Grūbā. This is a title of rank in the Saṅgha hierarchy of Kengtung.

131. Various bamboos. Four kinds are named:

Maibô (*Dendrocalamus giganteus*)--this is the famous elephant or giant bamboo, the biggest and tallest of the species, known to exceed one hundred feet in height and ten inches in diameter at the base;

Maipheu (*Gigantochloa macrostachya*);

Maipong (? *Dendrocalamus hamiltonii*);

Maibūn (*Gigantochloa albociliata*).

132. Observe . . . dāna. "Observe the sīla, eat, and give dāna": this is a stock phrase meaning "patronize the monastery regularly."

133. The great sīla. This is also called "uposatha sīla" or the "eight sīla," in which one undertakes to avoid: taking life; stealing; unchastity; telling lies; intoxicants; eating after midday; singing, dancing entertainment, and bodily adornments of any kind; sleeping on a high couch with a soft mattress. See also the introduction, under "The Lay Devotees."

134. Müngplau, Sakkarāja 934. Sakkarāja 934 (1572 A.D.) is in Tausan. Müngpau (or Müngplau) would have Sakkarāja 939 (1577 A.D.). The text states in paragraph 156 that Müngpau was an adhikamāsa year (see note 137). With proper references, such as those available in Kengtung or Thailand for this matter, it would be possible to check if Tausan Sakkarāja 934 or Müngpau Sakkarāja 939 was an adhikamāsa year.

135. Mingaung [?]. The name in the text is "Mengkung," and "Mingaung" is the nearest Burmese equivalent I can think of. Around 1572-1577, the Burmese king was Bayinnaung (1551-1581), one of the most famous in Burmese history, who subdued Chiengmai in 1558 and Ayudhyā in 1562 and 1565. This mention of the fight in the text may have been a minor battle later, and Mingaung could be the name of a local Burmese commander or a prince.

136. Möng Pāḍ. The *Yonaka Chronicle* states on page 83 that one Muang Pāṣtông (read "Pāttông") is east of Chiengmai. I take this to be the same Möng Pāḍ of the text.

137. Adhikamāsa. Adhikamāsa may be liberally translated as a "leap month." It is an intercalendar month added to the lunar calendar in Burma and in Thailand. In Kengtung, when this occurs, the additional month is placed between months Nine and Ten, and the normal Month Nine is then called "First Month Nine" and the added month "Second Month Nine." The vassā, which normally begins on the full moon of Month Nine, then begins on the full moon of Second Month Nine.

It is well known that, although Cuḷa Sakkarāja is a lunar era, a formula has been adopted from ancient times whereby the new year occurs about the same time as the solar year, i.e., every year has 365.25 days which we divided into twelve lunar months normally and into thirteen months after every three years with an intercalary day added after every other three years.

The text states that in the adhikamāsa year of Müngplau (Müngpau), the vassā should commence in Month Ten. This is the Second Month Nine of modern usage. Perhaps such disputes as narrated in the text were responsible for naming Month Ten as Second Month Nine? But, then, did that year have a Month Thirteen?

138. Cleansing ceremony. This ceremony is fully described in paragraphs 67-75.

139. Gavampati. Gavampati was an arahantā during the lifetime of the Buddha. He was one of the earliest converts, having been ordained soon after Yasa Thera, who himself had been converted after the five Pañcavaggī. Gavampati Thera once stopped a flash flood on the river Sarabhū in Sāketa, where a multitude of bhikkhus was camping on a sand bank. In Burma, Gavampati Thera is known to be a "patron saint" of the Môns.

140. Popularity potion. This is a very thick kind of ointment made of beeswax with some sesame oil and other ingredients. The oil is to make the wax pliable while the other ingredients are to make the ointment effective. During the process of making and after, the master will recite certain mantras so many hundred times according to his formula. The ceremony for the making process is quite elaborate. For example, the master must undertake to observe the five sīla; he must have had a bath and wear clean clothes; he must sit within a small enclosure fenced with slender split and plaited bamboo strips, called "rājamāḍ," at the four corners of which are tied sugar cane with leaves, tender banana trees, and the *Eugenia* branches. In this enclosure the ceremony of boiling the ointment over a small fire and making it potent is performed. When ready, the ointment is put away in small containers with lids to be given out to selected favorites. The forefinger is used to take a very small amount of the ointment from the container to apply it to the lips, while simultaneously reciting, perhaps with closed eyes, the gāthā given by the master, as if saying a prayer. From now on the subject will have every confidence in himself when he meets his sweetheart or people such as government officials, judges, influential persons, etc. Whatever is spoken by him will be believed!

141. Sādhu. This word of often translated into English as "well done," or "very well," but it has not quite the same meaning. A Buddhist in Theravāda countries often says "sādhu" after hearing a lecture on Dhamma, or after a dāna or meritorious act. Even on hearing some good news for the spiritual side of his life, a Theravādin bhikkhu or layman often utters the word "sādhu."

At the end of a dāna offering or some meritorious act in Burma, the chief dāyakā (donor) will announce aloud the formula: "O you human beings, devās, brahmas and all sentient beings, please share and share and share the fruit of this meritorious act." The whole audience will then respond by proclaiming aloud, "Sādhu! Sādhu! Sādhu!"

142. Ban and bōk. This paragraph speaks of two bans and one bōk. Ban and bōk are official titles. The three are Ban Kuang ("kuang," absent-mindedness or delirium), Ban Hum ("hum," popular), and Bōk P̱ākp̱aen ("p̱ākp̱aen," protruding mouth).

143. Sakkarāja 702. Sakkarāja 702 falls in Koḍsī. In the *Jengtung State Chronicle* Prince Ceḍbantū came to Kėngtung in Koḍyī Sakkarāja 712. In the year Müngmeḍ Sakkarāja 729, he was stabbed to death by a retainer who had served him well but was ignored when new appointments and promotions were made.

144. The Saṅgkhān departs. This is the ceremony of "sending off" the old year (see also note 96).

145. Buddhavaṁsa Sutta. This sutta is in KN:14.

146. Written . . . night. This last and brief sentence is in a different handwriting, similar to that of the following four documents.

147. Sanjüm. Sanjüms belong to the Môn-Khmer ethnic group. Other "tribes" of this ethnic group to be found in Kengtung State are: Va, Samdāu, Daiydôy, Aen, and (formerly, I suspect) Yāng. These peoples are believed to have settled in Kengtung before the Khüns and Shans. The village tract of Möngküy (Möng Küy) of the text is the chief domain of the Sanjüms.

148. The two sides. The two sides are called "Internal" and "External." The former are the Saṅgha, representatives of the Three Gems; and the latter the laity headed by the ruler and his administration. The Pali phrase for the two sides is "antarabāhira," as used in paragraph 219.

149. Beg-pardon silver. It is important for Buddhists to ask for forgiveness of their parents, teachers, and elders in a simple and short ceremony on appropriate occasions such as the New Year in April or the Pavāraṇā in October. In one's daily dealings with one's benefactors one may have wronged them by deeds, words, or thoughts, consciously or unconsciously, and it is desirable to beg their forgiveness to avoid accumulating bad kamma.

In the old days officials, high and low, felt the same way towards their rulers, and hence the biannual "beg-pardon" ceremony at the latters' courts during the New Year and the Pavāraṇā. In the case of Kengtung and other Shan States, officials and chiefs had to come from townships or substates and villages, far and near, and a small tax was levied for the expenses of the journey to the capital. In the 1930s this tax in Kengtung was about five U.S. cents per household.

The "gold flowers" and "silver flowers" proferred to the prince would also be made from this tax.

In the days of the Burmese kings, Shan princes went to Ava for the "beg-pardon" ceremony at the palace, and a small tax was levied for the purpose. This is the "beg-pardon silver" referred to in the text.

The Burmese word for beg-pardon is "kāntô" (pronounced "kadô") from which is derived the Khün or Shan "kandô."

150. Nammon khāuhnān hnāyōy. This is the name given to the quality or fineness of the silver bullion used instead of coins in the old days.

One viss is approximately 3.6 pounds. "Viss" seems to be an Indian term and is understood in India and Burma. The Khün word for viss is "jôy."

151. Within and without. The purpose of dividing the three viss of silver for inside and outside the state, as mentioned in the text, is not clear. Perhaps some words have been left out.

152. Ājñādham Bracau. This is the highest title for the head of the Saṅgha in Kengtung of recent times.

153. Great crime. The word in the text is "mahādōḍ," from "mahādosa," applicable to a crime punishable with death, or something almost as severe.

154. Rai cultivation. This is the notorious slash-and-burn cultivation well known in Southeast Asia.

155. "Nakkhatta" (Sanskrit "nakṣatra") is translated into English as "a lunar mansion" or "the constellation of the lunar zodiac." The Khün "rökfā" ("rök," constellation or auspicious moment; "fā," heavenly) is synonymous with "nakkhatta," which has become part of Khün vocabulary. In literary style "nakkhatta rökfā" is the accepted phrase.

Some reference books speak of twenty-eight nakkhatta. Some have twenty-seven. A Shan book on the horoscope has twenty-seven. Burmese astronomy seems to have twenty-seven. It matters a great deal whether the number is twenty-seven or twenty-eight nakkhatta.

The usually accepted twenty-seven nakkhatta are numbered and named as follows: (1) Assayuja, (2) Bharaṇī, (3) Kattikā, (4) Rohiṇī, (5) Magasiraṁ, (6) Addā, (7) Punabbasu, (8) Phussa, (9) Asilesā, (10) Maghā, (11) Pubba-phaggunī, (12) Uttara-phaggunī, (13) Hattha, (14) Cittā, (15) Sāti, (16)

Visākhā, (17) Anurādhā, (18) Jeṭṭhā, (19) Mūlaṁ, (20) Pubb-āsāḷha, (21) Uttar-āsāḷha, (22) Savaṇa, (23) Dhaniṭṭhā, (24) Satabhisaja, (25) Pubba-bhaddapadā, (26) Uttara-bhaddapadā, (27) Revatī.

According to the text, Month Seven full moon falls on nakkhatta Anurādhā which is the seventeenth in the serial number. Since Month Seven waxing 1st falls on Kattikā, the third nakkhatta, the full moon (fourteen days away) will fall on nakkhatta 17, viz., Anurādhā. When one knows the nakkhatta on which the beginning of the lunar month falls, then one is able to fix the nakkhatta of any particular day of that month.

A combination of the nakkhatta day, and the day of the week on which one is born, will determine one's character and fortune in the world. This the horoscope formula.

If one has to count the twenty-eighth nakkhatta before coming to the first again, the twenty-seven nakkhatta horoscope will go awry, unless there are two sets of formulae, one for the twenty-seven and the other for the twenty-eight nakkhatta. Twenty-seven is the accepted number in Burma.

The *Pali-English Dictionary* opines that the twenty-eighth nakkhatta may have come about because one nakkhatta (Orion, number 5) "bore two names," Magasiraṁ and Aggahayanī.

156. Somḍec Seṭṭha Paramapôbitra. This is another term by which a ruling prince of Kengtung is referred to by the Saṅgha, meaning "the supreme excellent one worthy of respect."

157. Khemāraṭṭhamahāsīha Pavarasudhammarājā Bhummindanarindādhipati. This is the full title of Prince Mahākhanān, who ruled from 1813 to 1858. He is known to have been a great organizer and legislator, although blind since 1824 (Mangrāi 1969:65). His chief fame stems from the fact that he signally defeated three attacks on Kengtung City by Thai northern armies commanded by a Bangkok prince, Kromluang Vongsādhirāja, during the dry months of 1849, 1852, and 1854.

Figure 4

Figure 5

Figure 6

Figure 7

Figure 8

Figure 9

Figure 10

Figure 11

Figure 12

Figure 13

Figure Captions

Figures 4-10 are reprinted courtesy of the author. Figures 11-19 are prints made from glass negatives taken during the first decade of this century. They were obtained by the author while doing research in London in 1959.

4. Looking through the P̱āḍaeng Gate into the city of Kengtung. Vat P̱āḍaeng is about three hundred yards outside this gate.

5. The entrance to Vat P̱āḍaeng, dating to about the turn of the century. The traditional tile roofing in the upper roof has been replaced with more durable, but less beautiful, corrugated tin sheets.

6. The vihāra and cetiya of Vat P̱āḍaeng, known as Sīhaḷarattārāma in the *P̱āḍaeng Chronicle* (actually the Pali name of the Nikāya or sect), and as Jayamantārāma in the inscription (the name of the monastery itself). On the ground, at the corner formed by the vihāra and the plinth of the cetiya, is the stone inscription mentioned in the introduction to the *P̱āḍaeng Chronicle*. At the upper right can be seen a few leaves of the monastery's Boḍhi tree, also mentioned in the chronicle.

7. A typical cetiya of Kengtung, in the compound of Vat Khemin.

8. Vat Rājathānhlōng Hōkhōng, Kengtung, called Vat Brahmai Hōkhōng in the *P̱āḍaeng Chronicle*. According to the *Jengtung State Chronicle*, the original Vat Hōkhōng was founded soon after 1350. The gate was built in the late 1930s, replacing the older and more picturesque one which resembled the gate of Vat P̱āḍaeng (see Fig. 5). The vihāra was built on the plinth of an older one destroyed by the great fire that consumed a large part of the city within the walls in 1906. To the left is the uposatha hall; the overly ornate eleven-tiered roofing called the prāsāḍ was built after World War II, replacing the older roof (without a prāsāḍ) which was more in harmony with that of the vihāra. A portion of the roof of the rōng can be seen behind the uposatha hall.

9. Mahābherī, the great drum of Vat Hōkhōng. This is the smallest (37.5 inches in diameter and 52 inches long) of three drums in Kengtung made from a single tree trunk. The largest (50 inches in diameter and 73 inches long) was formerly kept at the Old Court House (known as the Khemarat Club in the 1950s), but has since been moved to Vat Bracauhlōng which houses a replica of the sacred Mahā Myatmuni image of Mandalay. The third great drum (43 inches in diameter and 72.5 inches long) was made from

the middle portion of the tree trunk and is in the palace in Kengtung. Both faces of these drums are covered with cowhide. The drum stick (about 18 inches long) is made of turned wood and is kept in the hole in the cowhide seen at the side of the drum in the photograph. The striking of the great drum of a monastery in Kengtung on ceremonial occasions is accompanied by a pair of large cymbals and two large gongs (see the *P̄āḍaeng Chronicle*, par. 123 and note 94); or, it may be struck by itself when an assembly of the monastery's parishioners is needed, such as during the spring cleaning of the monastery or upon the death of a bhikkhu. The parishioners recognize the tone of their monastery's mahābherī.

10. The ādhāndham of Vat Hōkhōng with two kaṇḍa, or chapters (called "phūk" in Khün and Tai-Yuan), of a palm leaf manuscript "book" resting on its pegs. An ādhāndham is a carved and gilded wooden stand with two rows of three pegs each which receive a palm leaf manuscript in use. When a phūk of the manuscript is to be read, it is taken from the pegs; when the reader is finished, the phūk is replaced. When the whole "kap" of the manuscript is no longer needed, it is placed between two wooden slats and packed away, usually in cloth, sometimes in embroidered silk or brocade, and kept in the mondok or library. The palm leaves are not written upon with ink or pencil but have letters inscribed on them with a needle-sharp stylus. The size of each palm leaf is about 3.5 x 18 inches. The scribe sits on the floor with his left knee raised to support his left hand. He holds a batch of the leaves in his left hand with the thumb pressuring and controlling the batch (which may be .5 or .75 inches thick) according to convenience and habit. When inscribing is to be done, the stylus in the right hand (those were not permissive days!) is brought to rest on the left thumb just below the nail with the stylus point on the palm leaf, and the "writing" begins. Up to the late 1930s, many bhikkhus and senior sāmaṇeras, especially in the better-known monasteries of Kengtung, knew how to inscribe on palm leaves. A real expert could inscribe the palm leaf page almost as quickly as one writes on a piece of paper. Often a "thimble glove" with open ends (made of leather or layers of cloth) is worn over the left thumb. Before reading, the inscribed leaves are rubbed with vegetable or crude mineral oil which at once darkens the inscribed writing.

11. A portion of Tuṅga Market with the shrine house for the guardian spirits of the bazaar. The hats worn by women in the picture were discarded in the early 1930s.

12. Tombs of five ruling princes of Kengtung, namely, from right to left: Mahākhanān, Mahābrohm, Saeng, Kôngdaiy, and Kôngghamfū. In the old days ruling princes were cremated at Kāḍtung or Tuṅga Market, a portion of which can be seen in the picture. The ashes of these five princes were put into urns, entombed in the

brick-and-mortar structures on plinths, and topped with "lotus buds." This same Tuṅga Market has witnessed a few executions of bad rulers, as described in the *Jengtung State Chronicle*.

13. Vat Indapupphārām showing the gate with its guardian crested lions, the uposatha hall (or "sīmā") immediately behind the low wall to the left, and the huge and impressive vihāra. The rōng (dormitory for bhikkhus and sāmaṇeras) is on the other side of the vihāra. The ornate decorations on the roof ridges of the buildings are typical of monasteries in Kengtung. The monastery gate is also typical and its roof offers shade to weary travelers. The story of this "Vat In" is given in paragraphs 107 and 111 of the *P̱āḍaeng Chronicle*.

14. The inner front door of the vihāra at Vat Indapupphārām. The outer door is out of the picture to the right. Most vihāras have only one main front door, but all have side doors.

15. Main front door of the vihāra of one of the monasteries in Kengtung City. The rōng adjoins the vihāra on the right.

16. A panoramic view of Bāngaen, in the Samdāu (Three Kings) Hills, thirty-five miles northeast of the city of Kengtung, showing part of the village and the monastery on the high ground. The Samdāu Hills people are among those mentioned in paragraph 100 of the *P̱āḍaeng Chronicle*. Samdāu men were known for their fierce loyalty to the ruling princes of Kengtung and they provided fighting men whenever needed. These Samdāu Hills are also mentioned in the *Jengtung State Chronicle*.

17. Shwegyaung (a Burmese name meaning "golden monastery") on the main road at Sawlon, in the trans-Salween Kayah (formerly Karenni) State. The surroundings, the ornate carvings, and the beautiful Burmese architecture reflect the prosperity of the area at the turn of the century, a result of the teak trade between Karenni and Moulmein, at the mouth of the Salween.

18. An uposatha hall, called a "thein" in Burmese (from Pali "sīmā"), in the middle of a stream in Hsataw, another trans-Salween town of old Karenni. This photo was also taken at the height of Karenni's prosperity (see Fig. 17). The *P̱āḍaeng Chronicle* speaks of sīmā rafts in paragraphs 24 and 33.

19. Part of an old cetiya in Laikhā in the central part of the Shan States. Note the ornate friezes. It is a great pity that such beautiful structures have been allowed to go to rack and ruin, and new constructions always erase almost completely the old beauty and workmanship.

Figure 14

Figure 15

Figure 16

Figure 17

Figure 18

Figure 19

THE JENGTUNG STATE CHRONICLE

INTRODUCTION

I have written at some length in my translation of the *P̄ạdaeng Chronicle* about the State of Kengtung, its people the Khụ̈ns, the ruling prince and his court, the monasteries, and Khün script. In translating the *Jengtung State Chronicle* I have used the same method of literal translation as far as it is compatible with good English and the same romanized transcription as illustrated in the chart accompanying the translation of the *P̄ạdaeng Chronicle* (Fig. 2). It would have been much easier and taken much less time to render a free translation, but I feel that that would have robbed it of the original Khün flavor. For example, it is much better to say, as in the original, such and such a ruling prince "has accomplished his accumulated merit and gone to heaven" rather than the simple English "he died."

The *Jengtung State Chronicle* is but one of the many chronicles of the bigger Shan States whose historical periods date back to the thirteenth century. In translating this chronicle, and three or four more others to come, one of the aims is that the translations will be supplementary to the national history of Burma. History books on Burma tell us about the "Maw" or "Gwe" Shans without revealing the origins of these peoples. The chronicles of Hsenwi and Mụ̈nghmau tell us the "Mau" Shans belong to Mụ̈nghmau, which was once a powerful state. "Gwe" Shans are not mentioned in any Shan chronicle, but they are known to have come from beyond the present-day Va States through the Namting River and to have hired themselves out as mercenaries. From the *Chronicle of Hsenwi* it was the crown prince of Mö̈ngmit who, by the order of "Cau Vông" ("Chinese emperor"), led the Chinese delegation to demand tribute from Narathihapate of Pagan, who put forty of the fifty members of the delegation to death with consequences well known in history. "Cau Vông" may have been only the governor of Yunnan. From this it will be seen that Shan chronicles supply interesting details to the main history of Burma, besides recording detailed events in their own states. It is up to diligent scholars to verify the truth or otherwise of those records.

Astrology and Horoscopy

It is unfortunate that I know next to nothing about the world of astrology and horoscopy, generally known under the terms "hūrā," or "horā," with the result that I am unable to interpret in full the horoscopic terms that invariably follow the birth or accession of every ruler. My queries to Kengtung in this direction have not produced satisfactory response; nor is it easy to obtain the needed information from this distance, as astrology or horoscopy is a class of complicated learning by itself. I have tried my best to give the literal meaning to all the Pali and Khün words and phrases in this connection, and if one follows them closely it will be seen *how* the good or bad fortune, under such-and-such planet combined with Lagana (the ascendant sign) and compounded with signs of destructiveness or fruitfulness as found in the book under the appropriate section, has come about, without understanding the reason *why*. This is the chief weakness of the translation. But I can assure the reader who can't comprehend the hūrā terms that this is also the lot of the average reader in Khün and that few bother to understand more fully unless one is a real expert on the subject.

Jengtung and Kengtung

I have used "Jengtung" throughout the translation instead of the standard spelling "Kengtung." In Khün script the word begins with palatal *j* rather than gutteral *k*, which is how a native of Kengtung pronounces it. When the British came into the Shan State after they had conquered Mandalay, they came to the Western Shan States before encountering any native of "Jengtung." Through the structure of their dialect, many Shans pronounce the word "jeng" (city), which precedes the second syllable in the names of many towns and cities in Kengtung and northern Thailand, as "keng," which of course is incorrect, though some Shans do pronounce the first consonant somewhere between *k* and *j*--a sort of quick glide, rendered as "kyeng." By the time the British came to write the name of the city or state of Jengtung, they had adopted the Shan "Kengtung." From the sixteenth century on, the Burmese have used "kyaing" for the syllable "jeng." When the Burmese chronicles refer to Chiengmai and Lānjāng they say "Zinmae," and "Linzin"--the consonant *z* being the Burmese pronunciation of their own palatal *j*, which is a direct transcription of the Tai-Yuan and Lao *j*. Hence my adoption of "Jengtung" as the correct spelling in this translation.

Dates

Most year names and Cuḷa Sakkarāja in the *Jengtung State Chronicle* agree, but not a few of them are at variance with the correct names and Cuḷa Sakkarāja in my "Chart of the Sixty Cyclical Year Names and Cuḷa Sakkarāja" (Fig. 3). It is easy for a scribe, after copying many pages, to be confused with year names having the same beginning or ending, such as Ḍapgai and Ḍapsai, Pükyī and Püksī, Kaḍmeḍ and Koḍseḍ, Rōngpau and Rōnghmau, and so on. It is not easy to correct them arbitrarily. For example, in paragraph 141 it is said that "Dāu Ghamfū, a son of Brayā Lau, was born in the year Koḍseḍ Sakkarāja 862, Month Eleven waning 10th night, Wednesday Daiy Kāgai, nakkhatta constellation 6. . . ."

Now "koḍ" denotes that the ending numeral must be 2, but in the chart 852 is in Koḍseḍ, while 862 is in Koḍsan. Which is the correct year name or Cuḷa Sakkarāja? It is not possible to be definite until we know that ". . . Month Eleven . . . constellation 6. . . ." belongs to the right year name and Cuḷa Sakkarāja. This can be done by referring to what is known in Kengtung as the "Great Calendar," available in a few monasteries over there. The Great Calendar has the month, day, weekday, Daiy day, and nakkhatta constellation shown against the first day of each lunar month, thus enabling the student to work out the correct details of any day of the month within any Cuḷa Sakkarāja of any year name. With Ann Arbor half way around the world from Kengtung it is not easy to refer every discrepancy to the Great Calendar. What I intend to do on my return to Burma is to edit all the dates in the *Jengtung State Chronicle* and investigate certain textual discrepancies. For the present, the chart is included here for reference, and with the dates of the reigns of princes preceding and succeeding a particular one, some correction can be made, although total satisfaction cannot be obtained in all cases.

Names

Even for one well versed in Khün script, its strengths, and weaknesses, it is not easy to follow the different names of some of the rulers. Paragraphs 160 and following are a case in point. A crown prince was known by the names of Cau (Prince) Āyghamdāu, Cau G̱hamdāu, Fā Āy, Bhayā G̱hamdāu, and when he succeeded to the throne he received the title of Brayā Sudhammarājā, which later became Brayā Dhammikarājā, and at the end of his reign was called Mahā Dhammikarājā. All that one can do in such cases is to read with caution and concentration.

Lvas

There seems to be little doubt that the original inhabitants of the valley of Kengtung were Lvas or Vas of the Palaung-Va branch of the Môn-Khmer ethnic stock (as is traditionally believed), and many of their cousins, namely, the Daiydôys, Samdāus, Aens, Sanjüms, etc., are still found on the hills of Kengtung. The descendants of the original Lvas are now in the village of Bāng̱ham on the hills northeast of the Kengtung valley and they are known as the Vas of Bāng̱ham, whose chiefs were last invited to participate in the coronation ceremony of Prince Kônkaeu Intraeng in 1897 (see note 45).

While the *Jengtung State Chronicle* does not mention where the Lvas fled to when they were defeated by forces of Mangrāy and

Māngghum and Māngghen, *Prajum Bongsāvadān*, volume 61 (PB61), mentions on page 139 that they fled towards Möngkhlōy, Möngyāng, Möngkā, and Möngkhā, which are all on the routes to the present Va States. The tradition among the Vas of the Va States is also that they fled, or were driven out of, the Kengtung valley, and came to their present habitation through those routes. I reproduce below four paragraphs of a paper entitled "Comments on the Wa Tribe," written as a report by my friend, a Baptist missionary in the Va States before the war, the late Mr. Harold M. Young, when he was appointed Assistant Resident in the Va States from 1946 to 1948, and submitted to his superior, the Resident at Lashio, Northern Shan States.

> The Wa is the only tribe in Burma that claims to have come from the South. They do not have the appearance of the true Mongolian. The other races of Burma are Mongolian in features and their traditions and historical records show that they immigrated from Central or Northern China at one time or other. The Wa have a slight negroid look, thick lips but not the curly hair. The women in many sections keep their hair parted in the middle and look like red Indian squaws. There is no written history but records and traditions have been handed down from father to son by word of mouth. It seems quite definite from these records that they did come up from Southern Burma and in recent years coffins have been found in caves in the southern Shan States, which substantiate the claim that the country was inhabited by the Wa. They settled for a long period in the Eastern Shan States before finally reaching the territory they now occupy. The city of Kengtung is the only walled town in the Shan States and the Wa were the early settlers there. According to their old records they built the wall and the twelve gates--also the great moat which was intended as an obstacle in fighting rather than to be filled with water--and lived there 300 years. They called the lake in the valley Nawng Tung and later the name Kengtung was given the city in connection with the name of the lake.
>
> According to both the Shan and Wa historical records, a combined army of Shans and Siamese finally succeeded in driving the Wa out of their valley stronghold in Kengtung and they were forced to move Northward to Mongkha, a place halfway between their city and the present Wa States. Here they began at once to build another town on the banks of the Nam Lwe river. They had only completed

digging part of the moat when another Shan army was sent against them. This time the fight was a long and bloody one as the country was mountainous and easy to defend, but shortage of food and failure of crops, weakened their resistance and the Wa were finally driven out of Kengtung State and sought refuge in the mountain fastnesses which were destined to become their permanent home. It was due to this turn of events that the Wa turned from the ways of the plains to become one of the most hardy and feared of the mountain tribes.

In Kengtung state there are several tribal groups of Wa known as the Tai-loi, Sam-tao, Sam-htean, En and Sawn. Their long isolation has only created a slight dialective difference in their languages spoken. The Sam-htean may be the only exception as they have a wild temperament like the Shans. All these groups live in the mountains and have given up the ways of the plains. They are not war-like, but this is due to the fact that they have not been independent but under the Shan chiefs. The En and Sawn adhere the closest to the Wa customs and keep animal heads in place of human skulls.

The Wa in the Wa States proper are divided into two main groups, the wild or headhunting Wa and the so-called tame Wa. The wild Wa still adhere to the practice of headhunting and in some circles it has seemed to be on the increase, but Christian mission work has had great effect on these practices and many have given it up.

(This paper is now in the private collection of Mr. Julian Daglish of London, who was in charge of the police force in the Northern Shan States from 1946 to 1948, and I am grateful to him for his permission to use the report.)

This paper agrees with the account of the routes taken by the Lvas given in *Prajum Bongsāvadān*, volume 61 (which Mr. Young could not have read at the time he composed his report because he had not yet been to Thailand), but I would like to add my comment that there are other cities in the Shan States which have walls, in many cases originally constructed by orders of the court at Ava, and that it is not clear what is meant by "records" in the sentence, "There is no written history but records and traditions have been handed down from father to son by word of mouth," and elsewhere. The Siamese in the paper were obviously the forces of Mangrāy. Mr. Young credits the Shans (in this context, the peoples of Tai stock) with "a wild temperament," which is also unclear. If by that it is meant that they are not tameable by newly imported faiths, he is right; and whatever other implications the phrase may connote, and whether it is true or not, will be plain to the reader of the translations of the *Pādaeng Chronicle* and the *Jengtung State Chronicle*. Certain it is that throughout the eight-hundred-odd years of their history the Shans have never been known to indulge in human headhunting as a pastime.

Legends and Chronicles

the *Jengtung State Chronicle* can be divided into two distinct parts, legendary and nonlegendary. It will be noticed that before the chronicle proper starts in paragraph 99, events are interlaced with legends and supernatural happenings, many of which find parallels or similarities in *Prajum Bongsāvadān*, volume 61, which is the chronicle of Chiengsaen from earliest times. It is not easy to come to a definite conclusion as to which is the copy of which, because the accounts, although similar, are not exactly the same. It is somewhat tantalizing to read those similar accounts in both chronicles in that when one is about to exclaim that this is a good and credible account with the proper sequence of events, the very sequence ends abruptly and some disconnected episode creeps in; or, when one is about to say that the account in this chronicle has been copied from that chronicle, differences come in. However, many events in the legendary part of the *Jengtung State Chronicle* are nonlegendary and are supported by similar events in the *Prajum Bongsāvadān* (61) and in *Tamnān Mūlasāsanā Chapap Vat Pādaeng*. From paragraph 99 to the end is the chronicle of Kengtung State proper, and the remarkable thing about this part is that no supernatural happenings are recorded, even though one finds superstitious beliefs here and there.

States and Kingdoms

If the *Jengtung State Chronicle* ended in the seventeenth or eighteenth century I would not hesitate to translate the word "mӧng" as "kingdom" and "brayā" as "king." Any kingdom, regardless of size, can be translated only as "mӧng" and kings and emperors of ancient times have been translated as "brayā" in Thai, Tai-Yuan, and Khṻn chronicles. Ruling princes of Kengtung have been called "brayā" or "rājā" or "rāja" in Pali terminology, and many of them have the title "Khemādhipati Rājādhirāja," which means "master of the Khema Kingdom, king of kings." The Burmese chronicles often refer to Kengtung, Jengrung, Hsenwi, Laos, and Chiengmai as "taing" or "pyī," both having the connotation of sovereign states with the implication or understanding that the paramount sovereign is at Pegu or Ava. Burmese kings referred to the rulers of Kengtung and other premier Shan States as "our sons" or "our royal nephews," and Burmese court language was used extensively in the courts of Shan rulers. Rulers of Laos and Chiengmai, formerly known as kings, used to deal with those of Kengtung as equals.

But, since the *Jengtung State Chronicle* continues into a later Burmese period and the period of British rule down to 1935, and since one must have a perspective sense of history, I have chosen to use uniformly throughout the translations "ruling prince" or "ruler" for "brayā," and "state" for "mön̈g." When the British took Mandalay they had already given the nomenclature "state" to various "independent" administrative units in the Shan States that had direct dealings with the Burmese court. This had precedent in India where hundreds of Indian states became British protectorates. This term in English is extremely convenient and flexible. Kyong, a village tract of twenty-four square miles near the modern town of Kalô, and Kengtung with its twelve-thousand-odd square miles, are both called states. In my translation of the *Jengtung State Chronicle* I have decided to accept the English term "state" to refer to Kengtung State as the administrative unit of the whole state, and this could be taken to be Khemaraṭṭha or Khema Kingdom of old, or the Khün country, or a district or province as it now is in Burma.

THE JENGTUNG STATE CHRONICLE

TRANSLATION

Humbly and gratefully dedicated
to the people of the State

(*Jengtung State Chronicle*, writing on front cover)

The year Koḍsaṅā Cuḷa Sakkarāja 1292, Month Five waxing 3rd ṅight, Thursday, nakkhatta 25. This book of the chronicle of successive princes who have ruled the State of Khemaraṭṭha, that is, the Khün State, beginning from Gopāḷa, Bhayā Kāhām (the king who was carried by the crows), one after another, until the reign of Prince Ratana Kônkaeu Intalaeng, is the property of Bhayā Jae, of Jengcan, Khāngkāḍ, [and] created for the house and for future posterity. Whoever borrows it for reading please return it soon. Do not ever lose it.

The *Jengtung State Chronicle*

1. Srisukhasvassadī siddhikān [Hail to auspicious happiness and success], the chronicle of the state of Jengtung will now be told.

2. Eko duggata gopālo Bārāṇasiyaṁ vasati [There was a poor cowherd who lived in Bārāṇasī]. There was a poor cowherd who lived in Bārāṇasī and earned a living by looking after people's cattle every day without a break. Whenever that cowherd opened his food packet he always gave some rice balls[1] to the crows.

3. At that time this state of Jengtung was known as Dammilāp,[2] also as Ôngpū,[3] and also as Caṇḍavajira.[4] The king of Caṇḍavajira having died without issue to continue the line of succession, the ministers, officials, and people assembled to look for, but had not yet found, a person of royal blood to ascend the throne, and they therefore had not yet performed funeral rites for the dead king.

4. The crows that had eaten the rice balls of the poor cowherd, wishing to reward his generosity, came to the cowherd and said, "We will make you king of a country; what do you have to say?" Hearing such words from the crows, the poverty-stricken man was very pleased and said, "If I really became a king I would slaughter enough cattle to feed you to your satisfaction." The crows then extracted a firm promise from the man and made him weave a basket reinforced with rattan loops and lines. Into the basket the poor man was made to go, and the crows caught hold of the rattan lines with their beaks and flew away. Arriving at Caṇḍavajiragvām at midnight the crows placed [the cowherd] on the throne[5] in the middle of the palace and flew [2] away.

5. Rattiyā vivassane suriya sugamanampatti [at the end of the night the sun comes up], when night had ended and dawn came, that cowherd put on royal apparel and sat on the throne. When the ministers, officials, and people saw such a sight they asked questions then and there. The cowherd replied, "O, you ministers and officials, the powerful devās headed by Brayā

Indā, seeing that this state had no one of royal blood to continue succession to the throne, considered thus, 'Our nephew should succeed to the throne as king of this state; then the people and the state would prosper in times to come.' So saying [the devās] had the crows invite me, brought me through the air, and placed me on the throne in this palace, as you all have seen."

6. When the ministers and officials heard those words they were wonder-struck and together exclaimed, "Sādhu" [very well!]. The astrologers were then called to foretell the future. [The astrologers] said that all would be well, but that one hundred years hence great, torrential rains would fall in this state for seven days and seven nights. The poverty-stricken cowherd was then crowned as king of the country. [Having become king, the cowherd] slaughtered a cow or a buffalo a day for the crows to eat to their satisfaction. After some time the number of cattle was depleted and an animal would be killed every two or three days reducing [3] gradually the amount of feed to the crows, and eventually the crows did not have enough to eat and became angry. The crows then agreed among themselves to abandon the king by deception in some uninhabited region.

7. The crows went and spoke to the king, saying, "There is a larger country than this one which has no ruler; we will take you there to be king of that country." Possessing low intelligence but unlimited greed, the king believed the beguiling words of the crows and blissfully bade farewell to the ministers, officials, and ladies of the palace, saying, "We have to be away from the kingdom, from parents and relatives for a spell, but we will come back in the near future." So saying he let the crows carry him away in the same manner as before. The crows took the cowherd and abandoned him on an uninhabited island in the ocean, taking leave of him with the words, "You stupid king, you did not keep your promise, and here you shall stay." Having said so all the crows flew away.

8. Not long after the departure of Brayā Caṇḍavajira Gopāla the state encountered a calamity of great, torrential rains which fell for about seven days and seven nights. Water rose everywhere, forests and mountains everywhere came down in landslides blocking river courses, and the country was submerged by the rising water, while ministers, officials, and the people had nowhere to stay and separately [4] migrated to faraway foreign lands.

9. Brayā Gopāla, who was abandoned by the crows on a midocean island, suffered great hardships and lived for a long time on yams and fruits, harking back with regret and sorrow to the kingdom which he had formerly enjoyed. He died of sorrow and

his soul returned as a spirit to Caṇḍavajiragvām where he saw the whole country was under water, devoid of any human being, and he took birth in the womb of a golden mother crab. He was born as a golden crab, big in size and beautiful in complexion, and all the crabs raised him to be their king. That crab was the overlord of all the crabs in that lake for a long time until the son of the fāvông[6] by the name of Tuṅga Rasī came down and drained the lake dry. By then, having nowhere to live, the crab burrowed into the foot of the mountain by the river flowing out of the drained lake and became the guardian spirit of the tail end of the state. That mountain has been known as Dôypūkhau [the mountain the crab entered] until the present day.

10. Here will be told how Tuṅga Rasī, son of the caufāvông, came down and drained the great lake of Caṇḍavajira.

11. When the Lord Omniscient had attained the Enlightenment for twelve vassā, the state of Caṇḍavajira was flooded and became a great lake known as Dammilāp. There were seven places which remained unsubmerged: Dônhlōng 1, Mônprāsād 1, Cômsak 1, Srīmöng 1, Môntung 1, Yāngbrahrin 1, Cômg̱ham 1--these seven places were not flooded.[7]

12. Lord Buddha, the Omniscient, with a retinue of forty-nine arahanta disciples, [5] came to the Subhāsudebba Hill during his preaching tours and left behind eight hairs of his head. He then came to Cômḍôy and accepted honey from Gāng Āy-ūn, washed the lid of his alms bowl at Cômḍôy, came to Cômsak Hill and washed the alms bowl at Tuṅga Lake. In other words, the Lord came and received from Gāng Āy-ūn the dāna of food packet and honey which was suspended from a tree at Cômḍôy, and, when he had eaten, Mahā Ānanda Thera took the lid of his alms bowl to wash in the valley stream at the foot of the hill. The Lord then gave eight hairs of his head to Gāng Āy-ūn, grouping them at the place where he sat and made the prophecy, saying, "In future this valley will be named Mönglang, the valley stream will be named Namphū, and the place where I am now sitting will be named Cômḍôy." Having made the prophecy, the Lord came to the hill in the middle of the lake. Ānanda Thera took the Lord's iron staff[8] and planted it in the ground and took the alms bowl to wash in the lake at the foot of the hill where he saw three flocks of birds--one white flock, one black flock, and one variegated flock. As for the seven grains of rice remaining in the alms bowl, the mahāthera threw them into the lake and returned, whereupon the Lord gave a slight smile. Mahā Ānanda Thera reverenced Lord Omniscient and asked for the cause of the smile. Lord Omniscient asked, "O, Ānanda, what did you see?" The mahāthera reverenced and said, "Bhante, Lord Omniscient, I saw three flocks of birds--one white flock, one black flock, and one variegated flock." The Lord said, "O, Ānanda, after the Tathāgata has attained Nibbāna, there will be a hermit coming from the north who will drain away the water of this Dammilāp Lake which will become [6] a state in which there will be three groups of people--one group with very virtuous hearts, one group with hearts midway between virtue and wickedness, and one group with very wicked hearts. Six hundred and twenty-nine years after the Nibbāna of the Tathāgata a king will bring the Sāsanā and establish it in this state without a doubt." So saying, the Lord further uttered, "Khemaṁ subhikkhaṁ bhavanti [? bhavantu] niccaṁ janapaddaṁsavā [? janapadassavā] sassāni sabbaji [? sabbadhi] santu khemaranno jayaṁ bhavaṁ" [May there always be prosperity and abundance of food in the region; may there be crops everywhere; may there be victory for the Khema king]. Having said thus the Lord returned to Jetavanārāma there.

13. The narrative in brief of the prophecy for the Khün state is ended.

14. One hundred and fifty years after the Nibbāna of the Lord, there was a fāvông by the name of Vôngtīfāng with enlightened wisdom whose powers extended one hundred yojana above and one hundred yojana below [the earth's surface] and to whom all kings and princes in the world always sent royal gifts. The fāvông had one thousand and four wives, all of whom were daughters of kings and princes, and one thousand and four sons, each princess having one son. Every one of the one thousand sons was well-versed in the Vedas, shooting with bows and arrows, horsemanship, and spear and javelin throwing, but the [remaining] four princes studied neither the various branches of knowledge nor the arts of war as desired by their parents --they only wanted to go forth[9] to become hermits. The caufāvông, the father, ordered them to be confined, four princes in four lock-up houses, and the palace cooks were ordered to give them food every day. The four princes practiced meditation by the kasiṇa methods[10] in their lock-ups, and after seven months attained lokiya jhāna[11] and moved through the air to the habitation of all hermits. The caufāvông sent men to look [for the princes] everywhere. [7] The men, having seen the habitation of the hermits, returned to report in every detail to the caufāvông, the father. Having learned [the truth], the caufāvông said, "My sons want to be hermits and have already gone forth, let my sons be hermits."

15. The four hermits practiced the Brahmavihāra without lessening their diligence, and every one of them attained samāpatti jhāna.[12] Wishing to visit places in all directions the four lords went to take leave of the fāvông, their father. The caufāvông, who was the father said, "Should you four princes see places suitable for settlement, do come back and tell Father." Thus enjoined [the caufāvông].

16. The four hermits moved through the air to one mountain named Jhāydhāy Jhānbhô,[13] which had three peaks, and saw the image of Mahā Kassapa[14] there.

17. [One hermit] went round to see the foothills in the east, which were wonderfully extensive, and, seeing a red sandalwood tree, rested under it. The devatā who guarded the eastern mountain came and asked the hermit, "What is the lord's name?" The hermit was inspired by that sandalwood tree to say that his name was Candasikkhatuṁ. The devatā created out of red sandalwood a hermitage, an alms bowl, a staff, and a tālapatta,[15] and offered them as dāna to the hermit. The hermit stayed there to look after the image of Mahā Kassapa.

18. The second hermit went along the mountainside in the south, saw a cliff of radiant stone, and rested there. The devatā who guarded the southern direction came and asked, "What is my lord's name?" Inspired by the stone, the hermit said, "My name is Subhāna Rasī." That devatā made out of radiant stone an alms bowl, a staff, and a tālapatta, and created a hermitage for the hermit to reside in.

19. The third hermit went along the mountainside in the west, saw a white sandalwood tree, and rested there. The devatā who guarded the western direction came and asked, "What is my lord's name?" The hermit spoke according to the sign of the white sandalwood, saying, "My name is Candana Rasī." The devatā made out of white sandalwood an alms bowl, a staff, and a tālapatta, and created a hermitage for the hermit to reside in.

20. The fourth hermit went along the mountainside in the north, saw crystal stones, and rested there. The devatā who guarded the northern direction came and asked, "What is my lord's name?" The hermit said his hame was Phalika Rasī. The devatā created out of crystal stone a hermitage, an alms bowl, a staff, and a tālapatta, and offered them as dāna to Phalika Rasī.

21. The four hermit brothers made a solemn agreement with one another, saying, "On days of new moon and full moon, let us assemble at [the hermitage of] our eldest brother, Candasikkhatuṁ." The hermits had this solemn agreement between them, and, each having made a wooden bell to strike in worship of the image of Mahā Kassapa Thera, stayed the vassā on that mountain. After the vassā the hermits stayed on until the cold season was over. Then, together, the hermit brothers moved through the air and arrived at Aḷāvī state at dawn--that was why it had been named Jengrung [city of dawn].

22. The four hermits went on their way and came to a crystal cave, and the hermit named Phānaphalika was so delighted with the cave that they rested there for fifteen days. Then they traveled [further] and reached a high ground above the water, which has been [9] named Yāngfū Dônhlōng[16] until now. The four hermits traveled [further] and reached Cômsak Hill[17] and saw the writing and the mark of the staff which Lord Omniscient had planted into the ground [for all] to see. The writing read, "Truly, in time to come, a hermit named Candasikkhatuṅga Rasī will come from the north and drain this lake dry, and a future kingdom will arise bearing the name of that hermit."

23. Having seen [the staff mark and the writing] the hermits traveled through the air to the south and came to rest on a mountain summit and saw a rock with the shape of an elephant. It has been named Dôyjāng [elephant mountain] until the present time. The hermit by the name of Pabhāna Rasī returned through the air to make a solemn resolve and with his staff drew a channel to make water flow to the south for the first time.

24. After staying there for seven days, [the hermits] went through the air together to a mountain by the name of Āyrupnāy and stayed there for three vassā. [There] they saw a column as big as a palm tree, tall as the sky, red as the flame of the fire. When they went through the air to see it, they met a hermit who was two hundred and fifty years old, to whom they paid their reverence, and together they saw the relics of Lord Buddha, radiant, beautiful, and excellent. The five hermits then traveled through the air to the ocean and selected five giant shells, [each measuring] five vā[18] in length and breadth, and they pierced the five shells with their staffs and brought them, returning through the air to the Lord's relics. They started the construction of a cetiya with four shells, and, covering these with the fifth shell, a cetiya was constructed [over them]. [The cetiya has lasted] until the present time.

25. At that time [the lake] was still a great sheet of water measuring six yojana. The hermit by the name of Subhāna Rasī said to Binla Rasī thus, [10] "You will drain this lake so that settlements will arise [in its place] to look after the Lord's relics." Accordingly, the hermit made a solemn resolve and drained the brimming lake with the staff of radiant stone, and together they returned through the air to the mountain Āyrupnāy. The hermit who was the elder brother, looking at the future, gave that mountain the name of his younger brother as Dôy Subhāsudeb [and it has been known by that name] until now. There they stayed for three vassā, after which they came

together to the mountain Cômtung and went to have a look at the lake, but it was not dry, and the water merely seeped through the mountain ridges. That is why it has been named Dôy Sanjüm[19] until now. The four hermits then returned to the Phānaphalika cave and named it as Tham Phāsaeng [cave of precious stones] because of Phalika Rasī.

26. It was then that the hermit by the name of Candasikkhatuṅga Rasī made a solemn resolve, saying, "If this lake is to become a state in the future [in which] the Sāsanā will prosper, may this khaukhem rice[20] sprout as a seedling." So saying, he broadcast the khaukhem rice into the water at one place and seedlings came up. The hermit made [another] solemn resolve, saying, "If this lake really dries up, may there be a [small] lake in the middle of the city." So saying, the hermit brought his red sandalwood staff in order to draw a channel to the north. Saying, "The state will be teeming and prosperous in the future," he drew a channel to the north and the water flowed forcefully northwards without a break until the water dried up.

27. The hill on which the hermit stayed and made his solemn resolve is called Cômsak because the Lord planted his staff there and composed the writing. The place where Mahā Ā- [11]
nanda Thera washed the alms bowl and saw the three flocks of birds has become a lake called Hnöngtung. When the water of that [great] lake dried up, Gopāla, the golden crab, went along the water current, entered a hill, and disappeared there. [That hill] was called Dôypūkhau [the mountain the crab entered]; now it is called Dôybūkhau ["dôy" = "būkhau" = hill or mountain].

28. There was a nāga lady who always gambolled in that lake, and when the lake had been drained by the hermit she came out [of her underground dwelling] and saw no water but a hermit staying there. She approached the hermit and reverencing him inquired after everything. The hermit spoke to the nāga lady telling her about the Lord's prophecy regarding himself. The hermit gave instructions to the nāga lady, saying, "You must guard this place so that it will become a prosperous state throughout the five thousand vassā of the Sāsanā. Let no harm come to it." Receiving the hermit's words, the nāga lady said, "Should an enemy come to molest the state in order to destroy it, I will guard and protect it against any destruction." Thus did the nāga lady receive the instructions of the hermit and go to reside at the Phāyang Hill.[21]

29. The place where the hermit sowed the seed of khaukhem rice which sprouted into seedlings is now called Tāklā.

30. When the hermit had started the draining process but the lake was not yet dry, the entry of the vassā was near. On the full moon day of Month Eight, the hermits Candasikkhatuṅga Rasī and Pabhāna Rasī stayed at the Phāsaeng Cave, Subhāna Rasī went to the mountain Subhāsudebba, and Candana Rasī went to stay at the Cômsrī[22] Cave. The four hermits who were brothers stayed on [? in their respective places] for seven [12] years and the lake water dried up and [the old lake basin] was suitable for the construction of a city, except at the foot of the Sak Hill, as the hermit had wished. [This is the Hnôngtung or Tuṅga Lake within the present-day city of Kengtung].

31. The four hermits returned to their father in the Vông country and told him everything about the suitability of establishing a city. The fāvông who was the father, having been so informed, gave orders to one leader by the name of Kvāndö and to five hundred families to come down with the hermits and build a city. They first settled at Hnôngdö-ôn and cultivated rice. The paddy stalks were three cubits high and the paddy ears one cubit and four fingers long, but there were no rice grains in them. They decapitated pigs and chickens as sacrifice to the spirits. No matter how much the sacrifice was made there were no grains in any year. After three complete years the state's guardian spirits were not pleased and a great many [of the Kvāndö people] died. The spirits spoke [through a medium], saying, "We do not like the Chinese and are opposed to the construction of the city by them; we shall construct one ourselves in the future." The spirits came and spoke thus, and all the Chinese fled. The place of the Chinese construction was called Hôkvāndö and is known as Kvān Hnôngdö in the present day.

32. Three years after that a seed of the striped gourd was born at Hnôngtāng, with its vines climbing and creeping on trees everywhere and bearing many fruit. After three years its fruit grew to the size of small nuts and fell to the ground bursting and scattering [their seeds] all over. [That is why the places] are called Bāndōn, Khobô, Hnôngkhôn, until the present time. The [seeds of the] gourds scattered and fell into the footprints of oxen, buffaloes, elephants, rhinoceroses, and [from them] are born the Lvas who inhabit the whole country. There was one person who was very big, tall, and handsome, and they raised him to be the leader, the lord of them all. They built villages and towns and among themselves created [13] village heads and regional chiefs. The person whom they had chosen as their leader was named Māngyôy, and [he] came and lived at that Jengkaeu[23] as their overlord for the whole state. One person was Gāng Jengtāng, one person was Gāng Jenghlek, one person was the gāng at Vengyen, one person was the gāng at Būya, one person was Gāng Māngkhem living near

Hnôngtung, one person was Mānglön living at Mānglön, one person was Māngjhô living at Phājhô--these eight gāng or eight māng were the chiefs of all Lvas, their subjects numbering eighty thousand, and they constructed villages and towns, cultivating yams and roots there for seven years.

33. Here will be told the origin of the birth of Brayā Mangrāy.

34. At that time a brayā dham ["brayādham," king of righteousness] was born by the name of Vôngtīfāng who was very powerful, and great princes and kings of the Jumbū [Jambudīpa], every one of them, went to pay reverence [to him] except one country. Brayā In [Indra or Sakka], seeing that that country did not pay reverence, came down and asked [the people of that country], saying, "A brayādham has been born, why have you not been to pay him reverence?" They said, "It is true we have not been to pay reverence because we have no king whom we could obey. The water reaches the bodies and our heads reach the same height[24]--no one would obey anyone, and that is why we have not been to pay our reverence." Brayā In said to them, "From now on when you see anyone born without father, without mother, you should consecrate him as the chief, the lord to rule over all of you." So saying, he returned to his palace in the heaven of Tāvatiṃsā where he commanded one devaputta and one devatā, saying, "You two go down and be the lords of those people."

35. The two, devaputta and devatā, came down and stayed at the foot of one sandalwood[25] tree at Möngfāng there. When [14] the people saw the devaputta and devatā staying there, they went to ask, saying, "Where have the two lords come from?" Then, the devaputta said, "We two are without father, without mother. We are born here." They came back and said, "We saw one man and one woman staying at the foot of the jujube tree [*Zizyphus jujuba*]; let us go together and bring them to be our lords, as the devatā[26] has told us."

36. Thereupon, the people harnessed four royal Sindhu horses to a state chariot [phussaratha] and, striking up music, let the horses go towards the east. After [the people] made three reverential rounds [padakkhiṇa] of salutation, the horses headed east and reached the foot of the jujube tree, big and tall, having [a girth of] eighteen closed hands [about five feet]. The horses skirted the foot of the tree towards the east and, having seen the two devarājās, kneeled down in front of the royal brother and sister.[27] The populace, having seen the peerless beauty and handsomeness [of the two devās], made obeisance and asked about everything, playing music in worship. They talked to one another, saying, "They must have come up from the earth here." "The man must have been born by supernatural power." "The woman must have been born by magical power." They invited them to rule over the country. The two devaputtas accepted the invitation, mounted the chariot and returned by the same route to the city where they ascended the palace, and sat on the gem-studded throne and ruled the country with glory and power. The lord used supernatural clothing, implements, and utensils with a crown and gem-studded earrings, all supernatural, with no one to rival--it was a great wonder.

37. [15] The devarājā reigned with great glory, subjugating small nations, tributary states, small villages, and large countries totaling ten thousand paddy fields, well known throughout small and great kingdoms. He constructed villages and towns, demarcated boundaries, appointed ministers and officials to rule over provinces, small and big. When these had been done, ministers and officials of small and big provinces came together and performed consecration and marriage ceremonies, placing the two royal persons on a mound of gems[28] as independent sovereigns. The lord enjoyed the wealth of the kingdom, ruling over one million paddy fields of fifty-seven [provinces][29]--happy, secure, and prosperous.

38. At that time the blessed and excellent royal elephant of the sovereign was being looked after and guarded every day by the mahouts. One day the royal elephant escaped from its stable. The mahouts went in search of the elephant but did not find it anywhere. They followed the elephant's footprints which entered a stream, circumambulated one place, and returned to the original position. They followed the elephant's footprints and returned to their starting point in the city. The mahouts reported the matter to the king, saying, "Sire, we followed the footprints of the excellent royal elephant; the footprints circumambulated one place, describing a circle, and returned by the same route. It was a wonder." Having heard those words the king said, "I will [personally] go and see the elephant's footprints." So saying, he took ministers and officials and the populace as retinue and followed the footprints of the elephant. The brayā had people measure the [circumambulation] of the elephant's footprints, and it was seven hundred vā. The brayā ordered the people to construct a city there.

39. On return to Möngf̲āng the brayā arrived at a locality where a villager on a foray into the forest had found a tortoise and brought it back. Seeing the brayā in their midst, the villager brought out the tortoise [16] and presented it to him. The brayā made him the chief of the village, which has been known as Bān Rôytau [village of the tortoise's trace or footprints] for that reason. The place of the elephant's circumambulation, where the brayā gave instructions for a city to be built, has been named Veng Jengrôy.[30]

40. Before long the queen became great with child and after ten months gave birth to a boy with beautiful features and the strength of thirteen elephants. His father, the brayā, had an iron cradle made [for him] because he was so naughty. When the prince grew up, the brayā who was the father gave him the name of Mangrāy for that reason. Prince Mangrāy was born with great glory, handsome features, and great strength. He also was intelligent and learned, able to deliberate arguments of the common people and settle them with great justice. Even the devās rained down popped rice in worship of him. There were two men who were counselors [of the prince] on all affairs, because the two were endowed with intelligence and learning and capabilities; they had discipline and a clear knowledge of the Piṭaka and of mundane and supramundane matters. The prince made them royal pages of the left and of the right.[31]

41. One day the prince went out hunting in the forest alone to look for a golden stag but did not see one. He ate his meal on a rock. He [later] cleansed his body and retreated to the city. At that time there was a female bear which saw Prince Mangrāy eat his meal and cleanse his body. She came and drank that water and a feeling of joy went through her body, and she thought thus, "I am going to have a baby," and ran away. Before long, that bear was pregnant for ten months and gave birth to a boy with beautiful features. The mother bear [17] brought up the child who grew up and, because of the power of the devās and past accumulated merit, was proficient in [human] speech. The child of the bear asked his mother, saying, "O, mother, two of us are not the same. Why are you, mother, a bear, and I a human?" The mother bear told her child everything, saying, "You are truly the son of Mangrāy." Realizing that he was the real son of Mangrāy, the prince told his mother, "I am going to look for my father." So saying the prince went in search of his father and actually arrived and told Lord Mangrāy everything. Lord Mangrāy believed the [boy's] words and saying "You are truly my son," named him Khun Dö̈ng, from the fact that the female bear came and drank the liquid that remained [dö̈ng] on the rock.

42. Having grown up, Khun Dö̈ng wished to go to his mother, and, taking some young men with him, he went in search of his mother. He reached a big forest near a lake. A nāga lady came out and played in the lake and saw Khun Dö̈ng with his handsome features, whereupon, desiring him as her husband, she shielded the eyes of his followers and took Khun Dö̈ng away. Not seeing the prince anywhere, the young men betook themselves home.

The nāga lady, on the other hand, took Khun Dǒng away to be her husband, and they lived together there.

43. One day, the nāga lady, wishing to go and sport in that lake, spoke to her husband thus, "I am going to sport in the lake with my retinue; please do not go and see me; please stay here." So saying, she had Khun Dǒng stay in bed and stitched the mosquito net to the mattress, thereby forcing him to stay there, while she went [18] and played in the lake with her retinue. At that moment the prince, wishing to see his wife at bath, took a small knife and cut away the thread and came out to look for his wife; he only saw snakes, all looking alike, and he was unable to recognize his wife; he therefore returned to his bed as before. After sporting in the lake, the nāga wife came and opened the mosquito net and saw the trace of the knife cut. She told the prince, saying, "You are not true to your word. I shall not allow you to live with me. I now have a three-month old child [within me] whom I will press out for you." So saying she pressed out her child and, wrapping him in the leaves of maidüng [*Dipterocarpus tuberculatus*], gave him to her husband. She then pressed milk [from her breasts] on to the düng leaves and said, "When the milk is no more you will bring our son and leave him at the foot of the tree over there." Having left instructions with her husband [the nāga lady] went down [into the cave] there.

44. The prince came away from the lady, carrying his son back to the city. When the milk was no more he placed the son at the foot of the düng tree, and she would come out to suckle the child every day.

45. When the lord kumāra grew up he asked his father, "Who is my mother?" The father said, "Your mother is a nāga lady living in a cave in the forest near the lake over there." So saying, the prince named the son Khun Düng because the nāga lady who was the mother wrapped him with düng leaves, and he was named Khun Düng[32] for that reason.

46. Having grown up and wishing to see his mother, the prince took leave of the father and went to his mother. The nāga lady who was the mother asked [him] questions and, having learned that he was her own son, she was very pleased and said, "You must first go and see your grandfather over there; whatever your grandfather gives you, do not accept it; only ask for a magical bronze pot and a city-creating magical hook[33]--you must try to obtain these two things." So saying, she sent him on. On arriving in the grandfather's presence he told him everything about the situation. The king of the serpents who was the grandfather [19] residing in the deep water, on seeing the grandson, was very happy and exchanged greetings with him.

Prince Khun Düng, the grandson, asked for the magical bronze pot and the city-creating magical hook, and the king of the serpents gave him everything. Having obtained the supernatural articles, Khun Düng took leave of the serpent king and came out [of the watery abode]. On arriving at one place the prince saw a forest of mixed trees and rattan vines, whereupon he brought out the supernatural articles given by the serpent king and wielded the magical hook, and the place was transformed into a city, and he resided there. That prince having been born of a heavenly egg of serpent descent, the city has been called Mönghvāy[34] until the present time.

47. The king of devās came and created Mangrāy as supreme head of all Lānnā, in the year Rāycai, Month Eight full moon, Wednesday, Daiy Kāpsan at noon and the constellation was 27 [Revatī], [and] cooking stones [used as a trivet] of Brayā Mangrāy turned into gold that day. The brayā of Labūn moved to a new city and was prosperous in every way according to his wishes. Brayā Mangrāy devised a stratagem to take Jenghmai. At the age of fifteen he brought the daughter of the brayā of Labūn to be his wife. At sixteen [he] had one son called Khun Gong. At eighteen [he] again had another son called Khun Lang. From the age [? reign] of devarājā, the grandfather and Brayā Mangrāy and Khun Döng, the ṣon, and Khun Düng, the grandson, [there were] twelve successive reigns of the line of the heavenly egg of the serpent king, until the reign of Cau Kaendāu, who had two sons, one named Cau Möngpün, one named Cau Japūng, [the latter] had seven sons, the youngest of whom was named Cau Mungmöng, [and he] had three sons, one named Cau G̱hāmyōng, one named Cau Phāyū, and the younger brother was named Cau Künā who was as clever as Brayā Mangrāy.

48. The first narrative of Mangrāy is here completed.

49. Here will be told [20] a little of the chronicle of Jenghmai,[35] the one million rice fields of fifty-seven provinces.

50. One hundred and seven years after Lord Buddha, the Omniscient One, had attained Nibbāna, there were two hermits who saw that Jenghmai was without a ruler, that the country was suitable for the establishment of the excellent Buddha-Sāsanā which would become prosperous in time to come, and that ways and means should be found to place a ruler in that country. Thus, they [the hermits] thought, and they saw Nāng Cāmmadevī, who possessed great accumulated merit. [She] was the daughter of Brayā Ārammaken of Āravō kingdom, and the wife of Brayā Srīsubrahmarājā, the crown prince [uparājā] and son of Brayā Ārammaken, sharing the same father as the princess. [When the] princess had been in pregnancy for three months the crown prince who was the husband went forth to become a hermit. The

princess underwent the dukkha of having to be separated from the loved one and of having to be an abandoned wife. [It was] then [that] the two hermits approached Brayā Rammaken, the father, and the prince who was her husband, and asked for Princess Cāmmadevī to be the ruler of Jenghmai. Brayā Rammaken, the father, and the prince hermit, the husband, gave permission in accordance with the wishes of the princess. Being a lady, weak in physical strength and fearful of future dangers, the princess requested from the hermits a promise [of assistance when needed] and the two hermits gave the promise of assistance in every way. Having learned of the princess' consent to go [to Jenghmai], the two hermits brought her up to be the ruler of the kingdom and consecrated her by seating [her] on a mound of gold[36] and constructed for her the bell tower, the ceremonial tower, and the sun tower. The queen constructed villages and towns with appropriate grades and classifications, together with places of worship, and named the capital Haribhuñja which later lengthened to Haribhuñjayanagara.

51. When the queen had completed ten months of pregnancy, [21] she gave birth to two sons on the same day, the elder named Mahantāyassa and the younger, Nandayassa.

52. One day the queen wished to bask in the sun [and ventured out]. At that moment a crow came and flew at her; she was terrified and ran back to the palace. Whenever she wished to bask in the sun, the crow would come and fly at her. The queen asked the astrologers to work out what this portended. The astrologers reverenced her and said that the incidents would not affect her in any way, but that the crow came and flew at her at that spot because there was a sacred object there. The queen asked what sacred object was there and that the astrologers should work it out properly. The latter said that there were sacred relics of the Lord at that spot. She said, "If that is true you should bring them out and build a great cetiya [over them] at that spot." The astrologers said that the Lord's relics were there without a doubt, but that three rings of yons[37] [machine, Pali "yanta"] had been constructed to guard them, making it difficult to bring out the relics, and that in order to obtain the relics a person must be found capable of cutting the cords of the yons; then only would [the relics] be obtained.

53. The queen sent for a master who could cut the cords of the yons, and he came. The master compounded his medicine and, having put it in a jar, recited magical incantations into it scrupulously and gave instructions [apparently to the astrologers], saying, "When I have cut the yon cords, the yons will come and cut off my neck without a doubt. When my neck has been cut off, please dip it into the medicinal compound and connect it [to my body] as before." The master dug deep into the ground and saw the yons with blades revolving nonstop [around the relics]. The master cut the [outer] yon cords and a yon came fluttering out and cut his neck off. The astrologers took the master's body and dipped it in the medicinal compound and reconnected [the head and the body], and he came to life as before. The master again went to the middle ring and cut the yon cords and the yon came fluttering out and cut off his neck as before, and they dipped his body in the medicinal compound and reconnected [the head and the body] as before. The master then went into the innermost ring and [22] saw the cords of the ever-revolving yon and severed them. The yon came fluttering out and cut off the master's neck, and went on the slam into the compound jar and overturn it, making it impossible for the people to find the medicinal compound into which to dip [the master's head], and the master definitely died there.

54. The yons were no more, and the people dug deeper into the ground and saw [? miniature] golden boats, one atop another, silver and gold pedestal trays, one atop another, and a rounded pedestal tray with a conical cover containing the relics amidst precious gems. Inside were one hundred thousand gold [approximately 270 pounds] which the people took out to build a great cetiya at that place. From then on the kingdom was happy and prosperous.

55. At that time there was a Lva named Laṅgo, who was the overlord of all Lvas, residing in Usupabbatta [arrow mountain], and he was very strong and powerful. When that Lva learned that the queen had come to reside in the kingdom he had a desire to have Nāng Cāmmadevī as his wife. He therefore tied a letter to the neck of a lance and threw the latter so that it fell in the middle of the city. They [the people] took the letter and presented it to the queen. When she learned that the Lva man had a desire to have her, she thought to herself thus, "The Dammilva is base and low; no matter how powerful he may be, he is not suitable for me. Were I to reply with brief words it would not be proper; I must think of means to demolish the power of the brayā of the Lvas," and she wrote a reply saying that her sons were still small, but that when the two sons were a little older and able to comprehend human language[38] she would accept him. She tied [the letter] to the neck of the lance and threw it away [back]. After that she stitched a longyi[39] out of white cloth and wore it as the inner garment until it was soiled; then, having cleaned it properly, stitched it into a hat and tied it to the lance neck and hurled it up to Usubbha Mountain as a present for the Lva chief. The brayā of the Lvas saw the hat and, thinking it was very beautiful, put it on his head with a delighted heart and [23]

thought: "This lady is really fond of me." He again wrote a letter and tied it to the lance neck and hurled it, but the lance fell at the foot of the hill without reaching [the city] because his power had declined. Since then it has been the custom for women to wear white inner longyis until now.

56. When the queen learned that he [the Lva chief] had lost his power, she prepared an army and asked the two sons to make war, and [the sons] were victorious over Brayā Laṅgo, the Lva chief, [and the Lvas] were utterly destroyed and fled. That mountain was named Dôy Lvavôd [mountain of Lva extinction] for that reason. That city was known as Veng Lvabung [city of Lva hurling (the lance)] for that reason, which later was corrupted into the name Labūn.

57. The elder son of Cāmmadevī by the name of Mahantāyassa succeeded his mother in ruling over Jenghmai. Queen Cāmmadevī ruled over Jenghmai for fifty-three years, dying at the age of ninety-two. The younger son by the name of Nandayassa was told to go and rule over Kherānagôn [Khelāṅga-nagara]. Prince Mahantāyassa succeeded his mother for twenty-seven years and died. A son by the name of Puññarājapuḍ succeeded his father for thirty years and died. At that time the Sakkarāja was 560; the Lord had attained Nibbāna for 110 vassā. Brayā Dhammaruddha terminated the Sakkarāja that year.[40] At Sakkarāja 1, Nāng Cāmmadevī became the monarch reigning over Jenghmai. After forty-nine reigns of rulers the dynasty came to an end.

58. The narrative about Jenghmai is here concluded as a chapter.

59. Here will be told about Jengtung state, inhabited by the Lvas.

60. Regarding the great lake Dammilāp which Caṇḍasikkha-Tuṅgarasī had drained dry for the construction of villages and towns, the Chinese tried to settle there but were not successful. The striped gourds gave birth to a low people like the Dammilas [Damiḷas] and they became Lvas, inhabiting the country, every place, [24] everywhere. Wishing to bring and establish the Sāsanā [in Jengtung], the devatās by supernatural powers placed a golden stag in the pleasure garden of Brayā Mangrāy. His heart having been inspired by the devatā, Brayā Mangrāy had a desire to go hunting wild game. He therefore collected four hundred hunters and, having made preparations regarding snaring nets, hunting horns, hunting dogs, rice, water, salad ingredients, onions, garlics, chilies, salt, all complete, led the host out of the city in order to go hunting.[41]

61. He came across the stag created by the devatās, having hair like gold, having eyes like great sapphires, having horns like cat's eyes. Having seen [the stag], the brayā gave chase, following it tantalizingly close. The stag [sometimes] acted as if it was lame in the leg, and the brayā chased it for seven days; the powers of the devatās led him to give chase over long distances. He reached a place where he thought he had caught up with the stag and dived to seize it, but failed. That region is now known as Möngn̈ôm ["n̈ôm," to cover something with one's body, as a hen does her eggs]. He did not give up, but chased the stag further away. The region was known as Mönglai up to now ["lai," to chase or hunt]. Brayā Mangrāy chased the stag towards the south; the stag leapt onto a cliff and the brayā hurled a spear but missed it by two fingers. The spear cut the face of the cliff making a mark there just behind the stag's footprint. The hill has been named Dôylai up to the present time. ["Lai" is from "lai-reng," which means "in consecutive order."] The imprints of the stag and of the spear are still there now. The stag sped towards the west and the brayā, following its footprints, reached a hill called Phālāy [variegated cliff] and saw a large, extensive valley suitable for constructing a city, but it was inhabited completely by the subject people, the Lvas. The brayā cut figures of a dog and a man carrying a spear, a snaring net, a hunting hook, and a hunting horn on the rock surface of Phālāy Hill. He then followed the track of the stag up to the Hōmöng River and obtained a jungle stag. The brayā felt weak and tired; he therefore took a rest, [25] made a minced venison salad, and ate it for his midday meal. He cut off the roots of the onions and garlics, which fell to the ground and became the [onion and garlic] seeds in that region, which up to now has been named Mönglāp ["lāp" is a salad of meat and vegetables], and it has had onions and garlics from that time. Having eaten his meal, the brayā again followed the track of the stag towards the northeast up a hill, and, cornering the stag at an embankment, hurled his spear at it. A rock created by the devatās cropped up, the stag stepped onto it and fled. That rock still bears the footprints of the stag to this day. The stag's track then disappeared and in vain did the brayā look for it. The stag entered a cave on the summit of Dôy Mungmöng [roof of the state]. That hill was known as Dôy Kwāngghamcuk [the hill on which the stag stood]; it is now called Dôy Cukgham.

62. Brayā Mangrāy proceeded further but did not see the track of the stag anywhere and gave up the chase there and the place has been named Dôy Lai up to now. The brayā collected his forces and returned home. There Brayā Mangrāy spoke to the gathering of ministers and officials, saying, "I went to hunt a golden stag and saw one country in the north all inhabited by the Lvas where we should make appropriate constructions. We shall take our forces to fight [the Lvas] and drive them all away and will create villages and towns." So saying he gave royal orders to the two sons, Khun Gong [? and Khun Lang], giving them a force of five thousand men to fight the Dammilas [Damiḷas] of Tuṅga country until they were vanquished. The two princely brothers obeyed the orders of the royal father and came up with forces there.

63. That year Mahā Liko heading eight bhikkhus brought the Sāsanā up from Ayodhiyā and established it in the kingdom of Jenghmai of the million rice fields.

64. Khun Gong brought his forces to fight [against the Lvas] at Baby Elephant Hill. The Lvas could not prevail against Khun Gong, and had to disperse [26] and withdraw. Prince Khun Gong gave chase to the Lvas until one locality was reached. Here his wife, whom he had brought along, gave birth to a child, and, because of compassion, he rested. The wife gave birth to a child in a war camp and he was a boy [and was] named Janañjeyyayuddha. [They] rested there for one month, [and the place has been] named Möngbak[42] ["bak," rest] until now.

65. Khun Lang arrived with his forces and the Lvas came out to fight but could not prevail against the prince and retreated. Khun Lang followed them and established himself at one place, and that place has been called Mönglang to this day.

66. As regards Khun Gong, when his wife had completed her month,[43] he brought his forces to fight but did not win. Khun Lang did not help--he merely looked on. When Khun Lang fought, Khun Gong also did not help--he merely looked on. Hence the saying: "Tok Gong gô ḍū Gong; tok Lang gô ḍū Lang" [When it is Gong's turn, merely look at Gong; when it is Lang's turn, merely look at Lang]. They could not defeat the Lvạs and went down to report to Brayā Mangrāy. [Mangrāy] was furious and reprimanded Khun Gong and Khun Lang and deprived them of their ranks and positions.

67. The year after that the brayā sent for two Lvas living at Dôydung and spoke to them, saying, "There is one Lva in the north, will you go and fight him?" Of the two Lvas, one was named Māngghūm, one was named Māngghen. The two reverenced Brayā Mangrāy, saying, "You desire us to go and fight; it will not be easy to win a victory, but we will try. Should an opportunity come for victory, we would send you a message and only then should Your Majesty bring up forces to fight." The brayā said, "You are of the same Lva race and can understand each other's language; go and try with a stratagem."

68. Māngghūm and Māngghen received the royal orders of their lord and fled with their families to Māngyôy. Seeing the arrival of Māngghūm and Māngghen, Māngyôy asked, "What causes two of you to come here?" Māngghūm and Māngghen said, "Two of us have incurred the wrath of Brayā Mangrāy and both of us have come to my lord for refuge; please do not let us die." [27] Māngyôy believed them completely and allowed them to establish a city there.

69. Whatever the two said or managed was approved by Māngyôy. After a stay of three years, there was nobody above Māngghūm and Māngghen, and the two wrote to Brayā Mangrāy saying, "Bring armed forces to fight." And Brayā Mangrāy brought up armed forces to fight. Māngghūm and Māngghen took out a force as if to give a real battle, [but instead] sent a letter to Māngyôy saying that the enemy forces were too great to overcome and that unless [Māngyôy] ran away all would perish. Māngyôy could not run fast enough and was captured, but he was not killed--he was only imprisoned. Those Lvas who could not run away came and submitted, saying, "We beg to be the humble subjects of the kingdom's hills." Māngyôy was made their chief and they were told to [? go] and live at Mungmöng Hill ["mung," to cover like a roof; "möng," state, kingdom, etc.], where the golden stag had stood up, and it was named Bāngham [golden village].

70. Because Māngyôy started a new line as the chief of the region, [he was re-]named Mānggham for that reason. An oath of allegiance was administered to the Lvas, saying, "Here shall you stay. If you should so much as turn or tense your bodies all of you would perish and die. And when you hear the croaking of the frogs, big and small, you shall be ill with diseases." They accepted everything. And after his victory over the Lvas, the brayā returned to his kingdom with his forces. At that time the state became deserted.

71. Here will be told about Brayā Mangrāy's efforts at conquering Jenghmai.[44]

72. The brayā reflected: "I will try [to conquer Jenghmai] with wisdom and stratagem." So saying he talked to a Lva who lived at Dôydüng named Hmünfā, saying, "We will ask you to go and take the city of Jenghmai, will you be able to do it or not?" Hmünfā paid reverence, saying, "[I] will go and try. When the time is ripe [I] will send a message to [28] Your Majesty; you could then go with an army and attack." He then packed up and went to Jenghmai where he paid reverence to the brayā, saying, "I have incurred the wrath of Brayā Mangrāy and he is going to kill me; I beg to come for refuge as Your Majesty's subject." The brayā believed that it was true and took him into his service, giving him the name of Saenfā, and whatever he did in affairs of state was after the brayā's heart in every way.

73. He [Saenfā] urged the people to make a dam [of wood and bamboo] across the Maebing River in the south so that all the rice fields above [the dam] were flooded. When the people objected, he would say, "Your lord of earth has given the orders to do it this way; it is not what our Brayā Mangrāy would do." Everyone of the populace could not but raise his hands to pay reverence to Brayā Mangrāy. Brayā Bā [Yībā of Haribhuñjaya], ignorant of the plot against him, praised him [Saenfā] further and gave him a new title of Saen Fāfôngbing [overlord of the waves on the Bing]. When the brayā asked him to tell the people to fetch timber for the palace, he verily told the people to fetch timber for the palace, making people haul the posts to the city. When [a post was] tied [with ropes for hauling] by the root end, he said that would be tying the head of the brayā. When tied by the top end he said that would be tying the feet of the brayā. He made them tie [the posts with ropes] at the center and haul them across the rice fields. When the people objected, he would say, "Your lord the brayā has given the orders to do it this way; it is not what our Brayā Mangrāy would do." Everyone of the populace raised his hands to pay reverence to Brayā Mangrāy. He [Saen Fāfôngbing] knew that the hearts of the populace were revolting against their prince and sent a message to his lord, Brayā Mangrāy.

74. Brayā Mangrāy gave orders for setting an army on the move to attack Jenghmai then and there. At that time Saen Fāfôngbing undertook to lead the [Jenghmai] army to fight Brayā Mangrāy as if he meant to do it seriously. He sent a message back to Brayā Bā, saying, "If you are going to flee, flee immediately; if not, you will die. We are [29] all one." Brayā Bā fled and reached a hill, and he was so angry that with his sword he cut a rock into pieces like hay. And he wept there; that hill has been named Dôy Bāhai [the hill where Bā wept]. The brayā went to his younger brother, named Brayā Bôn, ruling the southern region. [They] brought forces to fight against Brayā Mangrāy, but they did not win and the two brothers died there.

75. From the time Nāng Cāmmadevī came from Āravo kingdom and ruled Jenghmai there had been thirty-two monarchs ending with the reign of Brayā Bā and Brayā Bôn, without a successor. Having conquered the kingdom of Lānnā, Brayā Mangrāy gave orders for sculptures to be made of Brayā Bā and Brayā Bôn and the sword with the blade as big as a bullock pack, and these were kept on the surface of the rock.

76. The narrative about Brayā Mangrāy's conquest of Jenghmai is here ended as a chapter.

77. The narrative about the Khün state will now be told.

78. After the conquest of Jenghmai, Brayā Mangrāy gave orders for the construction of villages and towns in Jengtung. Brayā Mangrāy had astrologers come up and inspect the countryside everywhere. The astrologers said it was not auspicious to construct the city at Jenghlek [site of the present airfield], as there would be no royal offspring [there], the city would have to depend on other places for subsistence, and prosperity would be mediocre. They went to inspect Jengtāng [not very far from and to the northwest of the present city of Kengtung] where the astrologers worked out and said it was not auspicious as there would be no royal offspring and the population would not be teeming. They came to inspect Jengkaeu [present city] which was the [old] habitat of Māngyôy. The astrologers said it was auspicious; there would be an unbroken line of the royal family; there would be elephants, horses, oxen, and buffaloes in abundance; there would be glory for the state and radiance for the Sāsanā; and the population would be teeming; but wealth would be moderate, sufficient for consumption, spending, and dāna; this city and this state would have an age of fifty Dhaiy years; at the completion of fifty years, it would be well to perform the renewal ceremonies of the horoscope of the kingdom and the city. Furthermore, worship should be offered to the nāga lady [to] whom Tuṅga Rasī had given instructions to guard the state so as to maintain stability, and whatever misfortunes [30] there were for the state would then disappear totally. So spoke the astrologers, and the people together constructed villages and towns and a city there.

79. From then on, however, no prince who came to rule could live long, he would die, his life would be short, and there was no stability. The people went to reverence and report to the lord, Brayā Mangrāy. Brayā Mangrāy, the lord, reflected thus: "It is said that this state was the site of the lake drained by a hermit so that a state would spring up; because the lake was drained for the construction of a state by a saintly one replete with sīlas, it is meet that it should be a state of the Saṅgha; then only all would be well." So saying, the brayā commanded a son whose name was Namthūm to come and govern the kingdom, and then had Thenhong [Haṁsa Thera] and Thencan [Canda Thera] take along four images of the Lord. When they arrived at one place, one image fell into the water, and they therefore brought only three. [When the royal party] arrived in the city [of Jengtung] the state was offered as dāna to the Saṅgha, who asked for the eight boons. The brayā gave everything to the Saṅgha except the seven crimes, which were not granted to them, and these are: theft of gold and silver articles; intercourse with virgins and female servants; causing disputes among states; murder for larceny; murder of traders and merchants; murder of administrative chiefs; and poisoning members of the royal family. These were not allowed to the

Saṅgha and the Saṅgha lords said they were not interested in them.

80. The brayā had a palace built at Jengkaeu at the old site of Māngyôy's house there. When the golden palace had been built, the Lvas living in Bāngüng and Bāngham were brought down [from their hills] to sit and eat their food on the gem-studded throne in the palace. While they were eating, the Lvas were driven out and the brayā took their place.[45]

81. Having sat on the golden palace [that is, having been consecrated as king on the throne] the brayā asked the Saṅgha and the astrologers to examine the [horoscope of the] kingdom in every respect. "This state belongs to the nām ["nāma," or name, mental formation, the intangible] of Monday; we are Yōn, belonging to the nām of Rāhū; hence the likelihood of instability. It is said that a group of the great Khüns have come and settled in the southern direction; let [31] them be brought here for us to inspect them." The great Khüns were then brought [before the Saṅgha and astrologers]. They wore black jackets mixed with white and had their hair cut at the hair line. The Saṅgha said thus, "These people are compatible with the state's nām." Thereupon, the brayā had the gong sounded amongst the people, urging them to give up the Yōn dress and to cut their hair in the manner of the great Khüns. [The great Khüns] numbered sixty-nine and the Saṅgha had cowrie shells paid to every one of them except their chief, who was not paid; sixty-eight cowrie shells were paid out, no less and no more, as tokens [of auspiciousness] for the nām of the state, which would thrive, and the lord of earth and the populace would have long lives. So it was said, and they paid out sixty-eight cowrie shells, and no more, and the lives of the populace would be stable and long and the kingdom prosperous and happy.

82. Some time after that, word reached the Chinese emperor that a people had come and settled in that state completely and successfully. The emperor deputed one Chinese named Yu Ve-ya to come down [to Jengtung] to demand tribute, saying, "You must give one thousand carrier poles[46] of rice and one thousand elephant tusks. If that is not possible, give ten elephants and one hundred thousand silver."

83. Brayā Namthūm, lord of the state, thereupon ordered two elders, Kvāndö and Hmünjai, heading [a party] to go and negotiate with the Chinese, saying, "Now the Chinese emperor maintained that he had his son drain the lake to establish villages and towns. [This] we do not know, we do not see, because there are hermits everywhere. We do not know whose son has come and drained this lake. You have come walking on the earth [like ordinary mortals] and we cannot believe you. You talk nonsense. If it were true as you maintained, you should have come through the air like the hermit; then only would we believe you. If you cannot come through the air, we cannot pay any tribute to you." The Chinese could say naught, but were furious and returned to reverence and report to the emperor [32] about everything. The emperor was also furious and moved an army down to make war with the words: "Do not give up until you have conquered that state. If you really cannot win [in battle], go and dam up [the river] to create a lake as of old."

84. The Chinese came down in force. The populace went out to give battle but could not prevail against the Chinese, and all retreated into the city. The lord, Brayā Namthūm, gave orders for the city to be guarded with vigilance everywhere. The Chinese could not take the city by frontal attack, and, feeling exhausted, they held a war council, saying, "Together we shall dig a tunnel into the city, and when they come out to fight us we shall enter the tunnel until we reach inside of the city, and take them in the rear, then only shall we defeat them." So saying they dug the tunnel every day, and the Chinaman who was their commander had a chair brought to sit to supervise the digging every day.

85. Brayā Namthūm had a crossbow brought and placed in position at Yāngbrahrin and made a solemn invocation, declaring, "If this state is not destined to be a vassal of the Chinese, may the devās, Indra and Brahmas, who stand guard over this kingdom guide this missile so that it will strike to death the Chinese commander." Having spoken thus, [the brayā] gave the order to fetch a stick to strike the trigger of the crossbow and the Chinaman who was the commander was shot dead there.

86. The Chinese did not give up, and saying, "The dammed-up water will rise and flood them out; unless they run away they will all perish," went to dam up the river. At that time the brayā gave orders for a raft to be made from arundo reeds [*Arundo donax*], [on which were placed three] cooking stones made from mollusk shells, a steamer pot made from the chrysalis of a scarab beetle, and a [glutinous] rice pot made from the whorl of the pod of dö̈ngkā [*Oroxylum indicum*], and, after an invocation to the devās, the raft was floated down the river until it stopped at the place where they [the Chinese] were damming the river. Lightning struck that place,[47] and many Chinese died; [the rest] could not stay and all fled. Henceforth the state became happy, prosperous, and stable without a break.

87. The narrative about Brayā Namthūm's accession is completed as a chapter.

88. Here will be told [33] about Brayā Mangrāy.

89. One day Brayā Mangrāy dreamed that the sun fell into the palm of his hand; the brayā caught hold of it and handed it to the queen who received it with her hands; and there daylight came. The brayā asked the astrologers to work out what would happen. The astrologers, having worked it out and become enlightened, reverenced the brayā, saying that nothing would happen, but that the lord brayā would have a son without a doubt. After that the queen, having been pregnant for ten months, gave birth to a son with very handsome features. When he grew up, Mangrāy, the lord, gave him the name of Brayā Sing [Singha] and allowed him to rule the kingdom of N̈ōnyāng [Jengsaen]. From then on the kingdom was very prosperous and happy.

90. There were three village boys who were out roaming together when they saw a wasp hive on the top of a tree and said to one another, "Let us take this wasp hive and eat it [the larvae]," and made a vow among themselves that anyone who climbed [the tree] and did not get [the hive] must be killed. Having made the vow, [one boy] climbed up [the tree] but he was stung by so many wasps that he had to come down. Another went up, was stung by the wasps, and came down as before. The third boy went up, and, though stung, did not come down until he had dropped the hive, from which he obtained a precious stone with the likeness of a wasp. He came down and promptly killed the other two. The parents of the two reported the matter to the brayā asking permission to kill [the murderer] as he had done the other two. Brayā Sing said, "The two are already dead, never mind, it matters not, in any case, if either of them is killed. This boy had successfully climbed [the tree]; had he failed like [the] others, all of them should be killed. As for this boy I will adopt him as a son to direct military affairs." [The brayā] adopted him as his son, and the kingdom became very prosperous and happy until word reached the Chinese emperor that [the kingdom] would submit to none. The emperor sent men to find out, and they [the kingdom of Brayā Sing] said, [34] "We will not submit; we are not vassals of the Chinese." The Chinese were angry and went back to report to the emperor who ordered an army to come down to subjugate the kingdom. Verily the Chinese brought down an army to make war.

91. At that time Brayā Sing ordered Prince Āysaengtô [prince of the wasp stone] to lead forces to give battle, and he defeated the Chinese. The Chinese were routed. Prince Āysaengtô returned to reverence the brayā, saying, "I will follow them and fight in their country. If we do not beat them in their own country they will always come and attack us and we shall never find peace." The brayā agreed with Āysaengtô, who then led an army to fight the Chinese and won. The Chinese were defeated and ran away to the Wông kingdom. The emperor was about to go out and fight when the palace, the arm-supporting cushions, and leaning cushions were full of wasps everywhere. The emperor was terrified and could not go out to fight, and thought, "We should welcome [him] with the kingdom." So saying he came out to submit and gave one of his daughters in marriage [to Āysaengtô].

92. Prince Āysaengtô ruled over the Wông kingdom and had three sons. When the sons grew up, Āysaengtô asked the ministers and officials if there was a country that had not submitted to him. The ministers reverenced the brayā and said, "There is one kingdom by the name of Maentātôk which has not yet submitted to us."[48] Then the lord desired to go and fight Maentātôk and left word with his children and wife, saying, "I am going to war with Maentātôk, and should my merit not help and I get killed, let my three sons go and rule over the Daiy [Tai] country. The royal line on the father's side being the criterion, let my first son go and rule over the kingdom of Aḷāvī [Jengrung]; let my second son go and rule over the kingdom of Bôlaem--these two kingdoms are to be their mother's fiefs which pay tribute to the [35] mother, and, when they [the sons] have children and grandchildren, let them come and report and let the mother send them diapers; let my third son go and rule over the kingdom in succession to Brayā Mangrāy, who is the grandfather over there. These three children of mine must be united--if a war comes to the south help one another to cut it up and if a war comes to the north help one another to carve it up. Three of you must be the three tripod cooking stones. Let China be China; let the Daiy realm remain the Daiy realm; do not despoil each other; respect the territorial integrity of each other."

93. Having said so [Āysaengtô] led his forces to fight the brayā of Maentātôk, and verily he was victorious but had not yet captured the city. They [Maentātôk] put up a false stone bridge, and, not knowing that it was to trap him, Brayā Saengtô urged his elephant to go over the bridge, which immediately collapsed, and the brayā fell from the elephant and was killed beyond doubt.

94. Not so long after, the queen who was his wife did not discard her husband's instructions and let her children depart to rule over the Daiy country over here as instructed by the husband: the eldest came to rule the kingdom of Aḷāvī, the second came to rule the kingdom of Bôlaem, the third came to rule the kingdom of the Khüns.

95. Aḷāvī and Jengtung built a monastery as a frontier between them; [? two] human beings facing each other were buried alive;

a solitary post was buried at that place and a solemn agreement was made, saying, "In future may he perish who destroys this agreement and by force seizes the land and frontiers [of the other]. If the subjects of one state, in running away from suffering to seek happiness, cross over the boundary and are beyond the boundary pillar, they must not be taken. Anyone guilty of intercourse with virgins and female servants, of theft of silver and gold pedestal trays, of causing disputes among states [? treason], of making illegal use of the state seal, anyone guilty of the [above-mentioned] crimes must be surrendered by the state in which he has taken refuge. If war comes to the south, help each other to cut it up; if war comes to the north help each other to carve it up. When heat [fire or mortal danger] comes from the Laos, let the Khün state be the fence, let the Lü state be the roots and yams; when cold [arctic freeze or mortal danger] comes from the Chinese, let the Lü state be [36] the fence, let Jengtung state be the roots and yams. May the side that destroys this solemn agreement perish." That monastery has been named Vat Yāngban [the binding gum] for that reason. The person [? persons] who was buried alive could not run away fast enough because of a withered leg [tīn ṅôy] and he was caught on a hill, which has since been named Dôy Ṅôy.

96. Bôlaem state also came to make a solemn agreement; no human being but a buffalo was made the witness--a buffalo was killed at that place, which has been named Dôy Gvāy [buffalo hill] for that reason.

97. The three states were very prosperous. Whenever a prince of one of the three states has completed his merit and gone to heaven [the other two] have to send tokens of mucus and tears [mourning] for that reason.

98. The narrative of the enthronement of the three princely brothers and their solemn agreement, solid and firm as the granite umbrella of Brayā Indādhirāja, is here completed as a chapter.

99. Here will be told the chronicle of Jengtung state from the time when the gourds burst and gave birth to the Lvas who inhabited the state when the Sakkarāja was 496. In Sakkarāja 591 Brayā Mangrāy chased the golden stag into Jengtung state. In 592 Brayā Mangrāy deputed Khun Gong and Khun Lang to fight the Lvas but did not defeat them. In Sakkarāja 605, Prince Mangrāy deputed Māngghūm to rule Jengtung state for four years, and [he] died. Māngghen succeeded in Sakkarāja 609 for six years and died.

100. In Sakkarāja 615, Brayā Mangrāy deputed a son named Prince Namthūm to come and rule the state. This prince, belonging to the Mangrāy family of Khattiya [kingly or warrior] caste, lord of the white umbrella, ruled for eleven years and died. In Sakkarāja 626, Prince Namnān succeeded to the state for fifty-three years and died. In Sakkarāja 679, Prince Sāmhmün-hōy succeeded to the state for seven years and died. In Sakkarāja 686, Prince Jāylok succeeded to the state for eighteen years and died. In Sakkarāja 704, Prince Sainān succeeded to the state for eighteen years and died. After that there was a long interregnum [37] because Jengtung state came under a misfortune.

101. Two astrologers--one a native of Bing region named Ghamröng and very accurate in foretelling by the chicken [bone] method, the other a southerner named Bunröng and very accurate in astrology--were asked by Prince Phāyū to examine the horoscope, nakkhatta constellations, and characteristic properties of the state. Having done [what was asked of them, the astrologers] approached and reverenced Prince Phāyū, saying, "This Khün state is a state with the Moon's nām, while rivers which flow northwards belong to the male nām; a female should [therefore] rule over the state; should a male rule over it, the Jaenmöng post ["jaen," to protect, to guard] should be erected. Every nobleman of five hundred rice fields should prepare the four state rafters and a brass post."[49]

102. The Saṅgha and wise men having examined [the horoscope of] the Khün state, Prince Phāyū had the five items of royal regalia made, together with articles of royal usage such as xylophones, harps, white umbrellas, the crown, and others. A golden palace was constructed, encompassed by walls with gates in the four directions. There were experts on elephants, experts on horses, experts on astrology, experts on divining by chicken [bones], experts on medicines, junior chefs, senior chefs, treasurers and merchants, [and] four nāyrôys [centurions]: Rôyrī, the most senior, Rôyrau, Rôyghôm, and Rộyfā, with as many servants and slaves as they liked. Hmün Ṅon, Hmün Gham-yai, Hmün Āynārāy, and Saen Môn were the chief ministers [to look after] possessions, gold, silver, gems, spears, swords, elephants, and horses. There were four [representations of] Lord Sabbaññū [Omniscient], namely the crystal image, ivory image, stone image, and the relics, together with the three divisions of the Piṭaka Dhamma. There were four mahātheras, having Mahā Haṁsāvati as the head, with Dasapañño, Dhammalaṅkā, Dhammatrailōk, and disciples totaling twelve.

103. Prince Phāyū went to Vat Jenglæ, poured libation water onto the palms of the four mahātheras in the presence of all members of the Saṅgha, and declared, "I hereby give the Khün state as dāna to the Saṅgha. Whoever is going to rule the state must offer [the Saṅgha] a restoration fee of ten thousand silver and one thousand gold [approximately 27 pounds of silver, 2.7 pounds of gold]. I will have my son rule Jengtung which has 7,500 rice fields, the Saṅgha, and the devatās. I beg the Saṅgha to administer [the state] on his behalf in such a way as to give blessings and prosperity to the state, and may it please my lords to preach all the Dhamma.

104. The age of Prince Cedbantū [son of Phāyū] was ten years[50] [38] when he came to rule Jengtung state in the year Koḍyī Sakkarāja 712, arriving at Jengtung City in Month One waning 6th night. In Month Three waxing 1st night, Daiy Koḍyī, Sunday, [he] ascended the golden palace in the afternoon. After offering the restoration fee of ten thousand silver and one thousand gold to the Saṅgha, Prince Cedbantū constructed Vat Brakaeu for Dhammalankā to live in, constructed Vat Hōkhōng for Dhammatrailōk to live in, constructed Vat Brakāng for Dasapaññō to live in, constructed Vat Cômdông for Mahā Haṁsāvati to live in. The four representations of Lord Sabbaññū were kept one at each of the [four] monasteries. The Dhamma Piṭaka was kept with Mahā Hong [Haṁsāvati] who headed the ordination, teaching, and preaching, and the establishment everywhere of the Sāsanā of the Pupphārām Sect.

105. Prince Cedbantū, whose title was Sattabandhurājā, was born in the year Püksī Sakkarāja 700, Month Four full moon, Monday, Daiy Rōngpau, nakkhatta constellation 8 [Phussa], predawn. In the year Koḍyī he came up [from Jenghmai] to rule Jengtung state.

106. The Sun and Mercury being rājayoga and coming before Lagana [ascendant sign], these were the reasons for his ruling the state; Jupiter and Rāhū were destructive; Lagana was in the realm of Jupiter; Saturn was kālakiṇī [goddess of adversity] to Lagana.

107. While [the prince was] residing in Jenghmai, the astrologers predicted that he would die at the age of fifteen, for which reason Prince Phāyū made him ruler of the state while still young. From the age of twelve he ruled the state for seventeen years. At the age of twenty-nine years he died as a result of assassination--because evil misfortune was atop Lagana, and the Moon was death--at the hand of an old retainer named Lauhyôm. He was ungrateful to Lauhyôm on whose back he, when young, used to play at riding on an elephant or a horse. He was encamping at Tuṅga Market preparatory to leaving for Jenghmai and making appointments of other officials, designating them as administrators everywhere. He gave Lauhyôm only the privilege of collecting market taxes. He [Lauhyôm] asked for Mönglai, but the prince refused. Lauhyôm was furious and stabbed the prince to death at Tuṅga Market there. If the prince had not abandoned the Khün state,[51] his his age would have reached forty-five before he died.

108. [39] Prince Āy-ôn, son of Prince Ceḍbantū, was born in the year Tauyī Sakkarāja 724, Month Ten waxing 13th night, Monday, Daiy Kārau, nakkhatta constellation 27 [Revatī], predawn. He succeeded his father at the age of fifteen. He had to leave the state[52] at the age of thirty-four because Rāhū was atop Lagana of the final stage. He had reigned for fourteen years [when he] killed Bōk Hnôngrāy.[53] The Sun and Mercury preceding Lagana were rājayoga; Lagana falling in the realm of Venus was counter-auspicious; Mars was nicca [permanence] atop Lagana. He died at the age of fifty because he built the city walls to encompass Hnôngdājāng and Yāngbrahrin. [He died] because he eventually followed the words of Bōk Hnôngrāy. His title was Ratanabandhurājā--he never listened to the advice of either deity or man.

109. Prince Bunjū, younger brother of Prince Ceḍbantū[54] and an uncle of Prince Āy-ôn, was born in the year Tauseḍ [Sakkarāja 744], Month Six waning 13th night, Tuesday, Daiy Rōngp̱au, nakkhatta constellation 26 [Uttara-bhaddapadā], time--early morning. His age was eight years when he succeeded to the state in the year Koḍsaṅā Sakkarāja 752. When the news came that the enemy had captured his elder brother and that the enemy would make war to conquer the state, he struck the great drum [mahābherī] so violently to summon the army that the drum striker broke in his hand. By the title of Āyyakābāhuṁrājā was Prince Khaenhlek [arms of iron] called. Fāvông [the Chinese emperor] dispatched state regalia, trumpets, Chinese drums, ivory umbrellas with gold handles, and the title of Prince Svaenfūj̱hö.

110. Because Rāhū was daiy [independence], [he] acquired mahā-uccā [great height, honors, etc.]; Mars and Venus were in front of Lagana creating yoga [auspiciousness]. [The prince] died after thirteen years' rule.

111. Prince Yīghamkhā, younger brother of Brayā Khaenhlek, was born in the year Kāpcai Sakkarāja 746, Month Ten waning 13th, Thursday, Daiy Tauseḍ, nakkhatta constellation 8 [Phussa], predawn. In the year Sakkarāja 765, when his age was twenty, he succeeded to the state with the title of Brayā Kaeumadhu. [40] The Sāsanā was brought up from the south and established by the lord named Indamoli in the year Münggai Sakkarāja 769. Fire consumed Hōep̱un in the year Koḍyī Sakkarāja 772.

112. That year the Khün state had a great drought and the brayā asked astrologers concerning the drought and absence of rainfall. The astrologers reverenced the brayā, saying, "This

Khün state is a state with the Moon nām. It is meet that a representation of Rāhū with the Moon in its mouth be made, sand cetiyas be constructed on the Saṅgkhān's day of departure,[55] and then men, elephants, and horses be readied to go in procession to pay reverence [to the above] on the bank of the Khün River. All high officials headed by Brayā Kaeu proceeded with forces to worship and invite four bhikkhus of Vat Cômdông to recite the Buddhavaṁsa[56] [on the bank of the Khün River]. [When the recitation] reached Kakusandha, the rain fell and thunder rolled, rumbling and loud. The bhikkhus escaped the rain by taking refuge at the roofed bridge there. [That bridge] has been named Khōfārō [the bridge where the sky leaked] up to the present. Because of the glory of the Three Gems and because astrologers made that representation of Rāhū eating the Moon, the rain fell very heavily, cooling the state. Brayā Kaeu then said, "This is an auspicious field of victory which should be a place of worship for future rulers." The tradition has thus been established up to the present that on the departure day of the Saṅgkhān, Rāhū eating the Moon is to be worshiped, state astrologers are to recite the Buddhavaṁ[sa Sutta], and sand cetiyas are to be constructed. In the year Koḍyī Sakkarāja 772, the rain fell and the sky leaked [that is, rain fell heavily].

113. During the reign of Brayā Khaenhlek, the elder brother, Dāu Hōhūk, was deputed to go and answer Chinese riddles. The Chinese melted down the gold presents and they cracked. Saying, "You are really vassals of the Chinese and are deceitful," the Chinese put Hōhūk in stocks for three months before releasing him and [Jengtung] had to pay tribute to the Chinese. During the reign of the younger royal brother, when the Chinese and the Burmese were at war with each other, [the prince] sent one thousand cups of liquor to await the arrival of the Chinese and sent one thousand cups of liquor to await the arrival of the Burmese, as if they would really fight each other, but by the stratagem of giving presents to the Chinese and the Burmese, the war [41] was stopped. The Chinese were delighted and, saying that they were indebted to the Khün state, suspended the tribute in the year Müngrau during the reign of the younger royal brother.

114. Brayā Kaeu ruled for thirteen years and died in the year Rāysan Sakkarāja 778. No tribute has been sent to the Chinese from the reign of this prince until now.

115. Prince Sām, the youngest brother, was born in the year Rāyyī Sakkarāja 748, Month Nine full moon, Thursday, Daiy Kaḍhmau, nakkhatta constellation 20 [Pub-āsāḷha], time--late morning --and succeeded to the state at the age of thirty-four, [received] consecration in the year Kaḍgai, Month Nine waxing 7th night, Thursday, Daiy Kaḍgai.

116. Ghosts came and haunted the golden palace since the year Rōnggai, Month Nine waxing 2nd night, Tuesday, Daiy Tauseḍ, nakkhatta constellation 13 [Hattha], time--midday. The bhikkhus of Jenglæ were invited to exorcise, but [the situation] became worse.

117. This prince's title was Brayā Kôngratanabherī. He was uparājā [crown prince] at the age of twenty-three, residing at Jengbāu. [He] built Vat Yānggham, entitled Suvaṇṇapupphārām, for [Mahāthera] Dhammalaṅkā to reside in. In the same year and the same month [he] built Vat Jenglæ of the same size [as Vat Yānggham] with artisans imported from the west [cis-Salween] and completed it at the same time [as the construction of Vat Yānggham]. He was twenty-five years old when he had the monasteries built. From Kuson, Saendong encompassing Yāngbrahrin, had the out-flow end of the Dājāng Lake filled up and had bricks made and fired for battlements [of the walls] throughout, in the year Koḍseḍ, Month Six full moon, nakkhatta constellation 12 [Uttara-phaggunī], Sakkarāja 792. This prince was a mertiorious prince, and he built monasteries everywhere. Brayā Kôngratanabherī ruled the state for twenty-five years; his age was fifty-nine when he died in the year Kāgai.

118. Prince Sāmsrī, son of Brayā Kôngratanabherī, was born in the year Koḍyī Sakkarāja 772, Month Nine full moon, Thursday, Daiy Kaḍhmau, nakkhatta constellation 20 [Pub-āsāḷha], time--late morning. He succeeded to the state at the age of thirty-four in the year Kāgai.

119. The ghosts had been haunting the palace since the year Rōnggai Sakkarāja 733 [799 is probably the correct Sakkarāja, taking the dates of the last reign into consideration] until the year Kāgai [42] Sakkarāja 803. The bhikkhus of [Vat] Jengrom came to exorcise, but [the situation] became worse. The bhikkhus of [Vat] Jenglæ and [Vat] Yānggōng were fetched to exorcise, [and the palace] was habitable intermittently. The bhikkhus ran away in the year Kāpcai Sakkarāja 806, and the bhikkhus of [Vat] Bôghok were invited to come and reside as the head at Vat Jengbon in the brass pavilion, and the monastery was called Siṅhārattarām.[57] In Month Eight waxing 5th night, Thursday, Daiy Kaḍhmau, the great vihāra and the uposatha hall were built. The prince was consecrated in the year Kāpcai Sakkarāja 806 with the title Srīsudhammacuḷāmaṇīrāja. The bhikkhus of Jenglæ and Yānggham fled to the southern state [Lānnā or Tai-Yuan states]. The Ḅaḍæng Sect of the Sāsanā came to be established during the reign of Brayā

Srīsudhamma. [He] ruled for fifteen years and at the age of fifty-nine years died in the year Rōngmeḍ.

120. Caubrayā Āylaughamdā was born in the year Koḍseḍ Sakkarāja 792, Month One full moon, Saturday, Daiy Tauyī, time--late morning, nakkhatta constellation 2 [Bhāraṇī]. At the age of twenty-six he succeeded to the state in the year Rāycai Sakkarāja 818 with the title Candapuṇṇarājā. He had five sons, because Jupiter was putta [son], Rāhū was bandhu [kinsman], Saturn was suhajja [amiable friendship].

121. He had ruled up to the year Ḍapgai Sakkarāja 817 when Lānnā Jenghmai sent as rājabhiseka [consecration] presents two elephants loaded with rājabhiseka paraphernalia. Brayā Candarājā in return sent four horses and the five royal regalia to the lord of Jenghmai in the year Rāycai.

122. Brayā Āylaughamdā Rājanarindā ruled for eighteen years and died in the year Ḍapsai [should be Kāsai] when he was forty-three years old. The embankment of the Āhraen Lake collapsed in the year Kāhmau--Mӧ̈ngkhôn South was all covered with sand and tree trunks.

123. Prince Āylau was born in the year Tausan Sakkarāja [43] 814, Month [?] waxing 2nd night, Daiy Kāpcai, nakkhatta constellation 16 [Visākhā], at dawn, and succeeded his father in the year Kāpsaṅā Sakkarāja 836 with the title of Brayā Ādittarājā. Gem mines and gold mines came into being everywhere during that period, and elephants and horses were abundant because Saturn, being mahā-uccā [great height], was united with Lagana. He succeeded to the state while still young because Mercury, being rājayoga, was united with Lagana; tending to quarrel and be angry with one another because Venus, being kālakiṇī [goddess of adversity], was united with Lagana.

124. In the year Rōnggai Sakkarāja 853, the body of the cetiya of Vat Cômdông collapsed, and, during Month Five waning, there were three great fires and the golden palace was completely burned, because teja [glory] was kālakiṇī to Lagana. Brayā Ādittarājā fled to reside at Jengbāu that year.

125. In the year Taucai Lānnā, Jenghmai sent a deputation to test the Khün state: a royal document was written on a small booklet in invisible characters and placed in a square box with no trace [of how it should be opened]. [The deputation] was instructed to give [the box] to the Khün state. Seeing [the box], the Khün people said, "The Yōns sent a whetting stone for us to sharpen swords." No one knew anything [about it], and it was given to the two sects of the Saṅgha. Not a single lord knew; only one Mahā Ñāṇauttama knew: he passed a strand of female hair through the stone [box] and was able to open it, but the message was invisible, and it became visible only when he exposed [the booklet] to the sun, sprinkled slate pencil powder over it, and then blew away the powder. Then there were only alphabetical characters, without any spelling, which could not be read with any intelligence. He [Ñāñauttama] deciphered it and gave it to the brayā who had it read correctly to the deputation which then returned to tell Jenghmai, saying, "There still are wise pundits [among the Khüns]; we cannot hope to conquer their state." And they did not come.

126. In the year Kaḍsai Sakkarāja 871, Brayā Āditta [44] headed the whole state in constructing the Cômdông cetiya with a plinth of six vā [approximately eighteen feet] in length and a height of thirteen vā [approximately seventy-eight feet]. Headed by Brayā Āditta the whole state collected thirty thousand gold [22.5 viss, approximately eighty-one pounds] which was beaten into caṅkō sheets, loaded on a cart, and hauled to the cetiya. From the base of the kongken, including Māngāng, to the tip of the finial, all was of gold caṅkō sheets.[58] It was called the Gold Cetiya for that reason. Another source says that lord of earth collected twenty thousand gold [approximately fifty-two and a half pounds].

127. Brayā Ādittarājā ruled the state for thirty-four years and at the age of forty-nine died in the year Kaḍhmau, Month Three waxing 1st night. He was disposed of [cremated] at the Tuṅga Market. In his existence as a guest residing at Cômsak,[59] this prince ministered to the needs of Lord Omniscient [Sabbaññū]. He placed a sunshade above the head of the Lord, and that was why he possessed no glory but had abundant accumulated merit.

128. Prince Cômsak, younger brother of Brayā Ādittarājā, [also] named Prince Hnôkaeu, was born in the year Rāysan, Month Eight waxing 9th night, time--midmorning, nakkhatta constellation 13 [Hattha]. He never won any battle because the Moon was in the retinue of Rāhū, resulting in the destruction of the state and disturbances. The retinue fell within the domain of Jupiter which was enemy to Lagana.

129. In Month Four waxing 1st night, he [Hnôkaeu] persuaded his nephew to enter the gold building [strongroom] saying he would give the latter presents. The nephew, unsuspecting, went in without his jacket. His enemies were going to kill him [the nephew]; he fled into the forest of Yānggōnglōng, went forth to become a lordly one [bhikkhu] and during Month Five fled to Mönglaem. The peoples of Möngloe and Möngyāng were all unitedly for the nephew. The prince of Mönglaem by the name of Brayā Lāpfā sent a force to help the royal nephew. Prince Jenggông, a cousin and son of an uncle, that is, son of Prince Möngtök, also supported him [the nephew].

130. The brayā sent for Ban Jengṅām to come and help and asked him to take a force to combat the enemy at Dāböm.[60] [Ban Jengṅām and his force] could not prevail against the enemy and came fleeing and took refuge at P̱āḍaeng. The other side set fire to the whole of the small palace. Month Six [45] Prince Sāyghô arrived with the people of Mönglaem. After the new year in Month Seven, they executed Prince Cômsak and Ban Jengṅām at Tuṅga Market. [Cômsak] was executed even though he had gone forth and had become a bhikkhu because Saturn and Rāhū were pinning Lagana between them. He had ruled for one year and five months when they executed him.

131. Prince Sāyghô, son of Brayā Lau [i.e., Āylaughamdā or Ādditta-rājā] and lord of the Hlek rice fields, was born in the year Püksaṅā Sakkarāja 820, Month Three waxing 3rd night, time--waking up from sleep, nakkhatta constellation 8 [Phussa]. At the age of thirty he succeeded to the state in the year Rōngmeḍ Sakkarāja 873 with the title of Brayā Sivijeyyarājā who ruled for three years.

132. He was fond of loafing early and returning late [at night]. He was fond of trapping and fishing [by the net-casting method], of hawking--he would hawk even in monasteries. He reverenced not the Three Gems, nor did he uphold the kingly duties, and he outraged the traditions of the state. Headed by the Saṅgha, the state counsellors advised him, but he would not listen to anybody.

133. They [the enemies] burned down the residence of Prince Jenggông, younger brother of the brayā, and he fled into the palace. In Month Five, the brayā, the elder brother, sensing danger, asked him to take refuge at P̱āḍaeng. During Month Six he [the younger brother] escaped to Jenghmai.

134. In the year Kaḍmeḍ Sakkarāja 885, all commoners headed by the state counsellors attempted to capture the brayā; he escaped to P̱āḍaeng and went forth to become a bhikkhu. They all arrested Prince Sāyghô, namely Brayā Sivijeyya, and executed him at Tuṅga Market on the day Rōngmeḍ, with Brayā Saenpāknôm as the person who executed the brayā, because Mars and Rāhū were in the same mansion as Lagana.

135. Prince Saibrom, son of Brayā Lau [Āylaughamdā or Ādittarājā] and lord of Tök rice fields, was born in the year Püksaṅā, Month Ten waning 1st night, Tuesday, Daiy Ḏapgai, nakkhatta constellation 22 [Savaṇa], time--midmorning. At the age of thirty-four he succeeded in the year Kaḍmeḍ Sakkarāja [46]

885. He ruled for over one month because the Sun and Venus were rājayoga of the medium class.

136. Lord of Jenghmai by the name of Brayā Kaeuyôḍjengrāy deputed Saen Yī to lead an army consisting of one hundred and thirty thousand men,[61] three thousand elephants and seven thousand horses to come in support of Prince Jenggông. In Month Seven waning 5th night, Saen Yī and Prince Jenggông entered the city with their force. The lord [Saibrom] escaped to Lōe Yāng [Möngl ōe, Möngyāng], and some to the Lü state. The Yōns defeated the Khün state that year, the Yōns staying in the city for five days because the Moon was a vassal and that state is ruinous to Lagana.

137. The Khüns mustered together five thousand men and came to fight in the direction of Jenghlek, but were unsuccessful, and they went to seek help partly from the Lüs and partḷy from the Yeus [Shans, known to Thais and Tai-Yuans as Ṅio]. Fāghamraep [Khamhaepphā of Hsenwi] brought a contingent to help. Hmün Benglōng, Hmün Ṅaen, and Fāghamraep brought forces to fight Saen Yī. The Lüs, Lōes, and Yāngs took Jenggông in the rear. Saen Yī was defeated and fled. Hmün Benglōng and Hmün Ṅaen led in driving out the Yōns up to Hinkông--a great number of the Yōns were killed and very many elephants and horses lost. The defeated Saen Yī retreated to Jengsaen. Brayā Kaeuyôḍjengrāy ordered the execution of Saen Yī at Jengsaen and allowed Prince Jenggông to rule Möngbhyāk [a substate and sixty miles south of Kengtung City].

138. This Prince Sāmjenggông, who was the [third] son of Brayā Lau and brother of Prince Sāyghô, was born in the year Müngrau [no mention of the sakkarāja], Month Ten waning 1st night, Thursday, Daiy Rāysan, nakkhatta constellation 10, at midnight. He had to flee the state to Jenghmai. The lord of Jenghmai gave him an army of one hundred thirty thousand men and one hundred forty thousand elephants and horses, commanding him to rule over the Khün state. The populace was not pleased, and he fled to Lānnā and went to rule Möngbhyāk. Because Jupiter, being srī [luck], was together with Lagana, he did not rule the state permanently; because the populace was not pleased, he had to go and reside at Möngbhyāk for that reason.

139. [47] Prince G̱hamhmū, son of Āylau, was born in the year Tausẹd Sakkarāja 864, Month One waxing 14th night, Tuesday, Daiy Kāgai, nakkhatta constellation 1 [Assayuja]. This prince was a younger brother of lord of earth and lord of Khāk rice fields. He clashed with the Khün state and fled to the Lüs because the Moon was the enemy against the Lüs, Rāhū was nicca [permanence] before Lagana; he fled to Lānjāng because Venus

shared the mansion with Lagana; he went to stay in Jenghmai because the Sun, Mars, and Mercury were destructive to Lagana; because Jupiter was maraṇa [death], an inborn disease nearly killed him.

140. Brayā G̱hamhmū ascended the golden palace [succeeded] and resided there for one month and seven days. The populace was not pleased and he had to flee.

141. Dāu G̱hamfū, a son of Brayā Lau, was born in the year Koḍseḍ Sakkarāja 862, Month Eleven waning 10th night, Wednesday, Daiy Kāgai, nakkhatta constellation 6 [Addā]. At the age of twenty-four Fāghamraep was camping at Sāmsāu [at the foot of modern Cômsrī Hill]. Hmün Benglōng, Hmün Ṅaen, and Fāghamraep together went to invite the Rājakhanān [lord royal bhikkhu] Brahrin, namely Dāu G̱hamfū, who was son of Brayā Āditta and younger brother of Brayā Sivijeyya, to leave the Saṅgha Order in order to rule the state [with] the title of Brayā Kaeuyôḍfānarindā.

142. Hmün Benglōng was [made] lord of Saen rice fields; Hmün Ṅaen, lord of Khāk rice fields, in addition to Lāmhmünlāi rice fields; Fāghamlaep obtained a great number of Yōn elephants and horses, and returned to his state with his forces, taking with him Lāmhmün of Jeng-ing who had been guilty of a crime. Brayā Kaeu presented Fāghamraep with Möngbeng [a substate of Kengtung about sixty miles to the west].

143. Brayā Kaeuyôḍfānarindā, after five years of succession, was consecrated in the year Münggai, Month Nine waxing 13th night.

144. In the year after [the succession], [namely] the year Kāpsan Sakkarāja 886, Mönglōy and Möngyāng rebelled against Brayā Kaeu. The prince ordered Möngkā to lead a force to capture the lord of Möngyāng who escaped [but he was] pursued and captured, [48] after which Möngkā was given the overlordship of the Yāng rice fields.

145. Brayā Kaeu ruled with a meritorious heart and built monasteries everywhere, old places became new, [and the state] was very prosperous. In the year Rāyseḍ Sakkarāja 889 [actually 888], [Lord] Mönggham [? Möngrā or Mönghā] headed [a deputation] taking a royal letter and two horses to Jenghmai and presented them to Brayā Āadditta, son of Brayā Kaeujengrāy there.

146. In the year Rōnghmau Sakkarāja 893, Month Eight, the people of Möngbeng rebelled and Fāghamraep was brought to help. Victory came only after some strenuous actions. Mönglaem came down to help, blocking the rear [of the enemy, of whom] a great number died of starvation. [The place] has been called Jôybôngyōm [meaning not clear] up to the present.

147. In the year Kāsai Sakkarāja 895, Month One, Brayā Āditta of Jenghmai dispatched paraphernalia for the consecration ceremony to Brayā Kaeuyôḍnarindā together with [other] gifts.

148. In the year Müngsai Sakkarāja 919, Brayā Kaeu asked for the hand of a daughter of Brayā G̱hamraep. [She was his wife] for one month and died in Month Twelve. During Month Seven a monastery was built over the site of her cremation.

149. In the year Püksaṅā Sakkarāja 920, Month Seven waxing 2nd night, Mangbrarā Hongsā [king of Haṁsāvati-Pegu of Burma, namely Bayinnaung], having taken Möngnāy, went to war with Jenghmai. On Month Six waxing 11th night [the Burmese] circumambulated the city. On the full moon of Month Six [the Burmese] captured the city, entering it by way of Hrolin after a great deal of confusion, fighting, and killing. After appointing Brayā Maeku to rule over Jenghmai as before, Mangbrarā [corrupted from the Burmese "Maṅtara," king of righteousness or of Dhamma] returned home.

150. In the year Kaḍmeḍ, Brayā Kaeu deputed Khônnö to head a delegation which included ten lordly ones [bhikkhus] to Hongsā.[62] The mangtarā was delighted and gave a large number of presents including the three Piṭaka to be kept in the state.

151. In the year Koḍsan Sakkarāja 922, Month Eight, Brayā Kaeu was gravely ill and asked for Bōk Möngsang to head a delegation to offer the state as dāna to the Saṅgha and to speak thus, "The state counsellors left word that whoever out of these four persons is as capable as I of ruling the state [49] so that both the state and the Buddha Sāsanā would be prosperous and happy, [that person] should be appointed to rule the state." The Saṅgha accepted the state but had not yet appointed anyone to rule when, on Month Ten waxing 10th night, Brayā Kaeu became very critically ill. At that time Saenmöng and others came on elephants to see Brayā Kaeu, dismounted the elephants at the Great Khōng [grounds in front of the palace], and entered the golden palace. There Saenmöng brought out the five items of the royal regalia and state apparatus, loaded them on his elephant, and kept them at his house.

152. Brayā Kaeu succeeded to the state at the age of twenty-four because Rāhū was together with Lagana; Jupiter was ahi [enemy] in [the realm of] kālakiṇī [misfortune]; Mars was mahā-uccā [great height] supporting Lagana of the final stage. On

Month Ten waxing 12th night Brayā Kaeu died at the age of sixty-one in the year Koḍsan Sakkarāja 922.

153. Kaeubunnam, son of Brayā G̱hamfū, was born in the year Rāysan Sakkarāja 898, Month Three waning 13th night, two days prior to new moon, Friday, Daiy Ḍappau, at midday, nakkhatta constellation 16 [Visākhā]. Bhayā Saen led the state counsellors and the Saṅgha to install Lord of Möngkā, namely Kaeubunnam the son, at the age of twenty-five years, on the throne to succeed his father in the year Koḍsan with the title of Brayā Ratanabhummindanarindā Khemādhipatirājā.

154. In the year Kāpcai Lānnā, Jenghmai rebelled against Mahādham [King Bayinnaung of Burma]. The mangtarā came and captured Jenghmai and then came to Jengsaen. On Month Three waxing [the Burmese king] went after a white crow as far as Möngsāng and Mönglōng and captured it during that Month Three. [The king] asked Fā Ime to take Lānjāng, which he did; asked Fā Bae [? prince of Prae] to take the Lü state, which he did, but [he] did not capture the ruler.

155. Fā Mangtarā had a message dispatched to Brayā Kaeubhummindanarindā to go [to him] saying, "We would like our son, lord of the golden palace of Jengtung, to come and meet us [hold hands and lace fingers] here in Jengsaen." [50] Brayā Ratanabhumminda took a big force and went in the year Kāpcai Sakkarāja 926 during Month Three. And Fā Mangtarā was delighted and gave a great number of royal presents.

156. In the year Ḍappau Sakkarāja 927, the Laems came down to fight the peoples of [Möngh-]Lōy and [Möng-]Yāng who were defeated by the Laems. The Laems went away by way of Möngdü and returned home forcing all the populace of Möngphaen to with them.

157. In the year Münghmau Sakkarāja 929, the Lord of Lānjāng deputed Bhayā Jeyyaṅākvā and Bhayā Baladebbajeyya to lead a force of four hundred thousand men to come and ask for the hand of Nāng Kaeurūpdip. The Khüns all fled. Lord of earth fled to stay with Gāng Jengkūm. The Khün state was deserted at that time. Having obtained Nāng Kaeu the Lāos retraced their steps without harming anyone, not breaking a tree or plucking any vegetable. Brayā Kaeu fled to stay at Möngkhā for a while, and when the state became normal the state counsellors invited him to return as of old.

158. In the year Püksī Sakkarāja 930, the Möngṅaen people rebelled and killed the father of a minor wife [of Brayā Kaeu]. Brayā Kaeuratanabhumminda lost to them Bōk Nôy. A lord of Mongṅaen who was nicknamed Bhayā Hāngoḍkaecau [brave chief is disloyal to his lord] approached the Laems for help. [They] went and fought against Bhayā Möngyāng and killed him. The queen of Brayā Kaeu who was the daughter of Bhayā Yāng was enraged and reverenced Brayā Kaeu, asking him to kill all officials and commoners--men were not to be spared and women were to be made slaves. Some people sold [the slaves] and obtained silver to put in their treasure chests.

159. In the year Kodsanā Sakkarāja 932, Brayā Kaeuratanabhumminda commanded Bhayā Saen of Cômsak and Bhayā Hlek of Jengcīn, his son-in-law, with Bhayā Saen as the commander, to go with forces to war against the southerners [Ayudhyā, in this case] in aid of the mangtarā. Together with the Lü people, [51] Lānnā, people of Bông [?], and the Burmese, [they] fought against the southerners. There was a great deal of fighting and a great many men, elephants, and horses died. Bhayā Hlekkaeu was very brave--he rode an elephant to combat with a leader of the southerners and killed him. The mangtarā was very pleased and gave him a riding elephant and presents, and he has been named Brayā Thaencaihān Khaenhlek of Jengcīn until the present. Having conquered the country [Ayudhyā] the mangtarā returned home with his armies.

160. In the year Kāpsed Sakkarāja 935 [936, to be correct], a comet covered the whole sky, reaching the horizon. The mangtarā thought of the lord and sent a letter saying, "We would like our son, the heavenly lord of the golden palace of Jengtung, to come to us as we, the father, wish to see him." Brayā Ratanabhummindanarindā went that year with his younger brother, Dān Brommarājā of Jenggông, and son, Prince Āyghamdāu, at the head of ten high officials and two hundred thousand soldiers.

161. That year the state experienced a great drought. After a ceremonial bathing of the Buddha images during Month Nine, silver was hurriedly dispatched after [the delegation]. When they reached the mangtarā, he presented them with ten elephants headed by the chief elephant named Kaeughamlōn. [They] stayed [in Hongsā, or Pegu] for over one month and returned.

162. In the year Tausanā Sakkarāja 944, the mangtarā again sent a royal command calling [Jengtung] to go to Kosambī [Hsenwi]. The peoples of the Lü, Laem, and Lānnā states also went. Brayā Kaeuratanabhumminda commanded Prince Ghamdāu, lord of Yāng rice fields, Bra Vengkaeu, Bhayā Hānkhaenhlek, the brayās of Möngbeng and Möngbū, to lead forces to fight as far as Möngnampād, which was secured.[63] Jenghmai came to fight against Fā Āy [Ghamdāu] but was not successful; [he] deserted his troops and fled to Jenghmai. The Khüns fought as far as Möngnā and killed Fā Möngnā, acquiring elephants, horses, and an enormous amount of silver and gold.

163. In the year Kāpsan [Sakkarāja 946], Bhayā Khaenhlek went to present men, elephants, and horses to the mangtarā, who was greatly pleased, and gave eight elephants together with horses and men and a great amount of silver and gold to be presented to Brayā Kaeu.

164. [52] In the year Rāyseḍ [Sakkarāja 948], Prince Uparājā of Hlākhōng and Bhayā Khaenhlek led a force to Mönghūn [a substate of Sipsôngbannā Jengrung]. Bhayā G̱hamdāu of Möṇgyāng, Bhayā Kaeu of Möngkôy, Bhayā Sivijai of Möngkā and Fā Vengkaeu of Mönglaem led another force to Möngjae [another Sipsôngbannā dependency]. [They] challenged the Lüs to elephant combats; not a single man came forward for the combat; and they returned the way they came.

165. In the year Pükcai Sakkarāja 950, Bhayā G̱hamdāu escorted Nāng Inkaeu to Hongsā; the mangtarā was delighted and gave ten elephants, with Prāsāḍ as the chief elephant.

166. In the year Tausī Sakkarāja 954, Bhayā [G̱ham]dāu went to preach moral lessons to the Möngṅim lord who was disloyal to the Fālōng [great ruling prince] of Mönglaem; [Möngṅim] submitted; [G̱hamdāu] returned with the black horse [named] Jāunān.

167. In the year Kāsai [Sakkarāja 955], Uparājā of Hlākhōng died.

168. In the year Ḍapmeḍ Sakkarāja 957, Bhayā Khaenhlek, who was the Saenmöng, died that year.

169. Brayā Kaeuratanabhumminda came to the throne at the age of twenty-five. He was indiscriminating in sensual pleasures. The cause being nicca [permanence], he took a daughter to wife, in the same manner as Brayā Bhān of Jengrung and Brayā Lok of Jenghmai. He was fond of disguising himself as a humble commoner and went about the state. Because mittayoga [yoga of friendship] was of the middle stage and Saturn was tanu-lagana [fortune of the subject of horoscope is on the rise] he ruled for thirty-seven years and died at the age of sixty-two, in the year Rāysan, Month Two waning 4th night, Daiy Tausaṅā, at dawn. As he was dying, he left instructions for his son, Bhayā G̱hamdāu, to succeed him, and the limit of his age came to an end there.

170. Prince G̱hamdāu, son of Prince Bunnam--Brayā Kaeuratana--was born in the year Koḍsan Sakkarāja 922, Month Ten waning 8th night, Thursday, Daiy Kāpcai, nakkhatta constellation 4 [Rohiṇī], midmorning. In the year Rāysan Sakkarāja 958, when his age was thirty-six years, he received consecration on Month Seven full moon, Saturday, Daiy Rāysan with the title Brayā Sudhammarājā.

171. [53] In the year Püksed̤ Sakkarāja 960, Month Eleven waxing 11th night, Sunday, Daiy Kāgai, Brohmmarājā of Jenggông, the uncle, rebelled against lord of earth, the nephew, and together with the younger brother of Bhayā Sudhamma, Bhayā Saen of Jeng-ing, Bhayā Jengsaen of Möngkhôn, Möngn̄en, and Möngjem--these were all the chief [conspirators]. [They] tried to get lord of earth in the golden palace, but five men of Kānôy [Möngkā] were killed and they withdrew from the golden palace. Lord of earth did not give in and came out and struck the great drum [which was heard] all over the city. The populace learned that lord of earth was still alive, and the people near the palace rushed into the small palace compound, while members of the Saṅgha came at dawn and made Bracau [Bhayā] Jengsaen, younger brother of Uparājā of Hlākhōng, the uncle [of lord of earth], come to the side of lord of earth and lead men to get Brohmmarājā of Jenggông and burned down his house at noon. Bhayā Saen of Jeng-ing fled to the Yōn lord of Jenghmai, but he was ordered to be killed at Möngbeng. The lord of Möngkā fled to P̱ādaeng. In Month Four, the lord of Möngyāng, son of Brayā Sudḣammarājā, took a force to kill Prince Jengsaen of Hlākhōng and drove [the lords of] Möngkā, Möngn̄en, and Möngjem to the Lüs, having succeeded in killing Möngkhôn.

172. In the year Kad̤gai [Sakkarāja 961], the lord of Hrōkhôngföe-rai of Möngsād̤, Rājavang Hlū, fled [from his state to Jengtung] with twenty elephants which he presented to lord of earth, including the chief elephants named Kaeuphālôm, Cômcai-hlek, and Comcaibek. Brayā G̱hamdāu Sudhammarājā was very powerful.

173. In the year Kod̤cai Sakkarāja 962, the lord of Lānjāng state presented [Sudḣammarājā] with twelve elephants and [he] was annointed with the title Brayā Dhammikarājā.

174. In the year Rōngp̱au [Sakkarāja 963], the southerners were coming to war, but at Jengdau, Nared̤ [? Nares] fell from an elephant and died, and they ran away. The year after that, when the son had succeeded, [54] Fā Nāusrīsak [? governor or prince of Tanāusrī][64] was sent to make amends and led a delegation to present ten elephants with the elephant Drongnārī as the chief elephant. At that time Lü, Laem, Mengbong, and Ava each came to attend the consecration ceremony of the title dhammikarājā, because Saturn was uccā; Venus was the fertile field. The mangtarā adopted [Dhammikarājā] as a son, loving him more than all lords and princes. At that time the Khüns of Jengtung lived in happiness and tranquility, both freemen and slaves could do business and commerce, rice was abundant and fish was cheap, prosperity came with [the

ruler's] great power and glory, and a Vejayanta[65] palace was built in the city of victory.

175. Mahā Dhammikarājā ruled for twenty-four years, and, after bringing prosperity to the people and the Buddha Sāsanā and having built Suvaṇṇarāma [monastery], died in the year Koḍseḍ [should be Koḍsan] Sakkarāja 982, Month Eleven, at the age of sixty.

176. Prince Ghāk, younger brother of Prince Ghamdāu, and uparājā [crown prince], was born in the year Ḍapgai Sakkarāja 937, Month Six waning 3rd night, Monday, Daiy Kāpau, nakkhatta constellation 25 [Pubba-bhaddapadā], time--late at night. At At the age of thirty-five he succeeded with the title Brayā Kaeuphāpnarindā.

177. In the year Rōnghmau [actually Rōngrau] Sakkarāja 983, Month Twelve waning 5th night, the ruler of Möngnāy and Bhayā Lān who came as state guests staying in the same residence, together with Prince Mönglön, the uparājā of Cômdông rebelled against Brayā Kaeu. [The latter] brought the Laems to help but was unsuccessful. The mangtarā Fāsuddho [King Thālun of Burma] commanded Fāmangrāy Côthāng [Burmese: Minye Kyôhtin] to lead a Burmese contingent [to Jengtung] and captured Möngnāy then. Many Khüns, headed by the uparājā of Cômdông [? and] Prince Mönglön were taken down [to Burma]--all those who were disloyal were taken.

178. In the year Ḍappau Sakkarāja 987, the Lüs rebelled against the mangtarā [and the latter] dispatched an army to Möngjae. Brayā Kaeunarindā also went to stay at Möngjae. At that time Bhayā Jengröng and Bracau Möngnung, and the peoples of Möngbok and Möngkhā in the west, [55] all rebelled against Brayā Kaeu. [Brayā Kaeu] gave Möngnung and Möngrön to the Burmese to be taken to Ava. After defeating the Lüs, the Burmese also returned home.

179. The sons of the state [people] and Möngnāy people rebelled against Brayā Kaeu's rule because teja [glory] and srī [splendor] turned destructive to Lagana and the ground of Mercury gave way; he was not captured because Lagana was in the realm of [the horoscope of] Fāsuddho who came to help, and because Venus was together with Lagana, Mars was kālakiṇī [goddess of calamity] and maraṇa [death]. Brayā Kaeu ruled for seventeen years and died in the year Münghmau [Müngpau for] Sakkarāja 999 at the age of seventy-two. At that time the Khün state was beset by fighting and suffered greatly.

180. Prince Āy-ūn, son of Brayā Kenggham[66] and lord of the Ghāk rice fields, was born in the year Rōngpau Sakkarāja 964,

Month Five waning 4th night, time--midmorning, nakkhatta constellation 16 [Visākhā]. When he was twenty-four years old, Bhayā Saen and the Order of the Saṅgha, together with the Burmese, installed Prince Möng[ghāk], son of Brayā Kaeu, on the throne in the year Püksī Sakkarāja 1000 with the title Brayā Suriyarājā. After the consecration [the title] was changed to Brayā Ādittarājā. He had to leave the state to go to Jenghmai because the Moon and Jupiter were satrūyoga [junction of enemies] coming before Lagana. Prince Bhom was ordered to be executed because Saturn was face to face with Lagana. Month Four new moon, the uparājā was executed. Month Five new moon, Bhayā Jengsaen was cremated at Jengṅām. [The brayā] ruled for twenty-three years and died in the year Kodyī, Month Two waning 10th night.

181. Prince Ingham, son of Prince Jenggông, was born in the year Tausan Sakkarāja 934, Month Four waxing 7th night, Monday, Daiy Ḍapmeḍ, nakkhatta constellation 3 [Kattikā]. Lord of the Ṅom rice fields, he joined the uparājā and Möngnāy in rebellion. Fā Suddho took him to Hongsā. He came and resided in Ava and [56] was allowed to return to the state and received consecration to rule the state in the year Rōngrau Sakkarāja 1022, with the title of Ratanagandha. He ruled for eighteen years and died.

182. Prince Oksing was born in the year Kārau, Month Nine waning 7th night, Daiy Ḍappau, time--predawn, nakkhatta constellation 5 [Magasiraṁ]--Jupiter was srī [goddess of luck] being destructive to Lagana. [He] had the power to defeat the Burmese because Mars and Venus were mittayoga [union with friendship] in the same mansion as Lagana and Saturn was teja [power] to Lagana.

183. He succeeded to the throne in the year Kaḍrau Sakkarāja 1040, when Bhayā Saenlōng of Jengcīn led the whole state, civilian as well as the Saṅgha, in installing him [as ruler] Prince Lāmhmün, the second son, in Month Two with the title Surindarāja. Prince Möngkhāk was installed as uparājā.

184. In the year Taucai on the day of the departure of the Saṅgkhān [New Year's Eve during April] the earth quaked ten times [and continued to do so] until the middle of the vassā. Cetiyas collapsed, buildings [of bricks] collapsed, one hundred eighty bhikkhus, sāmaṇeras, and laymen died, a great number of people were wounded, the heads of the chief Buddha images of [Vat] Ṗāḍaeng and Vat Yānggōng collapsed and fell down, and many other Buddha images were damaged. The whole state, told to perform great meritorious deeds, offered the state as dāna to the two gaṇā [Saṅgha parties, namely the Forest and

Garden sects] for seven days, at the completion of which [the state] was restored to the administration as before.

185. In the year Kāpau, Fāmöngnāy [ruling prince of Möngnāy] with followers came to take refuge under royal protection. Brayā Surindarājā possessed great glory and power without peer, and there was no one, either within or without the state, to rebel against his authority, nor did he go to submit to the mangtarā of Ava. Brayā Surindarājā ruled for seven years and died in the year Rāysī, Month Twelve waning 5th night, at the age of forty-two.

186. Prince Mönghlek, namely Kaeubūnmā, son of Mahādhammikarājā, was born in the year Kaḍhmau Sakkarāja 952, Month Nine [57] waning 4th night, Saturday, nakkhatta constellation 24 [Satabhisaja], time--midnight, and succeeded [Surindarājā]. He was consecrated with the title of udeyyatraisaṁvacchara, also known as Prince Jahlemāng[67] [Burmese: "Calemaṅ"] and came to the throne in Sakkarāja 1027, when the Moon was lābha [acquisition] [and] Saturn was kattuṁ ["katumba," property of the subject of horoscope]; long life because Lagana was in the realm; [he] fled the state and an interregnum occurred because Mars was antagonistic to [?] Lagana, Mercury was srī and putta [child]; [he] succeeded to the throne only through his daughter's support. He ruled for seventeen years and died at the age of eighty-four.

187. Prince Sāmplī was born in the year Kāpcai Sakkarāja 1016, Month Seven waning 3rd night, early after daylight, nakkhatta constellation 19 [Mūlaṁ]. This prince possessed great power and glory, rebelled against the Burmese in the year Pükcai Sakkarāja 1017, and was successful three times.

188. Prince Möngjün, who was the prince of Möngbī, was born in the year Tausan Sakkarāja 1024, Month Ten waning 12th night, Saturday, Daiy Kāpau, midmorning, nakkhatta constellation 5 [Magasiraṁ]. He was separated from his father because the Moon was in the realm which was destructive; returned to the state because the Sun and Venus were rājabandhu [royal connections or kinsmen]; he was fond of putting flowers of rice to the tips of hay[68] because he listened to royal pages; because Saturn was together with Lagana he was fond of listening to the Dhamma, performing meritorious deeds, and constructing monasteries; because Jupiter and the Moon attained fortune,[69] he ruled for eighteen years and died in the year Püksan.

189. The prince who was the younger brother was the son of the same father but of Yônghwe line born in Ava and named Maung Myo. He followed his father to the Khün state as he grew up. He was born in the year Ḍaprau Sakkarāja 1068, Month One full

moon, Saturday, nakkhatta constellation 27 [Revatī], predawn. He was lord of the northern Khôn rice fields and came to the throne at the age of fifteen in the year Kaḍpau Sakkarāja [58] 1092, Month Eight waxing 12th night, Tuesday.

190. This prince succeeded to the throne because Lagana was in the mansion of Leo; he succeeded only because he was born abroad --had he been born within the state he would not have succeeded. He ruled for eight years without the ten kingly duties and would not listen to the advice of ministers and officials or that of senior members of the Saṅgha because the Sun being atta [self] was nicca [permanence] and satrū [enemy]; Venus was kālakiṇī [goddess of misfortune]; Mars being the enemy of the field of fortune was kālakiṇī coming before Lagana; Jupiter was destructive to Lagana. He feared no consequences of [evil] actions in the supramundane world or mundane world, and acted any way that pleased him. There was nothing noble in him because his planet was nicca; and, although Mercury was srī [goddess of fortune], it was destructive. He was faithless and very evil because Rāhū [the dark planet] was in the mansion of Scorpio. He was not loved and had enemies because Mars and Venus were assayoga [? yoga of the horse] coming before Lagana and turning into misfortune and enmity. He would do evil deeds because Rāhū being death was in the mansion of Scorpio; he would perform meritorious deeds because Jupiter was mahā-uccā [great height] in front of Lagana; he might be evil or good because Jupiter was destructive to Lagana.

191. [The prince] was fond of hunting. Furthermore, he built a residence to the east of Möngjem and lived with [his] ladies there. He would make his subjects cut firewood and keep any good bullock that he saw. On a Tuṅga Market day the firewood would be carried [by pack bullocks] into the city, with two leading bullocks carrying the [bullock caravan] bells and lord of earth on horseback driving the bullocks into the palace. Moreover, [the prince] would make love to people's maiden daughters within the city. Any virgin wanting to be married could do so only after he had given permission. He would send pack bullocks to trade in betel nuts and salt. He would take any good and beautiful bullock from anyone without payment. He was so fond of being a doctor and of propitiating evil spirits and brahmas that he became a hungry demon, eating the commoners and subjects of the state. He was not in the habit of living in the palace but would live at Möngpong [where there is a hot spring] and Möngjem.

192. Eventually the people were dissatisfied and displeased and together they went to reverence Prince Saenmöng, granduncle of Prince Möngbī, and drove Prince Maung Myo [59] from the state of the lord of the golden palace that year. Prince Maung Myo went to stay with Bhayā Maen at Bān Dāy.

193. Prince Mӧngbī with the title of Titthanandarājā, the younger brother, having succeeded to the throne, sent a force to attack Prince Maung Myo at Bān Dāy and killed Bhayā Saen there. After that a royal order [appointed a Burmese envoy named Dhammasenā to come and settle affairs in Jengtung state concerning the flight of Prince Maung Myo, but without coming to any conclusion. Then Bhayā Sāmmӧng of Jengcīn][70] deputized Bhayā Bhān of Pāmān and a contingent from Yānggōng to take the case to the royal capital [at Ava] where the affairs were settled and royal orders gave the succession to Prince Mӧngbī whose title was Titthanandarājā.

194. In Sakkarāja 1111, a new monarch came to the throne[71] [in Ava], and a royal order summoned [Titthanandarājā] to the royal capital. At that juncture Prince Maung Myo fled to Jenghmai to hire the prince of Jenghmai to come [to Jengtung]. Led by Bingbāng, three hundred men came by jungle routes via Mӧnglung, through Mӧnghving and Mӧnghvae, arriving at the capital late at night. They set fire to the residence of the rājamādā [royal mother]. Then, when the city populace heard the sound of the great drum of the courthouse, they rushed to block the front and rear [of the enemy], and the Yōn were defeated and fled towards Cômsak foothills; some of them, ignorant of the directions, hid themselves north of Sālāghô, and our people killed many of them there.

195. Not long after that, Prince Maung Myo, unwilling to give up, came down with the peoples of Lōy and Yāng [Mӧnghlōy and Mӧngyāng] to attack Jengtung, but was unsuccessful and fled to the Lü state. As regards Prince Mӧngbī, he and the offshoots of gold and stems of gem [royal family] fled to Nājū at Hōṅā and later moved to Nāghā [and] Nāhvāy. Then Bhayā Sāmmӧng and Bhayā Jengsaen of Cômsak together invited Prince Mӧngbī to come and reside at Dāyā in Mӧngkhā, and sent Prince Mӧngsām, who [60] was the twelve-year-old son [of Mӧngbī], to the court at Ava.

196. [When Mӧngsām] reached the age of sixteen years, Maung Myo was summoned to Ava where he had a debate [with the former] but was defeated by Prince Mӧngsām's side. Prince Maung Myo was not satisfied and had another debate and was again defeated by Prince Mӧngsām, because princes Bīn and Kāng, sons of Prince Maung Myo, were bandits in Burma. Then Prince Maung Myo was confined to Ava.

197. Prince Kāngjhāy was the son of Prince Maung Myo by a girl from the village of Hlāykvang [three or four miles north of Kengtung City] and was sent to be Lord of Mӧngyāng.

198. At that time our state had no ruling prince and there was an interregnum for one or two years; only Bô Cemsan acted as the leader, residing in Kāngmöng[72] while the city was deserted.

199. After that the Burmese told Prince Maung Myo, saying, "Your sons are bandits; will you be able to catch them or not?" Prince Maung Myo undertook to go and capture them. The Burmese then sent Prince Maung Myo and Prince Möngsām up [to Jengtung] and they camped at Jengkā. Prince Kāng and Prince Bīn were not captured; the three Bômöngs would not submit; they were against each other. The Burmese sent Prince Maung Myo to Jenghmai and he died there.

200. As for Prince Möngsām, he went to fetch his parents, brothers, and sisters [relatives] and took them to the court at Ava. Prince Möngbī, the father, died in the following year at Mukjho City [modern Shwebo; Burmese pronunciation: "Mokso"]. After the funeral ceremonies had been performed, the great monarch [Burmese king] gave Prince Möngsām the revenue of Jenggūm Myo [unidentifiable] to enjoy. In the following year the Burmese established Prince Möngsām at Dāvī [ferry on the Khā (?) River] where his followers and subjects were collected and those who had fled to the Lü state were recalled; they all came back that year, while Prince Möngsām went down to Ava.

201. In the following year Sakkarāja 1102 [? 1112], the great monarch permitted [Prince Möngsām] to succeed to the throne of Jengtung at the age of twenty-two.

202. After four years reign, the great monarch commanded Tingjā-[61]-pō ["Htinshābō" in Burmese] and Myokmengmū [Myaukminhmū] to lead an army to fight against the Chinese. On arrival in Jengtung they ordered Prince Möngsām to go along. Prince Möngsām and Myokmengmū went up by way of Möngkhông and Möngvang; Tingjāpō went up by way of Jengrung. Myokmengmū and Prince Möngsām defeated the Chinese and obtained a great amount of war spoils, which the Burmese asked Prince Möngsām to present to the court [at Ava]. On the Jengrung front Tingjāpō was defeated by the Chinese and retreated. The Chinese followed him to Jengtung [City] which became deserted in the absence of Prince Möngsām. That was the year Kāmeḍ Sakkarāja 1125 and the Chinese took away to China all members of the royal family. The Chinese were victorious as far as Jenghmai over there. In Jengtung state the Chinese installed Prince Bīn as lord of earth for the three months of the vassā.

203. The Burmese and Prince Möngsām led an army to fight on the Jenghmai front and were victorious up to Jengtung during

Month Five. Möngyāng did not submit and an army was sent up to attack it by way of Ūmgaeng [west of Möngyāng]. After the fall of Möngyāng all the people who could not escape were brought down to reside in the Khün state.

204. In the following year, Prince Kāng, Prince Bīn, the Lüs, and the Laems were allied together, while at Möngyāng Prince Kāng was the leader. There they confronted one another but [the allies] would not come down when called [by Jengtung]. [The Jengtung side] then went up to attack but neither side would win or take flight. Prince Mönghlek and Bhayā Saenbhong led a force and came down [to Jengtung] through jungle routes and set fire to the city. [The Jengtung forces] were routed and fled to Möngsāt, whereupon Prince Möngsām went to Jenghmai and brought the fās [ruling princes] of Jengrāy and Jengsaen to help in the fighting. Having captured the city [of Jengtung] a force was dispatched to fight Prince Kāng and Prince Mönghlek. They fought at Möngkhāk and Möngnung. Prince Kāng brought a force through the Jô Pass to Kātpung [bazaar about three miles north of Kengtung City] where there was fighting for twenty-one days with neither side winning or fleeing. [Möngsām's men] withdrew to the safety of the city walls and they [the enemy] brought [62] men to lay siege to the city, but were unable to achieve victory over Jengtung and were routed and all fled to their separate states.

205. That year Jengtung state could not cultivate rice. The following year was the year Rāysed̩ Sakkarāja 1128 when there was a great famine. After that Prince Möngsām fell from the state [? left in disgrace] and went to reside in Ava. The Burmese then appointed Prince Kāng to rule the state for three years, but as his services to the great monarch were indifferent he was executed by the Burmese who then brought back Möngsām to rule as of old with the title of Cuḷāmaṇī Sirimegha Bhummindanarindā Khemādhipatirājā, and Prince Kôngdaiy, his sixteen-year-old son, was sent to be brought up at the court in Ava.

206. In the year D̩apsai Sakkarāja 1142, Month One waxing 8th night, Wednesday, the excellent lord by the name of Cuḷāmaṇī Sirimegha Bhummindanarindā Khemādhipatirājā marched with a strong force to attack Sipsôngbannā. The royal [Burmese] army, consisting of one thousand men with Tingjāp̱ō and Myokmengmū as commanders-in-chief, advanced by way of Dālô [about sixty miles northeast of Kengtung City on the Chinese side of the present-day border].

207. The Jengtung contingent attacked by way of Möngyāng and reached Möngjae and Mönghun [substates of Sipsôngbannā Jengrung] where the caugrahmôm [lord above the crown of the head, or highest lord] was taken seriously ill and returned, having appointed Bhayā Lāmhmün of Yānggōng and Bhayā Hyāu of Hnông-kung as commanders to lead the army to join the Burmese in Jengrung. The caugrahmôm arrived back at the capital on Month Five waxing 10th night. In the year Rāysaṅā Sakkarāja 1148, Month Six waning 2nd night, Saturday, at midnight, the caugrahmôm passed away. Sæn Lang and three followers were deputed as messengers to reverence [inform] Prince Kôngdaiy, the son, residing in Ava, to reverence the great monarch.

208. On the state side, Bhayā Sāmmöng of Jengcīn led state officials, big and small, in making arrangements [for the funeral] in accordance with custom and tradition since the reign of Prince Ceḍ-[63]-bantū, Sattabandhurājā, thus: The sides of the coffin were decorated with fifteen-tier gems. [The coffin-housing structure] had eight windows gilded and decorated with gem-studded floral designs. The plinth for the coffin [which is a kind of elongated Burmese throne narrowed midway at the waist] had fourteen-tier gems. The top [narrowing towards the waist] and bottom [expanding towards the foot] portions of the plinth were decorated with gilded and gem-studded floral designs of a "cow-face" hairpin.[73] The prāsāḍ [tiered roofing] of the coffin-housing structure had gilded floral designs of gold paint. The posts of the prāsāḍ and of the library were wrapped in velvet. Four devaputta images and four devatās were in a sitting position on bended knees. The coffin plinth was placed on a hassaḍīling [mythical bird with the strength of five elephants]; two king haṁsa birds stand on the [hassaḍīling] carriage. [The tradition] is thus.

209. Amūglī [Burmese: "ahmūgyī," principle leader] Nôrathā led the Burmese delegation of ten men from Ava and four men from the jagāy [Burmese: "citkae," commander of the Burmese garrison] of Möngnāy in bringing up the royal letter. On arrival they stayed at Jengṅām. The royal letter was opened and read[74] on the thirteenth. Paraphernalia presented by the great monarch consisted of: eight sets of aṭṭhaparikkhāra,[75] twelve bolts of kāsā [Banares] cloth, eight pieces of white sandalwood, eight pieces of red sandalwood,[76] one gold [drinking] water cover, one decorative gold sash-chain for the chest, one [? gold] belt, one pair of rings, four glass bottles of perfume, twelve thousand bullion gold [.9 viss, or approximately 3.24 pounds], lūk mangbyā [meaning not known, but it seems to be some article(s) of a spherical shape]. This was all.

210. On Month Three waning 12th night, all arrangements being completed, the caugrahmôm was taken away by way of P̱āmān, Jeng-cām, cutting across Hnongghai to the northern side of Tuṅga Market, and thence to the front of Vat Jengcan. [The funeral procession] was to have gone by the main road, but the Burmese military camp at Jengṅām did not allow it.

211. The pācan [sandalwood grove or cremation area] was encompassed with three courses of rājamāḍ[77] fencing, whose posts were wrapped in red cloth and the lotus bud on each post was gilded with gold leaves; [at the foot of each post] were planted banana saplings, sugar cane suckers, and gukgās,[78] with pennons, streamers, and water pots. This is in accordance with tradition.

212. When the funeral rites were over, the [new] caugrahmôm gave away presents [as follows]: Amūglī the leader--one silver-encased sword, one piece of woolen cloth; each of the four followers--a [? silver] woven betel box weighing three ticals, six viss of silver [approximately 21.6 pounds] of fineness one hundred/5 bahts; representative of the jagāy of Möngnāy--one [silver-]encased sword, one piece of cloth; each of the two followers--one woven betel box weighing three ticals, three viss of silver [approximately 10.8 pounds] of fineness one hundred/5 bahts. This is all.

213. Prince Cuḷāmaṇī Sirimegha Surindnarindā Khemādhipatirājā ruled for forty-four years and died in the year Rāysaṅā Sakkarāja 1148.

214. [64] In the year Müngmeḍ Sakkarāja 1149, Month Three waxing 10th night, the mangbrarā [Burmese king] appointed Prince Kông-daiy to come and rule the state at the age of eighteen with the title of Sārabyabhummindnarindā Khemādhipatirājā. After he had ruled for fifteen years, in the year Tauseḍ Sakkarāja 1164, Month Seven waxing 3rd night, citizens of Jenghmai brought up an army and attacked Jengtung and captured the person of the prince, members of the royal family, and subjects of the state and took them all down to Jenghmai, with the exception of Prince Dōngsaeng, the younger brother, that is, Prince Mahākhanān, who escaped to stay with his subjects at Sip-eḍ Sip-hā Bān,[79] where, with his family, he took refuge at P̲āngkeng.

215. Having collected together his followers and subjects who had not been taken away, he [Mahākhanān] led them to establish themselves at Mönghlōy and Möngyāng.

216. Headed by Prince Sārabya Bhumminda, members of the royal family, followers, and subjects who went to Jenghmai together reverenced the prince of Jenghmai asking permission to go up and settle in Jengsaen, and the prince of Jenghmai allowed them to go. Having settled in Jengsaen, the prince of the Khün state and his followers and subjects used to sally forth and attack continuously the Lüs, the Laems, Bôfā, and Manglön, and would return to Jengsaen again.

217. Prince Dōngsaeng Mahākhanān, the younger brother, who remained in Mönghlōy and Möngyāng, conducted defensive battles against the Burmese. Before long the monarch of Ava appointed Meng Mahāsura [Burmese: "Maṅ Mahāsūra," pronounced "Min Mahāthūra"] as the commander-in-chief at Möngnāy. [The commander] then marched forth with an army consisting of contingents from the nine caufās [sôbwas] of the western states and Burmese troops and went up to Mönghlōy and Möngyāng and attacked Prince Mahākhanān there. [The latter] fought defensive actions against the Burmese for a period of eleven or twelve years but he was unable to stand up to [65] the Burmese, and with his followers and subjects went to reside in Jengsaen, leaving behind only Saen Lāmban and Sip-eḍ Sip-hā Bān, Möngkhāk, and Möngnung.

218. Dāu G̲hamvang, who was Prince Mahākhanān's man, also remained; he did not follow [his master]. Together [those who remained behind] submitted to the Burmese, wrote a letter and dispatched a messenger to reverence Prince Mahākhanān at Jengsaen there.

219. Having learned [the contents of the letter] Prince Mahākhanān did not tell anyone. The southerners said they would take the person of Prince Mahākhanān to Jenghmai. The prince thought to himself, saying, "Should I go to Jenghmai I might be stranded there, the royal family would sink and perish, the excellent Sāsanā of the Lord would be abandoned, and the state would never rise again. It is meet that I should go to my state." Such was the thinking of the prince, and he talked to his followers and subjects who had accompanied him. Having decided to act as one, [the prince and his followers] collected their families and freed themselves from the southerners.

220. Having reached Möngyāng and arranged to acquire such presents as twelve elephants, the prince led a delegation and went to submit to the great monarch at Ava there. The great monarch, showing generosity and compassion, took no offense but handed over the elephants and the state,[80] allowing [the prince] to be the supreme lord of earth in the state of Jengtung in the manner of his ancestors, with the title of caufāhlōng [great lord of the heavens] Khemāraṭṭhamahāsiha Pavarasudhammarājā Bhummindanarindādhipatirāja.

221. Prince Dōngsaeng Mahākhanān came to the throne in the year Kāmeḍ Sakkarāja 1175. The elephant trappings and state paraphernalia which the great monarch who was named Paduṁ Mengbrarā [Burmese: "Paduṅ Maṅ," pronounced "Padōng Min," better known as Bodôpayā (1782-1819)] gave to Caufāhlōng Khemāraṭṭha-[66]-mahāsiha Pavarasudhammarājā are as follows:

twelve-cornered gold pedestal tray studded with gems, complete with internal outfit, 1; multi-petalled gold pedestal tray, studded with gems, 1; pedestal tray for pickled tea, studded with gems, 1; gold spittoon, 1; large pedestal trays for food, of beaten gold and studded with gems, 2; twelve-cornered gold bowl, studded with gems, 1; gold crown, 1; double-edged hand sword with gold-banded and gem-studded sheath, 1; gold sandals, 1 [pair]; fifteen-strand decorative sash-chain for the chest, 1; swords [with sheaths] wrapped in black velvet with nine gold bands and studded with gems, 4; white umbrellas with gilded ferrules and gold Boḍhi leaves as pendants on the three-tiered fringe, 4; "kȫng" [or "kö̈k"][81] with gilded tops [? ferrules], 4; totally gilded umbrellas, 4; [gilded palm leaf] fans with gilded long handles, 2; totally gilded carriage, 1; totally gilded rattan canes, 4; bull elephants, 2; cow elephants, 2; elephant-head cover cloth of gold threaded net, 1; gem-studded gold tassel [? for elephant trappings], 1; drum-shaped chair with gilded edge, 1; red drums, 14; "būhūlābhā" [? wind instruments], 2; small [Burmese] oboes, 2.

222. A palace[82] of twelve pavilions sharing the same floor, the upper portions of which were painted with cinnabar and the middle [? pavilion] had a prāsāḍ [tiered roof structure] which was totally gilded; the decorative designs on the roof ridge were gilded; the walls of the front chamber [under the prāsāḍ] were totally gilded; carvings of four king haṁsa birds, pillars and beams, were totally gilded; small bells whose ringers [inside the bells] had Boḍhi leaves attached were suspended onto the decorative designs of the roof eaves.

223. The throne was four cubits high, gilded and decorated with gems; two devaputta images each shouldering a sword were at the foot of the throne; [and the throne area] was surrounded by a railing whose turned balusters were painted with cinnebar.

224. The parapets and battlements of the city walls were to be constructed of kiln-baked bricks; there were to be bell and watch towers; the city gates were to be of stone.

225. These were the royal orders of Lord Alongmangbrarāglī Padummeng [King Bodôpayā (1782-1819)].

226. Prince Dōngsæng Mahākhanān came up from Ava and made Mö̈ngyāng his capital for one year.

227. In the year Ḍapgai Sakkarāja 1177, he came down to reside in the valley of Jengtung at Bān Nông, and the capital included P̱āhmai and Dônjai.

228. In the year Müngpau Sakkarāja 1179, he went to swear an oath of friendship [67] with the Lüs in Vat Yāngban.

229. The year Pükyī Sakkarāja 1180, the prince Mönglaem came [to Jengtung] and died.

230. The year Kaḍhmau Sakkarāja 1181, [Mahākhanān] came and established his capital at the great city [Jengkaeu].

231. The year Tausaṅā Sakkarāja 1184, full moon, Prince Mahākhanān offered as dāna one hundred sets of yellow robes and one hundred sets of palm leaf Dhamma scripture, and held a rocket festival at Farō. In the year Pükcai the Burmese minister of Yô rebelled. In the year Koḍyī Sakkarāja 1192, Month Four waxing 4th night, the excellent lord abbot of Vat Hōkhōng accomplished accumulation of merit [passed away]. The Lüs sent a delegation that year. The year Kāsai Sakkarāja 1195, Month Ten waning 8th night, Bhayā Sāmmöng of Sōnrau died. In Month Four orders were given for the city walls to be constructed.

232. In the year Ḍapmeḍ Sakkarāja 117 [*sic*], Month Ten waxing 14th night, the rājadevi [chief queen] died.

233. The year Rāysan Sakkarāja 1198 [Mahākhanān] went to wed the lady of Jengkhaeng state and brought her [to Jengtung] during Month Three.

234. The year Rōngpau Sakkarāja 1203, Princess Suvaṇṇā was taken to Ava.

235. The year Tauyī Sakkarāja 1204, Möngkāy and Möngyông rebelled against the Burmese residing at Yāngfārō.

236. In the year Müngmeḍ Sakkarāja 1209, Princess Sunandā was taken to Jengrung during First Month Nine.

237. The year Kaḍrau Sakkarāja 1211, Month Five waning 11th night, sixty-five hundred southerners attacked the Khün state. They came via Möngsāt through Möngbeng and through Namkāi and pitched camps at Dāsān, Jengfông, and Cômsrī. Month Six waxing 6th night, the southerners were defeated and fled.

238. In the following year the Burmese called Prince Saenmöng [crown prince] to Möngnāy.

239. In the year Taucai Sakkarāja 1214, Month Two, the lord abbot Ghūbā of Vat Jengyün accomplished his accumulation of merit.

240. [In the same year] Prince Soḍec Kummahlōng [Vongsādhirāj of Bangkok] collected an army comprising men from Ayodhiyā,

Rahaeng, Kambaeng, Möngtāk, P̱āpheu, and Mönghlom, and on Month Five waning 6th night reached Möng-[68]-bhyāk. On Month Five waning 13th night, [the enemy] arrived in the state [valley of Jengtung] and encamped at Bengsang. On the 14th night, Jenghmai [forces] besieged the city. The forces of Labūn [Lamphūn], Lagôn [Lampāng], Bae [Prae], and Nān came via Möngyông. The forces that came via Möngyông arrived in Jengtung only on Month Six waxing 10th night, and moved to surround the city, establishing themselves at Hōkhō Fārō, Yānglô, Bān-īḍ, and Cômsrī. On Month Six waning 1st night, the southerners of Ayodhiyā were defeated and retreated. People of the state followed and killed them as far as Nam-raeḍ; a great number of the southerners died and [we] captured a great number of their elephants and cannons.

241. The year Kāpyī Sakkarāja 1216, Kummahlōng Vongsādhirāj did not give in, and, having collected forces from Ayodhiyā, La-haeng [Rahaeng], Kambeng [Kambaeng], Möngtāk, P̱āpheu, Möng-hlom, Labūn, Lagôn, Bae, Nān, Jenghmai, Jengrāy, Nampāḍ, and Hlōngprabāng, came up via Möngyông, Jengkhaeng and came through [Möng]lāy and [Möng]n̈ôm, and encamped at Môntung on Month Six waning 13th night. On Month Seven waning 6th night, the southerners were defeated and escaped via Kaengnôy and Kaenghlōng. Khüns and Bôngs went after and killed many [of the enemy], capturing many elephants, cannons, and men. That year the Burmese army and the nine caufās of the west were called to help. That year the great jagāy of Möngnāy by the name of Mengglī Mahānôrathā, leader of the royal army and the nine caufās, encamped at Tung Market. The caufā of Lāy-khā encamped in the rice fields at the Nôngpha Gate. The fā-hoheng of Möngnông encamped on the hillock of Cômsrī.

242. The year Ḍaphmau Sakkarāja 1217, Month Three full moon, [Mahā-khanān] consecrated the uposatha hall with prāsāḍ roofing at Vat Hōkhōng, offered as dāna [to the monasteries] one hundred twenty karabük[83] trees, consecrated one hundred twenty images of the Lord, and held a rocket festival at Fārō. Month Four waxing 12th night, the bragrū of Vat Kōkhōng was broken [broke the vow of celibacy and was defrocked]. Month Five waxing 13th night, the excellent rājaguru, lord abbot of Vat Hōkāt, accomplished the accumulation of his merit and the funeral ceremonies were held at Dongkōy.

243. The year Rāysī Sakkarāja 1218, Month Three waning [69] 3rd night, Prince Mongghāk of Jengcām died.

244. The year Müngsai Sakkarāja 1219, Month Seven full moon, Prince Mönghlek consecrated the Lord's image and the vihāra of Cômsrī and held a rocket festival at the rice fields of Nôngphā.

245. Month Eight waning 11th night, Thursday, Daiy Müngpau, nakkhatta constellation 3 [Kattikā], time--towards dawn, Caumôm Mahākhanān accomplished the accumulation of his merit. Month Nine waxing 2nd night, his remains were placed in a casket within the gilded coffin. Prince Saenmöng together with ministers, high officials and low and their wives dressed in their best garments--junior and senior officials wearing gowns with large sleeves--performed the invitation ceremony of placing the prince's remains in the coffin, with Bhayā Rom as the master of ceremonies and Bōk Möngsang holding aloft the pedestal tray containing flowers and candles.

246. Regarding the work of cooking meals for public feeding, the palace slaves erected the cookhouse [of thatch and bamboo] and drew water; palace retainers set up cooking stones [used in place of trivets] and looked after cooking utensils and the fire; officials' wives and monasteries' parishioners did the actual cooking.

247. Month Eight waning 12th night, the parish nearest to the palace came to work, palace slaves drew water, palace retainers saw to the cooking utensils and the cooking fire. The thirteenth night was the turn of the parishes of Pamān and Jengcām to come and work; the fourteenth night, new moon, was the turn of the parishes of Hōkāt and Khāngkāt to come work; Month Nine waxing 1st night was the turn of the parishes of Asōk and Jengkhūm; Month Nine waxing 2nd night was the turn of the parishes of Bhakam and Jeng-ing; the day of Month Nine 3rd night was the turn of the parishes of Bhayāu, Nôynô and Bhakaeu to work; and so on until all parishes had had their turns, and a new start was made from the beginning.

248. The parish that came to work must also come and sleep to keep watch during the night. On the day when senior and junior officials [from the palace office] came [to be on duty], royal pages are to come to keep watch and to run errands. On the Sanām side [executive branch of administration] each high official must be attended by a secretary. Officials of the substates are to come and sleep one day and one night together with members of the parishes.

249. The construction of the wheels and frame [of the funeral carriage] was the responsibility of the three Bômöngs and state craftsmen; [70] the procurement of timbers and bamboos was the responsibility of the Bômöng of the parishes. Bômöng Jôn, Bômöng Jônglae, Bômöng Cūm, and heads of the parishes worked together. Construction of the [large, temporary] hall was the responsibility of state retainers. Hauling ropes [for the funeral carriage] was the responsibility of the state. Maipheu, maibô, and maijhāng [bamboos: respectively,

Gigantochloa macrostachya, *Dendrocalamus giganteus*, and *Dendrocalamus membranaceus*] for the posts for the pulpit throne, the library, and the funeral carriage, all are the responsibility of the state. Construction of the flat-roofed hall [for the public at the funeral] and the pavilion [for royalty and officials] was the responsibility of state retainers. Assistance to and feeding of the public and state guests were the responsibility of peoples of the hills and substates. One hundred strings each of cowrie shells and betel nuts [for ceremonial offerings] were the responsiblity of the people of the ferries and fisheries. Prāsāḍ [tiered roofs for the funeral carriage] was the shared responsibility among the three Bôm̈ongs and parishes.

250. Led by Bhayā Bhom, the state craftsmen worked according to ancient state traditions: the sides of the coffin were decorated with fifteen tiers of gems; the housing over the coffin had eight windows decorated with gilded and gem-studded floral designs. The plinth [which receives the coffin] had fourteen tiers of gems, the top and bottom portions of which were studded with "hnavo" pins of gems. The fluted narrowed waist of the plinth was gilded and decorated with chips of mother-of-pearl. The prāsāḍ above the coffin was decoratively painted in gold; the posts of the prāsāḍ over the library and those of the prāsāḍ over the pulpit throne were wrapped in velvet interspersed with gold rings. Four devaputta images stood beside the coffin, four lady devatā images were seated on bended knees with palms together raised in obeisance. This prince had not yet established a tradition, and therefore the coffin plinth was placed on a hassaḍīling bird; two king haṁsa birds stood on the carriage.

251. The pācan [sandalwood grove or place of cremation] and the place for firewood were surrounded by three courses of rājamāḍ fencing whose posts were wrapped in red cloth and topped with gilded lotus buds; [and at the foot of each post] were planted banana saplings, sugar cane suckers, and gukgā, together with [the bamboo stems of] pennons and streamers, and a water pot, in accordance with ancient tradition, thus.

252. On Month Twelve waning 7th night, the delegation from Möngnāy and Ava led by commanders Yecô [Burmese: Yekyô] and Yaemengthengmengcô [? Burmese: Yaeminhtinmincô], bringing the royal letter for the funeral, arrived, and a temporary residence for them was constructed at Tuṅga Market.

253. On the ninth night the royal letter was opened and read out as desired by the father, the great monarch. [71] There were only one ban [seven and a half tolas] of gold and ten bolts of Banares cloth. The Burmese were asked why they did not act according to tradition. The Burmese said, "We are ignorant of old traditions because we are a new government."[84]

254. Mönglaem came with traditional offerings with Bhayā Khaek heading a delegation consisting of the fā of Vengjai, fā of Kānghô, and fā of P̱ānmöng, totaling thirty men. They came with the [following] contributions: silver, one ban [seven and a half tolas]; horse, 1; silver bowl, 1--weight, thirty tolas; aṭṭhaparikkhāra,[85] one set; ten tolas of silver, to go with the parikkhāra. On their return, each of the officials was presented with a bolt of Banares cloth and a woven betel box, weighing thirty tolas, two boxes; three and a half tolas, two boxes; the followers were presented with nine bolts of Banares cloth.

255. As for the state of Svaenhvīfā Jengrung, there was a war on. Prince Svaenhvīfā of the East[86] came as far as Möngmā [a frontier village of Jengtung state] and deputed Bhayā Jeyyavong and Bhayā Pupphā of Jenglô, totaling ten men. They came with the [following] funeral contributions: silver, one ban; horse, 1; silver bowl, 1, weighing thirty tolas; brocade bolt, 1; aṭṭhaparikkhāra set, 1; silver pedestal tray, 1; these are all the funeral contributions. When the envoys were about to return, [Jengtung] gave Bhayā Jeyyavong: Banares cloth, one bolt; woven betel box, 1, weighing forty [tolas];[87] gave Bhayā Pupphā: Banares cloth, one bolt; woven betel box, 1, weighing three and a half tolas; the followers: Banares cloth, two bolts.

256. Jengkhaeng contributed: silver, fifty tolas; aṭṭhaparikkhāra set, 1.

257. On Month One waning 10th night, all arrangements having been completed for the prince to be taken down from the golden palace, all ministers, senior and junior officials, town elders, ladies of rank, officials of the substates and of the hills, headed by the Prince Bra Saenmöng [heir apparent] and the Prince Bra Mönghlekhlōng [heir presumptive], together invited [the remains of Mahākhanān] to descend from the palace: Saenhlōng Bōkmöngsang held aloft the pedestal tray of flowers and candles and Bhayā Rom intoned reverence. [72] Bhayā Rom intoned reverence; Bhayāhlōng Dep was the head, Müsang[88] held aloft the pedestal tray of flowers and candles inviting the prince to descend the palace.

258. Officials of the four substates of Mönghlōy, Möngkhāk, Möngbeng, and Möngyāng, wearing long coats in white, led the procession up to Hōkhōng. Headed by the Prince Saenmöng the whole state carried paraphernalia of elephants and state property to their places prepared in front of the house of Bhayā

Möngggham on Jhedān Main Road. State retainers constructed a [temporary] pavilion surrounded by flat-roofed halls. Ministers, senior and junior officials, officials of the substates, and royal subjects of the three Pākmü, within and without, held ceremonies and kept watch day and night.

259. On Month One waning 11th night, the caugramôm was taken along Jhedān Main Road, and, at the nearer corner of [the walls] of Vat Jengñām, was received with flowers and candles carried on a pedestal tray by Jāykaeu, younger brother of Bhayā Cā of Khāngkāt, acting on behalf of the Ban Nôykut and wearing a long coat in white.

260. On arrival at the sandalwood grove in front of the monastery, officials of the substates offered as dāna their shares of pañsukūla[89] robes to the Saṅgha lord abbots [as follows]: Möngyāng, one set; Möngdôy, one set; Hōdau, one set; Bānkông, Nônglāu, and Yāngkông, one set; Mönghlōy, one set; Möngkhāk, one set; Möngkā, one set; Möngkhā North, one set; Namying, Nambāy, and Donglae, one set; Möngbū, one set; Möngbeng, one set; Möngkhā South and Jenghlek, one set; Möngsim, one set; Mönglaeng and Hit-ung, one set; Möngphü, Yāngnô, and Möngpan, one set; Möng-ing and Möngsaen, one set; Möngmāng, one set; Möngleng, Dā-ô, and Dācaed, one set; Möngdin and Langsāt, one set; Möngbhyāk and Möngrāy, one set; Möngyông, one set; Möngkāy, one set; Möngvāk, Rairom, and [Möng]nôm, one set; Möngmā, one set; Phālāhlek, Yānghlōng, and Yāngpāu, one set; Bānthān, Yāngsing, Bānrôm, and Kampaen, one set; Mönglā, one set; Möngñen, one set; Dābing and Dābôm [ferries], one set; Möngdum, one set; [73] Bhayā Candajumbū of Naivang, one set; Bhayā Pupphā, one set; these are the sets of pañsukūla robes offered as dāna before the arrival [of the remains of the prince] at the sandalwood grove on the eleventh night.

261. The robes of the rājadevi, one set; high officials of the Sanām [executive branch], one set; the Pākmünôy, one set; the Pākmühlekyôy, one set; the Pākmühlōng, one set; these five sets of robes were offered as pañsukūla dāna on the twelfth night, the day of cremation [as follows]: one set to the Lord and four sets to the Saṅgha.

262. Bhayāhlōng Khaek Khattiyavong [? and] Mengcôcāu Nôrathā[90] has recorded [the above] for future reference as a tradition.

263. The year Müngsai Sakkarāja 1219, Month One waning 12th night, the funeral ceremonies of the caumôm were completed. On Month One new moon, ministers and high officials gave silver to the Burmese commanders headed by Mengthengmengcô [Minhtinmincô] as the amūglī of Ava Nalaengcung [undecipherable into Burmese] as follows: the amūglī, the commander, silver-sheathed sword, 1; woolen cloth, one piece; a member of the delegation, two men of the jagāy of Möngnāy, two couriers, two captains--each of these seven men was given one woven betel box, each weighing thirty [tolas]. As regards silver bullion, they were given three viss with the fineness of one hundred/5 bahts. Apart from this the twelve men were given a food allowance to reach Möngnāy and Ava, and fifty [tolas] of silver with the fineness of 9/50. The commander of the military establishment at Möngnāy was given a silver-sheathed sword, one piece of woolen cloth, and five viss, forty-six tolas of silver. Thus it is recorded.

264. This prince was born in the year Rōngpau Sakkarāja 1143, Month Ten waning 7th night, Saturday, Daiy Kāgai, nakkhatta constellation 3 [Kattikā], time--midmorning. He was named Prince Dōngsæng; he went forth to become a bhikkhu and was named Prince Mahānām; when he left the bhikkhuhood people called [74] him by the name of Prince Mahākhanān. The great monarch appointed him as brayā to rule over Jengtung with the title Caufāhlōng Khemāraṭṭhamahāsiha Pavarasudhammarājā.

265. He was led by the Moon to succeed to the state because the Moon was friendly to Lagana, becoming honor, glory, and great special acquisitions. Mars led Lagana in the first stage to become ahi [enemy]; Mercury was death as well as enemy to Lagana; Saturn and Lagana were together constituent parts of the body imperfect;[91] Jupiter being with Lagana [indicates] a fondness for great meritorious actions. In the middle stage Mars led Lagana to be bandhu [kinsman] and lābha [acquisitions], enemies submitted. In the last stage Mars was ahi, and many illnesses existed. He ruled the state for forty-two [actually forty-four] years from the year Kārau to the year Müngsai. His age was seventy-six years.

266. This somḍec brapencau [most excellent one who is the lord] came to the throne in the year Kārau Cuḷa Sakkarāja 1175. In the year 1180 he went up and swore an oath of friendship with the Prince of Svænhvīfā whose name was Mahāsuriyavongsārāja at [the border village of] Jenglô, and constructed the great monastery of Yāngban.

267. In the year Koḍsī Sakkarāja 1182, royal commands summoned the lords of heaven to go down [to Ava]. From Jengtung, the somḍec brapencau went down; from Jengrung the Prince Svænhvīfā, Mahāvongsā, went down; from Monglæm, Prince Kūm went down; from Jengkhæng, the caufā went down. [The caufās] gave the numbers of men for military service to the Sōyluttô [Burmese: Shwehluttô, Council of Ministers]: Jengtung state, the number of men for service was 1,500; Jengrung, 2,500; Monglæm, 750; and Jengkhæng, 375. Thus it is.

268. This prince ruled for forty-four years and had five sons and two daughters: the eldest was named Prince Mahābhom, lord of the Saen rice fields, with the title of Khemāraṭṭha Mahāvoṅsarājā; next, Prince Saeng went down to serve the great monarch who appointed him to rule Möngmīḍ with the title of Gandhāraraṭṭharājā; the next prince was named Prince Ghamsaen, lord of Hlek rice fields, with the title of Khe-[75]-māraṭṭha Mahāsuriyavongsā Sihavararājā; the eldest daughter was named Princess Sunandā, who was raised to be the Jengrung princess; the younger sister was named Princess Suvaṇṇā who went down to wait upon the great monarch in Ava and became Queen Khemamahesī; the two [remaining] princes were the sons of the Jengkhaeng princess, the elder brother was named Prince Debbamaṇigham, and the younger brother was named Prince Jōtikông-daiy.

269. In the year Müngsai Sakkarāja 1219, Month Eight waning 11th night, towards dawn, he [Mahākhanān] died, having completed his accumulation of merit. On Month One waning 10th night, his remains were moved [out of the palace].

270. In the year Püksaṅā Sakkarāja 1220, Month Seven waxing 8th night, led by Cauhmôm Saenmöng and Cauhmôm Mönghlekhlōng, the royal family, ministers and high officials together arranged the following state gifts which are articles for the continuity of the royal lineage to be sent to Mönglaem according to tradition: elephant, 1; silver pedestal tray, 1, weighing 320; Burmese lime [for betel] box of gold, 1, weighing 30; woven betel box in gold, 1, weighing 2.25 tolas. As there was no elephant, silver was sent instead, [weight] 3 bans [22.5 tolas] with the fineness of [?]. Saenkhaek of Fākāng and officials of the substates of Möngkhāk, Mönghlōy, and Möngyāng together were deputed to go and present [the state gifts].

271. Articles for the continuity of the royal lineage for Jengrung are as follows: silver pedestal tray, 1, weighing fifty-one tolas; gold vessel [?], 1, weighing seven and a half [tolas]; silver-sheathed sword, 1. On Month Eleven waning 13th night, Bhayā Lāp, Bhayā Khaek, Saen Kāngdü, and Nāy Hmū took them and presented them to the son of the prince of Svaenhvīfā who was staying in the house of the old Dui Vang of Hôngghum. These have been recorded thus. The continuity of the reign of the excellent lord of earth of Jengtung state, whose title was Khemāraṭṭhamahāsiha Pavarasu-[76]-dhammarājā, has now come to an end. Itaraṁ, that is, the prince who will succeed hence, paraṁ in the future, is the responsibility of posterity to record.

272. Prince Mahābrohm was born in the year Kāpseḍ Cuḷa Sakkarāja 1176, Month Two new moon, Sunday, Daiy Müinggai, nakkhatta constellation 18 [Jeṭṭhā], midnight. He was lord of the Sæn rice fields, with the title of Khemāraṭṭha Mahāvaṁsa. He was consecrated and ruled at the age of forty-five in the year Püksañā Sakkarāja 1220, Month Four waxing 13th night, with the title of Khemāraṭṭhamahāsiha Pavarabrahma Sirisudhammarājā. He ruled for eighteen years until the year Rāycai Sakkarāja 1238, Month Twelve waning 12th night, when he died at the age of sixty-three. The funeral ceremonies were performed in the year Müngp̱au Sakkarāja 1239, Month Eight waxing 6th night.

273. Prince G̱hamsaen was born in the year Kāpsan Sakkarāja 1186, Month Twelve 1st night, Saturday, Daiy Müngp̱au, midmorning, nakkhatta constellation 1 [Assayuja]. He enjoyed the revenues of the Hlek rice fields with the title of Khemāraṭṭha Mahāsuriyavaṁsa Sihavararājā. At the age of fifty-two he accomplished his merit and went to heaven. This prince did not receive consecration.[92]

274. Prince Saeng, son of Prince Mahākhanān, was born in the year Pükyī Cuḷa Sakkarāja 1180, Month Nine new moon, Saturday, Daiy Rāysan, midmorning, nakkhatta constellation 8 [Phussa]. He was the fifth son. In the year [77] Sakkarāja 1204, at the age of twenty-five, he went down to Ava to serve the great monarch Prince Mangdūng [King Mindon of Burma].

275. In the year 1215, the sovereign, Mangdūng, gave his sister named Ratanadevi in marriage to Prince Saeng, whose title was Gandhālakhemāraṭṭha Mahājeyyarājā, so that she might be his partner by his side as queen, and appointed him to rule over Möngmīḍ [modern Burmese spelling: Momeik] and that was the reason why he was called the caufā of Möngmīḍ [when he came to rule Jengtung].

276. In the year 1238 Prince Mahābrohm, the elder brother, having accomplished his merit and gone to heaven, the younger brother Prince Kôngdaiy, having considered that it was right to invite Prince Saeng, his elder brother in Möngmīḍ, to come and rule the state, deputed high officials to go down and invite Prince Sæng in Möngmīḍ. [The latter] came up and arrived in Jengtung City in Sakkarāja 1139, Month Seven new moon. On Second Month Nine waxing 13th night, Monday, [Daiy] Müngrau, nakkhatta constellation 2 [Bharaṇī], he was consecrated on the throne with the title of Somḍecseṭṭha Mahāsihapavarabrahma Sudhammarājā.

277. [He] came to the throne because the Moon led [him there]; because Saturn was graseḍ [fertility] in pattaṇi [wife], he

regarded the wife as greater than self; because Jupiter was enemy of the Moon and at the same time became ahi, [he] could not stay in the state, but lived in Ava and Möngmīḍ for thirty-six years before he succeeded to the state.

278. During Month Ten the Burmese jagāy [Burmese: "citke," military commander], Mông Maṅa [? Maung Maṅa], with Burmese soldiers of black and red coats under his control, arrived in Jengtung City and, encamping at Dapmān [Burmese military lines, near the city's northeastern gate], they caused disturbances among the prince's subjects and common people in the state of Jengtung, by plundering their property, silver and gold. Prince Kôngdaiy, the caufā of Jengkhaeng who was [78] the son of Prince Mahākhanān, fearful that the state subjects would be ruined but that he might offend the great monarch should he take action [against the soldiers], went down to Ava during Month Twelve to seek an audience with the great monarch. [The latter] having been informed of all events, gave orders [to Prince Kôngdaiy who] was about to return, when Jagāy Mông Maṅa and his followers were alarmed and fled during the night in Month One. [The prince] arrived back in Jengtung City on Month Three waning 8th night.

279. During Month Four he [Kôngdaiy] arranged and gave orders to the state subjects of Mönghnö,[93] descendants of [the villages of] Kādf̣a and Hnôngnün, to go and establish settlements in Möngsinghlōng [Möngsing, now in northeastern Laos].

280. At that time Jengsaen state was without people, and our Jengtung state people went down to settle at Maebāncông, Hōygrai, Hōylai, and Maeghamhlōng. The Ayodhiyā people also came and settled there, mingling [with our people]. Our Jengtung side regarded the Nammaegham as the boundary, while the state of Yodhiyā side took Maisrīmōng at Hopong as a landmark and thence to Mangalo Hill, east of the Namyôy and the Maehōk up to the Mekhong; and in the west, starting from Maisrīmōng [the Yodhiyā boundary] went along the Dôydūng ridge and the Namyôy with Jengsaen in the east. [The two boundaries] therefore did not agree with each other.

281. In the year 1240 during Month Two, he [Kôngdaiy] moved some forces down and established military camps at Āybhayāhlek, Āyhrinkông, Āydindaeng, and Gungkāt, and Banjhāu at Möngbhyāk, with rice granaries established at Mönglen and Rônglük. The Yodhiyā state side deputed Hlōng Plasānsālāvudhasarasiḍyayānukān as the chief commissioner to lead military forces and establish one military camp at Dākhīhlek [79] and another at Hnônghvaen. There was no fighting. In the year 1241, Month Eight waning 3rd night, both sides came to have friendly talks and agreed to regard each other as brother states of love and affection: even if Jengtung state subjects went down to settle in the states of Jengsæn and Jengrāy, the Yodhiyā state side would have no objection; and even if Ayodhiyā state subjects came up to settle as far as Mönglen and Möngbhyāk, the Jengtung state side would raise no objection. This was the agreement and each side withdrew its military forces.

282. During Month Four, Prince Sæng of Jengrung state, with a retinue of high officials, arrived in Jengtung City. [Sæng] was on his way to receive royal orders from the great monarch at Ava. [At Jengtung they] went to the Sanām to ask for help in procuring provisions for the onward journey to Möngnāy and in composing [Burmese] letters. Remembering the oath of friendship between the two states, Jengtung state gave every help. On return [the Jengrung party] arrived in Jengtung City on Month Six waxing 2nd night and put up at Vat Jengcīn, and on Month Six waxing 12th night departed for Jengrung without saying a word of leave-taking--this was pride and haughtiness and came under akataññū, ingratitude.

283. In the year Koḍyī Cuḷa Sakkarāja 1242, Month Eight waxing 13th night, Prince Sæng, son of Prince Mahākhanān, whose title was Somḍecseṭṭha Mahāsihapavarabrahma Sirisudhammarājā, having ruled for four years and accomplished his merit, went to heaven at the age of sixty-three. On Month [?] waxing 10th night, he was cremated at Tuṅga Market.

284. During Month Six waxing, [80] a military force was sent up to attack Jengrung state of Sipsôngbannā. Prince Sæng could not withstand the attack and fled to take refuge in Mönglæm during Month Seven.

285. The year Rōngsai Cuḷa Sakkarāja 1243, Month Eight waxing 12th night, Wednesday, Daiy Kārau, nakkhatta constellation 16 [Visākhā], Prince Kôngdaiy, that is, the caufā of Jengkhæng, son of Prince Mahākhanān, succeeded to the throne with the title of Somḍecseṭṭha Pañcalaraṭṭhamahāsiha Pavarasirisudhammarājā Bhummindanarindā Khemādhipatirājādhirājacau.

286. In the year 1244, a military force was again sent up to attack Mönglæm. The Læms did not run away, nor did our Jengtung forces retreat. When the time for the beginning of rice cultivation came in Month Eight, he [Kôngdaiy] recalled the force.

287. In the year 1245 during Month One, a military force was again sent up to attack Mönglæm. The forces of Jengtung state were victorious and the Læms fled into the city. On Month Four waning 7th night, the end came only when the head of the dead Prince Sæng was obtained and the force was recalled.

288. During Month Five, a military force was dispatched to attack Mö̈ngsā̦d and [Jengtung] was victorious up to Mö̈ngsā̦d town where both sides established stockades. Our Jengtung side did not withdraw; the Sā̦d people did not retreat. When the time came for rice cultivation during Month Eight [Prince Kôngdaiy] thought it would serve no useful purpose to allow the men to remain so immobilized and called them back.

289. In that year of 1240, Lord Sovereign Mangdūng was gravely ill, and the ministers and [81] high officials had a secret conference and unitedly agreed to make Mangjhā Sībô [Prince Thibô] the crown prince, but, as they were afraid that other princes who were elder brothers would not agree, they arrested all the princes who were elder brothers and raised Mangjhā Sībô to be the crown prince. The queens who were the mothers of the arrested princes went to reverence the sovereign and informed him of the arrests of the princes, whereupon the king ordered the release of all the princes. Prince Thonze was appointed to rule the province in the upper Erāvatī.

290. Not long after, the princes were arrested again, together with their mothers and their men. At that time the monarch Mangdūng became critically ill and went to sleep on the cloth of brocade [died] on Month Twelve waxing 6th night. Prince Thibô became king, and on Month Four waxing 10th night the arrested princes were taken out and executed.

291. In the year 1243, during Month Eleven, the king told the Mö̈ngnāy queen to send men to summon the caufā of Mö̈ngnāy to Mandalay. At that time the queen thought thus: "Should I send men to summon the caufā of Mö̈ngnāy and he were to come, well and good; if he did not come I would be in trouble." Having thought thus, the queen secretly made her escape. The king sent men after her, brought her back, and kept her in confinement.

292. The caufā of Mö̈ngnāy, having heard the news, thought: "Should I go down the king would put me to death without a doubt. Even my elder sister, the queen, was imprisoned in that manner." He then went to consult with the caufās of the states of Mö̈nghnông and Rokcôk [modern spelling in English: "Lawksawk"], and having become one, they collected about three thousand soldiers and came in to attack the Burmese soldiers who were at Mö̈ngnāy and killed about four hundred of them. The Burmans who escaped, traveling day and night, went down to reverence [82] the king in Mandalay over there.

293. Having been informed [of the events], the king marshaled military forces to attack Mȫnghnông, Mȫngnāy, and Rokcôk. Ten elephants, one hundred fifty horses, and twenty-five hundred soldiers came up by way of Mȫngnāy; another contingent of twenty-four hundred men came up by way of Mȫnghnông; and there was fighting without a break during Month Three.

294. The caufās of Mȫngnāy and Mȫnghnông, unable to stand up to the Burmese forces, fled and came up to the caufā of Jengtung for protection, arriving on Month Four waxing 12th night, and reported to the caufāhlōng of Jengkhæng all the happenings: how the king sent up military forces to attack them, and how they could not withstand the Burmese soldiers and fled to Jengtung. Having heard everything, he [Kôngdaiy, i.e., the caufā of Jengtung] then discussed the matter [with Mȫngnāy and Mȫnghnông] thus: "This king has attained the position of sovereign and lord of merit and righteousness, but he has a despicable heart, and, placing grasping greed before all else and ignoring brothers and sisters, put to death all the princes who were his elder and younger brothers, and then ascended the throne. This is against the custom and tradition of the state. Later on, if someone went and reported against us, whether we had done any wrong or not, [the king] would put us all to death as he had done to the princes, and no state of any sort would be possible."

295. In the year 1246, during Month Eight, [the caufās] unitedly marshaled military forces of Jengtung state and sent them out to fight. They were victorious from Kôpheu Hoklāp to Mȫngsū, Mȫngcāng, and Mȫnghnông. A great stockade was established at Tūyā and there was incessant fighting with the Burmese forces. The Burmese soldiers were numerous and they came in from every hole and corner making the situation untenable [for the Jengtung forces]. On Month Seven waxing 7th night, the great stockade at Tūyā was overwhelmed during the day, and a great many subjects of our Jengtung state lost their lives. Our Jengtung side again dispatched troops for reinforcement. A stockade was established close [to the enemy]. [83] The Burmese forces did not run away; our Jengtung forces did not retreat; there was a battle once in every nine or ten days.

296. During Month Four, the caufās of Jengkhæng, Mȫngnāy, Mȫnghnông, and Rokcôk held a council [and deliberated] thus: "The fight between our troops against the Burmese does not seem to make any headway. There is one Burmese prince at Bôrameng [Moulmein] whom we should invite to come and head the army to the battle, then only the fighting would progress favorably in the future." Having decided thus, they sent men to invite Prince Sōylinpin [Shwelinbin] to come up, [and he] arrived in Jengtung City in 1247, Month Seven waning 12th night.

297. During that year of 1247 many ill omens which had never been seen before made themselves felt in Ava. These were: fire broke out in Mandalay in many places, although the entire city was not burned down; thieves and bandits were numerous; commoners would not obey the law, and hot words and quarrels were frequent, leading to chaotic conditions; tears came down from the eyes of the rājasīs [crested mythical lions] constructed by the king at the monastery west of the city; the great Arakanese image of the Lord gave out supernatural rays of light for all the city people to see; the image of the Lord at Sōygūgī [Shwegūgyī] at Sōypō [Shwebo] City shed tears of blood; mother bees made hives in the golden palace; dogs came into the great Sanām [Council Hall]; dogs barked and howled throughout the city during the night; many wild tigers came into the city; mother bees came and made hives at the Mahācedi Pagoda, which was constructed by the king; the king's white umbrellas in the golden palace swayed to and fro of their own accord; stars dropped from the sky to the earth incessantly.

298. As these omens appeared, the English foreigners ["Galā Ingalik"], during the waxing phase on Month One, marshaled powerful forces and came up by steamers along [84] the Nammaekeu [Erāvatī River].

299. The Burmese officials in charge of the city of Ñông-ū [Nyaung-ū, near Pagan] sent a letter to the king [informing him of the coming of the English along the Erāvatī]. The king called all the ministers and high officials together and said: "What are we to do about the English foreigners coming up with powerful forces? If we resist and fight we may not be able to defeat them." [The king] having considered thus, orders were given to the Burmese commanders of the garrisons along the banks of the Keu at Ava, Sagaing, and Prome not to fight the Galā Ingalik. Those garrisons did not give battle, and saying, "We are allies, we should have friendly talks as during the reign of King Mindon," allowed the forces of the English foreigners to come up along the Maenamkeu until the port of Mandalay was reached.

300. At that time, about twenty thousand English soldiers went and surrounded the golden palace of the king, while their commanders went up the golden palace for talks. The king then said: "The English country and Burma have been allies from time immemorial, that was why we did not fight but restrained our troops. Why did you disregard [this friendship] and come up to our golden palace?" The English commander reverenced the king, saying, "The English king has given orders to conquer Burma and to take the person of the king to the Galā country [India]."

301. At that time all the ministers and high officials were unable to think of anything; they therefore made a list of all the silver and gold utensils and articles and made them over to the commander with proper care. On Month One waning 9th night, when the hour was [85] three in the afternoon, the king and all the queens together went to the river port and boarded a steamer and by stages went to Rangoon [where they] rested for six nights. Then, they again boarded a steamer [and continued the journey] until they reached the Galā country where they were made to reside in the city of Maddarāj. They never set their eyes on their old residence, the golden palace, for a second time until the extinction of their pañcakkhandhā[94] [death] in the Galā country.

302. During Month Twelve of the year 1247, when it was decided to accept Prince Shwelinbin [as leader] to go out and fight, the caufās of Möngnāy, Mönghnông, and Rokcôk sent letters to the peoples in their various states regarding the acceptance of Prince Shwelinbin [as leader] to go out and fight, and the peoples in Möngnāy, Mönghnông, and Rokcôk came to know about all the business.

303. On Month Twelve waning 8th night, the caufās of Möngnāy, Mönghnông, and Rokcôk, and, on our Jengtung side, Bhayā Lāmhmün of Nôynô, appointed by the prince [Kôngdaiy], departed with military forces and Prince Shwelinbin. This coincided with the time when the English foreigners were about to come up to take Ava and take the king to the Galā country. Some Burmese soldiers had already gone down to Ava, and there was not much fighting. A great number of villages came in to submit; only a small number did not submit. On Month One waxing 10th night, the Burmese soldiers learned that the English had taken the king away, and they went down to Ava. All the substates came in to submit, and the caufās of Möngnāy, Mönghnông, and Rokcôk returned each to his own state.

304. On Month Three waning 11th night, Prince Jengkhaeng, son of Prince Mahākhanān, accomplished his merit and went to heaven. In the year 1248 Month Eight waxing 13th night, he was cremated at Tuṅga Market. This prince ruled [86] the state for five years but had not been consecrated.

305. In the year 1248, Month Eight, Prince Mahābyaggha Jōtikôngghamfū succeeded to the state with the title of Somḍecseṭṭha Mahābyaggha Jōtikôngghamfū Bhummindanarindā Khemādhipaṭirājādhirājacau.

306. In the year 1249, the states of Yodhiyā and Jengtung divided water and earth between them [marked boundaries]; beginning

with the Maesāy as the boundary up to Möngyôn, Möngsāḍ, and Dôylāng.

307. On Month Five waxing 12th night, officials of Möngsāḍ came in to offer Möngsāḍ as a substate of Jengtung state.

308. In the year 1250, Month One waxing 4th night, Sōylānpō [Burmese: Shwelānbo], leading the people in Mönghyu, Möngleng, and Pongkun, came and requested to be a substate of Jengtung state, after which Sōylānpō himself received a high honor and position and was raised to be Bhayā Mungmöng as the leader of the prince's subjects and commoners in all Mönghyu, Möngleng, and Pongkun.

309. On Month Four waxing 8th night, headed by Jhüngkhae, the common people of the state of Saenyôḍ and officials of Mungmöng [or Saenmöng] offered their states to be the substate of Jengtung state.

310. In the year 1252 the Galā Ingalik entered the state.

311. Prince Mahābyaggha Jōtikôngghamfū was born in the year Kāpseḍ Cuḷa Sakkarāja 1236, First Month Nine waxing 4th night, Wednesday, Daiy Ḍapmeḍ, time--towards noon, nakkhatta constellation 10 [Maghā]. He ascended the throne of the state in the year Rāyseḍ Cuḷa Sakkarāja 1248 with the title of Somḍecseṭṭha Mahābyaggha Jōtikôngghamfū Bhummindanarindā Khemādhipaṭirājādhirājacau. He ascended the throne because he was led by Mercury to it; because Mercury, being tanu [horoscope subject], became graseḍ [fertility], he had glory and fame to which foes submitted--Mönghyu, Möngsāḍ, Saenyôḍ, and Saenmöng came in for protection as substates, because Mercury became srī [87] and bandhu; the Moon, which was the age, was in the same zodiacal sign as Lagana and Jupiter was destructive--he did not live long.

312. In the year 1257, Month Six waxing 14th night, at the age of twenty-two and after a reign of nine years, he accomplished his merit and went to heaven. In 1258, Month Eight waxing 13th night, his remains were taken to Tuṅga Market and cremated.

313. The year 1258, Prince Kônkæu accepted the state. In the year year 1259, Month Eight waxing 12th night, Saturday, Daiy Rōngpau, nakkhatta constellation 16 [Visākhā], Prince Kônkæu Intraeng, son of Prince Jengkhæng, received consecration and ascended the throne of the state with the title of Somḍecseṭṭha Paramadebindapobitra Mahāratanajoti Sirisudhammavarajeyyā Sihaḷameghamaṇī Pavaraseṭṭhārājā Bhummindanarindā Khemādhipatirājādhirājacau.

314. In the year 1260, Month Three, the prince, accompanying the commissioner of the government [of Burma], went out to demarcate the boundary with China. On the Chinese side there were Taudhāy, as the head, and Ḍenp̲īn. [The boundary line] began from the Namhlak, Hlabhuk, alōng the boundary of Möngphaen, Möngyāng, to Dā-āng, down to Latīp, going out to Bānnôy, Kāngbengnāng, Möngva, Jengkhāng, Bānj̲hô, Bānf̲āy, Mönghlōy, along the Namn̈a until the Mekhong was̲ reached. On the British side there were the commissioner and the prince heading the officials; on the Chinese side there were Taudhāy and the Prince of Svaenhvīfā heading the officials; and they went to have a conference at Mönglōng [a substate of Jengtung]. When that had been done the prince returned to Jengtung City during Month Eight of the year 1261.

315. In the year 1262, during Month Three, the royal elephant, Bukaeu, was in musth and, greatly maddened, entered the city during the night and killed four persons and then went to rest at the cemetery grove Saenphī of Bānyāngkaeu. The assistant superintendent [British resident], fearing that it might gore more people to death, went out and shot it.[95]

316. In the year 1268, Month Eight 12th waxing night, the prince built the golden palace and completed the construction in the year 1269, Month Four waxing 12th night, and ascended [88] the new palace that day.[96]

317. In the year 1268, Month Eight waxing 12th night, a fire which started from Adīju spread to the rōng and the vihāra of Vat Hōkhōng, and on to [houses] along J̲hedānhlong Street, to Vat Jengn̈ām, Vat Jengcan, Jhedānkāḍ, crossed the city wall and spread to Tīnp̲ā and as far as Ḃān Hānghnôngkaeu.

318. In the year 1270, Month Eight waxing 3rd night, Ājññādhambracau of Vat Hōkhōng completed his accumulation of merit.

319. In the year 1283, Month Seven waning 1st, the prince offered the dāna of one hundred thirty sets [of palm leaf books] of Mahā Vessantara [Jātaka] and other Dhamma stories, and consecrated images of the Lord at Vat Jengkhūm.

320. In the year 1291, Month Six waxing 14th night, the prince offered the dāna of Mahā Vessantara [Jātaka] and other Dhamma stories, five sets of aṭṭhaparikkhāra and consecrated the great Arakan image of the Lord [a replica of the Arakan Mahāmuni image of Mandalay] at the great Vat Brasing of Hōkhōng.

321. This prince had a great accumulation of merit and was very fond of performing meritorious deeds.

322. The [prince's] chief wife, named Caunāng Padummā, had two children, a girl and a boy: the girl was the elder, named Caunāng Debbakaisôn, and the boy was named Cau Brohmlü, who became the Prince of Mönghlek [heir presumptive].

323. The second wife, named Nāng Fông, had six children: the eldest child was Cau Kôngdaiy who became the Prince of Saenmöng [heir apparent]; the second child was Cau Intrā, who died in Sībô; the third child was Cau Phāpmöng; the fourth child was Cau Khunsük, who was born during the war between the English and the Germans and was named Khunsük [lord of war] for that reason; the fifth child was Caunāng Bōsvan; the sixth child was Caunāng Fôngkaeu.[97] These are the children of Nāng Fông, the second wife.

324. The third wife, named Nāng Bōdiphlōng, had five children: the eldest child was Caunāng Vaenkaeu who went to be the daughter-in-law of Rokcôk state, the second child was Caunāng Suvaṇṇagandhā, the third child was Caunāng Vaendip, the fourth child was Cau Singjeyyarāj, and the fifth was Cau Kaeumāmöng. [89] These five are the children of Nāng Bōdiphlōng, the third wife.

325. The fourth wife had two children: the eldest child was a boy, Cau Sāymöng, and a girl, Caunāng Canfông. These are the children of Nāng Daeng, the fourth wife.

326. The fifth wife had two children: one was Caunāng Fôngnōn and the second was Cau Bunvāḍvongsā. These two are the children of Nāng Bunyōng, the fifth wife.

327. The sixth wife, Nāng Bōdipnôy, had two children: one was Caunāng Hnot [later named Bōnōn], and one was Cau Yôḍmöng. These two are the children of Nāng Bōdipnôy, the sixth wife.

328. All these are the children of Prince Kônkaeu who had ruled over this state.

329. Prince Kôngdaiy, the eldest child of Nāng Fông, married a princess of Sībô state by the name of Caunāng Kyāñun. Prince Brohmlü, the eldest child of Caunāng Padummā, the chief wife, married a niece of the cauhlōng [ruling prince] of Lagôn Lambāng, by the name of Caunāng Debbavan. Caunāng Debbakaisôn was married to Cau Hônggham, who was the son of Caunāng Debdhiḍā, daughter of the caufā of Jengkhaeng and wife of the myōjā of Jenggham.

330. Prince Ratana Kônkaeu Intraeng was born in the year Ḍapgai Sakkarāja 1237, Month One waxing 3rd night, Monday, Ḍaiy Münghmau, nakkhatta constellation 17 [Anurādhā], early

morning [after daybreak]. At the age of twenty-two he came to the throne.

331. In the year Müngrau Sakkarāja 1259, Month Eight waxing 12th night, he was consecrated with the title of Somḍecseṭṭha Paramadebindabopitra Mahāratanajoti Sirisudhammavarajeyyā Sihaḷameghamanī Pavaraseṭṭhārājā Bhummindanarindā Khemādhipatirājādhirājacau. This prince ruled the state for thirty-eight years. In the year 1297 he was ill from Month One waxing 6th night until Month Nine waning 6th night when he accomplished his merit at 9 o'clock and 35 minutes [a.m.].

332. Because Mars was uccā, Venus and Saturn were grasẹd and became mūntrī [abundance], the Moon was leading Lagana, Saturn was srī, Mars and Saturn being in the same zodiacal sign were mahā-uccā [supreme], Mars led [him] to the throne, and that was [also] why he had many sons and daughters.

333. This prince possessed a great accumulation of merit, moral discipline, and a mind bent on meritorious deeds. He built monasteries everywhere. He was handsome. Because the Moon was in the same zodiacal sign as Lagana, he had many children and grandchildren, and he was very powerful.

Notes

1. Khau-neu, or glutinous rice, has been the staple grain of all Tai peoples from ancient times, with the exception of Central Thais who came under external influences from early days. To the Shans, Khüns, Lüs, Læms, Tai-Yuans, and Laos the ordinary rice (kau-cāu) as known to the rest of the world was of recent introduction. In eating glutinous rice one takes a handful of it from the container of woven bamboo, or silver for those who could afford it, with one hand from which the other hand will take a mouthful of it and roll or manipulate it into a ball or lump before eating it with curries on the "table." Hence "rice balls" or rice lumps in the text.

2. Dammilāp is derived from Pali "Damiḷa" (the Tamils of South India) and Khün "lāp" (level, open space). The original inhabitants of the Kengtung valley are believed to have been the Vas or Lvas whose complexion is dark like that of the Tamils. The Lvas are equated with the ancient dark and "low" Damiḷas, the ancient enemy of Buddhist Sinhalese and, by implication, of good Buddhists everywhere. Hence Dammilāp, the land of dark-skinned Lvas. That the Dammiḷas are not highly esteemed can be seen in paragraphs 55 and 62.

3. "Ông" is a depression, a concavity; "p̲ū" is crab. Probably the name alludes to the valley of Kengtung that was the home of the legendary golden crab. Legendary crabs are also mentioned in the Chiengsæn chronicle but in a different setting.

4. While the names "Ôngp̲ū" and "Dammilāp" seem appropriate enough as names for Kengtung at the time, "Caṇḍavajira" (fierce thunderbolt) is usually a personal name of an individual, e.g., a mahāthera is so named in the *P̲āḍæng Chronicle* (par. 12).

5. The Burmese and Khün or Shan idea of a throne is not the Western one of a huge, decorated chair with arm rests on which the king sits with his feet resting on a cushion; rather it is a raised dais five or six feet in height with the top measuring about three and a half by four or five feet. A six-inch-thick mattress covered with velvet is placed on it for the king to sit cross-legged on ceremonial occasions.

6. "Fā" is a term whereby a ruler is referred to; "vông" comes from Chinese "huangte" (emperor). "Fāvông" is always understood as referring to the Chinese emperor.

7. These places are within Kengtung City except Dônhlōng which is outside it, about a mile to the northwest.

8. The usual iron staff for bhikkhus in Burma measures about four and a half feet with a wooden handle. The diameter of the iron rod is about three-eighths of an inch, flattened for three or four inches at the end. It was the fashion for a bhikkhu to carry such a staff, especially when on long overnight journeys. Ancient ascetics in India are known to have carried such staffs, probably for digging up edible roots and yams and as a general tool to help the austere living. Since World War II such staffs are seldom seen with bhikkhus in Burma.

9. The word used here is a well-known term for a man to become an ascetic in the Buddhist sense, derived from the Pali "pabbajjā," literally meaning "the going forth," or, more fully, "agārasmā anagāriyaṁ pabbajjā," (the going forth from home to the homeless life).

10. There are ten kasiṇas as aids to meditation: earth, water, fire, wind, blue, yellow, red, white, space, and consciousness.

11. Lokiya (mundane) jhāna (absorption or trance, which is not the exact meaning) tends to lead the disciple (of meditation) on the path to attainment of supernatural powers, while lokuttara (supramundane) jhāna leads one on the path to Nibbāna.

12. Samāpatti (attainment) is the name for the eight jhānas--four rūpa (fine-material) jhānas and four arupa (of the immaterial sphere) jhānas--and a ninth attainment, nirodha-samāpatti (attainment of cessation or Nibbāna).

13. This seems to be a Chinese name.

14. A traditional belief in Kengtung is that the undecomposed remains of Mahā Kassapa Thera are on some unidentified peak in Southwest Yunnan, China. Mahā Kassapa was one of the chief disciples (mahāsāvaka) of the Buddha and was the president of the first Saṅgāyanā (Buddhist Council) to recite and edit the Tipiṭaka under the patronage of King Ajātasattu of Rājagaha.

15. Tālapatta is sometimes translated as "fan," made of palm leaves and usually carried by bhikkhus of Theravāda countries for shielding their faces on ceremonial occasions, such as recitals or dispensing of the five sīlas.

16. This is in the valley of Kengtung, about a mile northwest of the city.

17. Cômsak is the hill in Kengtung City, southwest of the Tuṅga Lake, on which stand, at present, the government rest house and the Roman Catholic mission. In ancient times the foot of the hill must have been on the lake itself; now it is about two or three hundred feet away.

18. One vā is a measurement equivalent to that of the outstretched arm of a man, from the tip of the middle finger of one hand, across his body, to the tip of the middle finger of the other hand. In modern times, one vā is taken to be six feet in Burma or two meters in Thailand.

19. "Dôy," mountain; "san," ridge; "jüm," to seep out. This mountain ridge, about four thousand feet above sea level, can be seen from the road to Loimwe, a military station from the British days, fifty-six hundred feet high, twenty miles south of Kengtung City. The monastery subjects in the *Pādaeng Chronicle* live mainly on this ridge and are called Sanjüms, ethnically belonging to the Palaung-Va stock.

20. A kind of hardy rice still grown, I understand, in the Sipsôngbannā area.

21. Until the 1930s, the protection of this nāga lady was often ceremonially invoked in times of stress for the state of Kengtung.

22. Cômsrī Hill is just outside the western Kengtung city wall.

23. The present city of Kengtung was once known as Jengkaeu.

24. This is the literal translation of the phrase "Nam beng tō hō beng kan," meaning "all are equal and uncontrollable."

25. This should be the jujube tree. In Khün writing "mai dan" (jujube) can easily be mistaken (in this case by the scribe) for "mai can" (sandalwood).

26. Devaputta is definitely a male, but devatā, as illustrated here, is applicable to either a male or a female devā.

27. Husband and wife.

28. Compare this to the consecration of Queen Cāmmadevī of Haribhuñjaya (Lambūn) when she was made to sit on a "heap of gold" in the *Jinakālamālī* (JKM, p. 100).

29. In the *Prajum Bongsāvadān*, vol. 61 (PB61, p. 100 ff.) and the *Yonaka Chronicle* (YC, p. 242 ff.), the coming of Lau Caṅkarāja (or Cakarāja) by "opapātikajāti" (birth without cause) is almost the same as the coming from heaven of the two devās mentioned here; but the "brayādham" was King Aniruddha of Pagan, and not Vôngtīf̄āng of China. The establishment of the Cuḷa Sakkarāja (CS) was attributed to this Aniruddha. See the *P̱āḍaeng Chronicle* ("Introduction") regarding the establishment of the Cuḷa and other sakkarājas.

30. This is the founding of Chiengrāy mentioned in PB61 (pp. 104-5) and in the YC (p. 245).

31. By tradition a prince or a king has his two closest and most trusted officers styled as those of the left and of the right, with the latter taking precedence over the former. "The senā [minister or general] of the left, the senā of the right" is quite a well-known phrase--comparable to the Western term "right-hand man." The chief disciple of Lord Buddha on the left was Moggallāna Mahāthera and that on the right was Sāriputta Mahāthera. "Left" is mentioned before "right," just as "small" is mentioned before "big" in Tai terminology.

32. The stories of Khun Dӧng and Khun Dӱng are also found in PB61 (p. 110). The story of Khun Dӱng is again found in the *Mӱnghmau Chronicle* and the *Hsenwi State Chronicle* under the same circumstances.

33. The magical brass pot ("hmôdông baucāy") can produce any amount of food to feed whole armies or cities.

The city-creating magical hook is of the shape of the elephant hook of a mahout, I imagine, and when the owner wishes to create a city at a suitable locality, it is wielded to and fro until it gets stuck in a suitable tree. The wielder then sleeps the night at the foot of the tree, and when he wakes up the next day, a city, complete with walls, battlements, and gates, will stand before him (PB61:113).

34. There seems to be little connection between the prince's serpentine ancestry and Mӧnghvāy, which means "the city of rattan." This Mӧnghvāy is near Muangfāng, northeast of Chiengmai and near the border of Burma.

35. What follows (pars. 49-58) is actually the story of Haribhuñjaya (Lambūn), and various incidents and names in it could be compared to those in the JKM (pp. 96-110) and the chronicle of the great cetiya of Haribhuñjaya, an edition of which was printed in Buddha Sakkarāja (BS) 2512 (1969) by Śivabôn Company, Ltd., Bangkok, for distribution at the funeral of Nāng Candragam Vuḍḍhikul at Lampang on February 15, BS 2512.

36. See also note 28 and paragraph 37.

37. Compare this with the story of Emperor Asoka and the three yons guarding the Buddha's relics, in *U Kalā Mahāyāzawingyi* (U Kalā, sections 116-117, pp. 78-79).

38. This is a way of saying, "When my sons have attained full manhood. . . ."

39. Female skirt or sarong worn throughout Burma, northern Thailand, and Laos.

40. Brayā Dhammaruddha is the "king of righteousness" (brayādham), Anuruddha of PB61 (p. 99) and of YC (p. 242), who is obviously the Anuruddha (or Aniruddha) of Arimaddana Pugarama (Pagan, "the land that has vanquished its enemies"), but the assumption here that he terminated the sakkarāja (Mahā Sakkarāja [MS] or Saka Era [SE]) is wrong. It was King Poppa Sôrahan (613-640 A.D.) who did it (*Glass Palace Chronicle* [GPC], p. 53) when Mahā Sakkarāja had reached 960 and the new Burmese era, Cuḷa Sakkarāja, was established.

41. We have been told that when Genghis Khan was on a hunting expedition it was really a large military maneuver with wild beasts as the enemy (Lamb 1968). Perhaps hunting on a big scale by princes was the fashion of the time in all Asia. Mangrāy lived about this time, and the distance between his capital at Chiengsaen and Kengtung was but five fast marches. A hunting expedition by Mangrāy with four hundred followers is not impossible. (Hunting season in the Shan States is between February and June, when the undergrowth of hills and jungles is parched and often set afire by humans who give little thought to the disastrous consequences of their acts.)

42. In the PB61 (pp. 132-34) version of Mangrāy's chase, Mö̈ngbak was named after a rest there by Mangrāy. The old travel route between Kengtung and the Thai border passed through Mö̈ngbak, about two marches from Kengtung City.

43. It was the custom among the Tai peoples that after childbirth a mother must stay in bed for one month. This was known as "staying the month," and is still practiced among some village Tais.

44. Here again, as in paragraphs 49-58, the scribe has mistaken Haribhuñjaya for Jenghmai.

45. This ceremony was last performed in 1897 when Prince Kônkaeu Intraeng was consecrated as lord of earth of Khemaraṭṭha Tuṅgapurī.

46. One carrier pole carries two baskets.

47. The "scientific" explanation of this incident lies in the superstitious belief that any extraordinarily abnormal or unnatural doing perpetrated by mere mortals, such as an incestuous act, is frowned upon by the unseen, which will put a stop to it with a lightning strike. In the present case the raft of reeds and the cooking contrivances on it are "unnatural." This, together with the invocation to the state's devās before the raft's floating, brought on the lightning.

48. In the 1930s, when I began reading this chronicle, I was told that Maentātôk is the modern Tengyweh (or Tengyueh, now called Tengchung--25.02N 98.28E). Recently, Bra Sāmī Saeng (? Dhammasiri), lord abbot of Vat Sāimöng of Tachilek opposite the Thai border town of Maesai, with whom I discussed the identity of Maentātôk (or Möngmaen, for short), categorically stated that in Sipsôngbannā the present-day Puerh (23.05N 101.06E) was known as Möngmaen. In his younger days the lord abbot was a native of Mönghun, a substate in one of the twelve bannās of Kenghung (Jengrung). Both Tengyweh and Puerh are in S.W. Yunnan, China.

49. This is not real brass metal alloy, but the timber of a species of *Erythrina*, perhaps *Erythrina stricta*, which is called in Khün or Shan "mai dong" (brass tree).

50. Twelve years old according to paragraph 107, which is somewhat confirmed by paragraph 105, stating that he was born in the year Püksī CS 700. Püksī should be read as Pükyī to which CS 700 belongs. It is easy for a careless scribe to write "sī" for "yī" in Khün script. Real confirmation can only be had when the month, day, and nakkhatta constellation can be ascertained to belong to that year.

51. According to *Tamnān Mūlasāsanā Chapap Vat P̱āḍaeng* (TMP, p. 7), Ceḍbantū was about to leave Kengtung for Chiengmai in order to succeed his father, Phāyū, who had died and left word that Ceḍbantū should succeed him; Künā succeeded to the Chiengmai throne only after Ceḍbantū was murdered.

52. According to a chronicle of Kengtung written on palm leaves in my library in Burma, Āy-ôn was involved in a war between Chiengsaen and Chiengrāy on the one hand, and Ayudhyā on the other, and was captured by the latter and made chief mahout of its king. This seems confirmed by the sentence, "When the news came that the enemy had captured his elder brother. . . ." TMP (p. 10) confirms the capture.

53. I was told this story during my boyhood, and have since read about this this Bōk Hnôngrāy in the chronicle on palm leaves referred to in note 52. In a council of senior ministers discussing the best way of building the city walls, Hnôngrāy, a junior officer, ventured an opinion that the walls should encompass such and such localities, including Hnôngdājāng and Yāngbrahrin. For daring to speak that much he was executed. Before he died he laid a curse that any ruler who followed his word about the walls should perish. This story was also quite well known among the novices in the monasteries in the 1920s and 1930s.

54. In view of note 52 and a few lines later in this paragraph, Bunjū seems to be the younger brother of Āy-ôn.

55. See also the *P̱āḍaeng Chronicle*, paragraph 195.

56. Buddhavaṁsa (Chronicle or Lineage of Buddhas) is the fourteenth work in Khuddaka Nikāya (KN) of the Sutta Piṭaka, and it contains accounts of twenty-four Buddhas from Dīpaṅkara to Kassapa. Each chapter is an account of a Buddha. Kakusandha is the first Buddha of the present bhadda kappa (world cycle) and is the twenty-second in the Buddhavaṁsa.

57. This is the well-known Vat P̱āḍaeng.

58. Caṅkō is the beaten sheet of metal. Kongken is a circle in the māngāng which is the pennant (of metal) attached to the top of the cetiya just below the lotus-bud-shaped finial. In the present case, the caṅkō sheet is rolled into a cone, the top of which is the lotus bud, to be fitted to the masonry top. The gold pennant is attached to the conical part.

59. See paragraph 12.

60. A ferry on the Lōy River.

61. *Chiengmai State Chronicle* (CSC), printed by the Thai prime minister's office in Bangkok in BS 2514 (1971), mentions this incident on page 71 but states that forces headed by Saen Yī numbered a little over twenty thousand. It is interesting to note that the *Jengtung State Chronicle* exaggerates the number of men in a foreign army, as in this case and again in paragraph 157 in which the Laos were supposed to have dispatched an army of four hundred thousand men to Kengtung. On the other hand, the number of five thousand men in the Kengtung force (par. 137) sounds credible enough. But then in paragraph 160 Kengtung is supposed to have sent two hundred thousand men--or perhaps two hundred is meant. In paragraph 62 Mangrāy sent

a force of a credible five thousand to fight the Lvas after his vain stag chase.

62. Hongsā is Haṁsāvati (Pegu) which was the famous royal capital of Bayinnaung of Burma (1551-1581).

63. This is the fight referred to in the *P̱āḍaeng Chronicle* (par. 155).

64. It seems hardly possible that Tanāusrī (? Tenasserim--at that time under Ayudhyā) would be sending a delegation to Kengtung, but that is what the name Nāusrīsak suggests.

65. Name of the palace of Indra in the Tāvatiṁsa heaven.

66. Kengg̱ham could be another name of the preceding ruler Prince G̱hāk whose name suggests he was the lord of G̱hāk rice fields, which after his death would pass on to his son. Prince G̱hāk was known as Brayā Kaeu. Later in this same paragraph it is mentioned he was the son of Brayā Kaeu.

67. Most probably the court at Ava had made him a ruler of the township or district of Sale in Central Burma before he succeeded to the throne at Kengtung. Probably, too, his daughter was a minor queen at the court, as a few lines further on in the text his horoscope states that he came to the throne "through his daughter's support."

68. This is the literal translation, the exact meaning of which is not clear, and letters to Kengtung on this and other astrological points remain unanswered.

69. The word in the text is "ken," which in a certain context has the same meaning as "grô" (fortune or the planet). One's grô can be bad or good, as in "grôdī" or "grôrāy," but by itself "grô" usually denotes bad luck. It is the same with the "ken." "Grôken" often means bad luck. Whether "ken" has a different meaning in horoscopes, I am unable to tell. Information on horoscopy from my sources in Kengtung remains very unsatisfactory.

70. The passage in brackets was copied from another copy of the *Jengtung State Chronicle*. It is quite obvious the scribe of my copy left out the passage and without it the paragraph would suffer.

71. This could well be Alaungpaya, founder of the Konbaungset dynasty of Burma. History books give the beginning of his reign as from 1752, when the last king at Ava, Mahādhammarājādipadi (1733-1752), died. The year of the coming of the "new

monarch" is given by the chronicle as CS 1111 (1749 A.D.) which was about the time Alaungpaya was preparing to resist the Talaing tax collecting columns. CS 1111 may be wrong, but paragraph 200 clearly indicates that Kengtung had to deal with Alaungpaya, the new king, at Moksobo (modern Shwebo), the temporary new capital.

72. Kāngmӧ̈ng means "middle of the state" and this term refers to the group of villages about two miles north of Kengtung City. They are more in the "middle" of the valley of Kengtung than the city, which lies to the south of the valley. Kāngmӧ̈ng has always been the chief source of strength to the city in men and food.

73. Hairpins of the Khüns (Lüs and Laems) for ceremonial full dress have two types of heads (called "faces" because they are flat). One is to be "stuck" in front and the other in the back of the hair knot whose base may be as large as three and a half inches in diameter and three inches high. The shape of the face of the front hairpin is round (about two inches in diameter), and that of the back one is equilaterally triangular (about two and a half inches high). It is the back hairpin which is called "cow-face," but the triangular lines are broken by very slight arcs or curves of floral design of the pin face.

74. It was a custom in Burma during the British rule that if a dead person was a government official, an order from his departmental head would be read, releasing him from government duties, just before his coffin was buried. I presume the royal letter here was read in the same way. This custom is no longer in fashion now, illustrating the impermanence of traditions.

75. The eight requirements of a bhikkhu: the three robes, the alms bowl, a razor, a needle, the girdle, a water strainer.

76. Red sandalwood (*Pterocarpus santalinus--Leguminosae*) or white sandalwood (*Sirium myrtifolium--Leguminosae*) has been an ingredient of perfumes, incense, and cosmetics since ancient times. One special use of the two sandalwoods in Burma is for scenting water for religious and ceremonial purposes, and is obtained in this way: a small piece (about three inches long and one-half inch thick) is rubbed with water on a round stone with a groove at the rim (made for this purpose). After some five or six minutes the water in the groove becomes a thin paste impregnated with fragrance from the very fine powder of the sandalwood in the water. The scented water in the groove is then transferred to a silver bowl. With three or four such transfers the whole body of water in the bowl becomes scented, ready for such uses as an offering to monasteries or for

ceremonial watering of one's elders during the water festival of the Burmese New Year.

77. This word comes from the Pali "rājamagga" (king's way). On both sides of such a "king's way" (or auspicious road for the Saṅgha or distinguished person to walk) is temporary thin bamboo lattice fencing. Such fencing is called rājamāḍ fencing, and it is about three feet high and is also erected as a special enclosure, as in the text, or on a special route, usually of short stretch, through which important personages such as ministers, or, more often, members of the Saṅgha out on special alms receiving, will pass through.

78. I do not know the English name for this plant which has large leaves like those of the canna and seed pods at the roots underground. The slightly oval-shaped pods have elongated ridges (maybe ten or twelve per pod) which make them thick, and they come in clusters, each the size of two fists held together. At the right state the seeds, brownish-black, are edible and sweet in taste. Both the seed pods and the seeds have a slight aroma of cardamom. Possibly gukgā belongs to the cardamom family. The plant grows to a height of four or five feet.

79. This village tract is also known as Sip-eḍ Mô̂n Sip-hā Mô̂n (eleven hills fifteen hills) near Mö̈nghlō̄y and Mö̈ngyāng in the northern part of Kengtung state.

80. "Āpjāng dānmö̈ng" (hand over the elephants and give away the state) is a phrase meaning to hand over the state or kingdom. Elephants are inevitably mentioned because they formed such an important part of the state trappings and apparatus. The phrase is repeated in a slightly different form in paragraph 221.

81. In spite of my queries to Kengtung, the meaning is obscure.

82. This could hardly be a royal gift from Ava. Most probably it is the specifications for a palace to be built in Kengtung, in the same manner as the throne in the next paragraph. The court at Ava always prescribed specifications for such things and their royal trappings to the various grades of ruling princes in the Shan States.

83. This has been explained at some length in note 96 of the translation of the *Pāḍaeng Chronicle*.

84. The government of King Mindon (1852-1878).

85. See note 75.

86. Jengrung of the Twelve Thousand Rice Fields (Sipsôngbannā) is cut into two by the Mekhong River. The capital city of Jengrung itself is on the west bank. Apparently the then ruling prince had been driven to the eastern half of the state.

87. The text does not say what weight this "forty" is. Further research is needed to settle once and for all the weights mentioned in the chronicle. There will be no further comments on weights of silver or gold articles.

88. In the former Kengtung royal household three groups of palace pages took turns in coming to the palace to serve their prince. Each group of several dozen young men of good families was called Pākmü, and three senior officers in charge of the three groups were called Saenhlōng Bōkpôṉg, Sænhlōng Bōkkök, and Sænhlōng Bōkmöngsang, who, in abbreviated form, were known as Müpôṉg, Mükök, and Müsang, respectively. By scribe's mistake, what Bōkmöngsang did in paragraph 257 was repeated in the last seventeen words, because Saenhlōng Bōkmöngsang and Müsang are one and the same person.

89. Robes offered to members of the Saṅgha at a funeral are called paṅsukūla robes. "Paṅsukūla" means "rags from a dust heap." During the Buddha's lifetime some members of the Saṅgha had their robes stitched from such "rags from a dust heap" and from shroud cloth. Later, robes were allowed by the Buddha to be donated by lay devotees to the bhikkhus. The stitches of modern robes are believed to be a reminder of the former ancient days when robes were stitched from rags.

90. It is not clear whether Bhayāhlōng Khaek Kattiyavong had the Burmese title of Mengcôcāu Nôrathā or whether the two names denote two officials, one Khün and one Burmese, who collaborated in recording the foregoing events.

91. Prince Mahākhanān became blind in Ava in 1824. See Mangrāi (1969:65). When he gave an audience to the British representative, Captain W. C. McLeod from Moulmein, in February 1837, he had been blind for thirteen years. He continued to rule the state until his death in 1857.

92. From paragraph 276 it is clear that this prince did not even succeed.

93. Mönghnö means "northern states" and the term is used to refer to Chinese Shans from regions north of Kengtung and Mönglæm who migrated to Kengtung during the eighteenth and nineteenth centuries. Their places of origin are generally known to have been Möngkā, Möngban, Möngpô, Möngting, Möngmæn, and Küngmā.

See also the map and paragraph 102 of the translation of the *P̱āḍaeng Chronicle*.

94. In Buddhist terminology a living being is made up of the "pañcakkhandhā" (five groups of existence), and this term has been adopted as indigenous vocabulary in all Theravāda countries. The five groups are: corporeality, feelings, perception, mental formation, and consciousness. When the pañcakkhandhā function no more, it means life has come to an end.

95. This episode occurred in 1900 and was still talked about in the 1930s, and it was the loss of a fine elephant that was discussed. The emotion of the ruling prince could be compared to that of a sheik forced to consent to the killing of his beloved war horse. What would have happened if the British had not been there? Compensations would have been paid to victims' relatives and Bukaeu spared. Different times and different philosophies on human lives. It was said that if he had not been shot Bukaeu would have come out of his "musthy" state in a day or two. The only way of dealing with an elephant in musth is to detect signs of trouble early and shackle its legs to posts in its stable or camp.

96. This palace was built after the prince's attendance of the Delhi Durbar in 1901 when Edward VII became Emperor of India, hence its Indian-looking style of architecture; it is still standing and is being used as government offices.

97. Bōsvan and Fôngkaeu are the fourth and fifth, with Khunsük as the sixth and last child of Nāng Fông.

WORKS CITED

Aung Thaw, U. "Later Evidence of Pyū Culture." In Burmese. Paper read at the Research Congress of Burma, Rangoon, 24 March 1966.

Barua, G. C., ed. and trans. *Ahom-Buranji*. Calcutta, 1930.

Billard, R. "Les cycles chronographiques Chinois, dans les inscriptions Thaïes." *Bulletin de l'Ecole Française d'Extrême Orient*, vol. 51, no. 2 (1963), pp. 403-431. This is useful for converting the Cuḷa Sakkarāja year, month, and day into A.D. equivalents.

Buddhaghosa, Bhadantācariya. *Visuddhimagga* [The path of purification]. Translated by Ñaṇamoli Bhikkhu. Colombo, 1956.

Burlingame, E. W., trans. *Buddhist Legends*. Harvard Oriental Series. PTS. London, 1969. Translated from the original Pali text of the Dhammapada Commentary.

The Burma Research Society Fiftieth Anniversary Publications 2. Rangoon, 1960. Contains all the issues of the *Journal of the Burma Research Society* referred to in the introduction to the *P̱āḍæng Chronicle* translation.

Chan Htoon, U. "Address to the Sixteenth Congress of the International Association for Religious Freedom." Rangoon, 1958. Delivered 12 August 1958, under the auspices of the University of Chicago.

Chiengmai State Chronicle [Tanānbüنmuang Chiengmai]. Bangkok, BS 2514.

The Chronicles of Chiengmai, Nagôn Lampāng, Lambūjaiy, and of Bradhātu, Dôy Sudeb, Lampānghluang, and Haribhuñjaiy. Bangkok, BS 2512.

Coedès, G. *The Indianized States of Southeast Asia*. Translated by S. B. Cowing. Honolulu, 1968.

References to the various suttas in the Sutta Piṭaka are standard and so well known that no mention is made of them in this list.

Colquhoun, A. R. *Amongst the Shans.* London, 1885.

Elias, N. *Introductory Sketch of the History of the Shans.* Calcutta, 1876. See, in particular, "*Möngmāu Chronicle* or 'The Story of Mung-mau.'"

Gāngsö of Möngsū. *Cātisarañān.* Edited by Sobhaṇa Thera of Möng-hnông. Rangoon, 1972. The title is from Pali "Jātissarañāṇa" (Knowledge of births), and the author was a well-known Shan poet of the late nineteenth century.

Geiger, W., trans. *The Mahāvaṁsa.* PTS. London, 1964.

Glass Palace Chronicle. See Pe Maung Tin, and Luce.

Griswold, A. B. *Wat Pra Yün Reconsidered. Journal of the Siam Society* Monograph, No. 4. Bangkok, 1975.

Griswold, A. B., and Prasert ṇa Nagara. "Epigraphic and Historical Studies, No. 10: Lödaiya of Sukhodaya and His Contemporaries." *Journal of the Siam Society*, vol. 60, no. 1 (1972), pp. 21-152.

Hall, D. G. E. *A History of Southeast Asia.* New York, 1970.

Hall, D. G. E. *Historians of Southeast Asia.* London, 1962.

Halliday, R. *The Talaings.* Rangoon, 1917.

Harvey, G. E. *History of Burma.* London, 1967.

Hmannan Mahāyāzawindawgyi. 3 vols. Mandalay. Vol. 1, CS 1318 (1963); vol. 2, CS 1319 (1964); vol. 3, CS 1317 (1962).

Hsenwi State Chronicle. Unpublished. 139 pp. Concertina-pleated-type folding book of Shan paper, copied after World War II, 18 x 7 inches.

Htin Aung, Maung. *Burmese History Before 1287: A Defence of the Chronicles.* Oxford, 1970.

Htin Aung, Maung. *A History of Burma.* New York, 1967.

Jayatileke, K. N. *Early Buddhist Theory of Knowledge.* London, 1963.

Jengtung State Chronicle. In Khün. Copied 1930.

Jinakālamālī(pakaraṇaṁ). See Ratanapañña Thera.

Kaccāyana. *Kaccāyana-Vyākaraṇa* [Pali grammar of Kaccāyan]. Edited by L. N. Tiwari and B. Sharma. Banaras, 1962.

Lace, J. H., and Roger, A. *List of Trees, Shrubs, and Principal Climbers, Etc., in Burma.* Rangoon, 1922.

Lamb, H. *Genghis Khan.* Bristol, 1968.

Ledi Sayadaw, Mahāthera. *Vipassanā-Dīpanī* [The manual of insight]. Translated by Sayadaw U Nyana. Rangoon, 1965.

Luce, G. H. *Old Burma--Early Pagan.* Vol. 1 (Text). New York, 1969.

Luce, G. H. "Countries Neighbouring Burma." *Journal of the Burma Research Society*, vol. 14, no. 2 (1924), pp. 138-205.

Luce, G. H. "The Tan (A.D. 97-132) and the Ngai Lao." *Journal of the Burma Research Society*, vol. 14, no. 2 (1924), pp. 100-137.

Luce, G. H. "The Ancient Pyū." *Journal of the Burma Research Society*, vol. 32, no. 3 (1949), pp. 239-53.

Luce, G. H., and Pe Maung Tin. "Burma Down to the Fall of Pagan." *Journal of the Burma Research Society*, vol. 29, no. 3 (1939), pp. 264-82.

Lu Pe Win, U. "Burmese Calendar." *Journal of the Burma Research Society*, vol. 50, no. 2 (1967), pp. 223-44.

Lu Pe Win, U. Review of *Old Burma-Early Pagan*, by G. H. Luce. *Journal of the Burma Research Society*, vol. 54, no. 1-2 (1971), pp. 1-30.

Mahāsī Sayādaw. *The Satipaṭṭhāna Vipassanā Meditation.* Translated by U Pe Thin. Ėlgin, Ariz., 1957.

Mahāvaṁsa. See Geiger.

Mangrāi, S. S. *The Shan States and the British Annexation.* Reprint. Ithaca, 1969.

Maurice, D., trans. *The Lion's Roar.* New York, 1967. An anthology of the Buddha's teachings from the Pali Canon. Includes rules for sāmaṇeras (pp. 65-71), and summary of the Pāṭimokkha rules (pp. 69-92).

Milinda's Questions. Translated by I. B. Horner. London, 1969.

Mūlasāsanā. See *(Tamnān) Mūlasāsanā*.

Ñāṇamoli Thera. *Ānāpānasati* [Mindfulness of breathing]. Translated. Kandy, 1973. From Majjhima Nikāya 118 and Pali Commentaries.

Nārada Thera. *The Dhammapada*. Colombo, 1972. Pali text and translation with stories in brief and notes.

Nikam, N. A., and McKeon, R., ed. and trans. *The Edicts of Asoka*. Chicago and London, 1959.

Nyanaponika Thera. *The Heart of Buddhist Meditation*. London, 1972.

Nyanatiloka Thera. *Path to Deliverance*. Colombo, 1959.

Nyanatiloka Thera. *The Word of the Buddha*. Colombo, 1952.

Paññasāmi. *Sāsanāvaṁsa* [The history of the Buddha's religion]. Translated by B. C. Law. London, 1952.

Pe Maung Tin, and Luce, G. H., trans. *The Glass Palace Chronicle*. Rangoon, 1960. Translated from sections 102-147 of the *Hmannan Mahāyāzawindawgyi*.

Po Lat, U. *Shayhaung Myanma Yazawin Hnint Yinkyay-hmu Thutethana* [Researches in ancient Burmese history and culture]. In Burmese. Rangoon, 1962.

Prajākickāracakr, Phryā. *The Yonaka Chronicle* [Bongsāvadān Yonok]. In Thai. National Library edition. Bangkok, 1961.

Prajum Bongsāvadān [*Vol.*] *61*. In Thai. Department of Fine Arts edition. Bangkok, BS 2479. Contains the chronicles of Jiangsaen and Prince Siṅhanavati (the Lion Prince).

Prajum Tamnān Bradhātu [*Vol.*] *1*. In Thai. Bangkok, BS 2485. Contains the chronicles of six well-known cetiyas in northern Thailand, viz., Dôydung, Bradhātu Haribhuñjaiy, Lampāng Luang, Cumbitnagara, Dôypūbhūdap, and Jôhae.

Prajum Tamnān Bradhātu [*Vol.*] *2*. In Thai. Bangkok, BS 2510. Contains the chronicles of four well-known cetiyas in Thailand, viz., Banom, Nagarasridhammarāj, Dôysudeb, and Jaehaeng.

Premchit, Sommai. *Tamnān Mūlasāsanā Chapap Vat P̱āḍaeng*. Transliteration Series, Vol. 9. Chiengmai, 1967.

Rāhula, W. S. *What the Buddha Taught*. New York, 1974. Contains a collection of illustrative texts translated from the original Pali, including the Satipaṭṭhana Sutta (Majjhima Nikāya 22).

Ratanapañña Thera. *Jinakālamālīpakaraṇaṁ* [The sheaf of garlands of the epochs of the conqueror]. Translated by N. A. Jayawickrama. PTS. London, 1968.

Rhys Davids, T. W., and Oldenberg, H., trans. *Vinaya Texts*. Reprint. Sacred Books of the East, edited by F. Maxmüller. Banaras, 1968. Complete translation of the Vinaya Piṭaka. There is another translation of the Vinaya Piṭaka by I. B. Horner, in six volumes, entitled *The Book of Discipline* (PTS series, London).

Sāsanāvaṁsa. See Paññasāmi.

Shattock, E. H. *An Experiment in Mindfulness*. New York, 1972.

Shway Yoe. *The Burman: His Life and Notions*. New York, 1963.

Soni, R. L., trans. *Life's Highest Blessings*. Mandalay, 1956. An elaborate translation of the Maṅgala Sutta.

Soni, R. L. *A Cultural Study of the Burmese Era*. Mandalay, 1955.

(Tamnān) Mūlasāsanā. Department of Fine Arts edition. Bangkok, BS 2481.

Tamnān Mūlasāsanā Chapap Vat P̱āḍaeng. See Premchit.

Tet Htoot. "The Nature of the Burmese Chronicles." In *Historians of Southeast Asia*, edited by D. G. E. Hall, pp. 50-62. London, 1962.

Than Tun. "Mahākassapa and His Tradition." *Journal of the Burma Research Society*, vol. 42, no. 2 (1959), pp. 99-118.

Than Tun. "Religion in Burma, A.D. 1000-1300." *Journal of the Burma Research Society*, vol. 42, no. 2 (1959), pp. 47-70.

U Kalā Mahāyāzawingyi. 3 vols. Rangoon, 1960.

Vickery, M. "The Lion Prince." *Journal of the Siam Society*, vol. 64, no. 1 (1976), pp. 326-77.

Visuddhimagga. See Buddhaghosa.

Warren, H. C. *Buddhism in Translations*. New York, 1972. An anthology of translations selected from the Sutta Piṭaka, Vinaya Piṭaka, *Jātaka*, *Milinda Paṇhā*, and *Visuddhimagga*.

Wells, K. E. *Thai Buddhism: Its Rites and Activities*. Bangkok, 1975.

Yonaka Chronicle. See Prajākickāracakr.

Prehistory in Southeast Asia

Bayard, D. T. "Excavations at Nö̈n Nok Thā, Northeast Thailand: An Interim Report." *Asian Perspectives*, vol. 8 (1972), pp. 109-143.

Burmese Socialist Programme Party. *Acheypya Myanma Naingṅanye Thamaing* [The basis of Burmese history]. In Burmese. Rangoon, 1970. Volume 1. Pages 56-99 deal with the Stone Age and caves in Burma, including the famous Padā-lin Caves.

Gorman, C. F. Associated Press report. *Ann Arbor News*, 2 November 1975.

Gorman, C. F. "Excavations at Spirit Cave, North Thailand: Some Interim Interpretations." *Asian Perspectives*, vol. 8 (1972), pp. 79-107.

Honan, W. H. "The Case of the Hot Pots." *New York Times Magazine*, 8 June 1975.

Solheim, W. G., Jr. "Northern Thailand, Southeast Asia, and World Prehistory." *Asian Perspectives*, vol. 8 (1972), pp. 145-62.

Solheim, W. G., Jr. "Prehistoric Archaeology in East Mainland Southeast Asia and the Philippines." *Asian Perspectives*, vol. 8 (1972), pp. 47-58.

Solheim, W. G., Jr. "New Light on a Forgotten Past." *National Geographic*, vol. 139, no. 3 (1971), pp. 330-39.

Dictionaries

The Concise Oxford Dictionary. 5th edition. Oxford, 1974.

Hoke Sein. *Pāli-Burmese Dictionary*. 4 vols. Rangoon. Vol. 1, 1954; vols. 2-3, 1956; vol. 4, 1959.

Judson's Burmese-English Dictionary. Century edition. Rangoon, 1953.

Ling, T. O. *A Dictionary of Buddhism*. New York, 1972.

McFarland, G. B. *Thai-English Dictionary*. Stanford, 1960.

Malalasekera, G. P. *Dictionary of Pali Proper Names*. London, 1937.

Nyanatiloka. *Buddhist Dictionary: Manual of Buddhist Terms and Doctrines*. Colombo, 1972.

Rhys Davids, T. W., and Stede, W. *Pali-English Dictionary*. PTS. London, 1972.

Simon, W. *A Beginners' Chinese-English Dictionary*. London, 1964.

Webster's New World Dictionary of the American Language. 2d College edition. New York, 1974.